MARRIAGE AT THE CROSSROADS

The institution of marriage is at a crossroads. Across most of the industrialized world, unmarried cohabitation and nonmarital births have skyrocketed while marriage rates are at record lows. These trends mask a new, idealized vision of marriage as a marker of success as well as a growing class divide in childbearing behavior: the children of better-educated, wealthier individuals continue to be born into relatively stable marital unions while the children of less-educated, poorer individuals are increasingly born and raised in more fragile, nonmarital households. Meanwhile, growing numbers of same-sex couples seek access to marriage as an important political and personal goal.

These trends have generated political controversy and pose a number of challenges for policy makers: Should access to marriage be extended? Should lawmakers increase or reduce government support for marriage? And, with marriage rates declining, what policies will best support families in their important function of caring for children? The interdisciplinary approach offered by this edited volume provides tools to inform the debate and to assist policy makers in resolving these questions at a critical juncture. Drawing on the expertise of social scientists and legal scholars, the book will be a key text for anyone who seeks to understand marriage as a social institution and to evaluate proposals for marriage reform.

Marsha Garrison is the Suzanne J. and Norman Miles Professor of Law at Brooklyn Law School and Secretary-General of the International Society of Family Law. She is the coauthor of *Family Law: Cases, Comments, and Questions* (with Harry Krause, Linda Elrod, & Tom Oldham 1998, 2003, 2007) and *Law and Bioethics: Individual Autonomy and Social Regulation* (with Carl E. Schneider 2003, 2009).

Elizabeth S. Scott is the Harold R. Medina Professor of Law at Columbia University School of Law. She is the coauthor of *Rethinking Juvenile Justice* (with Laurence Steinberg, 2008), which received the 2010 Society for Research in Adolescence award for the best social policy book.

Marriage at the Crossroads

LAW, POLICY, AND THE BRAVE NEW WORLD OF TWENTY-FIRST-CENTURY FAMILIES

Edited by

MARSHA GARRISON

Brooklyn Law School

ELIZABETH S. SCOTT

Columbia University Law School

CAMBRIDGE
UNIVERSITY PRESS

CAMBRIDGE UNIVERSITY PRESS
Cambridge, New York, Melbourne, Madrid, Cape Town,
Singapore, São Paulo, Delhi, Mexico City

Cambridge University Press
32 Avenue of the Americas, New York, NY 10013-2473, USA

www.cambridge.org
Information on this title: www.cambridge.org/9781107623705

First published 2012

Printed in the United States of America

A catalog record for this publication is available from the British Library.

Library of Congress Cataloging in Publication Data

Marriage at the crossroads : law, policy, and the brave new world of twenty-first-century families /
Marsha Garrison, Brooklyn Law School; Elizabeth S. Scott, Columbia University Law School.
pages cm
Includes bibliographical references and index.
ISBN 978-1-107-01827-3 (hardback) – ISBN 978-1-107-62370-5 (pbk.)
1. Marriage – United States. 2. Marriage law – Social aspects – United States.
I. Garrison, Marsha, 1949– editor of compilation. II. Scott, Elizabeth S., 1945– editor of compilation.
HQ536.M3243 2013
306.81–dc23 2012031092

ISBN 978-1-107-01827-3 Hardback
ISBN 978-1-107-62370-5 Paperback

Contents

Contributors — *page* vii
Acknowledgments — xv

Introduction — 1
Marsha Garrison and Elizabeth S. Scott

PART I: HISTORY, DEMOGRAPHICS, AND ECONOMICS – MULTIPLE PERSPECTIVES ON FAMILIES

1 **Red v. Blue Marriage** — 9
June Carbone and Naomi Cahn

2 **International Family Change and Continuity: The Past and Future from the Developmental Idealism Perspective** — 30
Arland Thornton

3 **The Division of Household Labor across Time and Generations** — 54
Margaret F. Brinig

4 **Marriage at the Crossroads in England and Wales** — 73
Rebecca Probert

5 **The Curious Relationship of Marriage and Freedom** — 87
Katherine Franke

PART II: EMPIRICAL RESEARCH ON FAMILY CHANGE

6 **Institutional, Companionate, and Individualistic Marriages: Change over Time and Implications for Marital Quality** — 107
Paul R. Amato

7 **Marriage and Improved Well-Being: Using Twins to Parse the Correlation, Asking How Marriage Helps, and Wondering Why More People Don't Buy a Bargain** 126
Robert E. Emery, Erin E. Horn, and Christopher R. Beam

8 **Fragile Families: Debates, Facts, and Solutions** 142
Sara S. McLanahan and Irwin Garfinkel

9 **Should Marriage Matter?** 170
Ira Mark Ellman and Sanford L. Braver

PART III: FAMILY POLICY AND LAW FOR THE TWENTY-FIRST CENTURY

10 **Forsaking No Others: Coming to Terms with Family Diversity** 201
Judith Stacey

11 **Why Marriage?** 224
Suzanne B. Goldberg

12 **Essential to Virtue? The Languages of the Law of Marriage** 241
Carl E. Schneider

13 **The Pluralistic Vision of Marriage** 260
Shahar Lifshitz

COMMENTS

14 **The Growing Diversity of Two-Parent Families: Challenges for Family Law** 287
Andrew J. Cherlin

15 **Legal Regulation of Twenty-First-Century Families** 303
Marsha Garrison and Elizabeth S. Scott

Index 327

Contributors

Paul R. Amato is the Arnold and Bette Hoffman Professor of Family Sociology and Demography at Pennsylvania State University. His research interests include marital quality, the causes and consequences of divorce, and psychological well-being over the life course. He has published more than 100 journal articles and book chapters, along with four books, including *A Generation at Risk: Growing Up in an Era of Family Upheaval* (1997) and *Alone Together: How Marriage in America Is Changing* (2007). He received the Reuben Hill Award from the National Council on Family Relations for the best published article on the family in 1993, 1999, 2001, and 2008. He also has received the Distinguished Career Award from the Family Section of the American Sociological Association, the Stanley Cohen Distinguished Research Award from the American Association of Family and Conciliation Courts, the Ernest Burgess Distinguished Career Award from the National Council on Family Relations, and the Distinction in the Social Sciences Award from the Pennsylvania State University.

Sanford L. Braver is a Professor Emeritus at Arizona State University, where he served in the Psychology Department for 41 years, and he is currently a Research Psychologist at University of California, Riverside. He received his PhD in Social Psychology at the University of Michigan. His primary research interest is in the dynamics of divorcing families. To support this work he has been the recipient of 18 competitively reviewed, primarily federal, research grants, totaling more than $28 million, and is currently Principal Investigator of grants from the W.T. Grant Foundation and the National Institute of Mental Health. His work has been published in more than 110 peer-reviewed professional articles and chapters, and he is author or coauthor of a graduate-level statistics textbook, the edited book *Six Degrees of Social Influence*, and the acclaimed 1998 book *Divorced Dads: Shattering the Myths*. He serves on the Editorial Boards of *Family Court Review* and *Fatherhood*. His work has been quoted widely in news media, including *U.S. News and World*

Report, *Kiplinger's*, *Redbook*, *New York Times*, *USA Today*, and *The Wall Street Journal* and was featured in a segment of ABC News' 20/20.

Margaret F. Brinig is the Fritz Duda Family Chair in Law at the University of Notre Dame and the Associate Dean for Faculty Research. She earned her BA in History in 1970 from Duke University, a JD from Seton Hall University in 1973, and an MA (1993) and PhD in Economics (1994) from George Mason University. She has taught at George Mason University School of Law and at the University of Iowa College of Law, where she was the William G. Hammond Professor of Law. Professor Brinig is the author of textbooks on Family Law and Quantitative Methods for Lawyers, two edited collections, and a handbook for Virginia family lawyers. In 2000, she published two books: *From Contract to Covenant: Beyond the Law and Economics of the Family* and *Law, Family, and Community: Supporting the Covenant*. She has also written more than eighty articles and book chapters and has worked with coauthors in law, economics, sociology, medicine, and public health from all over the United States and Canada. Professor Brinig has been active in the American Association of Law Schools (for which she has been an officer in the Family Law, Socioeconomics, and Law and Economics sections), the Canadian and American Law and Economics Associations (for which she has served on both Executive Committees), the International Society of Family Law (for which she has long been the newsletter editor and an elected member of the Executive Committee), and the American Law Institute (for which she was a consultant to the Principles of Family Dissolution). She referees for numerous journals and presses in law and economics, including the *Journal of Legal Studies*, the *American Law and Economics Review*, and Yale University Press.

Naomi Cahn is the John Theodore Fey Research Professor of Law at George Washington University Law School. Her areas of expertise include family law, adoption and reproductive technology, and international women's rights. She has written numerous law review articles on family law, feminist jurisprudence, and other subjects and has coauthored several books, including, with June Carbone, *Red Families v. Blue Families* and, with Fionnuala Ní Aoláin and Dina Haynes, *On The Frontlines: Gender and the Post-Conflict Reconstruction Process* (2011). *Test Tube Families: Why the Fertility Market Needs Legal Regulation* was published in 2009, and she is working on a book tentatively titled *The New Kinship: Donor-Conceived Family Connections*. She is a Senior Fellow at the Evan B. Donaldson Adoption Institute, a member of the Yale Cultural Cognition Project, and a Board Member of the Donor Sibling Registry. Prior to joining the faculty at George Washington in 1993, Professor Cahn practiced with Hogan & Hartson in Washington, DC, and as a staff attorney with Philadelphia's Community Legal Services.

June Carbone is the Edward A. Smith/Missouri Chair of Law, the Constitution and Society at the University of Missouri at Kansas City. She previously served as

Associate Dean for Professional Development and Presidential Professor of Ethics and the Common Good at Santa Clara University School of Law. She received her JD from the Yale Law School and her AB from the Woodrow Wilson School of Public and International Affairs at Princeton University. She teaches Property, Family Law, Assisted Reproduction, and Bioethics. She has written *From Partners to Parents: The Second Revolution in Family Law* (2000); the third and fourth editions of *Family Law*, with Leslie Harris and the late Lee Teitelbaum (2005, 2009); and *Red Families v. Blue Families*, with Naomi Cahn (2010).

Andrew J. Cherlin is Griswold Professor of Sociology and Public Policy at Johns Hopkins University. In 1999, he was President of the Population Association of America. In 2003, he received the Distinguished Career Award from the Family Section of the American Sociological Association. In 2005–2006, he was a Guggenheim Foundation Fellow. His research interests include the well-being of parents and children in low-income families and the changing nature of marriage and family life over the past century. His recent articles include "The Deinstitutionalization of American Marriage" in the *Journal of Marriage and Family* and "Family Instability and Child Well-Being" in the *American Sociological Review*. He is the author of *The Marriage-Go-Round: The State of Marriage and the Family in America Today* (2009).

Ira Mark Ellman's principal scholarly interests are in family law and the use of social science in policy making by legislatures and courts. He served as Chief Reporter of the Principles of the Law of Family Dissolution, published in 2002 by the American Law Institute, and is the senior author of a leading text on family law used at more than forty law schools. Among his current projects are an empirical investigation into how people make judgments about the level of child support payments they believe the law should require an absent parent to pay and a book about the difficulties inherent in making family law policy. Professor Ellman is an affiliate faculty member of the Center for Child and Youth Policy at the University of California at Berkeley and an official Observer on the Drafting Committee for the Commissioners on Uniform State Laws that is considering revisions to the Uniform Premarital Agreement Act. Following graduation from law school, Professor Ellman served as a law clerk for Justice William O. Douglas of the U.S. Supreme Court. He has been a member of the faculty at Arizona State University Law School since 1978. He has visited for a semester or more at the Hastings College of Law, Brooklyn Law School, the Institute for Social and Policy Studies at Yale University, and both the Earl Warren Institute and the Center for the Study of Law and Society at U.C. Berkeley. In the fall of 2010, he was a Visiting Fellow at Trinity College, University of Cambridge.

Robert E. Emery is Professor of Psychology and Director of the Center for Children, Families, and the Law at the University of Virginia. His research focuses on family relationships and children's mental health, including parental conflict, divorce, mediation, child custody, family violence, and associated legal and policy issues. He has authored more than 125 scientific publications and several books including *Marriage, Divorce, and Children's Adjustment*; *Renegotiating Family Relationships: Divorce, Child Custody, and Mediation*; and his guide for parents, *The Truth about Children and Divorce: Dealing with the Emotions So You and Your Children Can Thrive*. He is the coauthor of *Abnormal Psychology*, with Thomas Oltmanns. Dr. Emery has discussed his work on the *Today Show*, *Good Morning America*, *The Jane Pauley Show*, and *National Public Radio*; in *Newsweek and Time* magazines; and in many other print and electronic media. In addition to his research, teaching, and administrative responsibilities, Dr. Emery maintains a limited practice as a clinical psychologist and divorce mediator.

Katherine Franke is a Professor of Law at Columbia Law School, where she also directs the Center for Gender & Sexuality Law. She is among the nation's leading scholars in the area of feminism, sexuality, and race. In addition to her scholarly writing on sexual harassment, gender equality, sexual rights, and racial history, she writes regularly for a more popular audience in the Gender and Sexuality Law Blog. She is also on the Executive Committee for Columbia's Institute for Research on Women and Gender and teaches at a medium-security women's prison in Manhattan.

Prior to joining the law faculty at Columbia, she taught at Fordham University and the University of Arizona. Her legal career began as a civil rights lawyer, specializing first in HIV discrimination cases and then race and sex cases more generally. In the past twenty-five years, she has authored briefs in cases addressing HIV discrimination, forced sterilization, same-sex sexual harassment, gender stereotyping, and transgender discrimination in the Supreme Court and other lower courts.

Irwin Garfinkel is the Mitchell I. Ginsberg Professor of Contemporary Urban Problems at the Columbia University School of Social Work, co–founding director of the Columbia Population Research Center, and the co–principal investigator of the Fragile Families and Child Well-Being Study. He has authored more than 180 scientific articles and 12 books on poverty, income transfer policy, program evaluation, single-parent families, and child support. His most recent book is *Wealth and Welfare States: Is America a Laggard or Leader?* (2010).

Marsha Garrison is the Susan J. and Norman Miles Professor of Law at Brooklyn Law School and an expert on law and policy relating to families, children, and reproductive technology. Her research and writing span a broad range of topics including marriage, cohabitation, parentage determination, the economics of divorce, and child welfare decision making. Much of her research is interdisciplinary, applying social science and economic data to legal policy issues. She also conducted widely cited empirical analyses of judicial decision making of divorce and the impact of changes in New York's divorce laws. Professor Garrison has coauthored two widely used casebooks: *Family Law: Cases, Comments, and Questions* (6th ed., 2007) and *Law and Bioethics: Individual Autonomy and Social Regulation* (2d ed., 2009). Her scholarship has been published in a variety of books and leading law journals. Professor Garrison is the Secretary-General of the International Society of Family Law. She is also a member of the Advisory Board of the *Journal of Law and Family Studies* and the International Advisory Board of the *Child and Family Law Quarterly*.

Suzanne B. Goldberg is Clinical Professor of Law, Director of the Sexuality & Gender Law Clinic, and Director of the Program in Gender & Sexuality Law at Columbia Law School, where she also teaches courses in civil procedure. Professor Goldberg has written extensively on family law matters and morals-based justifications for lawmaking, and more generally on procedural and substantive barriers to equality. She has published articles in leading law reviews, including the *Yale Law Journal*, *UCLA Law Review*, *Columbia Law Review*, and many other legal journals. Through Columbia Law School's Sexuality & Gender Law Clinic, Professor Goldberg has also submitted numerous amicus briefs in family law cases, including one that will be reproduced in a forthcoming article in the *Columbia Gender Law Journal* entitled "Family Law Scholarship Goes to Court: Functional Parenthood and the Case of Debra H. v. Janice R." Prior to entering academia in 2000, Professor Goldberg spent a decade as a senior lawyer with Lambda Legal, an LGBT/HIV civil rights advocacy organization in the United States.

Shahar Lifshitz is a law professor at Bar-Ilan University Law School. He is also a Senior Research Fellow at the Israel Democracy Institute, where he co-directs the project on Human Rights in Judaism. Professor Lifshitz was a visiting scholar and Berkowitz Fellow at New York University Law School in 2005–2006 and a visiting Professor of Law and Distinguished Fellow of Jewish Law and Interdisciplinary Studies at Cardozo Law School in 2006–2007 and Spring 2009. He was also a Visiting Professor at Columbia Law School in Fall 2009. Professor Lifshitz's areas of academic interest are contract law, family law, law in multicultural societies, and Jewish law, especially the philosophical basis of these fields. Professor Lifshitz is the author of numerous publications. His books include *The Spousal Registry* (2007) and *Cohabitation Law in Israel from the Perspective of a Civil Law Theory of the Family* (2005), for which he was awarded the Bahat Prize. He is also the author of numerous articles in Israeli and American law reviews, including *Law & Contemporary Problems* (2011), *Boston College Law Review* (2010), *Washington and Lee Law Review* (2009), and *North Carolina Law Review*. Professor Lifshitz currently serves as the Vice Chairman of the Israeli Association of Private Law. Together with Israeli Supreme Court President Dorit Benish, Professor Lifshitz co-chairs the Forum for Cooperation between the Israeli Supreme Court and Israeli legal academia. Professor Lifshitz's previous work at IDI included formulating the family law chapter in IDI's Constitution by Consensus.

Sara S. McLanahan is the William S. Tod Professor of Sociology and Public Affairs at Princeton University and Faculty Associate of the Office of Population Research. She directs the Bendheim-Thoman Center for Research on Child Wellbeing, is a principal investigator on the Fragile Families and Child Wellbeing Study and Editor-in-Chief of *The Future of Children*. Her research interests include family demography, poverty and inequality, and social policy. She has written five books, including *Fathers Under Fire* (1998), *Social Policies for Children* (1996), *Growing Up with a Single Parent* (1994), *Child Support and Child Wellbeing* (1994), and *Single Mothers and Their Children: A New American Dilemma* (1986), and more than 100 scholarly articles. She currently serves on the Board of Trustees for the W.T. Grant Foundation, the Board of Trustees for the Russell Sage Foundation, the National Advisory Committee for the Robert Wood Johnson Foundation Health and Society Scholars, the Advisory Board for the National Poverty Center, and the Advisory Board for the Pew Charitable Trust Economic Mobility Project. She is a former President of the Population Association of America and has served on the Board of the American Sociological Association, the Population Association of America, and the National Academy of Sciences Board on Children, Youth, and Families. McLanahan was named the James S. Coleman Fellow of the American Academy of Political Science in 2005 and received the Distinguished Scholar Award from the American Sociological Association Family Section in 2004.

Rebecca Probert is professor of law at the University of Warwick, where she teaches family law. Her research has focused primarily on the history of marriage and cohabitation (see, e.g., *Marriage Law and Practice in the Long Eighteenth Century: A Reassessment* [Cambridge University Press, 2009]; *The Rights and Wrongs of Royal Marriage* [2011]; and *The Legal Regulation of Cohabitation, 1600–2010: From Fornicators to Family* [Cambridge University Press, 2012]), but she has also written on family law more broadly (see, e.g., *Cretney and Probert's Family Law*, 8th ed., 2012) and has edited a number of collections of essays on family law topics (*Landmarks in Family Law* [2011] and *Responsible Parents and Parental Responsibility* [2009], both with Stephen Gilmore and Jonathan Herring, and *Sharing Lives, Dividing Assets* [2009], with Joanna Miles).

Carl E. Schneider is the Chauncey Stillman Professor for Ethics, Morality, and the Practice of Law and is a Professor of Internal Medicine at the University of Michigan. He was educated at Harvard College and the University of Michigan Law School, where he was Editor in Chief of the *Michigan Law Review*. He served as law clerk to Judge Carl McGowan of the U.S. Court of Appeals for the District of Columbia Circuit and to Justice Potter Stewart of the U.S. Supreme Court. He became a member of the Law School faculty in 1981 and of the Medical School faculty in 1998. Professor Schneider has written extensively in several fields, including bioethics, professional ethics, professional education, family law, and constitutional law. Schneider is the author of *The Practice of Autonomy: Patients, Doctors, and*

Medical Decisions (1998), which examines how power to make medical decisions is and should be divided between doctors and patients and analyzes the role of autonomy in American culture. As one reviewer said of the book, it uncovers a "great hole . . . for all to see: the failure of autonomy not only as reality but even as ideal law." He is also the author of two casebooks: *The Law of Bioethics: Individual Autonomy and Social Regulation*, with Marsha Garrison, and *An Invitation to Family Law* (2006), with Margaret Brinig.

Elizabeth S. Scott is the Harold R. Medina Professor of Law at Columbia Law School. Her areas of scholarly interest are family and juvenile law, and she has published extensively in legal and social science journals on marriage, divorce, child custody, adolescent decision making, and the legal regulation of juvenile crime. Much of her research is interdisciplinary, applying social science research, developmental theory, and behavioral economics to legal policy issues involving children and families. With Laurence Steinberg, she is the author of *Rethinking Juvenile Justice* (2010), which received the 2010 Society for Research in Adolescence award for the best social policy book. Professor Scott is also the coauthor of two widely used casebooks in Family Law and Children in the Legal System. Scott was a member of a John D. and Catherine T. MacArthur Foundation Research Network on Adolescent Development and Juvenile Justice, an interdisciplinary research group that, over a ten-year period, conducted studies of adolescents' competence to stand trial, desistance from criminal activity, and public attitudes toward youthful culpability. She was a founder and co-director of the Center for Children, Family and the Law at the University of Virginia, an interdisciplinary center that promotes research and informs policy makers and practitioners on issues relating to children and families. Scott has also served on numerous task forces and committees dealing with legal policy toward families.

Judith Stacey is Professor of Sociology and Professor of Social and Cultural Analysis at New York University. Her research examines changes in family, sexuality, and society. Her publications include *Unhitched: Love, Sex and Family Values from West Hollywood to Western China* (2011); *In the Name of the Family: Rethinking Family Values in the Postmodern Age* (1996); *Brave New Families: Stories of Domestic Upheaval in Late Twentieth Century America* (1990, new edition in 1998); as well as "(How) Does the Sexual Orientation of Parents Matter?" coauthored with Timothy Biblarz, *ASR* (2001), and "How Does the Gender of Parents Matter?" coauthored with Tim Biblarz, *Journal of Marriage and Family* (2010). She served as an expert witness in the Canadian same-sex marriage case and in lesbian adoption and gay family rights cases in the United States.

Arland Thornton is Professor of Sociology at the University of Michigan and Research Professor at the Population Studies Center and Survey Research Center. He is also a faculty affiliate at the University's Center for Middle Eastern and

North African Studies, Center for Chinese Studies, the Weiser Center for Emerging Democracies, and the Center for South Asian Studies. Thornton is a social demographer with a long record of sponsored research and publication. He has served as president of the Population Association of America and currently holds a MERIT Award from the NIH. He has received four awards for his books as well as a Distinguished Career Award from the American Sociological Association. Thornton has contributed substantially to the understanding of intergenerational processes and forces affecting marriage, cohabitation, and living arrangements. This work has culminated in an award-winning 2007 book (with William Axinn and Yu Xie) titled *Marriage and Cohabitation*. He has also coedited a book on the role of ideational forces in international family change (Jayakody et al. 2008) and is currently directing a panel study in Nepal investigating the impact of ideational factors on marriage and fertility behaviors in that country. During the past decade, Thornton has devoted considerable time and energy to studying developmental idealism and its influence in many areas of the world. His 2001 presidential address to the Population Association of America focused on this topic, as does his award-winning book entitled *Reading History Sideways: The Fallacy and Enduring Impact of the Developmental Paradigm on Family Life* (2005). Of particular importance for Thornton's current work are the ways in which values, beliefs, and people have been and are being distributed around the world.

Acknowledgments

The idea for this book grew out of numerous conversations over lunch in a small restaurant in the West Village – about family law issues generally, and about the future of marriage at this interesting historic juncture. As family law experts who share a belief that social science research can inform the legal regulation of families, we thought that an edited volume on "marriage at the crossroads," that brought together the leading social scientists studying families and leading family law experts could make an important contribution to the literature. We were delighted that virtually every scholar we invited to contribute to the book accepted our invitation, and we are extraordinarily grateful to all of our contributors for making this project such an amazing success. We are also grateful to the Columbia Law School and to the Henry Schneider Memorial Fund for funding a wonderful and productive conference that brought the authors together to present and discuss chapter drafts. The Columbia Center for Gender and Sexuality Law was a co-sponsor of the conference and Vina Tran provided invaluable assistance in its organization. We thank Dean David Schizer, of the Columbia Law School, and Interim Dean Michael Gerber, of Brooklyn Law School, for their enthusiasm about the project and for their financial support. We are grateful to our research assistant, David Berman, and to Peter Graham, who carefully organized the chapters into a coherent manuscript. Our Cambridge University Press editor, John Berger, was terrific; his enthusiasm for the book and guidance at critical points were invaluable. Finally, we are grateful to Shana Meyer who managed the production process with efficiency and good humor.

Introduction

Marsha Garrison and Elizabeth S. Scott

Today, marriage is at a crossroads. Across the industrialized world, young adults are marrying later and increasing numbers may not marry at all. Married couples, for several decades now, have also faced a relatively high probability that their relationships will terminate in divorce. These changes have affected children as well as adults. The proportion of children born outside of marriage has grown dramatically, and children born within marriage face an increased risk of parental divorce or separation. Moreover, marriage itself has changed in important ways, from a lifelong institutional union to a companionate relationship, the strength and duration of which are determined by the individual preferences of the parties. Public attitudes toward these trends are generally accepting; a majority of Americans in a recent survey were positive or neutral about couples (including gay couples) living together and having and raising children outside of marriage.

Interestingly, as traditional marriage has declined, the movement to extend the right to marry to same-sex couples has acquired substantial momentum and become an important focus for advocates in the gay and lesbian community. A number of nations and several American states have legalized same-sex marriage; others have created an alternate status that confers some or all of the rights and obligations of marriage. This issue has generated controversy. Those who favor extending marriage to same-sex couples see marriage as a core social status, access to which is an essential aspect of full membership in society. Social conservatives who favor an alternate status – or no status at all – agree that marriage is a core social institution, but argue that extending access to same-sex couples will irreparably weaken marriage. At the same time, some gay and lesbian advocates argue that marriage is a gendered and outmoded institution and that the gay community should not make the right to marry a key political goal.

Controversy has also surrounded the decline of opposite-sex marriage. Some commentators have argued that the decline of marriage is a troubling social problem, while others see the trend as nothing more than a sign of the growing irrelevance of an obsolete institution. Some who see a problem view the changes as evidence of moral decline, while others focus on the relative instability of nonmarital cohabitation as compared to marriage (and of remarriage as compared to first marriage). Family stability is associated with a range of benefits to children and instability with a range of risks. And both the risk of parental breakup and the number of different family arrangements that children experience as they grow to adulthood has skyrocketed. Moreover, particularly in the United States, a growing class divide in marriage and family life may exacerbate socioeconomic disadvantage. Less educated and lower-income individuals are far more likely to have children outside of marriage than those who have more education and higher incomes. Indeed, as Sara McLanahan and Irv Garfinkel suggest in this volume, Murphy Brown, the target of condemnation by Vice President Quayle in the 1980s, is a myth; only very small percentage of college-educated professional women have children outside of marriage.

While the association between marriage and relational stability is clear, whether marriage itself contributes to that stability has been less obvious. It could be that couples who do not marry have preexisting characteristics that would produce relational instability whether or not their relationships are formalized through marriage. And even if marriage plays a causal role in promoting family stability, it is not obvious how policy makers should respond. Should government actively promote marriage and marital childbearing? Or should government extend the public benefits and private rights that now accompany marital status to couples that have not married?

No consensus has yet emerged about the appropriate legal and policy response to these important changes in family structure. Policy makers in the United States, both at the national and state levels, thus far have tended to favor retaining the traditional pro-marriage approach, offering benefits and privileges to married couples that are not available to other families. Other marriage promotion policies have been favored as well. The 1996 federal welfare-reform legislation that provided incentives to the states to increase two-parent families and reduce nonmarital childbearing was based on an underlying marriage-promotion policy. More recently, the George W. Bush administration launched an initiative designed to support "healthy" marriages through relationship-skills education and the reduction of tax and benefit "penalties" that might deter marriage. Many states have also launched their own marriage-promotion initiatives. Outside the United States, however, marriage promotion has been much more controversial, and policy makers have sometimes rejected laws that treat marriage more favorably than other family relationships. For example, the Canadian Parliament has revised both tax and old-age pension laws so that the same standards apply to married and "common-law" partners. Canada is far from unique. Several nations have extended some or all of the entitlements available to divorcing marriage partners to one or more groups of unmarried couples: Some countries have established an alternate status available to same-sex couples, heterosexual couples, or both, through registration. Others schemes are conscriptive; the couple's rights and obligations at separation are determined retrospectively through fact-based analysis.

For example, New Zealand has extended *all* of the personal rights and obligations of marriage to couples who have been "de facto partners" for three years.

This volume, authored by social scientists and family law scholars, explores alternative policy paths forward at this critical juncture. Debates about marriage and family policy have often been ideological and political; the volume captures the complexity of the debates through contributions by authors with widely varying perspectives. But the book also aims to inform the debates by situating them within an interdisciplinary framework grounded in social science research. This approach reflects our belief that, although family policy is – and should be – influenced by social and political values, it should also be shaped by empirical evidence. Over the past generation, social scientists have produced a large body of research that has contributed in important ways to our understanding of family formation and functioning. Family law and policy informed by this research evidence (some produced by contributors to this volume) can more effectively support families in fulfilling their important functions of caring for children and other dependents. Empirically grounded analysis also offers a neutral lens that, by enhancing understanding, may sometimes even produce consensus across ideological divides.

Part I of this volume offers historical background on marriage and its regulation, as well as demographic and cross-national perspectives on changes in marriage and in family structure. In Chapter 1, legal scholars June Carbone and Naomi Cahn explore "blue" (liberal, egalitarian) and "red" (traditional, culturally conservative) patterns of family formation and dissolution to inform and enrich our understanding of recent trends, including the growing class divide in marriage behavior in the United States. They identify the cultural and demographic roots of these divergent patterns and chart their comparative advantages and policy implications. Sociologist Arland Thornton (Chapter 2) analyzes the impact on family life in the developing world of "developmental idealism," namely the Western European insistence that consent, equality, and freedom are fundamental human rights. He describes a pattern of resistance, modification, and hybridization across a range of cultures and offers some predictions as to how these cultural clashes will develop and be resolved in the future. In Chapter 3, Margaret Brinig, an economist and legal scholar, describes the economic model of marriage and uses it to explore changes in the allocation of household labor in marital and nonmarital households. Using data from several waves of the National Survey of Families and Households, she charts shifts in household labor patterns and relates them to the economic model of marriage. Rebecca Probert, a legal historian and legal scholar from the United Kingdom, in Chapter 4 describes current demographic and legal trends in the United Kingdom and continental Europe, focusing specifically on cohabitation, marriage, and divorce. She describes both variation within Europe and the ways in which the general European pattern differs from that evident in the United States. In Chapter 5, Katherine Franke, a legal scholar, offers an historical perspective on today's same-sex marriage movement by comparing the experience of African-American freedmen who first obtained the right to marry in the immediate post–Civil War era. She asks why the right to marry, rather than employment rights, educational opportunity, or political participation, emerged for both groups as the preeminent vehicle for gaining equality and dignity and suggests, based on the experience of the freedmen, how marriage rights can also constrain freedom.

Part II focuses on research by contributors (mostly social scientists) on family change and the public's response to that change. Several chapters in this part examine the impact of marriage and other family forms on adult partners and their children, illuminating the economic, social, and psychological links between family form and the well-being of family members. Paul R. Amato (Chapter 6) explores the evolution of marriage, describing three types of marriage that can be observed in contemporary society: traditional institutional marriage, companionate marriage, and individualistic marriage. He then compares the three types and finds companionate marriage to be associated with greater marital satisfaction and stability than the others. Robert E. Emery, Erin Horn, and Christopher Beam in Chapter 7 investigate whether the association between marriage and various health and happiness benefits results from marital status or from individual characteristics by comparing the marital histories and experiences with clinical depression of fraternal and identical twins who share childhood experience and some or all of their genes. They report that their data support the proposition that the marital benefit is not an artifact of selection. In Chapter 8, using data from the Fragile Families and Child Well-Being Study, a major longitudinal research project in the United States, Sara McLanahan and Irwin Garfinkel examine the causes and consequences of increased rates of cohabitation and nonmarital birth; they also offer policy recommendations, ranging from reduced incarceration to tax strategies, to increase the likelihood that children will grow up in stable families and minimize the harms associated with instability if it cannot be avoided. Finally, in Chapter 9, Ira Mark Ellman and Sanford L. Braver – a legal scholar and a psychologist, respectively – probe public attitudes toward family change and family obligations. They present survey evidence on public attitudes toward marriage as reflected in decisions about post-separation support and property division. They report that marriage plays a role in public attitudes toward these obligations, but not a determinative role.

Part III focuses on important contemporary policy debates, with several authors probing the legal implications of the recent changes in marriage and family life. In Chapter 10, Judith Stacey, a sociologist, draws on her ethnographnic research on families around the world to illustrate that a wide range of relationships can fulfill the important child-rearing and social support functions of families. She argues that formal, state-sanctioned marriage inappropriately privileges some families over others and proposes abolishing marriage as a legal status. Suzanne B. Goldberg (Chapter 11) and Carl E. Schneider (Chapter 12), both legal scholars, explore the debate over extending the right to marry to same-sex couples. Goldberg probes the arguments advanced by gay advocates for and against making the right to marry a high political priority. She endorses the view that marriage rights are important for their tangible benefits and as a powerful statement of social equality. But Goldberg rejects the contemporary relevance of the claim that allowing access to marriage for gay couples has the potential to transform marriage, suggesting that modern legal marriage is already based on equality norms. Schneider describes the declining role of morality in public discourse about marriage and family and analyzes the implications of this rhetorical shift on the debate over same-sex marriage. He considers whether same-sex marriage would serve the classic marital socializing function for gays and lesbians, as some gay advocates have argued, and how it would affect that function for heterosexuals. In contrast to Stacey, Shahar Lifshitz (Chapter 13), a legal scholar, argues against the abolition of formal marriage (what he calls the "private-neutral" approach), but also rejects the "public-channeling" approach that favors continuing to make marriage the only means of formalizing an intimate relationship. Instead, Lifshitz proposes a "pluralist" approach under which the state would make available to couples in intimate partnerships a range of legal-status options. This approach, Lifshitz argues, is the best means of protecting the key values of pluralism and autonomy and accommodating the important public and private interests at stake in designing family-status institutions.

The book concludes with two comments. In Chapter 14, sociologist Andrew Cherlin summarizes and reflects on the various contributions to this volume. We follow Cherlin's comment in Chapter 15 with an analysis of the evidence provided by the contributors, probing the policy implications and offering some tentative recommendations.

A generation from now, marriage and childbearing may seem quite different than they do today. Will marriage be less or more important as a family form? Will lawmakers have increased or reduced government support for marriage? Will couples who cannot marry today have gained access to marriage? Will formal marriage alternatives have expanded? Will some or all of those who do not marry be treated like those who do marry? The interdisciplinary approach offered by this volume provides tools to analyze and, hopefully, assist in resolving these policy questions about marriage at a critical juncture.

PART I

History, Demographics, and Economics – Multiple Perspectives on Families

1

Red v. Blue Marriage

June Carbone and Naomi Cahn

Marriage has long been a symbol of union – a union between husband and wife, a compact between the couple and the community concerning support for children, and an institution that, even as it changed or cloaked inconvenient facts about sexuality or paternity, forged shared meanings about family life. Today, however, marriage has increasingly become a symbol of disunion.

The disunion involves divorce and the disappearance of permanence as a defining feature of marriage. It extends to a dramatic increase in nonmarital births, as marriage has become an optional rather than mandatory aspect of child-rearing. And, in the United States today, marriage is increasingly a symbol of what divides us: regionally, economically, racially, politically, and ideologically.

These disagreements over the meaning and future of marriage start with fundamental changes in the role of marriage in ordering family life and extend to profound divisions about how to respond. Marriage "as we knew it" in the halcyon days of the 1950s was a product of two periods that have now passed: the industrial era that separated home and market and its final iteration in the relatively brief period at the end of World War II when the United States dominated world manufacturing. The nineteenth-century industrial era had moved the productive activities formerly associated with farm and shop, food and clothing production, out of the home. In response, the middle class promoted a new ideal that changed the couples' relationship from a hierarchical one that subordinated wife to husband to a more companionate and complementary one. In accordance with this ideal, the wage-earner husband handled the impersonal world of the market while the wife oversaw a redefined domestic realm whose principal purpose became the moral and educational instruction of children (Carbone 2000). While the middle-class model had long set the standards by which others were to be judged, it reached its height during the prosperous 1950s, a period in which a larger part of society could realize the advantages of stay-at-home moms in the nuclear families of newly constructed suburbs.

As the industrial era gave way to the information economy, the new economy remade women's roles, eliminated the highly paid jobs once available for less skilled men, and challenged the ideology of the family of the separate spheres. The information economy has simultaneously increased the demand for women's labor in the workforce and created labor-saving devices (and McDonald's) that reduced the amount of time devoted to the home (Carbone 2000). Perhaps as fundamentally, the birth control pill and abortion have remade the terms of sexual engagement: early marriage is no longer necessary to contain the consequences of women's sexuality. These changes have, in turn, transformed family life (Cahn and Carbone 2010; Goldin and Katz 2002; Hymowitz 2011).

Investment in women's income potential now pays off, and the new economy, while continuing to generate high-paying jobs for the most successful men, has increased income inequality for the country as a whole and has increased women's overall opportunities more than men's. With greater opportunities for the best-educated, the age of marriage has risen and, with it, the stigma of nonmarital sexuality has waned (Carbone 2000). In addition, as women enjoy more autonomy, they have greater ability to determine which relationships to embrace, which to leave, and which partners, if any, to include in rearing children. Within this context, marriage becomes a choice that can be redefined to express individual preferences or changing expectations about family roles.

In the midst of the transition, however, marriage no longer necessarily rests on shared experiences and understandings. The divisions start with geography. The age of marriage has increased everywhere, but it has increased most dramatically in the wealthiest and most liberal parts of the country (Cahn and Carbone 2010). The increase in the age of marriage also corresponds to a dramatic drop in teen births, decreases in fertility, and greater commitment to controlling childbirth through contraception and abortion. Birth rates in the Northeast resemble those in Northern Europe (at 1.8 in Massachusetts and Connecticut, they are below replacement) while remaining much higher in Utah, the South, and Southwest because of a combination of immigration, much younger average ages of marriage, and lesser access to contraception and abortion (Cahn and Carbone 2010).

The divergences increase with consideration of race and class. The most recent statistics show that both marriage and divorce have declined (Wilcox 2010). In fact, the average figures cloak dramatic differences for the college-educated middle class and what used to be the more marriage-oriented working class. The decline in marriage rates has been far more precipitous for those without a college education. And marriage has effectively disappeared in some communities; 96 percent of children born to African-American high school dropouts, for example, are born outside of marriage. At the same time, the divorce rates for college graduates have steadily declined since the late 1970s, returning to the levels of the mid-1960s (Wilcox 2010; McLanahan 2004). Yet, they continued to climb for everyone else, slowed only by the Great Recession (Wilcox 2010). In addition, while college graduates marry later than nongraduates and have relatively low overall fertility rates, they still overwhelmingly raise children within two-parent families, and the likelihood that their children will live with both biological parents has increased over the last thirty years. For everyone else, the connection between marriage and child-rearing has eroded, with the intact two-parent family emerging as a marker of class (Carbone 2010:2).[1]

The differences become a chasm when viewed through the lens of ideology. We have argued that the changing marriage patterns of college graduates reflect a new, "blue" middle-class strategy (Carbone 2010): invest in women as well as men, postpone marriage until after the couples establishes financial independence and emotional maturity, hold the line on nonmarital births through an embrace of contraception and, if necessary, abortion, and adopt more flexible attitudes toward gender and family roles. Those who embrace this strategy have more resources to invest in their children and enjoy more stable family relationships.

The new model, however, is an affront to the "red" values associated with traditional religious teachings, and the advice to postpone marriage and childbearing until completion of postgraduate internships rings hollow for those who will not attend college. The red elite associated with more conservative, religious, and traditionalist parts of the country has accordingly opposed the new model and used its opposition to forge political alliances that link the traditionalist working class most threatened by these changes to a conservative business elite. The result has stalled acceptance of the symbols of the new family model, such as same-sex marriage, and blocked more systematic access to contraception and abortion, disproportionately affecting the reproductive decisions of the poorest women (Carbone 2011:560–563).

The clash between the two groups, which Justice Scalia has termed a "culture war," is a fight to establish the dominant terms of family life and the meaning of marriage within it (Cahn and Carbone 2010). If one or the other group won, it would set the terms of assistance for those on the losing end of the new economy. In the midst of the clash between red and blue, however, each side fights to undermine the other's proposals to systematize norms through either abstinence or marriage promotion, on the one hand, or more effective access to contraception, the morning-after pill and abortion, and assistance for children, on the other. In the context of these divisions, marriage has emerged, not as a potential rallying cry for a new era of union, but as a marker of regional, class, and ideological differences.

This chapter first examines the process of family change and its connections to the changing economy. Second, it describes the way family changes play out along regional and class lines. Third, it considers the relationship between family changes and ideological divisions, describing the differences between strategies that seek to link women to men through control of sexuality versus those that would promote women's autonomy and insist on neutrality toward family form. Finally, the chapter

[1] The marital birth rate for women with some college education in 2006 was 80 percent; it was 58 percent for high school graduates and 45 percent for women who did not have a high school diploma (Cohn 2009:16).

will conclude that changes in the family magnify the increasing inequality in society, and that the class-based nature of changes in marriage will guarantee increasing disinvestment in the next generation as a whole.

FAMILY CHANGE, CHANGING COMMUNITIES, AND THE CHANGING ECONOMY

Marriage, as a matter of union or disunion, has long corresponded to the country's political and economic climate. Early New England colonists came to the New World to escape the domination of the Church of England. They adopted judicial divorce at a time when it took an Act of Parliament to dissolve a marriage in the home country (Estin 2007). By 1800, all of the Northern states permitted judicial divorce. In contrast, the Southern states, settled by English plantation owners and the more traditionalist Scotch-Irish, remained firmly opposed to divorce (Estin 2007). They did not adopt judicial divorce until after the Civil War, and even then opposed the liberalization occurring in other states through the end of World War II. The founding fathers dealt with these divisions by assigning family law firmly to the states. Justice Felix Frankfurter observed in 1942 that the Constitution of the United States reserves authority over marriage and divorce to the states, and "each state has the constitutional power to translate into law its own notions of policy concerning the family institution." He stated that "neither the crudest nor the subtlest juggling of legal concepts could enable us to bring forth a uniform national law of marriage and divorce" (*Williams v. North Carolina*, 304).

Nonetheless, family law enjoyed a brief period of greater uniformity in the 1960s and 1970s; initially, the changes in the family affected the country as a whole. The United States emerged from the shaping events of the Depression and World War II as a prosperous nation. Income inequality, which had peaked during the 1920s and remained high through the war, fell sharply during the 1950s (Noah 2010). Economists now term the period from 1941 to 1979 as the "Great Compression"; during this period, the income of each part of American society – rich or poor – grew at roughly the same rates (Bartels 2008; Goldin and Margo 1992). The increased prosperity – and greater equality – set the stage for the "baby boom," the dramatic increase in the birth rate that began with the return of the troops from World War II and lasted until the advent of the "sexual revolution" and widespread use of contraception. While Americans think of the 1950s as a period of time-tested family values, Stephanie Coontz emphasizes that:

> In fact, the "traditional" family of the 1950's was a qualitatively new phenomenon. At the end of the 1940's, all the trends characterizing the rest of the twentieth century suddenly reversed themselves. For the first time in more than one hundred years, the age for marriage and motherhood fell, fertility increased, divorce rates declined, and women's degree of educational parity with men dropped sharply (Coontz 1992: 23).

These changes, although they partly reflected "good times," also marked the unheralded beginning of the sexual revolution (Bailey 1988; Sanger 1995). Coontz notes that along with the increase in marital births came an 80 percent increase in the number of babies placed for adoption and a doubling of the percentage of white brides who gave birth within eight and a half months of the nuptials (Coontz 1992). Indeed, in 1960, 30 percent of all brides were pregnant at the altar – a percentage last seen in 1800 (Hirshman and Larson 1998). The results undid the sexual restraint that had served as the foundation for middle-class morality since the nineteenth century and threatened the educational achievement of American women just as the doors to greater economic opportunity were opening. Indeed, from 1960 to 1970, the average age of women college graduates with children under the age of five continued to *fall* (McLanahan 2004).

Over the decade from the mid-1960s to the mid-1970s, however, came a profound remaking of sexual practices. The revolution began with dramatically greater access to higher education. From 1960 to 1970, the number of college students doubled, and then increased an additional 42 percent in the 1970s (Rumberger 1984). Women increased enrollment rates faster than men, matching male college attendance levels by 1980 and today exceeding the percentage of men who graduate from four-year institutions (Stoops 2004).

College attendance, particularly in institutions far from home, made supervision of young women's sexual activity more difficult, and ill-timed pregnancy threatened to derail college completion and graduate school attendance. The increase in college attendance accordingly increased interest in access to contraception. Before ratification of the Twenty-Sixth Amendment in 1971, however, the age of majority in most states was twenty-one, and distribution of birth control to minors required parental consent, if state law permitted it at all (Goldin and Katz 2002). The combination of the change in the age of majority and the Supreme Court's extension of a right to contraception to single women in 1971 and minors in 1977 made it possible to dispense the pill directly on college campuses (Cahn and Carbone 2010), and in 1970, Congress authorized federal funding of family-planning services for all women (Luker 1997). Finally, in 1973, the Supreme Court guaranteed women a right of access to abortion in *Roe v. Wade*. Adoptions, which reached an all-time high in 1970, fell by half by 1975 (Boonstra 2006).

These changes remade women's lives in a dramatically short time. Economists Claudia Goldin and Lawrence Katz observe that the percentage of women who reported engaging in sex before the age of twenty-one grew from about 40 percent of those born in 1945 to more than 70 percent of those born a decade later (Goldin and Katz 2002). Moreover, whereas in the 1960s, half of the women who engaged in premarital sex did so only with their fiancés, by the mid-1980s, less than 25 percent of the women who reported having premarital sex did so only with men they expected to marry (Luker 1997). Yet, the increase in sexual activity corresponded with a "baby bust" that reduced overall fertility. The postwar increase in births, which peaked in 1957 at 97 births per 1,000 teens between the ages of 15 and 19, fell almost in half by 1983 to 52 births per 1,000 young women (Coontz 1992:202–203; Luker 1997:196). During this latter period, expectations about fertility changed. In 1963, 80 percent of non-Catholic female college students wanted three or more children, and 44 percent wanted at least four. By 1973, just 29 percent wanted three or more (and fewer actually had this many) – an extraordinary shift in a ten-year period (Carbone 2011).

Goldin and Katz emphasize that these changes were particularly dramatic for the college-educated. Of the women born in 1950 and entering college in the late 1960s, half were married by age twenty-three. For those born seven years later in 1957, and entering college in the mid- to late 1970s, fewer than 30 percent were married by age twenty-three (a year after the normal age of college graduation) (Goldin and Katz 2002). With later ages of marriage, more women attended graduate school. Between 1950 and 1970, the percentage of women in professional schools stayed flat, with no more than 10 percent in medicine (0.1), law (0.04), dentistry (0.01), and business administration (0.03). By 1980, however, the numbers had jumped to 30 percent in medicine, 36 percent in law, 19 percent in dentistry, and 28 percent in business (Goldin and Katz 2002).

The changes in the family affected the country as a whole. The shotgun marriages of the 1950s set the stage for the divorces of the 1970s. Between 1965 and 1985, every state in the country liberalized its divorce laws, and divorce rates moved steadily upward (Carbone 2000). Although college graduates were less likely to divorce than those with less education, the divorce rates increased at about the same rate for both groups – at least for couples married by the end of the 1970s (McLanahan 2004). Nonmarital birth rates also increased for the country as a whole through the end of the 1960s, a trend that accelerated for African Americans and the least educated in every racial category during the 1970s (McLanahan 2004). Starting in the 1980s, however, the country began to change in quite different ways and the changes no longer moved the country as a whole in the same direction.

THE SEEDS OF DIVISION: REGION, CLASS, AND FAMILY CHANGE

If the story of the 1950s and 1960s is the story of the Great Compression and a greater degree of national unity, the story of the 1980s and 1990s is an account of the Great Divergence (Noah 2010) – a story of the country moving apart economically, culturally, and politically. The story starts with a dramatic increase in economic inequality – one that increases the differences between classes, regions, and families. It ultimately extends, however, to profound differences in family form and the ideological responses to family change. The precise causes of the economic changes are a matter of ongoing debate (Hacker and Pierson 2010), but the unmistakable fact is that they almost certainly are related to the emergence of marriage as a marker of region and class.

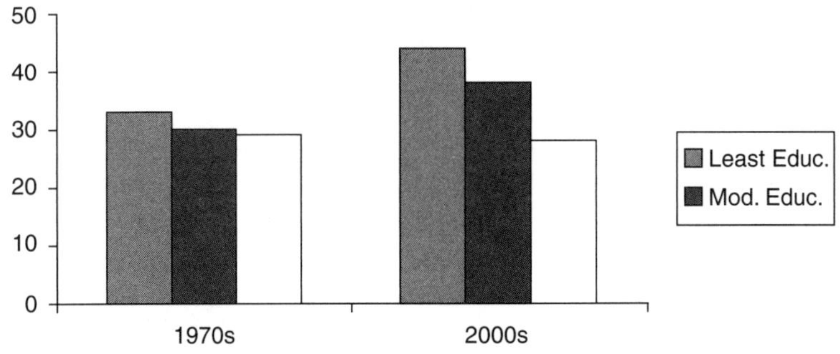

FIGURE 1.1. Percent of 29–60-Year-Old Men Unemployed at Some Point Over the Preceding 10 Years

Economic Change

Since 1980, the U.S. economy has changed substantially, creating dramatically greater rewards at the top, steady improvement for the college educated, stagnation for those without college degrees, and a loss of income in real dollar terms for the least educated. These changes have had the most negative effect on the least skilled men, as blue-collar manufacturing jobs have moved overseas, and at every level except for the top, they have improved women's positions vis-à-vis men.

Looking at the economy as a whole, economist Emmanuel Saez finds that income inequality in the United States is now at the highest level in a century (Carbone 2011:531). Between 1980 and 2005, the U.S. economy grew steadily, but 80 percent of the increase in income went to the top 1 percent of U.S. earners (Noah 2010). Indeed, those at the 99.99th percentile (about 13,000 people) increased their income between 1985 and 2005 by a factor of 5 (amounting to an increase of more than $4 million a year) and those at the 99.90th percentile tripled their incomes, while those below the 99.00th percentile showed relatively modest gains (Bartels 2008).

At the other end of the income scale, male high school dropouts earned only 70 percent in 1997 of what similar workers made in 1973 (Carbone 2011). White males in the middle of the income distribution scale saw their wages stagnate (Acemoglu 2002). The economic downturn made things worse (Boushey 2010). In August 2010, for example, the unemployment rate for high school graduates rose to 10.3 percent in comparison with a 4.6 percent rate for those with a bachelor's degree or higher. Laid-off college graduates find new employment more quickly, with median unemployment of 18.4 weeks, compared to 27.5 weeks for those with just a high school diploma (Dougherty 2010).

Job stability, which used to vary little for high school and college graduates, now varies more (Wilcox 2010:21, 55). The National Marriage Project found that during the 1970s, male employment varied little by class or education (Wilcox 2010). Today, as Figure 1.1 (Wilcox 2010:43) shows, unemployment rates have stayed the same for the college graduates, but increased substantially for other men.

	Least Ed.	Mod. Ed.	Highly Ed.
1970	67	73	73
2007	39	45	58

FIGURE 1.2. Percentage in Intact First Marriage, 25–60-Year-Olds, by Education and Decade

These changes set the stage for changes in family stress and marital prospects. During the period between 1980 and 2007, the only men whose earnings increased in real dollar terms were college graduates (Fry and Cohn 2010). Families farther down the socioeconomic ladder accordingly became much more dependent on women's income to maintain the same standard of living (Fry and Cohn 2010). At the same time, all women except for high school dropouts have seen their incomes increase, with the largest jumps for women college graduates (Fry and Cohn 2010). The result may affect not only the economic well-being of the affected families, but the terms of intimate partnerships (Carbone and Cahn, forthcoming).

Family Change

During the 1990s, scholars reported that the divorce rate, after climbing steadily for the last several decades, had finally leveled off (McLanahan 2004). Births to teen mothers also dropped sharply, falling the most for African Americans and other high-risk groups (Santelli et al. 2007). Both trends seemed to represent a national shift in intimate behavior, but in fact cloaked dramatic divergences.

The changes in divorce are in many ways the most dramatic. Divorce rates for both college and non-college graduates increased in the era in which no-fault divorce laws were first enacted. By 2004, however, the divorce rate for those with college degrees had steadily fallen, back to the levels of the mid-1960s – before the sexual revolution and no-fault reforms (Cahn and Carbone 2010; McLanahan 2004). For everyone else, divorce rates leveled off and then, for couples married in the early 1990s, resumed their rise (Cahn and Carbone 2010; Martin 2004:14, 34, fig. 1; McLanahan 2004; Figure 1.2). In other words, the change in divorce does not mean just that more educated couples are less likely to divorce; that in itself is not unusual. Rather, the divorce rates of the well off and not so well off are heading in opposite directions, increasing for one group and declining for another.

Paul Amato and colleagues (2007) provide an intriguing explanation of how the economy may interact with shifting mores to produce these changes. Amato sought to explain an apparent mystery: Why, with all the changes in the family, the decline in the number who marry, and the increase in divorce, were married couples not happier? Studies showed that marital quality appeared to remain the same over the last several decades, but Amato found that, in fact, these studies cloaked a double-humped curve that mirrored the divorce rates McLanahan and Martin found. Some couples were in fact substantially more satisfied with their marriages, but another group had grown much more discontented (Amato et al. 2007).

In explaining the results, Amato first observed that the effect of financial stress had increased. In 1980, he found, unsurprisingly, that those experiencing financial distress were more divorce-prone than those who did not experience financial distress. By 2000, however, those experiencing financial distress had twice the divorce risk of those who were financially stressed in 1980, and those who were not financially stressed had become even less likely to divorce. Moreover, Amato found that, in 2000, almost all of those marrying in their twenties reported financial distress, even though the economy was doing better than it had in 1980.

Second, he observed that women's employment exacerbated the relationship between financial distress and divorce. For higher-income families, two patterns produced relatively low levels of divorce proneness: a traditional breadwinner/homemaker one and a dual-earner model, with both spouses committed to full-time employment (with college graduate wives often in professional and managerial jobs). These couples spent relatively little time together, but also experienced relatively little conflict; the workforce participation of women in these marriages, which contributed to the couple's economic security, had generally beneficial consequences for the marriages themselves. In contrast, where the wife preferred to work outside the home part time or not at all, but needed to work full time because the family needed the income, the wife's employment likely added to family stress and the couple was very likely to be divorce-prone. Amato reported that:

> [D]ual arrangements are linked with positive marital quality among middle-class couples and with negative marital quality among working-class couples. Although the additional income provided by working class wives helps . . . their families, these financial benefits come at a steep price in the form of greater marital tension, low job satisfaction, and a desire to . . . decrease hours of employment or return to . . . homemaking (Amato et al. 2007:139).

Less educated women were more likely than middle-class women to prefer a traditional division of family responsibilities, but between 1980 and 2000, they had become less likely to be married to men who could earn enough to support them.

These changes also increasingly may have made marriage more unlikely. Perhaps the most common explanation for the increase in nonmarital births to poor women is linked to what Sara McLanahan and Christine Percheski refer to as a "marriage bar," which they define as "the standard of living a couple is expected to obtain before they marry" (McLanahan and Percheski 2008:261).[2] McLanahan and Percheski explain that:

[2] See McLanahan and Percheski 2008:261 (reviewing the claim that "family structure is an important mechanism in the reproduction of poverty and inequality"). See also Gould and Paserman 2002:279 (discussing the relationship between "male wage inequality and female marriage rates within cities").

> [I]f we assume that the bar is a function of the median income of married couples, the distance becomes even greater as marriage becomes increasingly concentrated among high-income couples. Thus, the decline in marriage among low-income populations likely has a negative feedback effect by raising the bar even further (McLanahan and Percheski 2008, p. 261).

The sociologists suggest that couples' willingness to marry does not rest on an absolute standard – the minimum necessary to maintain a household – but rather a relative one that ties marriage to the ability to "maintain a certain standard of living, that includes a house, a car, and stable employment" (McLanahan and Percheski 2008:261). The higher the median level of income in a community, the higher the minimum standard for marriage, and the greater the income inequality in a region, the greater the number of couples who will never meet the standard.

While the idea of a marriage bar is controversial as an explanation for the failure to marry (Wax 2007),[3] the emergence of class-based differences in attitudes toward marriage is not (Wilcox 2010). McLanahan and Percheski suggest that "[w]age inequality may also make men in the bottom half of the income distribution less attractive as marriage partners" (McLanahan and Percheski 2008:261). The male breadwinner role continues to define male success, and the loss of both status and income that comes with lesser employment causes many men who cannot meet the expectations associated with the breadwinner role "to be deemed as failures by society, themselves, and their partners" (McLanahan and Percheski 2008:261). The result may contribute to the increase in nonmarital births, which have now reached 41 percent of the American total.

Taken together, these changes increasingly make marriage a marker of class. The National Marriage Project found that in 1970, the likelihood that a person would be married did not vary much by class. Today, the likelihood that a person will be married is a direct function of education (Figure 1.2, Wilcox 2010:21, fig. 3).

Regional Change and Ideological Division

While the previously described class dynamic is evident across the country, regional differences in the patterns of marriage, divorce, and cohabitation have also increased. This has happened partly because of mobility; college graduates are more likely to move than those who do not attend college (Bishop 2008). Wealth has also been a contributing factor; the richer areas of the countries have gotten richer, and the technology centers that have shown the greatest increases in wealth also attract the most highly educated knowledge workers. Teen births, for example, have dropped significantly in some traditionally conservative states; for example, the Boston tech corridor has expanded in New Hampshire, "beltways bandits" have expanded

3 Wax observes that women rarely complain about men's lack of income, but rather about "criminal behavior, drug use, violence, and, above all, repeated and flagrant sexual infidelity" (Wax 2007:590).

further into Virginia, and the Research Triangle has attracted better-educated migrants to North Carolina (Cahn and Carbone 2010). Finally, cultural and social policies have been important; the most conservative states have done the least to reduce unplanned pregnancies and births (Cahn and Carbone 2010). Whatever the cause, regional data shows clear differences in marriage and family patterns – and these family patterns closely correlate with traditionalist (red) versus modernist (blue) political loyalties.[4]

During the 2004 election, for example, family composition provided one of the most reliable predictors of election results (Lesthaeghe and Neidert 2006, 2008). Political scientists generated a composite number describing family characteristics associated with modernist versus traditionalist cultures. Using this number, which included factors such as overall fertility (red), abortion rates (blue), cohabitation (blue), and later age of marriage (blue), the scholars analyzed the correlation with the electoral vote by state in the 2004 presidential election. The result was a .87 (a perfect match would be 1.0) correlation, the highest correlation of any demographic variable. In 2008, the comparable results were .83 – a little lower, but still a very strong relationship (Lesthaeghe and Neidert 2008).

The relationship between family form and political loyalty is almost certainly multidirectional. The wealthier, better-educated parts of the country where residents marry later, have fewer children, and accept nonmarital unions more readily are also more liberal. Even so, the wealthy in blue states are still more likely to vote Republican than the middle of the income distribution, but the middle of the distribution is more reliably Democratic than those with the same incomes in red states (Gelman et al. 2008). Journalist Bill Bishop (2008) explains that the concentration of people with similar political views has increased in recent decades, particularly for the college educated, who tend to be more mobile and to seek out cities and localities occupied by others who share their worldviews. These political and value differences tend to shape attitudes toward marriage, as well as responses

4 In *Red Families v. Blue Families*, we argued that conservative versus liberal political orientations overlap to a high degree with traditionalism versus modernist values. Political scientists define conservatives in terms of "a yearning for in-group unity and strong leadership," suspiciousness of other groups, and "a desire for clear, unbending moral and behavioral codes" that also includes a belief in the importance of punishing anyone who violated this code, "a fondness for systematization (procedural due process), a willingness to tolerate inequality (opposition to redistributive policies), and an inherently pessimistic view of human nature (life is 'nasty, brutish, and short')" (Alford, Funk, and Hibbing 2005:164–165). They characterize liberals in terms of comparatively "tolerant attitudes toward out-groups, a desire to take a more context-dependent rather than rule-based approach to proper behavior," greater empathy, less emphasis on strict punishment for violations of moral and behavioral rules, along with "suspicion of hierarchy, certainty, and strong leadership" and intolerance of inequality (*Id.* at 165). This chapter uses the terms "traditionalist" and "modernist" to refer to the values orientations that Alford et al. describe as conservative and liberal to be distinguished from political terms often used to describe views on other issues such as economic policy. We note, however, that while the U.S. political parties have not always differed in ideological terms, they increasingly do so today. For a full description of the relationship between values preferences, political loyalties, and positions on religious and family values, see Cahn and Carbone 2010, chapter 4.

to falling marriage rates. The policies that result then further exacerbate regional differences.

In *Red Families v. Blue Families*, we argued that these differences reflect different orientations toward the new economy, gender, and the interaction between the two. The first, which we described as "blue," embraces the new middle-class strategy designed to meet the needs of the information age. The blue approach invests in the earning capacity of women as well as men, counsels a delay in marriage and childbearing until after financial independence and emotional maturity, views sexual activity as a matter of personal choice, and regards contraception as morally compelled and abortion as an acceptable, if still regrettable, fallback (Cahn and Carbone 2010). Accepted most unequivocally by modernists in cities and the more secular coastal areas, this approach uses the language of equality and tolerance in the public sphere. It sees responsibility, particularly responsibility toward children, as following from the creation of supportive environments that assist young adults in staying in school, avoiding improvident pregnancies and births, securing employment, and securing the resources they need to manage child-rearing. The blue model, in short, places less emphasis on family form (marriage by itself is not the answer) and more on creating an infrastructure (e.g., education, family-friendly jobs, access to contraception and abortion) that encourages the right choices.

The blue model, however, is in vocabulary, content, and tone an affront to traditionalists. Furthermore, the advice to postpone childbearing until financial independence and emotional maturity is easily read as advice not to have children at all by those on the losing end of the new economy. Those leading the "red" backlash accordingly call for the reaffirmation of traditional virtues and celebration of the identity of sex, marriage, and procreation (Cahn and Carbone 2010). Rooted in the more religious areas of the country and resonant with calls for certainty and adherence to timeless values, this model sees the move away from traditional family values as a moral crisis best addressed through calls for greater individual responsibility and public disapproval of those who stray. Promoting the right values involves insistence on parental authority and abstinence before marriage – often to the extent of excluding access to accurate information about contraception from high school programs. This approach includes reflexive opposition to abortion; in some regions, polls show a hardening of public attitudes and increasingly restrictive legislation (Carbone 2010:335). The net result is a system, championed by social conservative elites, that tries to channel sexuality and childbearing into marriage in an economy that fails to provide a financial basis that can sustain the resulting unions.[5]

5 While traditionalist ideology resonates more with traditional working-class values, the most recent studies show that the working class is increasingly skeptical of the possibility of making marriage work (Wilcox 2010). The divergence in views we describe here, like most other political views in the modern era, is greater among college educated elites, with college graduates in red states more likely to attend

These ideological differences both reflect and reinforce demographic differences. Consider teen birth rates, for example. In the 1980s, the lowest teen birth rates were in parts of the northeast and upper midwestern states such as Iowa, Minnesota, and North Dakota (Cahn and Carbone 2010). Today, the states with the lowest teen birth rates are all concentrated in the heavily Democratic northeast: New Hampshire, Vermont, Massachusetts, Connecticut, and Maine. States benefiting from the technology boom, such as New Hampshire, California, and Virginia (the only red state in the top group and one that voted Democratic in 2008), showed some of the largest teen birth rate declines (Kaiser 2011). In contrast, the states with the highest teen birth rates in the 1980s showed much less change during the next twenty years; they also have remained among the most conservative states politically (Cahn and Carbone 2010). These regional differences in birthrates, although they correspond to differences in culture and wealth that preceded the modern family changes, also reflect state policy. Abortion rates, for example, reflect state commitment to secure abortion availability; blue states accordingly have the highest abortion rates and are more likely to provide state funding, if necessary, to secure poor women's access. At the same time, the largest declines in abortion rates over the last fifteen years have been in the states that have shown the greatest commitment to expanding contraceptive access – New York, New Jersey, Massachusetts, Illinois, California, Oregon, Washington State, and the District of Columbia (*New York Times* 2007). Teen pregnancies also fell substantially during the 1990s, with 85 percent of the drop attributed to greater contraceptive use (Santelli et al. 2007).

These policies reinforce regional differences toward marriage. Blue states have the highest average ages of marriage (Cohn 2009) and, as we noted earlier, the lowest teen birth rates (Cahn and Carbone 2010). Moreover, most of the teen births that do occur in these states are nonmarital. In contrast, in the states with some of the highest rates of teen births – particularly in mountain west states such as Idaho and Wyoming – a much higher percentage of teen births occur within marriage (Cahn and Carbone 2010). Whether marriage prompts pregnancy or, as is more likely at younger ages, pregnancy prompts marriage, these early marriages produce high divorce rates and account for much of what Andrew Cherlin terms the Marriage-Go-Round – the dramatically high rates of relationship instability in the United States (Cherlin 2009; Mechoulan 2006).

The regional differences accordingly interact with race and class to vary the role of marriage in different parts of the country. The blue model, in which couples combine greater investment in education and earning power with later marriage, has firmly taken hold among college graduates and in the areas in which college graduates dominate. College graduates in more conservative regions may be more

church regularly, for example, than either college graduates in blue states or non-college graduates in red states (Gelman et al. 2008).

religious and traditional in their attitudes toward gender roles (and certainly toward political ideology), but they also marry later than in earlier eras and invest in their daughters' as well as their sons' earning capacity (Gelman et al. 2008). Working-class communities vary more, moving toward cohabitation rather than marriage in some regions of the country, whereas in other regions, early marriage remains the norm, followed by high rates of divorce and remarriage.[6] Moreover, the concentration of college graduates has also changed, with the percentage of college graduates increasing in urban and high-technology centers such as Austin and Boston, with lower concentrations in rural areas and rustbelt cities such as Cleveland; this gap is greater than it was a half-century ago (Bishop 2008).

Race, of course, further influences the regional patterns. For African Americans outside of the middle class, the link between marriage and childbearing was shattered two generations ago. Today, the African-American nonmarital birth rates are more than 70 percent of all births (Wilcox 2010). In poor black communities, marriage has effectively disappeared. Wilcox (2010) has found a nonmarital birth rate of 96 percent for African-American high school dropouts and 75 percent for high school graduates. In the better-off African-American communities where marriage remains important, divorce rates substantially exceed rates in comparable white communities. And while the nonmarital birth rate for white college graduate women has remained stable at 2 percent, it is climbing upward for African-American college graduates and now exceeds 25 percent (Wilcox 2010).

The structure of Latino families is changing more rapidly than perhaps of any other group. Latino fertility rates are much higher than those for African Americans, Asian Americans, or non-Latino whites. Overall U.S. fertility (at 2.1) exceeds replacement, unlike the patterns in much of the rest of the developed world, because of the high birthrate among Latinos (Wilcox 2010). The percentage of Latino births outside of marriage has risen steadily over the last decade and now exceeds 50 percent (ChildTrends 2010). These developments reflect, in part, the high poverty levels of Latino communities and the adjustment to immigration to the United States; fertility levels have fallen with succeeding generations and nonmarital births increased with the declining influence of conservative community norms of rural Latin America and elsewhere.

These differences – whether regional, urban, rural (Pruitt 2011), racial, or economic – challenge any effort to treat patterns of marriage and family in the United States as reflecting a single unified trend. At the same time, however, the impact of greater inequality, between as well as within regions, is affecting the role of marriage in the country as a whole. And the ideological differences that now drive the country's political system threaten to undermine any systematic, national approach to bolstering the declining health of our families.

[6] See, e.g., "Premarital Sex in America: A Q&A with Sociologist Mark Regnerus," http://www.utexas.edu/cola/depts/sociology/features/_features/premarital-sex-regnerus.php.

MARRIAGE AND CULTURE WAR

The nation is profoundly divided over whether reinvigorating marriage is a necessary solution to providing for children. It should not be divided, however, on the empirical question of whether the emergence of marriage as a marker of class is exacerbating inequality and undermining any prospect that the next generation will be as well educated or prosperous as their parents. And citizens should recognize that the ideological division about the role of marriage is blocking assistance to those at the losing end of the American economy.

The divisions over marriage start with the question of what marriage is and whether it is critical to family well-being. Traditionalists see marriage as a divinely ordained institution designed to order reproduction (Dobson 2004). Theorists such as James Q. Wilson seek to revive what he terms as the "authority" of marriage – that is, the sense that the formal union of a man and a woman for life is essential to family well-being and that nonmarital childbearing and the betrayal involved in leaving a spouse for a "trophy wife" should produce "shame" (Wilson 2002:217). Religiously grounded social conservatives see sex outside of marriage as "sinful." Others view reproduction outside of marriage as contributing to societal decay (Blankenhorn 2007), and the individualism that underlies the ability to tailor relationships to satisfy personal needs as self-centered and destructive (Wilson 2002). Social conservatives accordingly decry the move away from marriage as a product of individual moral failings and almost all of their solutions therefore involve reaffirming individual restraint and responsibility.

Modernists, who are more likely to be secularists, distrust references to sin, societally imposed morality, or institutional rigidity. Indeed, they often see marriage itself as an outmoded, patriarchal institution designed to police sexuality and subordinate women to men. They believe that individuals should be free to fashion the relationships of their choice and that if young people are nurtured and supported, they will make appropriate choices. In the meantime, society should not pass judgment and certainly should not attempt to coerce anyone into the oppressive institution of the past. Modernists accordingly not only welcome the recognition of committed relationships between gays and lesbians; they view recognition of same-sex marriage as a symbol of the transformation of marriage away from its patriarchal roots (Cahn and Carbone 2010; Carbone 2010).

Traditionalists and modernists tend to talk past each other and both often fail to address the needs of children. According to William Galston, there is a "mountain" of evidence that establishes that children do better in two-parent families (Carbone 2000:43, citing *Liberal Purposes: Goods, Virtues, and Diversity in the Liberal State* 1991:284). Moreover, even if the reason two-parent families do better is that they have more time or money, or that married parents tend to be older and better prepared, the impact on the next generation is the same (McLanahan and Sandefur 1994). As greater economic inequality determines the incidence of marriage, it necessarily exacerbates the inequality among children in the next generation.

The negative consequences for children occur partly for reasons that could be addressed through better-designed social programs. McLanahan's early work indicated that single-parent families did worse for two primary reasons: first, they had fewer resources (married parents tend have to have higher incomes than cohabitants and two parents have more income than one). Second, single parents provide less supervision than two parents. Finally, both single parents and cohabitants tend to be less stable than married parents, with a larger number of residential moves, school changes, and variations in household composition (McLanahan and Sandefur 1994). Government programs – Medicaid, subsidized child support, day care, and direct cash assistance – could soften the effect, but in today's political climate, conservatives are leading the charge to reduce or eliminate the programs that currently exist.

Moreover, the class divide in family formation enhances differences that stem from the cognitive environment of early childhood. Middle-class parents, who tend to be older, wealthier, and in more flexible jobs, have more resources to invest in their children's cognitive development. They are more likely to be able to afford high-quality day care, to read bedtime stories to their children, to enroll them in afterschool enrichment programs, and to provide a stimulating verbal environment. Single parents are more pressed for both time and money, and younger parents are often less educated and have less stability in their own lives. The class-based nature of marriage accordingly skews the differences in children's development from birth, differences that will later be magnified by the differences in the quality of schools and in access to higher education.

In another era, the answer might ultimately lie with ratifying new family norms. The blue model, despite its identification with tolerance and individualism, is ultimately based on a very traditional notion of responsibility toward children. The blue model does not pay much attention to who sleeps with whom, but it does view child-rearing as a critical responsibility; it accordingly recognizes the advantages of commitment for the couple and the children.

A blue world that places relatively little emphasis on promoting marriage per se still provides support and resources so that women and men can make more considered decisions about childbearing. The resulting policies seek to routinize use of contraception and guarantee access to abortion. They also provide greater assistance with employment and child care. Marriage rates would disappear as a measure of children's well-being. Poverty rates, relationship stability, and educational achievement would become the more important criteria for determining family health. Marriage would retain its importance, if at all, as a means to an end rather than as an end in itself.

The traditionalist emphasis on marriage as a unidimensional metric for family faces a conundrum. Early marriage – and efforts to contain sexuality – cannot work if the resulting unions founder because of financial stress and instability. Two solutions tend to promote greater marital stability: improve male employment prospects or discourage women's inclination to leave unhappy relationships. Sociologists such as Daniel Patrick Moynihan and William Julius Wilson tied declining marriage rates in the African-American community to the loss of jobs (Wilson 1997). Sociologists Brad Wilcox and Steven Nock linked the assumption of traditional gender roles to greater family stability (Wilcox and Nock 2006:1340). Other conservatives would reinvigorate the stigma associated with nonmarital sexuality and child-rearing (Wilson 2002). Restrictions on divorce and abortion, attacks on family-planning funds, and abstinence-only sex education all attempt to punish women for nonmarital sexuality and to insist on the importance of linking women to men in a symbiotic way. Within this model, men's and women's fates are linked through marriage as an institution that not only provides two parents for the resulting children, but encourages husband and wife to invest in each other. Kay Hymowitz's recent book, *Manning Up*, is one of a number of efforts to call attention to what she sees as the pernicious effect on men of enjoying sexual access to women without being required to "grow up" and assume greater responsibility for themselves and their families (Hymowitz 2011).

Neither red nor blue solutions are likely to fully address the needs of children without considering the impact of inequality directly. Marriage simply cannot work as a universal solution if a substantial part of the male population is chronically unemployed, in prison, on drugs, abusive, or simply depressed – and therefore unavailable for marriage. The class-based nature of marriage is a symptom of the remaking of society along class lines – a remaking that excludes large portions of the population from stable employment or meaningful social roles. In today's world, with minimal public support for families, the social class marriage gap both results from and increases inequality.

In theory, marriage could be remade in ways more likely to gain consensus. It could continue to serve as a powerful symbol of a couple's commitment to each other, a commitment that stands independent of sex, gender, or procreation. It could also continue to formalize readiness for childbearing, signaling that the marshaling of adequate resources from the partners' efforts and from kin and community is an essential part of successful parenthood. It could continue to distinguish the creation of families from more informal and temporary relationships. It can only do so, however, if marriage retains a core of shared meaning in our communities and our lives. And this is only likely to happen if marriage can transcend the regional, racial, class, and ideological divisions that stand in the way. In short, a full response must acknowledge the emergence of marriage as a marker of education and the rise of family instability as a distinctly American phenomenon that differs from the patterns of the rest of the developed world; American marriages are less stable than *cohabitation* in much of Europe (Cherlin 2009:25). Consequently, we cannot look at marriage in isolation. Any full reconsideration also requires consideration of the health of communities and institutions that support families in hard times and reinforce appropriate standards of behavior. These institutions weave together public and private protections, community assistance, and individual norms. Growing inequality is associated with a decline in community organizations, including church attendance in working-class neighborhoods. Community and family well-being are interrelated. Recreating the terms of stable relationships is more likely with greater societal equality, not only *between* men and women, but *among* men and women. The growing rates of inequality threaten the shared expectations that make stable communities possible.

New approaches must include reconstruction of the script for the middle class, prompting investment in careers and relationships that can withstand the stresses of career moves, children's illness, and geographic mobility. They also must address the destruction of the pathways that helped the working class aspire to the same combination of financial and family security. Rather than more finger-pointing and blaming single parents or same-sex marriage or loose morals for the decline of the family, the focus must be on reconstruction. What becomes important is the development of strategies to promote equal respect between partners, greater realism about parenting, more secure financial foundations for family life, and greater recognition of the importance of preparation and maturity. These will do more to ensure two-parent child-rearing than any emphasis on institutional form alone.

REFERENCES

Acemoglu, Daron. (2002). Technical Change, Inequality, and the Labor Market. *Journal of Economic Literature*, 40, 7–72.

Alford, John R., Funk, Carolyn L., and Hibbing, John R. (2005). Are Political Orientations Genetically Transmitted? *American Political Science Review*, 99, 153–167.

Amato, Paul R., Booth, A., Johnson, D., and Rogers, S. J. (2007). *Alone Together: How Marriage in America Is Changing*. Cambridge, MA: Harvard University Press.

Bailey, Beth L. (1998). *From Front Porch to Back Seat: Courtship in Twentieth-Century America*. Baltimore: The Johns Hopkins University Press.

Bartels, Larry M. (2008). *Unequal Democracy: The Political Economy of the New Gilded Age*. Princeton, NJ: Princeton University Press.

Behind the Abortion Decline. *New York Times*, January 26, 2007, available at http://www.nytimes.com/2008/01/26/opinion/26sat2.html?_r=1&scp=2&sq=abortion+contraception&st=nyt&oref=slogin.

Bishop, B. (2008). *The Big Sort: Why the Clustering of Like-Minded America Is Tearing Us Apart*. New York: Houghton Mifflin.

Blankenhorn, D. (2007). *The Future of Marriage*. New York: Encounter Books.

Boonstra, H.D., Gold, R.B., and Finer, L.B. (2006). *Abortion in Women's Lives*. New York: Guttmacher Institute. Available at http://www.guttmacher.org/pubs/2006/05/04/AiWL.pdf.

Boushey, H. et al. (2010). Memorandum of the Center for American Progress, New Census Data Reveals Decreased Income and Health Coverage 1, 4–5 (2010). Available at http://www.americanprogress.org/issues/2010/09/pdf/census_poverty_memo.pdf.

Cahn, N. and Carbone, J. (2010). *Red Families v. Blue Families: Legal Polarization and the Creation of Culture*. New York: Oxford University Press.

Carbone, J. (2000). *From Partners to Parents: The Second Revolution in Family Law*. New York: Columbia University Press.

Carbone, J. (2010). What Does Bristol Palin Have to Do With Same-Sex Marriage? *University of San Francisco Law Review*, 45, 313–356.
Carbone, J. (2011). Unpacking Inequality and Class: Family, Gender and the Reconstruction of Class Barriers. *New England Law Review*, 45, 527–568.
Carbone, J. and Cahn, N. (forthcoming). *What Really Happened to the American Family*. New York: Oxford University Press.
Cherlin, A. J. (2009). *The Marriage-Go-Round: The State of Marriage and the Family in America Today*. New York: Random House.
Child Trends (2010). Percentage of Births to Unmarried Women. Available at http://www.childtrendsdatabank.org/?q=node/196.
Cohn, D' V. and Livingston, G. (2010). "The New Demography of American Motherhood," *Pew Research Center*. Available at http://pewsocialtrends.org/2010/05/06/the-new-demography-of-americanmotherhood/
Cohn, D' V. (2009). "The States of Marriage and Divorce: Lots of Ex's Live in Texas," *Pew Research Cente*r. Available at http://pewresearch.org/pubs/1380/marriage-and-divorce-by-state.
Coontz, S. (1992). *The Way We Never Were: American Families and the Nostalgia Trap*. New York: Basic Books.
Dobson, J. (2004). "Eleven Arguments Against Same-Sex Marriage," *CitizenLink.org*, May 23. Available at http://www.family.org/cforum/extras/a0032427.cfm.
Dokoupil, T. (2009). "Men Will Be Men," *Newsweek*, February 21. Available at http://www.newsweek.com/2009/02/20/men-will-be-men.html.
Doughetry, C. (2010). "College Grads Expand Lead in Job Security," *Wall Street Journal*, September 20. Available at http://online.wsj.com/article_emailSB100014240527487043624045754796032094759961MyQjAx MTAwMDIwNjEyNDYyWj.html.
Estin, A. (2007). Family Law Federalism: Divorce and the Constitution. *William & Mary Bill of Rights Journal*, 16, 381–432.
Farber, H. (2008). "Is the Company Man an Anachronism? Trends in Long Term Employment, 1973–2005." In Danzinger, S. and Rouse, C. (Eds.), *The Price of Independence: The Economics of Early Adulthood*. New York: Russell Sage Foundation 56–83.
Fry, R., and Cohn, D'V. (2010). "Women, Men, and the New Economics of Marriage." Available at http://pewsocialtrends.org/files/2010/11/new-economics-of-marriage.pdf.
Galston, W. A. (1991). *Liberal Purposes: Goods, Virtues, and Diversity in the Liberal State*. Cambridge: Cambridge University Press.
Gelman, A. et al. (2008). *Red State, Blue State, Rich State, Poor State*. Princeton, NJ: Princeton University Press.
Goldin, C. and Katz, L. F. (2002). The Power of the Pill: Oral Contraceptives and Women's Career and Marriage Decisions. *Journal of Political Economy*, 110, 730–770.
Goldin, C. and Margo, R. A. (1992). The Great Compression: The Wage Structure in the United States at Mid-century. *Quarterly Journal of Economics*, 107, 1–34.
Gould, E. D., and Paserman, D. M. (2002). Waiting for Mr. Right: Rising Inequality and Declining Marriage Rates. *Journal of Urban Economics*, 53, 257–281.
Hacker, J. S., and Pierson, P. (2010). *Winner-Take-All Politics: How Washington Made the Rich Richer – and Turned Its Back on the Middle Class*. New York: Simon and Schuster.
Hirshman, L. and Larson, J. (1998). *Hard Bargains: The Politics of Sex*. New York: Oxford University Press.
Hymowitz, K. (2011). *Manning Up: How the Rise of Women Has Turned Men into Boys*. New York: Basic Books.

Isen, A. and Stevenson, B. (2010). *Women's Education and Family Behavior: Trends in Marriage, Divorce and Fertility* 12–14, National Bureau of Economic Research Working Paper No. 15725. Available at http://bpp.wharton.upenn.edu/betseys/papers/Marriage_divorce_education.pdf. *or* http://www.nber.org/papers/w15725.

Kaiser Family Foundation. (2011). "Teen Birth Rate per 1,000 Population Ages 15–19, 2008." Available at http://www.statehealthfacts.org/comparemaptable.jsp?ind=37&cat=2&sort=a&gsa=2.

Lesthaeghe, R. and Neidert, L. (2006). "The 'Second Demographic Transition' in the U.S.: Spatial Patterns and Correlates," *Population Studies Center*. Available at http://www.psc.isr.umich.edu/pubs/pdf/rr06-592.pdf.

Lesthaeghe, R. and Neidert, L. (2008). "Voting and Families: America's Second Demographic Transition," *New Geography*. Available at http://www.newgeography.com/content/00461-voting-and-families-america%E2%80%99s-second-demographic-transition.

Luker, K. (1997). *Dubious Conceptions: The Politics of Teenage Pregnancy*. Cambridge, MA: Harvard University Press.

Martin, S. P. (2004). "Growing Evidence for a 'Divorce Divide?': Education and Marital Dissolution Rates in the U.S. Since the 1970s." Available at https://www.russellsage.org/sites/all/files/u4/Martin_Growing%20Evidence%20for%20a%20Divorce%20Divide.pdf.

McLanahan, S. (2004). Diverging Destinies: How Children Are Faring after the Second Demographic Transformation. *Demography*, 41, 607–627.

McLanahan, S. and Percheski, C. (2008). Family Structure and the Reproduction of Inequality. *Annual Review of Sociology*, 34, 257–276.

McLanahan, S. and Sandefur, G. (1994). *Growing Up With a Single Parent: What Hurts, What Helps*. Cambridge, MA: Harvard University Press.

Mechoulan, S. (2006). Divorce Laws and the Structure of the American Family. *Journal of Legal Studies*, 35, 143–174.

Noah, T. (2010). "The United States of Inequality: Introducing the Great Divergence," *Slate.com*, September 3. Available at http://www.slate.com/id/2266025/entry/2266026.

Premarital Sex in America: A Q&A with Sociologist Mark Regnerus, *University of Texas at Austin Department of Sociology*. Available at http://www.utexas.edu/cola/depts/sociology/features/_features/premarital-sex-regnerus.php. (last visited June 7, 2011).

Pruitt, L. R. (2011). The Geography of Class Culture Wars. *Seattle University Law Review*, 34, 770–809.

Regnerus, M. D. (2007). *Forbidden Fruit: Sex and Religion in the Lives of American Teenagers*. New York: Oxford University Press.

Rumberger, R. W. (1984). The Market for College Graduates, 1960–1990. *Journal of Higher Education*, 55, 433–454.

Sanger, C. (2005). Girls and the Getaway: Cars, Culture, and the Predicament of Gendered Space. *University of Pennsylvania Law Review*, 144, 705–756.

Santelli, J. S., et al. (2007). Explaining Recent Declines in Adolescent Pregnancy in the United States: The Contribution of Abstinence and Improved Contraceptive Use. *American Journal of Public Health*, 97, 150–156.

Stoops, N. (2004). "Educational Attainment in the United States: 2003, Current Population Rep. 4." Available at http://www.census.gov/prod/2004pubs/p20–550.pdf.

Wax, A. L. (2007). Engines of Inequality: Class, Race, and Family Structure. *Family Law Quarterly*, 41, 567–599.

Wilcox, W. B. (2010). "When Marriage Disappears: The New Middle America, The National Marriage Project." Available at http://www.virginia.edu/ marriageproject/pdfs/Union_11_12_10.pdf.

Wilcox, N. B. and Nock, S. L. (2006). What's Love Got To Do With It? Equality, Equity, Commitment and Women's Marital Quality. *Social Forces*, 84, 1321–1345.
Williams v. North Carolina, 317 U.S. 287, 304 (1942) (Frankfurter, J., concurring)
Wilson, J. Q. (2002). *The Marriage Problem: How Our Culture Has Weakened Families*. New York: Harper Collins.
Wilson, W. J. (1997). *When Work Disappears: The World of the New Urban Poor*. New York: Random House.

2

International Family Change and Continuity

The Past and Future from the Developmental Idealism Perspective

Arland Thornton

INTRODUCTION

To look forward, as the crossroads metaphor of this volume suggests, we must consider the forces that brought us to the present. Also, we live in a globalized world and should take an international perspective, which requires national and subnational perspectives. This is an impossibly difficult task, but the advantages of an international perspective are well worth the downside associated with falling short. With both historical and international perspectives, I must describe things in very general terms, and examples and details must be limited.

Many material and ideational forces have produced current marriage and family patterns, and many forces will shape the future. I focus on ideational or cultural factors, with an emphasis on developmental idealism, because these factors are important and have not received adequate attention. My focus on the ideational does not suggest that I believe other factors are not important, as I believe that a full understanding of family change requires consideration of a broad range of ideational and material factors and their intersections.

CULTURAL MODELS

Cultural models help people understand the world and how it operates. They describe what is good and moral, provide motivations for actions, and specify appropriate means to reach desired ends (Fricke 1997; Geertz 1973). Cultural models prescribe appropriate behavior, relationships, and roles (Johnson-Hanks et al. 2011; Thornton et al. 2001). They reside both within people's heads and in the beliefs and values shared within communities. Cultural models are sometimes sufficiently shared that they are taken for granted. Multiple models can exist within the same community and within the same person. These models may be mutually reinforcing or conflicting, have important implications for decision making and behavior, and can change dramatically, especially across long time periods.

For thousands of years the peoples of the world have had their own local cultural models for understanding the world and how it operates. These local cultures have also provided schemas specifying appropriate behavior and relationships.

A large literature documents a culture that originated in northwest Europe and has spread throughout the world. This culture is often referred to as world culture and is different from the numerous local cultures around the world (Krücken and Drori 2009; Meyer et al. 1997). This world culture has its roots in Christianity but is different from Christianity, even being its own quasi-religion. It places the autonomous individual at the center of its rational worldview and emphasizes science, education, development, freedom, equality, justice, consent, and human rights. World culture has been a powerful international force for change, generating increases in school attendance and in homogenizing school curriculums, giving science enormous prestige, spreading support for human rights and for family planning, expanding women's roles, and advocating individualism (Barrett and Frank 1999; Berkovitch 1999; Bromley et al. 2009; Chabbott 2003; Cole 2005; Drori et al. 2003; Tsutsui and Wotipka 2004).

The literature often emphasizes the influence of world culture on change outside northwest Europe and its overseas migrant populations. This is a natural emphasis for a worldview originating in Christianity and northwest Europe, but such influences have also been powerful in northwest Europe and its diasporas (Thornton 2001, 2005).

An important element of world culture is developmental idealism, a set of ideas specifying the good life and how to achieve it. Developmental idealism indicates where social change is heading and that freedom and equality are human rights. It has direct implications for marriage and family life, and its dissemination has been a powerful force for change. Understanding developmental idealism is essential for understanding both the past and future of marriage and family.

Many mechanisms have spread developmental idealism internationally, including colonialism, Christian missionaries, education, mass media, foreign aid programs, government policies and programs, national and international nongovernmental organizations, and international treaties. As Luke and Watkins (2002) argue, such messages can spread because of the persuasiveness of the ideas and because powerful governments and nongovernmental organizations provide financial incentives and legal sanctions for their adoption. My emphasis is on the persuasiveness of the ideas, but I also mention the influence of money and power.

I do not endorse or reject developmental idealism or any of the world's local cultures as good or bad, or true or false. I present developmental idealism, its intellectual underpinnings, and its consequences only to understand how it has influenced past marriage and family changes and how it is likely to influence the future.

MODELS OF DEVELOPMENT

Models for Understanding the World

The ideas of modernity and development have been important in world culture. They have influenced thought in ancient Greece and Rome, Christian theology, the Enlightenment, and much social thought and policy of the nineteenth and twentieth centuries. The modernization model posited a trajectory of development with all societies passing through the same stages (Nisbet 1975/1969). The speed of modernization was assumed to vary, resulting in societies at different stages at the same time. Societies believed to be low in development were labeled as backward, undeveloped, traditional, or even barbarous, and societies believed to be developed were labeled as advanced, progressive, or modern.

It was commonly believed that societies of northwest Europe and its overseas migrant populations were the most modern, with other societies distributed at various lower levels (Thornton 2001, 2005). It was also assumed that the past situations of so-called modern societies could be observed within contemporary so-called traditional societies and that currently traditional societies would one day become like the advanced contemporary societies. The world was, thus, portrayed as dynamic, with northwest Europe and its overseas populations providing a goal or model for modernization.

The family attributes of northwest Europe were often labeled modern or developed, while many attributes in other places were labeled traditional, undeveloped, or backward. This occurred despite the fact that there were extensive family variations within northwest Europe and extensive family variations within and across other world regions. It also occurred despite the fact that some places outside northwest Europe, such as areas in eastern and southeastern Europe, had many family attributes seen as characterizing northwest Europe (Szoltysek 2011; Todorova 1997). The family attributes of northwest Europe that came to be seen as modern included little family solidarity, great individualism, low parental control over adolescent children, marriages arranged by mature couples through courtship, monogamy, gender equality, the absence of veils for women, and small and nuclear (or stem) households. In contrast, the following attributes were labeled as traditional: extensive family solidarity, little individualism, high parental control over adolescent children, marriages arranged at young ages by parents, polygamy, gender inequality, veils for women, and large and extended households. Also, in the late nineteenth and early twentieth centuries, northwest Europe experienced trends toward planned and low fertility, and this was labeled modern, while uncontrolled and high fertility was labeled undeveloped.

Industrial and urban societies with high degrees of education, technology, wealth, and health were called modern or developed, while societies with the opposite attributes were labeled traditional or underdeveloped. Scholars of the era argued that changes from traditional to modern societies would produce modern families and that movement from traditional to modern families would bring modern societies. These perspectives and conclusions have been exceptionally influential for centuries (Thornton 2005).

Models for Dealing with the World

The ideas and conclusions from developmental approaches form the basis for developmental idealism (Thornton 2001, 2005). Developmental idealism provides new goals and methods. It provides beliefs and values suggesting that modern families, as defined earlier, are good and should be striven for. It also indicates that modern society – including being urbanized, industrialized, highly educated, healthy, and wealthy – is good and should be striven for. It stresses that modern societies and modern families are causally interconnected in reciprocal relationships that give governments and individuals guidance about the means for achieving societal development and about what family changes to expect as a result of development. Also, the ideas of modernization and development specify that science, secularism, free markets, democracy, and the separation of church and state are modern, good, and causally connected to the other elements of modernity. Further, developmental idealism locates the highest point of development in northwestern Europe and its overseas populations, suggesting that these regions can serve as models for people elsewhere.

Developmental idealism specifies that freedom, equality, and consent are universal rights. This conclusion is based on the belief of numerous scholars in the past that at the most undeveloped stage of human life – sometimes called the state of nature – there were no societal elements such as laws, governments, and families, and that individuals were free and equal and had the power to consent or dissent (Thornton 2001, 2005). It was argued that freedom, equality, and consent not only existed in the beginning, but were human rights. It was also believed that, with the advent of society, these rights were abridged and only in the most advanced regions of northwest Europe and its diasporas were these rights later regained (Thornton 2001, 2005).

Developmental idealism not only defines what it sees as modern as good and moral, but it frequently views what it defines as traditional and undeveloped as bad, backward, and immoral. Thus, developmental idealism not only strives for the so-called modern and moral; it also fights against what it defines as backward and immoral.

Many elements of modernization models have come under heavy academic criticism during recent decades (Nisbet 1975/1969; Wallerstein 1991). The criticisms indicate that the developmental model is teleological and that its assumptions of uniform and directional change cannot be sustained. Despite these criticisms, many of the ideas associated with modernity are increasingly recognized as powerful forces internationally within governments and nongovernmental organizations (Krücken and Drori 2009; Latham 2000; Meyer et al. 1997). In addition, qualitative studies have identified the existence of modernization ideas, including developmental idealism, among laypeople in many international settings (Abu-Lughod 1998; Ferguson 1999; Osella and Osella 2006; Pigg 1992; Yount et al. 2010). Survey data also document that laypeople in many settings have development models and endorse many of the elements of developmental idealism (Binstock and Thornton 2007; Thornton, Binstock, and Ghimire 2008; Thornton et al. 2012).

Because the cultural models that have existed for centuries in local populations are often very different from developmental idealism, the introduction of developmental idealism is usually not simply followed by its adoption, but is resisted and modified, often producing a clash of cultures. Although the pathways of change and continuity vary, the international spread of developmental idealism has had enormous effects on many dimensions of life. Almost everywhere, there is resistance; the resisters have slowed change and succeeded in keeping many aspects of local culture. Nevertheless, almost everywhere there have been changes, with a common outcome being hybridization.

Although for centuries, northwest Europe and its overseas populations have been seen as identical with modernity, the emphasis on modernity and the contrast with other places brought these places an "other" to compare themselves to and to move away from. Thus, northwest Europe and its diasporas could emphasize as good the elements of its culture defined as the most modern and move further in that direction. Also, the Enlightenment principles of freedom, equality, and consent gained additional power for changing hierarchical and authoritarian aspects of Europe and its diaspora populations that had existed for centuries (Thornton 2005). As these populations changed, the definition of modernity itself changed, and modernity took on diverse and sometimes competing meanings.

Developmental idealism has influenced family and marriage in important ways. My purpose in this discussion is not advocacy but analysis; I do not endorse or condemn any of the elements of developmental idealism or their effects. Instead, my aim is to evaluate the influence of developmental idealism on past family changes and to analyze its relevance for the future. I also do not believe that developmental idealism is the only force producing family changes.

International Agreements

Important manifestations of developmental idealism and forces for its spread are international agreements or conventions. By the early twenty-first century, there were more than 100 human rights instruments in force (Simmons 2009:37). Almost all were adopted after World War II. They cover many topics, ranging from freedom from torture and servitude, to freedom of movement and assembly, and to freedom of religion and thought. Three United Nations conventions are particularly relevant to family and marriage: the Convention on the Elimination of All Forms of Discrimination Against Women (CEDAW); the Convention on the Rights of the Child

(CRC); and the Convention on Consent to Marriage, Minimum Age for Marriage, and Registration of Marriages (MC). All three are aimed at restructuring marriage and family relationships along the lines of developmental idealism.

The CEDAW provides for the equality of women and men in all aspects of life. It calls for the empowerment of women in all spheres through education, employment, and reproductive rights. Parent-child relations are also modified by changing female education, employment, and reproductive rights. All such movement is in the direction of developmental idealism.

The CRC specifies a wide range of rights for children. Boyle, Smith, and Guenther (2007) indicate that the central principles of the CRC are individualism and universalism, suggesting that children everywhere have the same universal rights. Boyle et al. (2007:273) indicate that these principles are "Western in their orientation" and directed toward the construction of modern individuals. The CRC separates the interests of children from those of their parents, emphasizing children as "autonomous, agentic, and responsible" (Boyle et al. 2007:267). Children are given the rights of free expression, thought, religion, and association (Simmons 2009). The CRC also protects children from what are seen as harmful cultural practices, with this protection aimed at practices sometimes found in Africa and Asia (Boyle et al. 2007).

The MC assumes that parents and children have different interests in children's marriages (Boyle et al. 2007). The Convention specifies that there should be complete freedom of spousal choice. It also specifies that young people should not marry until they reach adulthood, and it permits states to determine the appropriateness of marriages.

There is disagreement on whether international conventions change government programs and people's behavior. Recent studies using both statistical and case-study methods indicate that conventions are often effectual (Simmons 2009; Tsutsui and Shin 2008). Conventions can have effects because they carry normative significance and thus create international legitimacy for their principles; conventions educate, raise rights consciousness, empower people, provide tools to support mobilization, and change values.

SOME PAST EFFECTS OF DEVELOPMENTAL IDEALISM

Developmental Idealism around the World

I now discuss the effects of developmental idealism in several countries, beginning with China. Before the middle of the nineteenth century, most Chinese considered China to be the middle kingdom, or the center of the universe. Beginning in the nineteenth century, China experienced a long period of defeat and humiliation at the hands of Europe and Japan and launched its campaign to find and/or create "modern China" (Spence 1999/1990). In the late nineteenth and early twentieth centuries,

China sent numerous emissaries to Europe and North America to learn their secrets of wealth, technology, and power (Spence 1999/1990). These emissaries discovered the ideas of developmental idealism, and they and Europeans and Americans distributed these ideas inside China. Campaigns were launched, with considerable success, to eliminate foot-binding as a backward and harmful practice (Lang 1968/1946). White wedding dresses from Europe and North America were introduced and competed successfully with red wedding dresses previously prevalent in China – a remarkable occurrence considering that white was historically associated with death in China (Lang 1968/1946).

Both the Nationalist and Communist parties adopted many ideas of developmental idealism and worked toward the transformation of the Chinese family. The communist revolution in 1949 brought a new marriage law, implementing many elements of developmental idealism (Cartier 1996/1986; Whyte 1990). Family planning and low fertility were not initially included in the reform package of the Chinese Communist Party, but by the 1970s, China had launched its aggressive one-child policy to facilitate development. These programs have helped reduce arranged marriages, emphasis on the ancestral chain, concubinage, and the marriages of young children (Davis and Harrell 1993; Greenhalgh 1994). The campaign against the ancestral chain has been so effective that it has been possible in recent decades for some Chinese to reach adulthood without knowing about the ancestral chain and its previous centrality in Chinese society. In addition, the age at marriage has increased dramatically, and fertility has fallen to the very low level of 1.5 children per woman, on average (Guo and Chen 2007).

Many elements of the Chinese story exist in Turkey, although with important differences resulting from Turkey's own culture and interactions with Europe (Kavas and Thornton 2012; Nauck and Klaus 2008). The Ottoman Empire had been a world power, but during the eighteenth and nineteenth centuries, many Ottomans became fascinated with European wealth, technology, and power. This led to desires to adopt European ways, and innovations were made by many of the country's elite.

The Ottoman Empire collapsed after World War I, and a smaller Turkey emerged with a government that adopted many elements of developmental idealism as doctrine and policy. This policy was implemented and enforced over several decades, although it met significant resistance. The efforts of Turkey to enter the European Union have provided additional impetus for the adoption of European ways. These programs have been instrumental in the banning of veils from public institutions, increases in gender equality, the decline of parental control over young people, the rise of self-choice marriages, increases in age at marriage, and the decline of fertility to replacement level (Kavas and Thornton 2012).

Similar stories can be told for many additional countries. For example, within a relatively short time after Europeans discovered America, many native Americans were speaking European languages and were at least nominally Christian, with restrictions on many family attributes such as young marriage and polygamy. The colonization of Africa by Europeans led many Africans to become Christian and to be influenced by European ideals and norms. Japan also launched its own campaign of modernization. In Nepal, the endorsement of development is widespread, along with the desirability of family change to bring development.

Women and Veils

The battle to eliminate women's veils has occurred in many places besides Turkey. It was an active – and largely successful – program in Central Asia under the Russian Empire and Soviet Union (Northrop 2004). It was also an active program of the Shah's regime in Iran before the 1979 revolution. Elimination of veils and of gender segregation was added to the fight against terrorism in the twenty-first century as a justification for the European and American military presence in Afghanistan. Interestingly, several European countries that usually take great pride in their emphasis on freedom have taken steps to abolish the veil in public places (Erlanger 2010). This has been justified both as a security measure and as a way to eliminate backwardness and the repression of women.

Efforts to eliminate veils have met great resistance in many places and are losing traction in some places. The veil became a symbol of resistance against the Shah in Iran, and after the 1979 revolution it became compulsory. Counterreformers in Turkey have argued that freedom should include allowing women to wear the veil in public places. Similarly, there have been increases in wearing veils in other predominantly Muslim countries.

Family Planning

A powerful component of world culture is the international family planning movement. For centuries, high fertility and large populations were viewed positively, but during the late 1700s, European writers began to suggest later marriage and low fertility as explanations for European socioeconomic accomplishments (Malthus 1986/1798). Although such arguments initially gained little traction, an international family-planning program was initiated after World War II to increase age at marriage and the use of birth control, and to reduce birth rates (Barrett and Frank 1999; Donaldson 1990). Several factors motivated these programs, but a central justification was the belief that they would foster socioeconomic development.

Family-planning programs were not accepted and implemented immediately, meeting resistance in many instances. Some countries, including China, initially rejected the call for population control. In Malawi, family planning was legally banned in the 1960s (Chimbwete, Watkins, and Zulu 2005). The government of Kenya publicly endorsed family planning in the 1960s, but resisted implementing it (Chimbwete et al. 2005). Later, each of these countries – China, Malawi, and Kenya – implemented more vigorous family-planning programs.

Despite initial resistance, almost all so-called developing countries adopted programs by the 1980s, albeit with varying degrees of enthusiasm and effectiveness (Johnson 1994). In some programs – for example, at times, in China, India, and Indonesia – the government tried to take control of reproduction from individual couples. Government control mechanisms in these places included monitoring women's reproductive cycles, requiring government permission to have a baby, and forcing abortion and sterilization.

In 1994, the agenda shifted from population control to gender equity and reproductive health for everyone, including adolescents (Luke and Watkins 2002). Although the full story is more complex, from the viewpoint of this chapter, this was a change in priorities from one element of developmental idealism – low fertility – to other elements of developmental idealism – equality and freedom. Endorsement of this new emphasis in Ghana, Bangladesh, Malawi, Senegal, and Jordan was mixed, with some elements being rejected, at least initially, in some places (Luke and Watkins 2002). International financial resources were also important in motivating acceptance of certain programs, although such incentives were not always successful, at least in the short run. Interestingly, by the late 1990s, there was widespread endorsement of the family-planning element of the international population agenda in these countries (Luke and Watkins 2002).

Changes in marriage, contraception, and childbearing have been phenomenal. In many countries where women previously married as teenagers or earlier, average ages at marriage have extended into the twenties, even the late twenties. Contraception has become common, and abortion has been legalized in many countries. Fertility has declined substantially in most of the world's populations. Many countries have fertility levels at approximately replacement levels of slightly more than two children per woman. In some countries, especially in East Asia and Europe, fertility levels have fallen, at least temporarily, to 1.5 children or less. Overall fertility levels in the United States are at or near replacement, but are below replacement in some groups.

In parts of Europe many people have not only assimilated the belief that two children are better than three, but that zero or one is acceptable and may be preferable to two (Sobotka 2009). Recent surveys in Argentina, China, Egypt, Iran, Nepal, and the United States document that low fertility is seen by great majorities to be correlated with development, a product of development, and a factor producing development (Thornton et al. 2012).

Fertility at 1.5 children or less will have substantial effects if sustained over long periods. It would reduce populations by one-quarter or more each generation, with large reductions in working-age populations. Sustaining population levels would require substantial international migration that would change the ethnic composition of populations. Such low fertility, accompanied by low mortality at older ages, is also producing older populations.

Reproductive freedom has been an important theme across recent decades. Among its earliest successes was the nineteenth- and early-twentieth-century fight to eliminate restrictions on contraceptive devices. Increases in the effectiveness, number, and availability of contraceptive supplies have been a major story of the twentieth century, with governments shifting from opposition to support of contraception. In recent decades, abortion shifted from being a violation of norms and laws to being accepted and legal in many places. The legalization of abortion in the United States was made possible by the expansion of freedom and the discovery of a new right to privacy. As noted earlier, however, in some places reproductive freedom was deemed less important than fertility reduction, as the use of contraception and abortion was required.

Marital Timing and Processes

Efforts to increase age at marriage have extended beyond the international population control movement. For centuries child marriage and arranged marriage have been common in many parts of the world. In South Asia it was considered morally necessary by many for a girl to be married before her first menstruation, and some brides were even chosen before they were born. Such practices have been explicitly targeted for elimination, with mature marriage and self-choice marriage declared to be children's rights, with vigorous implementation programs (Boyle et al. 2007). There have been dramatic declines in child marriage and arranged marriage in many places.

The fight against child and arranged marriage has largely been absent from northwest Europe because initial conditions were different (Brundage 1987; Hajnal 1965; Macfarlane 1986). For many centuries, most marriages in northwestern Europe were contracted at mature ages by the bride and groom themselves – often with input by the couple's parents – a pattern supported by the Catholic Church. Common law marriages could be contracted merely by a couple living together and presenting themselves to the world as wife and husband. In fact, marriage historically required only the consent of the bride and groom, and legitimate marriages could occur in secret without rituals, licenses, witnesses, certificates, clergy, or government officials. This system led to many disputes of the he said/she said variety that arose over whether both parties had agreed to the marriage.

This free marriage system was severely criticized during the Protestant Reformation, and a 500-year campaign supported by both Protestants and Catholics was launched to tighten control over marriage (Brundage 1987). Reforms required licenses, certificates, witnesses, and church or government officials for a marriage to occur. Common law marriages were also prohibited in many places. These reforms were so effective in some places that many elements came to be seen as essential for marriage.

This 500-year effort to control marriage in Europe collapsed under the wave of freedom during the last half of the twentieth century, when the old norms requiring marriage to legitimize sexual relations, cohabitation, and childbearing were eroded (Thornton, Axinn, and Xie 2007). At first, love remained a requirement for sex, but later, for many, consent became the only requirement. Marriage also was no longer a marker for adulthood or a necessity for independent living. For some it became a valued but unnecessary status that could be achieved at some indefinite future time when the perfect partner, two dream jobs, generous incomes, and a very nice house were achieved (Cherlin 2004). Also, married couples were no longer expected to have children.

Throughout northwest Europe and its overseas populations, this newfound freedom and decreasing centrality of marriage have contributed to substantial postponement of marriage and childbearing within marriage (Thornton et al. 2007). It has also greatly increased sex, cohabitation, and childbearing outside of marriage. Although these trends began in northwest Europe and its overseas populations, they have recently spread to Southern and Eastern Europe and to parts of East Asia and Latin America (Cerrutti and Binstock 2009; Lesthaeghe 2010; Thornton and Philipov 2009). It is likely that they have or will spread to many other parts of the world, as developmental idealism becomes even more widely disseminated and accepted.

Divorce

The trend toward easier and more frequent divorce extends back to the Protestant Reformation, when the prohibition against divorce was challenged by reformers, although they stressed that it should be difficult and infrequent (Phillips 1988). The Enlightenment gave the trend toward easier divorce added impetus, as it emphasized that consent was not only required for the contraction of marriage, but that it could later be withdrawn and the marriage dissolved (Thornton 2005).

Freedom was particularly emphasized during the French Revolution, with its slogan of liberty, equality, and fraternity. Late in the eighteenth century, revolutionary France passed a law that essentially allowed no-fault divorce, although it was later revoked (Traer 1980; Phillips 1988). The French Revolution also produced a longer-lasting reform requiring equal inheritance (Traer 1980). Following the American Revolution – with its emphasis on freedom and equality – there was a less dramatic but more permanent easing of American divorce laws (Cott 2000). Divorce laws in Europe and its overseas populations became less restrictive following World War II, and public attitudes toward divorce have become more permissive (van de Kaa 1987; Thornton and Young-DeMarco 2001).

These trends have been accompanied by dramatic increases in the divorce rate and the number of single-parent families. With many divorced people remarrying, there has also been an important rise in the number of blended or reconstituted families. These trends have occurred recently in many places around the world.

Same-Sex Relations

Particularly important in the past two decades has been the expansion of the rights of people with same-sex orientation, an expansion in the United States associated with the new right of privacy. On the basis of the principles of freedom and equality, sexual acts between two people of the same sex were decriminalized and legitimated in a few decades. Gays and lesbians became more open about their sexual orientations and became more socially accepted.

Decriminalization of gay and lesbian sexual relations has also occurred in other countries. One recent example is India, where the country's highest court overturned the prohibitions against same-sex relations on the grounds that they violated the principles of equality and liberty (Timmons 2009).

The success of this movement can be seen in the recognition of same-sex marriages by several European countries, Canada, and several states in the United States. Also, a federal district court ruled in 2010 that California's ban against same-sex marriage violated the U.S. Constitution's guarantee of equal protection and due process (Dolan and Williams 2010). This decision will likely be appealed and reach the Supreme Court.

Grassroots Penetration

Many changes in ideas and behavior have permeated to the grassroots in many places. An educator in Nepal in 2008 informed me that he taught the UN Declaration of Human Rights and the Convention on Rights of Children to students in his classes. The children in his classes were learning new beliefs and values, being empowered by international norms, and gaining tools to challenge the authority of their parents. Many other elements of family and marriage change have penetrated to the grassroots, including those dealing with marriage timing and processes, family planning, veils, and polygamy.

Recent research provides evidence that a large proportion of ordinary people around the world understand the ideas of development, believe that many family attributes such as gender equality, low fertility, high ages at marriage, and intergenerational independence are correlated internationally with development levels, believe that development causes family change, and believe that modern families help bring development. Thus, endorsement of developmental idealism is evident in the beliefs and values of ordinary people (Binstock and Thornton 2007; Thornton, Binstock, and Ghimire 2008; Thornton et al. 2012a, Yount et al 2010; Thornton et al. 2012b).

Changes Can Be Slow but Extensive

It can take centuries for the principles of developmental idealism to be adopted because they often compete with well-entrenched beliefs, values, and social and economic arrangements. Many of the examples mentioned earlier illustrate this fact, and here I mention the long-term efforts for gender equality in European and North American societies.

In 1690, John Locke (1988/1690), a British philosopher, wrote that women and men came together in marriage as equals – a normative rather than descriptive statement for Britain in the seventeenth century. A few years later, Mary Astell (1970/1730, p. 107) asked the simple question, "If *all Men are born Free*, how is it that all Women are born Slaves?" (italics and capitalization in original), a challenge that has been heard around the world. Enlightenment writers declared that the status of women was an indicator of development levels in a society, and declarations were passed concerning the rights of women, for example in France in 1791 and the United States in 1848 (Thornton 2005).

In the late nineteenth century, women received the right to vote in certain American states, but this did not occur in federal elections in the United States and in most European countries until the early twentieth century. The rights and status of women have increased over the past decades. Community identity of wives separate from their husbands, substantial participation in the labor force, educational attainments of women that often equal and sometimes exceed those of men, and the acceptance of legal equality are some of the many changes in these countries during the past century. In addition, egalitarian attitudes toward women have expanded, equal rights for women are enshrined in international treaties, and gender equality is becoming an element of world culture. Recent studies document worldwide increases in women's status and egalitarian gender values (Dorius and Alwin 2009; Dorius and Firebaugh 2010). This does not mean that equality has been achieved, but the changes have been substantial.

A similar trend can be seen in Egypt (Abu-Lughod 1998; Yount and Rashad 2008). Egyptians have had substantial contact over the years with ideas legitimating female education, women's employment, nuclear families, and companionate marriage. Ideas about what constitutes proper family life have been transformed. Abu-Lughod (1998:261) suggests that "access to any sort of real 'tradition' has been made impossible by the historical cultural encounter with the West." Many aspects of developmental idealism are opposed vigorously in Egypt, but this opposition occurs within the context of a changed cultural reality.

CLASHES OF CULTURE

The spread of developmental idealism has created many cultural clashes because developmental idealism brings new values and beliefs that often contradict traditional beliefs and values. These clashes of culture occur at many levels: within countries, between countries, and within individuals and families. In addition, because developmental idealism contains several different elements, clashes occur within developmental idealism itself. Many of these clashes extend over many decades.

Within-Country Culture Clashes

In many ways the cultural clashes in the United States are a direct outcome of the spread of developmental idealism. As mentioned earlier, the world's people have for centuries had their own cultural models that have defined right and wrong. Western Europe and the United States are not exceptions, and culture and law in these regions have historically opposed contraception, abortion, divorce, same-sex relations, premarital sex, and cohabitation and childbearing outside of marriage. The increased acceptance and practice of these behaviors have elicited strong opposition and conflict.

The importance of abortion, divorce, same-sex relations, premarital sex, cohabitation, and childbearing for culture clashes and American politics is demonstrated by research showing that voting patterns are strongly related to the geographical distribution of family behaviors. As Carbone and Cahn (Chapter 1 in this volume) discuss, geographical distributions of votes in recent U.S. presidential elections and in statewide initiatives followed closely the geographical distribution of family attributes (Lesthaeghe and Neidert 2006, 2009). The blue-state/red-state distinction in elections is closely related to the extent to which the behaviors supported by developmental idealism are evident in particular jurisdictions.

International Culture Clashes

Cultural clashes extend around the world and are often associated with desires for an alternative, suitable, or moral modernity that is different from Europe and North America. Many see certain personal and family patterns in Europe and North America as immoral and corrupt, with these viewpoints probably enhanced by the exaggerated displays often produced in the American media that are available internationally. In the Middle East, for example, many people view modern personal and family attributes as largely compatible with their values, but they see European and American personal and family life as largely incompatible with their values; they view European and American personal and family life, and local people who adopt it, as immoral (Yount et al. 2010).

The views of people in the Middle East about the immorality of American personal and family life are related to their views of American morality in general. In recent surveys in Egypt and Saudi Arabia, respondents were asked to rate several countries on morality, and the United States was rated the lowest and France the second-lowest. In a youth survey in Egypt, the average rating of American morality on a scale from 1 to 10 was only 2.1, whereas the average morality ratings for Egypt and Saudi Arabia were, respectively, 6.5 and 7.2 (Thornton et al. 2010).

Such international clashes of culture can become intense when people outside Europe and North America perceive that these regions are imposing their immoral standards on them. This has taken many forms over the centuries as developmental idealism has conflicted with local cultural models. A recent example occurred in Malawi. Two gay men formed an unofficial marriage and were arrested and sentenced to hard labor. This provoked considerable international outrage, critical communications from international bodies, a visit from the UN Secretary General, and threats to cut off foreign aid. The Malawi government reluctantly reacted to this international pressure by pardoning the two men (Bearak 2010).

The clashes between developmental idealism and local cultures take another form when the beliefs and values of developmental idealism are arrayed against norms and behaviors that are defined by developmental idealism as especially backward. Several behaviors have been labeled and condemned as barbarous, with strong action taken to eliminate them. Polygamy, for example, has generated strong opposition as a barbaric practice (Thornton 2005, 2011). For millennia, polygamy was considered a legitimate form of marriage in many countries, sometimes viewed as the preferred form. But, for centuries, Europeans and Americans have passed laws and launched campaigns to eliminate the practice in numerous settings around the world, including several in Africa (Phillips 1953; Stacey, Chapter 10 in this volume).

In the nineteenth century, the U.S. Congress, over several decades, passed increasingly harsher laws to eliminate polygamy, which was practiced by Mormons, a small religious group (Thornton 2005). These laws were challenged as violations of religious freedom, but the Supreme Court declared that religious freedom did not extend to polygamous marriages. The primary rationale for this conclusion was that polygamy was a barbaric practice contrary to civilized ideals. The Supreme Court has continued to uphold laws prohibiting polygamy in the twentieth century.

Other local cultural beliefs and practices have been challenged around the world. Sometimes these are identified as "harmful cultural practices," and efforts to eliminate them reach into the lives of individuals worldwide. For example, a newspaper advertisement sponsored by the United Nations Children's Fund (UNICEF) in Malawi declares: "Stop Harmful Cultural Practices: Every child has a right to good health" (http://developmentalidealism.org/imagery/malawi.html). The harmful cultural practices were not specified, but it is unlikely that the advertisement was aimed at cultural practices in Europe or North America with negative health outcomes, such as smoking, consumption of junk food, excessive television viewing, unhealthy media messages, or the lack of exercise.

One particular cultural practice that UNICEF has targeted is female circumcision, also known as female genital cutting. This practice is widespread in some regions of the world and is currently targeted for elimination. Official statements condemning this practice, laws outlawing it, and campaigns against it have been implemented in several African countries (Boyle 2002; Yount 2004).

The strong cultural differences within and between societies raise the issue of alternative modernities. Cultural models supporting technology, wealth, health, education, airplanes, and computers are relatively widespread internationally, but cultural models about personal and family lives can be conflicting. These strong differences have led some to advocate alternative modernities and alternative pathways of progress.

Clashes of Cultures within Individuals and within Families

Clashes of culture can occur within families and within individuals. Individuals can accept both the values and beliefs of their local culture and the values and beliefs of developmental idealism, and the respective beliefs and values can clash. Developmental idealism may be easily rejected in favor of long-standing local values and beliefs when it is first encountered. As it becomes more familiar and is accompanied by external incentives and sanctions, developmental idealism begins to compete with local values and beliefs within the minds of individuals. These within-individual clashes can become intense.

There are many ways for within-individual culture clashes to be resolved. Either developmental idealism or the local culture can be rejected. Alternatively, there can be hybridization of values and beliefs, with the acceptance and practice of elements from both the local culture and developmental idealism. This hybridization may occur with the integration of disparate ideas into a coherent package, or the elements may fit together awkwardly. People may also adopt developmental idealism superficially and take different stances concerning it in different contexts. But the ability to pick and choose may be restricted by the fact that "modernity" and "traditionality" are sometimes seen as "packages" with an all-or-nothing character, with "modernity" in one dimension implying "modernity" in another.

Within families, cultural clashes can be especially contentious. As different family members differentially adopt or reject the elements of developmental idealism, there can be considerable family tension and conflict. Such clashes are often intergenerational, as young people adopt new ideas that are contrary to those of their parents. Such clashes can also occur among siblings, as they differentially accept or reject developmental idealism.

Clashes within Developmental Idealism

The existence of many different values and beliefs within developmental idealism creates numerous opportunities for clashes within developmental idealism itself. There are many ways such clashes may occur, but I focus primarily on clashes between the idea that personal and cultural freedom are important values and the idea that behaviors labeled as backward or barbaric should be eliminated. Although freedom may be considered a human right, other values can take precedence. If a particular cultural attribute is judged as barbaric, there are often efforts to limit freedom to practice it.

One example involves the clash between support for sexual freedom and opposition to polygamy. In many places in the United States today, individuals have the freedom to have sex with as many different- or same-sex consenting partners as they desire. Although adultery is often considered unacceptable, there are no legal sanctions against a married person having sex with someone other than her/his spouse in many places today. However, if two women are simultaneously married to the same man, the threesome can be both socially ostracized and criminally sanctioned in most jurisdictions in Canada and the United States. In fact, a man's sexual relationships with two women who each say they are married to him are condemned by a larger percentage of Americans than almost any other behavior (Thornton 2011). This clash between support for sexual freedom and the condemnation of polygamy is seldom acknowledged.

The province of British Columbia in Canada is one jurisdiction that both criminalizes polygamy and recognizes a potential conflict between anti-polygamy laws and the principles of freedom and equality. After hearing testimony from numerous proponents and opponents of a law criminalizing polygamy, a British Columbia court concluded in November 2011 that the perceived evils of polygamy trump freedom and equality; anti-polygamy laws were ruled constitutional within Canada (Supreme Court of British Columbia 2011). Polygamists in Canada and the United States have mobilized to advocate for the decriminalization of their form of marriage, with sexual freedom being an important component of their arguments.

Women's dress is the focus of another clash. Many people in Europe today would allow almost any dress, except if it covers a woman's face. There is intense political and legislative debate in several countries in Europe about the freedom for women to wear veils.

Another clash of cultures within developmental idealism involves female circumcision, which has been common in certain parts of the world for centuries, presumably because it was valued in these settings. Powerful international forces have labeled this practice evil and launched vigorous campaigns to prohibit it. To my knowledge there is currently no substantial campaign to eliminate male circumcision, a form of male genital cutting.

Of course, clashes between the principles of freedom and the protection of what is seen as the public good occur in many areas of life and not only within developmental idealism. For example, the freedom to shout "fire" in a crowded movie theater when there is no fire, to drive while under the influence of alcohol, and to print counterfeit money are all severely restricted. Many considerations enter into such decisions that do not directly involve developmental idealism.

FUTURE EFFECTS OF DEVELOPMENTAL IDEALISM

As we shift focus from the past to the future, we lose the advantages of hindsight and accept the difficulties of looking forward. I examine the future of family change and conflict within the lens of the developmental idealism perspective. The question is: How does understanding of the influence of developmental idealism in the past provide insights into the future?

Continuing Influence and Tension

My firmest prediction is that developmental idealism will be a powerful future force in (nearly) every part of the world. It has been an extremely strong force in the past and there are no signs of it weakening. In fact, with the increasing globalization of the world, developmental idealism's power may be increasing.

This suggests that many elements of developmental idealism will play out in the future in many ways that are similar to the past. Many practices defined by many in Europe and North America as backward and barbaric – for example, female genital cutting, polygamy, and women wearing veils – still exist in some cultures and will likely continue to be the targets of campaigns to eliminate them. In many places, fertility is still above replacement levels, couples marry at young ages, parents arrange their children's marriages, same-sex orientation is repressed, same-sex marriage is not legally recognized, contraceptives fail, gender inequality exists, and there is opposition to abortion. Developmental idealism will continue to oppose these cultural attributes well into the future.

These trends likely will continue to generate significant cultural clashes. As noted earlier, developmental idealism is being advocated among people with their own established beliefs and values. Many of these local cultural models continue to clash with developmental idealism, and these clashes will not disappear soon. It is easy to predict long-term continuation of these cultural clashes within countries, between countries, within individuals and families, and within developmental idealism itself.

Pathways of Future Change

The continued importance of developmental idealism and continued cultural clashes in opposition seems easy to predict. What are more difficult to ascertain are the particular decisions and pathways of future change and continuity. I will speculate on such directions, but I will primarily ask questions to consider as we think about the future.

I begin by asking what will happen if the U.S. Supreme Court considers same-sex marriage, as it likely will. Will the Court declare that same-sex couples have a constitutional right to marry? If the Court decides that states cannot restrict this right, will those who oppose same-sex marriage seek a constitutional amendment? And what will be the response of the American people? Similarly, will same-sex relations be decriminalized in Malawi and other parts of the world? And, if so, will same-sex couples in Malawi and elsewhere eventually be able to contract legal marriages? Such questions can be raised on many other issues in numerous places.

Possible Limitations on Developmental Idealism

I mentioned earlier the clashes between various elements of developmental idealism and discussed some ways that freedoms are restricted. It may also be useful to contemplate the possibility of other limits on freedom, equality, individualism, and the necessity of consent. One area where this seems relevant today concerns the rearing of children. At what point do children have the right to determine their own educational programs? What are the rights of parents in this determination? In many societies, age at marriage is increasing and age at sexual initiation is declining. Are there any legitimate limits on the minimum age for sexual intercourse that parallel the specifications of a minimum age for marriage? Or will children of any age have the right to have sexual relations with any other child, as long as the two are willing and able? These issues raise questions about the clash between individual freedom and society's interest in protecting children.

As mentioned earlier, in some places fertility rates are substantially below what is needed for population replenishment. Is there any limit on how low fertility can or will go? Will a new equilibrium – or new equilibria in different places – be found in age at marriage and in the number of people ever marrying? Or will age at marriage and the number of individuals who never marry continue to increase? Are there limitations on the number of marital dissolutions and will society reach an equilibrium in this regard? Are there limitations on the extent to which human beings can operate as individuals rather than as members of social units?

Challenges to European and North American Exports

I earlier discussed the exportation and, in some cases, imposition of European and North American values and practices in many parts of the world. Such exportation and imposition are often accomplished by identification of these values and practices as universal and modern. This exportation and imposition are also benefited by the designation of Europe and North America as advanced role models for societies seen as less developed.

This exportation of European and North American cultural models as universal and modern is frequently effective, but it is also sometimes criticized as simply foreign and inappropriate for a given society (Chimbwete et al. 2005). This seems to be true in many places, as people consider alternative models of modernity that may be more suitable than models in Europe or the United States. People outside these regions increasingly may ask why Europe and the United States should offer models defining what is moral and immoral in other societies. If this occurs, how much will it detract from the international power of developmental idealism? Will the exportation and importation of cultural models from Europe and the United States under the labels of universal, modern, and progressive values continue indefinitely into the future?

Many people in the Middle East and elsewhere disdain cultural patterns found in Europe and the United States and view them as immoral. In addition, the latter countries do not always support the side of developmental idealism. They can take inconsistent positions that are seen to be in their national interests. An example is the support of repressive governments supportive of European or American economic or political interests.

CONCLUSION

There is considerable evidence that developmental idealism and its integration into world culture have been important forces for family and marriage change around the world. Establishing causation definitively is always difficult, especially because cultural models and changes in those models are infrequently measured, but there are many reasons to believe there are causal effects. Developmental idealism is not the only force for change, of course, and its spread has been the locus of much resistance, tension, and conflict. But, over long time periods, its influence has been substantial, although local cultural schemas also guide the change and often persist in modified form. This understanding of developmental idealism and its influence provides a framework for understanding family change, resistance to family change, and cultural tensions within and between societies.

Developmental idealism also provides a useful framework for thinking about the future. There are reasons to expect that many aspects of the future will be like the past. The principles of developmental idealism will continue to be advocated, exported, imported, and resisted. Cultural clashes within and between countries, within individuals and their families, and within developmental idealism will continue. There will continue to be contradictions, and there may be limitations on how far developmental idealism can be implemented.

The past has been full of surprises. Any Rip van Winkle who was to awaken from a long sleep would be surprised – and probably shocked – by the many changes. The coming centuries will probably be as full of surprises as the last two centuries. The developmental idealism framework does not provide assistance in specifying what pathways are best for what people, but it does provide an overview of some of the issues that will enter into the international flow of change and continuity in marriage and family relations. It also helps us to understand the terrain of the journey. The framework also provides impetus for further research concerning the beliefs of policy makers and ordinary people about developmental idealism, the factors producing associated values and beliefs, the consequences for family and marriage change, and the implications of these issues for international relations.

REFERENCES

Abu-Lughod, L. (1998). Feminist Longings and Postcolonial Conditions. In Abu-Lughod, L. (Ed.), *Remaking Women: Feminism and Modernity in the Middle East* pp. 3–32. Princeton, NJ: Princeton University Press.

Astell, M. (1970/1730). *Some Reflections upon Marriage*. 4th ed. New York: Source Book.

Barrett, D., and Frank, D.J. (1999). Population Control for National Development: From World Discourse to National Policies. In Boli, J. and Thomas, G.M. (Eds.),

Constructing World Culture: International Nongovernmental Organizations Since 1875 pp. 198–221. Stanford, CA: Stanford University Press.

Bearak, B. (2010). Malawi President Pardons Gay Couple. *The New York Times*, May 29. Retrieved from http://www.nytimes.com/2010/05/30/world/africa/30malawi.html..

Berkovitch, N. (1999). The Emergence and Transformation of the International Women's Movement. In Boli, J. and Thomas, G.M. (Eds.), *Constructing World Culture: International Nongovernmental Organizations Since 1875* pp. 100–126. Stanford, CA: Stanford University Press.

Binstock, G., and Thornton, A. (2007). Knowledge and Use of Developmental Thinking about Societies and Families among Teenagers in Argentina. *Demografía*, 50(5), 75–104.

Boyle, E.H. (2002). *Female Genital Cutting: Cultural Conflict in the Global Community*. Baltimore: The Johns Hopkins University Press.

Boyle, E.H., Smith, T., and Guenther, K. (2007). The Rise of the Child as an Individual in Global Society. In Venkatesh, S.A. and Kassimir, R. (Eds.), *Youth, Globalization, and the Law* pp. 255–283. Stanford, CA: Stanford University Press.

Bromley, P., Meyer, J.W., and Ramirez, F.O. (2009). Student-Centeredness in Social Science Textbooks, 1970–2008: A Cross-National Study. Unpublished paper. School of Education / Department of Sociology, Stanford University.

Brundage, J.A. (1987). *Law, Sex, and Christian Society in Medieval Europe*. Chicago: University of Chicago Press.

Cartier, M. (1996/1986). The Long March of the Chinese Family. In Burguière, A. Klapisch-Zuber, C., Segalen, M., and Zonabend, F. (Eds.), *A History of the Family*, vol. II pp. 216–241. Cambridge, MA: Harvard University Press.

Cerrutti, M., and Binstock, G. (2009). *Familias latinoamericanas en transformación: desafíos y demandas para la acción pública*. Serie Políticas Sociales N° 147, Santiago de Chile, CEPAL.

Chabbott, C. (2003). *Constructing Education for Development: International Organizations and Education for All*. New York: RoutledgeFalmer.

Cherlin, A.J. (2004). The Deinstitutionalization of American Marriage. *Journal of Marriage and the Family*, 66, 848–861.

Chimbwete, C., Watkins, S.C., and Zulu, E.M. (2005). The Evolution of Population Policies in Kenya and Malawi. *Population Research and Policy Review*, 24, 85–106.

Clayton, J., and Banda, M. (2010). Malawian Gay Couple Steve Monjeza and Tiwonge Chimbalanga Face Jail. *Times Online*, March 22. Retrieved from http://www.timesonline.co.uk/tol/news/world/africa/article7070500.ece.

Cole, W.M. (2005). Sovereignty Relinquished? Explaining Commitment to the International Human Rights Covenants, 1966–1999. *American Sociological Review*, 70, 472–495.

Cott, N.F. (2000). *Public Vows: A History of Marriage and the Nation*. Cambridge, MA: Harvard University Press.

Davis, D., and Harrell, S., (Eds.) (1993). *Chinese Families in the Post-Mao Era*. Berkeley: University of California Press.

Dolan, M., and Williams, C.J. (2010). Gay Marriage Ruling Anchored in Factual Findings. *Los Angeles Times*, August 5. Retrieved from http://www.latimes.com/news/local/la-me-0806-gay-marriage-california-20100806,0,1544119.story.

Donaldson, P.J. (1990). *Nature Against Us: The United States and the World Population Crisis, 1965–1980*. Chapel Hill: The University of North Carolina Press.

Dorius, S.F., and Alwin, D. (2009). The Global Development of Egalitarian Beliefs – A Decomposition of Trends in the Nature and Structure of Gender Ideology. Working paper.

Dorius, S.F., and Firebaugh, G. (2010). Trends in Global Gender Inequality. *Social Forces, 88*, 1941–1968.
Drori, G.S., Meyer, J.W., Ramirez, F.O., and Schofer, E. (2003). *Science in the Modern World Polity: Institutionalization and Globalization*. Stanford, CA: Stanford University Press.
Erlanger, S. (2010). Face-Veil Issue in France Shifts to Parliament for Debate. *The New York Times*, January 27. Retrieved from http://www.nytimes.com/2010/01/27/world/europe/27france.html.
Ferguson, J. (1999). *Expectations of Modernity: Myths and Meanings of Urban Life on the Zambian Copperbelt*. Berkeley: University of California Press.
Fricke, T. (1997). Culture Theory and Population Process: Toward a Thicker Demography. In Kertzer, D. and Fricke, T. (Eds.), *Anthropological Demography: Toward a New Synthesis* pp. 248–278. Chicago: University of Chicago Press.
Geertz, C. (1973). *The Interpretation of Cultures*. New York: Basic.
Greenhalgh, S. (1994). Controlling Births and Bodies in Village China. *American Ethnologist, 21*(1), 3–30.
Guo, Z., and Chen, W. (2007). Below Replacement Fertility in Mainland China. In Zhao, Z. and Guo, F. (Eds.), *Transition and Challenge: China's Population at the Beginning of the 21st Century* pp. 54–70. Oxford: Oxford University Press.
Hajnal, J. (1965). European Marriage Patterns in Perspective. In Glass, D.V. and Eversley, D.E.C. (Eds.), *Population in History* pp. 101–143. Chicago: Aldine Publishing Company.
Johnson, S.P. (1994). *World Population – Turning the Tide: Three Decades of Progress*. London: Graham & Trotmann / Martinus Nijhoff.
Johnson-Hanks, J.A, Bachrach, C.A, Morgan, S.P., and Kohler, H.P. (2011). *Understanding Family Change and Variation: Toward a Theory of Conjunctural Action*. New York: Springer.
Kavas, S., and Thornton, A. (2012). "Adjustment and Hybridity in Turkish Family Change: Perspectives from Developmental Idealism." Paper presented at the annual meeting of the Population Association of America, San Francisco, May 3–5.
Krücken, G., and Drori, G.S. (2009). *World Society: The Writings of John W. Meyer*. Oxford: Oxford University Press.
Lang, O. (1968/1946). *Chinese Family and Society*. New York: Anchor.
Latham, M.E. (2000). *Modernization as Ideology*. Chapel Hill: University of North Carolina Press.
Lesthaeghe, R. (2010). The Unfolding Story of the Second Demographic Transition. *Population and Development Review*, 36, 211–251.
Lesthaeghe, R., and Neidert, L. (2006). The Second Demographic Transition in the United States: Exception or Textbook Example? *Population and Development Review*, 32, 669–698.
Lesthaeghe, R., and Neidert, L. (2009). US Presidential Elections and the Spatial Pattern of the Second Demographic Transition. *Population and Development Review*, 35, 391–400.
Locke, J. (1988/1690). *Two Treatises of Government; a Critical Edition with an Introduction and Apparatus Criticus by Peter Laslett*. Cambridge: Cambridge University Press.
Luke, N., and Watkins, S.C. (2002). Reactions of Developing-Country Elites to International Population Policy. *Population and Development Review*, 28, 707–733.
Macfarlane, A. (1986). *Marriage and Love in England: Modes of Reproduction, 1300–1840*. Oxford: Basil Blackford.
Malthus, T.R. (1986/1798). An Essay on the Principle of Population. In Flew, A. (Ed.), *Thomas Malthus: An Essay on the Principle of Population and a Summary View of the Principle of Population* pp. 67–217. New York: Penguin.

Meyer, J.W., Boli, J., Thomas, G.M., and Ramirez, F.O. (1997). World Society and the Nation-State. *American Journal of Sociology*, 103, 144–181.

Nauck, B., and Klaus, D. (2008). Family Change in Turkey: Peasant Society, Islam, and the Revolution 'From Above'. In Jayakody, R., Thornton, A., and Axinn, W. (Eds.), *International Family Change: Ideational Perspectives* pp. 281–312. New York: Lawrence Erlbaum Associates: Taylor & Francis Group.

Nisbet, R.A. (1975/1969). *Social Change and History*. New York: Oxford University Press.

Northrop, D. (2004). *Veiled Empire: Gender and Power in Stalinist Central Asia*. Ithaca, NY: Cornell University Press.

Osella, F., and Osella, C. (2006). Once upon a Time in the West: Stories of Migration and Modernity from Kerala, South India. *Journal of the Royal Anthropological Institute, 12,* 569–588.

Phillips, A. (1953). Marriage Laws in Africa. In Phillips, A. (Ed.), *Survey of African Marriage and Family Life* pp. 173–327. London: published for the International African Institute by Oxford University Press.

Phillips, R. (1988). *Putting Asunder: A History of Divorce in Western Society*. Cambridge: Cambridge University Press.

Pigg, S.L. (1992). Inventing Social Categories through Place: Social Representations and Development in Nepal. *Comparative Studies in Society and History*, 34, 491–513.

Simmons, B.A. (2009). *Mobilizing for Human Rights: International Law in Domestic Politics*. New York: Cambridge University Press.

Sobotka, T. (2009). Sub-Replacement Fertility Intentions in Austria. *European Journal of Population*, 25, 387–412.

Some Say They Don't Want Them. (2010). *The Economist*, March 27: 53.

Spence, J.D. (1999/1990). *The Search for Modern China*. 2d ed. New York: W. W. Norton & Company.

Supreme Court of British Columbia. (2011). Reference re: Section 293 of the Criminal Code of Canada, 2011 BCSC 1588, Docket S097767, Vancouver, November 23.

Szoltysek, M. (2011). Family Systems and the Genealogy of Eastern European Difference: An Insider's View. Paper presented at the Third European Congress on World and Global History. London, England.

Thornton, A. (2001). The Developmental Paradigm, Reading History Sideways, and Family Change. *Demography*, 38, 449–465.

Thornton, A. (2005). *Reading History Sideways: The Fallacy and Enduring Impact of the Developmental Paradigm on Family Life*. Chicago: University of Chicago Press.

Thornton, A. (2011). The International Fight Against Barbarism: Historical and Comparative Perspectives on Marriage Timing, Consent, and Polygamy. In Jaconson, C.D. and Burton, L. (Eds.), *Modern Polygamy in the United States: Historical, Cultural, and Legal Issues* pp. 259–297. Oxford: Oxford University Press.

Thornton, A., Axinn, W.G., and Xie, Y. (2007). *Marriage and Cohabitation*. Chicago: University of Chicago Press.

Thornton, A., et al. (2012a). "Knowledge and Beliefs about National Development and Developmental Hierarchies: the Viewpoints of Ordinary People in Thirteen Countries." *Social Science Research* (online).

Thornton, A., Binstock, G., and Ghimire, D. (2008). International Dissemination of Ideas about Development and Family Change. In Jayakody, R., Thornton, A., and Axinn, W. (Eds.), *International Family Change: Ideational Perspectives* pp. 19–44. New York: Lawrence Erlbaum Associates: Taylor & Francis Group.

Thornton, A., et al. (2012b). International Fertility Change: New Data and Insights from the Developmental Idealism Framework. *Demography*, 49, 677–698.

Thornton, A., et al. (2001). Recommendations. pp. 437–448 in *The Well-Being of Children and Families: Research and Data Needs*. Ann Arbor: University of Michigan Press.

Thornton, A., et al. (2010). Lay Views of the Development-Morality Nexus in the U.S. and Middle East: Adherence to Modernization, World-System, and Clash-of-Civilization Perspectives. Paper presented at the annual meetings of the American Sociological Association, Atlanta, Georgia, August 14–17.

Thornton, A., and Philipov, D. (2009). Sweeping Changes in Marriage, Cohabitation, and Childbearing in Central and Eastern Europe: New Insights from the Developmental Idealism Framework. *European Journal of Population*, 25, 123–156.

Thornton, A., and Young-DeMarco, L. (2001). Four Decades of Trends in Attitudes toward Family Issues in the United States: The 1960s through the 1990s. *Journal of Marriage and the Family*, 63, 1009–1037.

Timmons, H. (2009). Indian Court Overturns Gay Sex Ban. *The New York Times*, July 3. Retrieved from http://www.nytimes.com/2009/07/03/world/asia/03india.html?_r=1.

Todorova, M. (1997). *Imagining the Balkans*. Oxford: Oxford University Press.

Traer, J.F. (1980). *Marriage and the Family in Eighteenth-Century France*. Ithaca, NY: Cornell University Press.

Tsutsui, K. and Shin, H.J. (2008). Global Norms, Local Activism, and Social Movement Outcomes: Global Human Rights and Resident Koreans in Japan. *Social Problems*, 55, 391–418.

Tsutsui, K., and Wotipka, C.M. (2004). Global Civil Society and the International Human Rights Movement: Citizen Participation in Human Rights International Nongovernmental Organizations. *Social Forces*, 83, 587–620.

van de Kaa, D.J. (1987). Europe's Second Demographic Transition. *Population Bulletin*, 42, 1–59.

Wallerstein, I. (1991). *Unthinking Social Science: The Limits of Nineteenth Century Paradigms*. Cambridge: Polity.

Whyte, M.K. (1990). *Dating, Mating, and Marriage*. New York: Aldine de Gruyter.

Yount, K.M. (2004). Symbolic Gender Politics, Religious Group Identity, and the Decline of Female Genital Cutting in Minya, Egypt. *Social Forces*, 82, 1063–1090.

Yount, K.M., and Rashad, H. (2008). *Family in the Middle East: Ideational Change in Egypt, Iran, and Tunisia*. Oxford: Routledge.

Yount, K.M., et al. (2010). Lay Accounts of 'Modern' and 'Traditional' Family in Greater Cairo: A Test of Developmental Models of Family Life. Paper presented at the symposium on the Globalization of Modernization Theory: Clashes of Modernities and Moralities, University of Michigan, June 9–10.

3

The Division of Household Labor across Time and Generations

Margaret F. Brinig

GENDERED DIVISION OF HOUSEHOLD LABOR: ITS PERSISTENCE AND ITS EFFECT ON RELATIONAL STABILITY

When my parents married after World War II, neither was specialized, except by biology, for the marital and parental roles they would assume. My mother, who had a PhD in physics, could not cook anything except fudge. Other people had always cleaned for her and done her laundry. My father, a college graduate working for a family business, had also led a privileged life. He had never lived away from the structure provided by parents, college dormitory, and the U.S. Army. While he knew a fair amount about early forms of radar, he had never fixed up a house, rebuilt an engine, or mowed a lawn.

Nonetheless, because of the period and the area in which my parents settled (Milwaukee, never a hotbed of liberalism), they quickly developed a highly gendered division of household tasks. My mother did not work outside the home except, for a couple of years, as an adjunct professor. She did learn to cook (badly, except for party foods) and was in charge of delegating the cooking, cleaning, laundry, and grocery shopping. Even the children's chores were gendered. My jobs, when I was old enough to have them, were setting the table, clearing up, and doing dishes. My younger brothers' jobs involved raking leaves, mowing the lawn (with ever fancier riding mowers), and shoveling snow. I wasn't supposed to touch my father's tools; my brothers were encouraged to saw and hammer and solder.

When I married in the 1970s, already a law professor, I (and most of my women friends) thought, having read the accounts of Jessie Bernard (1982:247, 289), that our marriages would be different. We believed that, because we had major roles in the labor force, our husbands would take on housework and that both of us would parent. Wrong. I did the cooking, cleaning, laundry, and the lion's share of parenting; my husband took care of cars and fixing up the house. We both complained about what the other did. (And my husband, later to become my ex, said that he thought I'd stay home once the kids came along, just as his mother had).

Apparently, my experience was not atypical for my generation (Berk 1985; Coleman 1991:248–49; Coverman 1985:93; Ferree 1991:158; Hartmann 1981:379; Hood 1983; Model 1982:193; Ross 1987:830; Shelton 1992:112; Vanek 1980:277; Yogev 1981:868). (I know it was not atypical in the law professor world.) Joan Williams has written extensively and persuasively about the continuation of gendered inequality in the division of household and paid work (Williams 1996; 1998; 2000; 2001). Sometimes men did household jobs like laundry so badly that their exasperated wives or partners would give up and take over. Or they displayed such an amazing tolerance for dirt that, like the Little Red Hen, their partners just did the cleaning or washing themselves (Brinig 2000:98; Czapanskiy 1991:1456; Williams 1991:1620–21, 1623).

Eternally an optimist, I assumed that men were simply slow in adjusting to "the new marriage" in which both spouses worked and, as equal partners, shared household tasks relatively evenly (Goldscheider and Waite 1991:204–05). I believed that marriages in which chores were divided more or less evenly would be the happiest and most stable.

However, my own research, much of it conducted with Professor Steve Nock, shows that I was wrong. In an initial project, we explored whether egalitarianism in household labor did in fact stabilize marriage (Nock and Brinig 2002). For this project, we used the first two waves of the National Survey of Families and Households, perhaps the most widely utilized (at least at that time) dataset in sociology.[1] Here, in brief, is what we found:

First, when the initial (1987–88) wave of the NSFH was conducted, married couples were individually asked to report[2] the number of hours each spouse had worked during the last week both in the paid labor force and at home. Their answers revealed that, although women worked fewer labor-force hours than men, women

[1] The National Survey of Families and Households (NSFH), first administered in the United States in 1987–88, produced personal interviews with 13,007 respondents. The national sample included a primary cross-section of 9,637 households plus an oversampling of African-Americans, Puerto Ricans, Mexican-Americans, single-parent families, families with stepchildren, cohabiting couples, and recently married persons. One adult per household was randomly selected as the primary respondent. The average interview lasted one hour and forty minutes. Several portions of the questionnaire were self-administered to facilitate the collection of sensitive information and ease the flow of the interview. The spouse or cohabiting partner of the primary respondent was asked to complete a shorter, completely self-administered questionnaire. The second wave of NSFH interviews was conducted in 1992–94. It included primary respondents in Wave 1, their current and former spouses, and a focal child who was five to eighteen years of age and living in the household at the time of the first interview. The second wave included a detailed marital history sequence that we used to determine marital-status changes after the first wave. Our research relied on identical questions given to the primary respondent and his or her spouse/partner. The data reported here are restricted to couples in their first marriages at wave 1 to avoid problems associated with remarriages, stepfamilies, and ex-spouses.

[2] Each spouse was asked to respond to these questions:

more than made up for this deficit with household tasks (Nock and Brinig 2002:179 and table 10.3).

Second, even after accounting for inequality in hours spent on household work, the typical division of household tasks was highly gendered (Nock and Brinig 2002:176 and table 10.2). Women did significantly more cooking, laundry, cleaning, shopping, and chauffeuring than their husbands. Men did significantly more automobile-related and household fix-it jobs than their wives.[3]

Third, above-average hours devoted to "women's work," whether done by a wife or husband, appeared to destabilize the marriage, while above-average hours devoted to "men's work," whether done by a wife or husband, appeared to strengthen the marriage: Couples reporting above-average hours of women's work were more likely than the typical couple to separate or divorce by the next wave of the survey (1992–93); couples reporting above-average hours of men's work were more likely than the typical couple *not* to separate or divorce during this period (Nock and Brinig 2002:185, 280, 282 and table 10.4).

Fourth, I was wrong about how attitudes toward the division of labor affected marriage stability. All surveyed marriage partners were asked whether the division of labor in household and paid work was unfair to themselves, their spouses, or just about right. Unsurprisingly, if both spouses felt that the division of labor in their marriage was unfair to *themselves*, they were on the road toward breakup. But, surprisingly, spousal agreement that the division of labor was fair was also associated with a higher risk of divorce. Equally surprisingly, the most stable marriage type was that in which the husband thought the division of both paid and household work was unfair to his wife, and the wife agreed about paid work but disagreed about household work (thinking it was about right or unfair to her husband) (Nock and Brinig 2002:184 and table 10.5). Finally, one very stable group of couples did not answer the time-diary questions about household work, although they completed

"The questions on this page concern household tasks and who in your household normally spends time doing those tasks. Write in the approximate number of hours per week that you, your spouse/partner or others in the household normally spend doing the following things:

1) Preparing meals
2) Washing dishes and cleaning up after meals
3) Cleaning house
4) Outdoor and other household maintenance tasks
5) Shopping for groceries and other household goods
6) Washing, ironing, mending
7) Paying bills and keeping financial records
8) Automobile maintenance and repair
9) Driving other household members to work, school, or other activities.

See http://nesstar.ssc.wisc.edu/webview/index.jsp (Wave 1, Primary Respondent, Self-Administered Questionnaire, Household Tasks).

[3] Although women did more bill paying and driving, and the difference was statistically significant, the actual differences were very small, so small that it did not matter to which spouse these tasks were assigned.

the rest of the survey (Brinig 2010:53; Nock 2000). Apparently, these couples did not keep track of what each spouse was doing.

Using the same NSFH dataset, other researchers have explored whether unmarried, cohabiting couples' division of labor is like that of married couples (Ciabattari 2004:119). They have found that, although cohabiting women also do more household work than their male partners, the "gender gap" is smaller than that of married couples (Artis and Pavalko 2003; Ciabattari 2004:124; Gupta 1999; South and Spitze 1994). And a fair amount of research shows that, in recent years, men are doing more parenting than their fathers did (Sayer, Bianchi, and Robinson 2004:21 and table 2).

THE HOUSEHOLD DIVISION-OF-LABOR RESEARCH AND THE ECONOMIC MODEL OF MARRIAGE

Many of the NSFH findings are predicted by economic theory. The economic model of marriage posits that individuals search for mates just as they search for anything else seen as valuable and, hopefully, durable (Becker 1991:108–35). The model posits that, through dating, each individual decides his or her relative worth on the "marriage market" and what he or she wants in a marriage partner; each prospective spouse is assessed both in terms of his or her desirability and the likelihood that a marriage proposal would be successful given one's own characteristics. (England and Farkas 1986:99). Individuals consider whether a prospective spouse is the best attainable spouse or whether it is worth waiting for another, possibly better, spouse to come along (Bergstrom and Bagnoli 1993). In making this assessment, household division of labor plays only a minor part in decision making, to the extent it is considered or discussed at all; sexual compatibility, common interests and goals, the desire for children, geographic considerations, interactions with prospective in-laws, and other factors all play important roles (Brinig and Alexeev 1995). The assessment is also typically clouded by the delightful fog of "falling in love."

According to economist Gary Becker, even if a man and a woman have behaved similarly before marriage, they will specialize after marriage (Becker 1991:63; see also Allen 1992; Grossbard-Shechtman 1993). Specialization occurs because the couple realizes gains from each partner's "comparative advantage" in one or more functions.[4] According to Becker (1991:32–41), the spouse involved in market production divides time between labor (earning money to purchase goods) and leisure activities (spending money, or at any rate not earning more). The spouse engaged in household production divides time between the production of household (or "Z" goods) and leisure." In "Z" good production, the spouse transforms purchased goods

4 The concept is taken from David Ricardo's analysis of how countries benefit from international trade (Ricardo 1817). For a discussion, see Mankiw 2008:57.

into ultimate consumption goods (Gronau 1980). Becker (1975) predicts that even a tiny comparative advantage in household production will lead efficient spouses to specialize (Yu and Borzel 1984). He also argues that, because only women can bear children, they start life with a comparative advantage in household production that increases over time as growing girls make investments in "human capital" (i.e., education and training) that enhances their efficiency in household production, thus increasing the likelihood that they will follow a traditional, homemaker path (Becker 1973, 1974, 1991:37–39). By contrast, Becker posits that their future husbands are likely to make human capital investments that enhance their efficiency in labor-force production. According to Becker, this gendered premarital specialization makes young men and women more attractive mates (Becker 1991; Duncan and Duncan 1978), and it can produce gendered differences in comparative advantage even without biological differences (Hadfield 1999; Shelton and John 1993).

In Becker's simple search model, marriages fail when a search was hasty (as, for example, in the case of a "shotgun marriage" where the woman's premarital pregnancy curtailed the search) (Akerlof, Yellen, and Katz 1997; Becker, Landes, and Michael 1977) or when an individual's assessment of " personal value" and the desire for a quick marriage preclude a thorough search (as, for example, when one is the custodian of one or more small children (Chiswick and Lehrer 1990)). Likewise, a marriage may fail when the couple is not "assortatively mated" as, for example, when the marriage is not homogeneous with respect to religion or race (Becker, Landes, and Michael 1977). The economists of the family (and of family law) therefore predict early divorce (or, in flagrant cases of mismatch, annulment) when couples are surprised by a mismatch (Brinig and Alexeev 1995; Sayer, Bianchi, and Robinson 2004). They explain later divorce as the product of spouses' rational decisions that divorcing, with all its costs, is better than remaining married (Becker, Landes, and Michael 1977; Cohen 1987; Zelder 2002).

The costs of divorce are, of course, considerable. Divorce necessitates the expense of hiring lawyers, the difficulties of dealing with an angry mate, the pain of admitting one has made a mistake, and the loss of individually owned assets that were purchased with, or grew because of, his or her individual labor during the marriage (Starnes 1993). Divorce may reduce an individual's marriage-market value (Landes 1978; Peters 1986). Moreover, if a woman has specialized in household work, her reentry into the labor force may be seriously hindered because of outdated skills (Fineman 1991:70).

Children add to these divorce costs. Post-divorce, parents must still support their children despite the increased expense of maintaining two households (Brinig and Allen 2000). Children are also, to some extent, public goods: parents can enjoy children together when they remain together but, after parental separation, neither children nor time with them can be divided as can a bank account or household goods (Brinig and Allen 2000; Weiss and Willis 1985; Zelder 1993). For women, the presence of children may additionally augment age-based loss of marriage-market value (Cohen 1987) and thus hinder the possibility of finding a new marriage partner (Becker, Landes, and Michael 1977).

Economists have also analyzed the negotiations that may take place during a troubled marriage. Some have posited that a spouse may threaten to leave the marriage in order to extract a better deal for him or herself within it (Lundberg and Pollak 1984), but my research with Nock revealed that, although this strategy might work over the short term, it is unlikely to be successful over the long run (Nock 2000). Lundberg and Pollak (1993) also posit that an unhappy spouse may perform his or her specialized marital role at only the minimum level needed to demonstrate compliance with spousal obligation to an outsider.

This classic economic model of marriage and divorce has been criticized on a number of grounds. One critique focuses on the fact that the gender-based specialization posited by Becker and others assumes specialization between husband and wife, but not among women generally (Parkman 1992:29–32). Critics have complained that there is no obvious rationale for assuming that it is invariably less efficient for a woman to hire someone to do the wash or clean the house than to do it herself and that it does not make sense to except household work from labor-force specialization (Brinig and Carbone 1988:866; Brinig 1993–94:2472 and note 64).

Other critics of the specialization model, citing the vastly increased labor-force participation of married women over the last forty years, have urged that the model of marriage on which Becker relied is outmoded (Engel 1999:345; Parkman 1999:55; Sessums 1989:991; Smith 1990; Starnes 1993). Becker's role-specialization model neatly tracks labor-force participation data prior to 1970. During this period, married women – but not men – typically left the labor force shortly after marriage and/or childbirth and thereafter maintained lower rates of employment throughout the life course (Blau, Ferber, and Winkler 1998:91–119; England and Farkas 1986:150–51). But in recent decades, there has been a growing convergence of men's and women's life-course employment patterns.[5] Relying on these trends, critics of the specialization model have argued for a new model of marriage that assumes spousal individualism, equality, roughly equivalent spousal earning capacity, and the need for flexibility over the life cycle (Brinig 1993–94:2470–71 and note 59). Proponents of this more egalitarian marriage model have typically assumed that, as married women enter the labor-force, their husbands will take on a fair share of household tasks (Bryan 1992:482; Haas 1980; Hood 1983:183,189; Starnes 1993:126–27; Wax 1992: 672).

5 "From March 1975 to March 2000, the labor force participation rate of mothers with children under age 18 rose from 47 percent to a peak of 73 percent" (Bureau of Labor Statistics 2009a).

DIVISION OF HOUSEHOLD LABOR IN THE TWENTY-FIRST CENTURY

Another set of NSFH data, based on a third-wave survey in 2002–03, is now available.[6] A fairly large number of the couples originally surveyed were still in the sample. In this third wave, respondents were again asked to write down how much time they and their spouses/partners spent on paid and household work, enabling us to compare the responses of the same couples fifteen years after they participated in the initial survey. The third-wave survey also provides data about the children of these couples, who then were eighteen to thirty-four years of age and often in married or cohabiting unions themselves.[7] A summary of these responses appears in Table 3.1.

What did the third-wave survey reveal? As one would expect based on the patterns revealed by the Wave 1 survey, cohabiting couples continued to be more egalitarian than their married counterparts (Ciabatarri 2004:124 and table 2). But the gender gap for married couples did decrease. On average, married women decreased their weekly work hours by about an hour (from 35.99 to 35.01 per week), and married men increased their weekly work hours by more than three hours (from 16.67 hours to 20.33 hours). For women, this shift reflected an average reduction of about two hours per week in "women's work" (what Sayer and Bianchi call "core housework") and an increase, of about one hour per week, in "men's work." On average, men increased their women's work by slightly less than three hours per week and increased their "men's work" by about 36 minutes per week. Overall, the proportion of household

[6] As reported on the NSFH website, "These data include telephone interviews with the main respondent, the first-interview spouse/partner, and the 'focal child' now ages 18–32"; http://www.ssc.wisc.edu/nsfh/design.htm. The linked field report indicates that the third-wave reinterviews involved a subset of the original sample, including a mid-to-later-life sample of main respondents ages forty-five and older with no focal children and a parent sample composed of main respondents and their young adult focal children. Wave 1 spouses or partners of the main respondents were also reinterviewed. The total number interviewed was 10,069 (Sweet and Bumpass 2002).

To make sure I was not comparing different couples, I matched my wave 3 sample with the wave 1 sample used in my earlier research. As a result, only children of individuals in first marriages in wave 1 were included. Primary respondents and their spouses/partners in wave 1 were both included in my wave 3 sample, but they were sometimes in different marriages or partnerships.

[7] For some reason, the questions asked were not of the respondent, but the respondent's parent (or substitute) rather than the spouse. The pattern of responses looked typical for married or cohabiting households rather than the contribution likely for parents for an 18–34-year-old living with a spouse or partner. However, I was unable to find anyone currently at the Wisconsin Center for Social Research who could resolve this discrepancy. I therefore eliminated all the questions about partner/parent work and focused solely on questions about the respondent's work. I coded female respondents as a wife/female partner and male respondents as a husband/male partner. Although this approach reduced the number of observations, and may exaggerate the number of hours reported, I feel this is the best solution under the circumstances. There may be errors introduced because people may exaggerate how much work they do, or because prevailing social norms may have induced males to minimize the household work they put into some tasks that are "women's work." I do have results for the original datasets that I will gladly share, and they do not differ in substantial ways from using the answers that I know were respondents'.

TABLE 3.1. *Employment*

	Men		Women	
	Married	Unmarried	Married	Unmarried
2000	0.75778	0.68053	0.59435	0.64151
2001	0.75293	0.66234	0.59283	0.62864
2002	0.74644	0.64312	0.58717	0.61421
2003	0.74344	0.62608	0.58736	0.60150
2004	0.74628	0.62905	0.58369	0.60206
2005	0.75123	0.63414	0.58733	0.60552
2006	0.75225	0.64563	0.59205	0.60687
2007	0.7499	0.63905	0.59252	0.60631
2008	0.74214	0.62193	0.59235	0.59758
2009	0.71225	0.57162	0.58026	0.56508
2010	0.70676	0.56143	0.57391	0.55149

Source: Statistics were taken from the various series of Labor Force Statistics from the Current Population Survey, available at http://data.bls.gov:8080/PDQ/servlet/SurveyOutputServlet;jsessionid=62.

work done by women thus decreased over the fifteen years between Wave 1 and Wave 3 from 2:1 to 3:2.[8] But, as is obvious from these numbers, surveyed couples' division of labor was still gendered, even though there were likely fewer children at home and even though the married men and women in the sample worked at paid labor approximately the same number of hours per week.[9] Moreover, as Table 3.2 shows, 59 percent of married women in the general population are in the wage labor force, and an appreciable number of married women earn more than their husbands (Bureau of Labor Statistics 2009a).

What about the children of these couples? In Wave 1 (1987–88), the children were all less than eighteen years of age and therefore almost all were living at home. At Wave 3, almost all were living away from home. Many were married or cohabiting and, like their parents in Wave 1, they often had small children. Whether married or cohabiting, these adult children reported less total housework than their parents did. As Table 3.1 shows, young married men (that is, the married male children) reported doing more "women's work" than their fathers had reported fifteen years earlier, and

8 In contrast to the married couples I tracked from Wave 1 through Wave 3, I did not track the same cohabiting couples from Wave 1 to Wave 3 because there was such a high likelihood that, fifteen years later, they would either have married or split up (U.S. Department of Health and Human Services 2010:34 and table 18).

9 Wives reported an average of 36.02 hours of work in the last week and husbands reported an average of 36.63 hours worked in the last week. Consistent with other recent studies showing an increasing number of two-earner married couples with a higher-earning wife, the proportion of married women earning more than their husbands increased from 18% in Wave 1 of the NSFH to 25% in 2002, where it has remained.

TABLE 3.2. *Comparing household labor hours in the NSFH*

Household task	NSFH Wave I[a]		NSFH Wave 3[b]		NSFH Wave 3 cohabitants		NSFH married children[c]		NSFH cohabiting children[d]	
	Husbands	Wives	Husbands	Wives	Male	Female	Husbands	Wives	Male	Female
Preparing meals	2.05	9.71	3.0089	8.6879	3.7801	8.2057	3.2432	6.2486	3.7426	4.9963
Washing dishes	1.76	6.07	2.4507	5.6210	2.8429	5.5286	2.6667	4.7915	2.6140	4.0221
Cleaning house	1.59	8.13	2.1672	7.2219	3.0423	7.3592	3.1640	6.5157	3.3088	5.6324
Outdoor tasks	4.96	1.81	6.1811	2.8689	6.7465	3.0211	3.5266	1.4495	1.9338	.9081
Shopping	1.39	2.81	1.8865	3.2519	2.1901	3.4155	1.5765	2.5472	1.7721	2.2978
Washing, ironing	0.57	4.29	.8717	4.0908	1.4577	4.3732	1.6113	3.9349	1.8088	3.2279
Paying bills	1.36	1.6	1.5207	1.9026	1.7324	2.5704	1.3442	1.7861	1.3971	1.6838
Auto maintenance	1.84	0.18	1.2638	.1871	2.0563	1.0845	1.2584	.2139	1.0699	.3529
Driving others	1.15	1.39	.9789	1.1807	1.0845	1.0986	1.2530	1.9207	1.1581	1.4853
Total "women's"	7.36	31.01	10.3850	28.87	13.3131	28.8821	12.2617	24.03800	13.2463	20.1765
Total "men's"	6.8	1.99	7.44495	3.056	8.80282	4.10563	4.78502	1.663409	3.00368	1.26103
TOTAL	16.67	35.99	20.3296	35.01	24.9329	36.6568	19.64389	29.40825	18.8052	24.6066
Per couple										
Total "women's"	38.37		39.259		42.1953		36.29967		33.4228	
Total "men's"	8.79		10.501		12.9085		6.448426		4.26471	
Total hours	52.66		55.342		61.5896		49.05212		43.4118	

Notes: (a) There were 4,377 respondents in Wave 1 in first marriages who answered the household hours questions. Their average age was 29 years. (b) There were 4,271 married respondents in Wave 3 who answered the questions. Their average age was approximately 44. (c) There were 921 married focal children of the Wave 1 couples who answered the questionnaire. Their average age was 29. (d) There were 272 cohabiting focal children of the Wave 1 couples who answered the questionnaire. Their average age was 24.6.

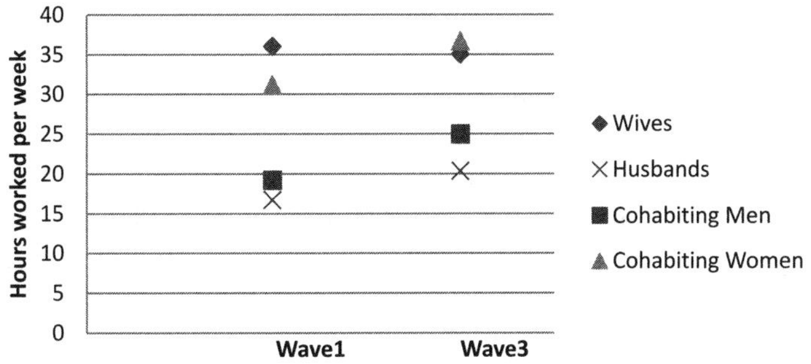

FIGURE 3.1 Married and Couples, Original Respondents

young women (both married and cohabiting) reported doing less household work than their mothers reported fifteen years earlier *and* less household work than their mothers currently reported. Although they typically reported that the female partner worked more hours than the male partner, the gender gap between married child partners was more like that of cohabiting parents in Wave 3, and the gap between cohabiting child partners had narrowed even more.

It is not obvious why the cohort of older women, who almost certainly have fewer children remaining at home, are continuing to spend so much time on "women's work." One possibility is that they are modeling behavior for children who remain at home, socializing them as Berk's *The Gender Family* (1985) would suggest. Another possibility is that, once a woman is accustomed to doing lots of women's work, she will substitute household work time in something she prefers, like cooking, gardening, and painting the house, for chores that are no longer necessary. Wave 3 women did seem to increase outdoor tasks, and they increased shopping and cooking

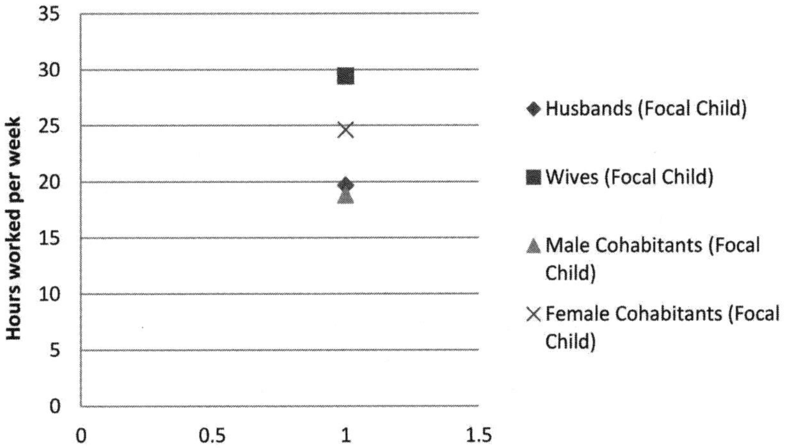

FIGURE 3.2 Focal Children, NSFH 3

time even more (although laundry actually remained about the same as it was in Wave 1).

The results of this research are consistent with earlier reports. Other researchers have also found that married women continue to do the bulk of the housework, despite having steadily increased their labor-force activity (Berardo, Shehan, and Leslie 1987; Biernat and Wortman 1991; Bryson et al. 1976). Minor reductions in women's household work and minor increases in men's household work are evident, but the magnitude of change is remarkably small.

TRENDS, QUESTIONS, AND POLICY ISSUES

So, given continued (although lesser) gender inequality in the division of household labor, we are left with several questions: Why did inequality arise? Why does it persist? Why do cohabiting couples report greater equality than married couples? What do these trends say about the economic theory of marriage? And what do they portend for the future of marriage and cohabitation?

Sociologists Goldscheider and Waite concluded their book, *New Families, No Families?* (1991: 202–03) by suggesting that Becker-style, specialized "old" families will not be possible for much longer:

> Why can we not return to the old balance of men's and women's work and family roles, which were "fair" to each in terms of hours, and which provided children with mothers who cared for them intensively and fathers who supported them adequately? . . . The major problem for women posed by "old families" is demographic. With the increase in life expectancy and the decline in fertility, homemaking is no longer a lifetime career for women as a group. Either there has to be a division within their adult lives, with about half their time devoted to raising two or so children to adulthood and half spent in other occupations, or women have to be divided into mothers and workers, or "real" workers and "mommy track" workers.

But although Goldscheider and Waite believe that more egalitarian families must be our future, they are less confident about the implications of such a shift: "We have suggested that such families have the potential to solve critical problems facing families today. But what do we really know about them? What effects does this pioneer family form have on marriages and families and on the men, women, and children who live in them? Are more egalitarian and sharing families possible? This is largely uncharted territory" (1991:204–05).[10]

So far, although egalitarian families seem possible, they clearly have not won the day numerically. Why would continued inequality persist? It no longer seems possible to blame the gendered nature of household labor on legal barriers. Alimony

[10] The term "New Family" was also used by Mary Ann Glendon (1985).

has long been available to either spouse,[11] and no-fault divorce enables women who might once have been unable to leave an unequal relationship to exit marriage without their husbands' consent. Theoretically, women have equal access to education and high-salary employment (Mather and Adams 2007; U.S. Bureau of the Census 2010.) Men have access to the Family Medical Leave Act, and at least some employers provide paternity leaves or flexible hours to enable paternal childcare.

These new rights have not yet produced major changes in behavior. Men rarely share parenting-leave opportunities with their wives (Lewis and Smithson 2007).[12] Gender inequality persists in marriages with adult children and childless marriages.

One possibility is biological; we might be "hardwired" to divide household work based on gender (Rossi 1977). But this form of predestination seems to be contradicted by the observed movement, however slow, toward more equality. It may also be contradicted by the same-sex couples now marrying or in civil unions, who also specialize but not along gender lines (Kurdek 2007).

Some feminist writers would argue, no doubt, that gender inequality in household labor occurs because men, still more powerful than women, want to keep things that way (Mannino and Deutsch 2007). This thesis seems to be corroborated by international data, which show both that women do less household work as they obtain relatively more power as measured by a complex formula[13] (Figure 3.3), and that they and their partners divide household work more equally (Figure 3.4; Knudson and Waerness 2008:105–06 and figures 1, 2). (In fact, the division is never very equal – the middle of Figure 3.3, approximately where Flanders is located, has women working twenty-five hours to men's eight, and the "best" has women working between twenty-five and thirty hours to men's fourteen.)

As long as those who do "women's work" for pay receive much less than men do for "their" work, little progress is likely to occur and gender hierarchy, reinforced by tradition and even by strict reading of the Bible, will stay in place.[14] However, if couples choose to cohabit and reject the religious view of marriage (which seems consistent with gender-role specialization), we may see less gender hierarchy; indeed, the cohabiting children of NSFH Wave 3 reported less specialization than their married

[11] *Orr v. Orr*, 440 U.S. 268 (1979). Alimony might have supported a specialization by women in household production, and economists tended to assume it did so (Becker, Landes, and Michael 1977; Landes 1978).

[12] This may be because a traditional ideal of full-time and uninterrupted work causes men who take advantage of entitlement programs to be undervalued and have their careers limited (Lewis and Smithson 2007).

[13] The calculation takes account of women's percentage of total parliamentary seats, managerial/administrative employment, professional/technical positions, and earned income (Knudsen and Waerness 2008:102).

[14] However, Wilcox (2004) found that these men tend to do more housework than the norm. Researchers who compared covenant and "standard" marriages in Louisiana made similar findings (Nock, Sanchez, and Wright 2008).

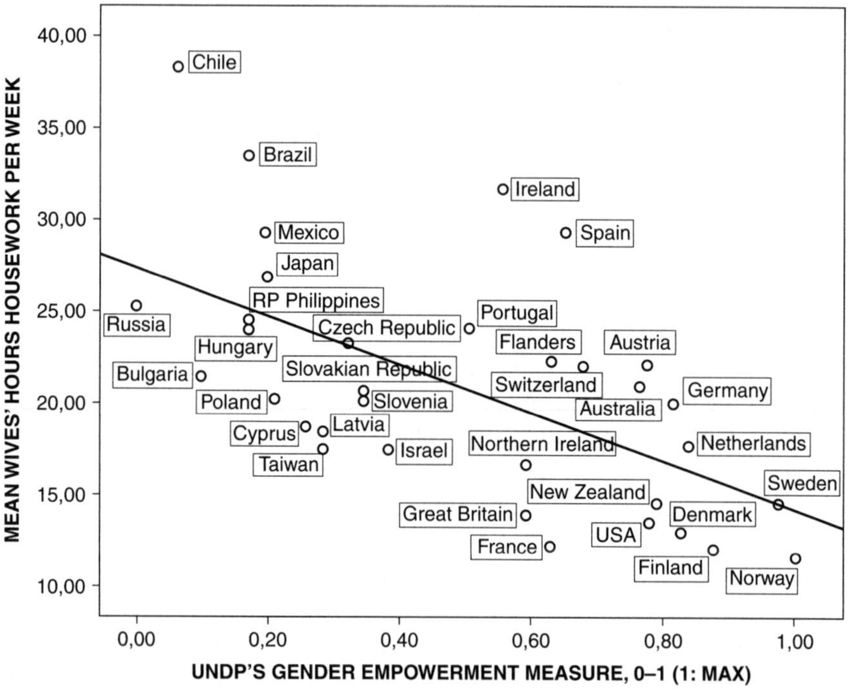

FIGURE 3.3 Wives' weekly housework hours by national gender empowerment level

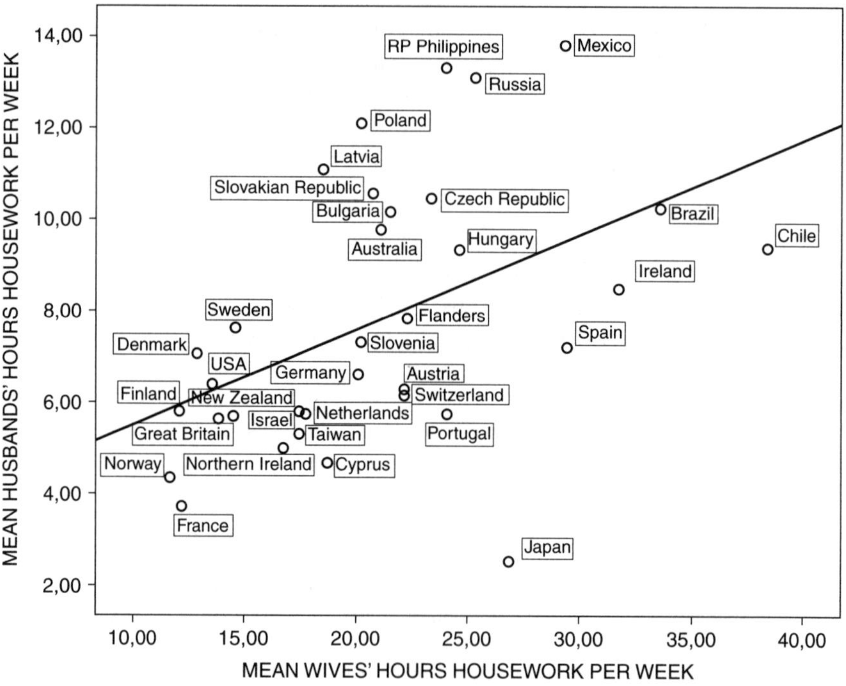

FIGURE 3.4 Average housework hours for wives and husbands across countries

contemporaries (although cohabitants are also younger, less likely to have children, and may someday marry). Most men and women do not really like quotidian, repetitive jobs;[15] couples who can afford to avoid them may also hire third parties (most often women) to take their place.[16] Such a hire may appeal to wealthy, educated couples, who are also more likely to be egalitarian. But it cannot alter a gendered balance of power within a relationship.

Finally – and I believe this is the most likely possibility – movement toward equality will slowly continue. Change within individual households requires change in societal norms as well, and societal norms change, at least at the beginning, at glacial speed (England and Farkas 1986:99; Nock 1999:139–40). That is, individuals are socialized into male or female gender roles and are "expected" to behave in ways consistent with their gender (Cunningham 2001). This socialization may cause men and women to derive gendered meaning from the unpaid work they perform (Bianchi et al. 2000; Erickson 2005), and these gendered meanings make it difficult for policy makers to nudge individuals toward equality. Put somewhat differently, even if we were to attempt to *force* household gender equality, this strategy is unlikely to work well; for example, the East Germans mandated gender equality, but although women's labor-force participation did thereafter increase, so did the divorce rate (Brinig 1998). When couples discover cooking as a hobby, an art form, or a shared pleasure, inequality may decline. (I don't foresee such a movement with cleaning or laundry, however.) The growing acceptance of same-sex couples, who cannot have a gendered division of labor (but may have a functional one if Becker's theory is correct), may also hasten an attitudinal shift (Kurdek 2007;[17] Schultz and Yarborough, unpublished). And the movement from a 4:1 ratio to a 2:1 ratio in the division of "women's work" from one generation of NSFH respondents to the next suggests that change is indeed under way.

It is not obvious what policy recommendations would usefully contribute to household gender equality, however. While valuing traditional "women's work" through higher market wages might cause people to dislike it less, the labor market is not likely to move in this direction given the number of workers, particularly those from poor countries, who are willing to work for relatively low pay in domestic, or domestic-related, jobs. And although cohabitation is associated with greater labor equality than marriage, the greater instability associated with cohabitation as compared to marriage (Cherlin, Chapter 14; McLanahan and Garfinkel, Chapter 8) suggests that the state should not promote cohabitation.

15 These tend to be stereotypically female, according to LaChance-Grzela and Bouchard (2010:769). The intermittent tasks are stereotypically male, and they are more flexible and less time-consuming (Claffey and Mickelson, 2009).

16 The NSFH coded work done by others. I have so far looked only at the division among spouses and partners.

17 Finding specialization in particular tasks by gay men but not lesbian women (both in childless couples).

From an economic perspective, marriage is more desirable than cohabitation because of its greater incentives to specialize; specialization produces efficiency gains both for the labor market as a whole and for the individual household. The persistence of the smaller gender gap among cohabiting couples demonstrates that marital incentives persist. However, the efficiency gains of specialization produce costs to the spouse doing the most household work, and these costs become particularly acute if the marriage ends. Even if the marriage endures for the lifetimes of the spouses, there is social cost in terms of gender inequality despite slow convergence in the non-leisure roles of men and women. Specialization in household tasks can often be avoided as long as a couple is childless because, with enough wealth, many chores can be contracted out to third parties. However, the arrival of children typically produces specialization that contracting does not abate. While substitute child care can take the place of a parent during the workday, it cannot replace parenting. Until parents share caretaking tasks more evenly, greater stability for children is likely to continue to come at some cost to absolute gender equality.

REFERENCES

Akerlof, G.A., Yellen, J.L., and Katz, M.L. (1997). An Analysis of Out-of-Wedlock Childbearing in the United States. *Quarterly Journal of Economics*, 9, 277–317.

Allen, D.W. (1992). What Does She See in Him? The Effect of Sharing on the Choice of Spouse. *Economic Inquiry*, 3, 57–67.

Artis, J.E. and Pavalko, E.K. (2003). Explaining the Decline in Women's Household Labor: Individual Change and Cohort Differences, *Journal of Marriage and Family*, 65, 746–61.

Becker, G.S. (1973). A Theory of Marriage, Part I. *The Journal of Political Economy* 81, 813–46.

Becker, G.S. (1974). A Theory of Marriage, Part II. *The Journal of Political Economy* 82, S11–26.

Becker, G.S. (1975). *Human Capital: A Theoretical and Empirical Analysis, with Specific Reference to Education* 2nd ed. New York: Columbia University Press.

Becker, G.S. (1991). *A Treatise on the Family*. Cambridge, MA: Harvard University Press.

Becker, G.S., Landes, E.M., and Michael, R.T. (1977). An Economic Analysis of Marital Instability. *Journal of Political Economy*, 85, 1141–87.

Bergstrom, T. and Bagnoli, M. (1993). Courtship as a Waiting Game. *Journal of Political Economy*, *101*, 185–202.

Berardo, D.H., Shehan, C.L., and Leslie, G. (1987). A Residue of Tradition: Jobs, Careers, and Spouses' Time in Housework. *Journal of Marriage and Family*, 49, 381–90.

Berk, S.F. (1985). *The Gender Factory: The Apportionment of Work in American Households*. New York: Barnes & Noble.

Bernard, J. (1982). *The Future of Marriage* 2nd ed. New Haven, CT: Yale University Press.

Bianchi, S.M. et al. (2000). Is Anyone Doing the Housework? Trends in the Gender Division of Household Labor. *Social Forces*, 79, 191–228.

Biernat, M. and Wortman, C.B. (1991). Sharing of Home Responsibilities between Professionally Employed Women and Their Husbands. *Journal of Personality and Social Psychology*, 60, 844–860.

Blau, F.D., Ferber, M.A., and Winkler, A.E. (1998). *The Economics of Women, Men and Work* 3rd ed. Upper Saddle River, NJ: Prentice Hall.

Brinig, M.F. (1993–1994). A Comment on Jana Singer's Alimony and Efficiency, *Georgetown Law Journal*, 82, 2461–80.
Brinig, M.F. (1998). Equality and Sharing: Views of Households Across the Iron Curtain. *European Journal of Law and Economics*, 7, 55–64.
Brinig, M.F. (2000). *From Contract to Covenant: Beyond the Law and Economics of the Family*. Cambridge, MA: Harvard University Press.
Brinig, M.F. (2010). *Family, Law, and Community: Supporting the Covenant*. Chicago: University of Chicago Press.
Brinig, M.F. and Alexeev, M.V. (1995). Fraud in Courtship: Annulment and Divorce. *European Journal of Law and Economics*, 2, 45–62.
Brinig, M.F. and Allen, D.W. (2000). "These Boots Are Made for Walking": Why Most Divorce Filers Are Women. *American Law and Economics Review*, 2, 126–69.
Brinig, M.F. and Carbone, J. (1988). The Reliance Interest in Marriage and Divorce. *Tulane Law Review*, 62, 855–905.
Bryan, P.E. (1992). Killing Us Softly: Divorce Mediation and the Politics of Power. *Buffalo Law Review*, 40, 441–524.
Bryson, R.B., Bryson, J.B., Licht, M.H., and Licht, B.G. (1976). The Professional Pair: Husband and Wife Psychologists. *American Psychologist*, 31, 10–16.
Bureau of Labor Statistics (2009a). *The Editor's Desk, Wives Earning More Than Their Husbands, 1987–2006*, Jan. 9, available at http://www.bls.gov/opub/ted/2009/jan/wk1/art05.htm.
Bureau of Labor Statistics (2009b). *Labor Force Participation of Women and Mothers, 2008*, available at http://data.bls.gov/cgi- bin/print.pl/opub/ted/2009/ted_20091009.htm
Chiswick, C.U. and Lehrer, E.L. (1990). On Marriage-Specific Human Capital: Its Role as a Determinant of Remarriage. *Journal of Population Economics*, 3, 193–213.
Ciabattari, T. (2004). Cohabitation and Housework: The Effects of Marital Intentions. *Journal of Marriage and Family*, 66, 118–25.
Claffey, S.T. and Mickelson, K.R. (2009). Equity but Not Equality: Commentary on LaChance-Grzela and Bouchard. *Sex Roles*, 60, 819–31.
Cohen, L. (1987). Marriage, Divorce and Quasi-Rents: Or "I Gave Him the Best Years of My Life." *Journal of Legal Studies*, 16, 267–303.
Coleman, M.T. (1991). The Division of Household Labor: Suggestions for Future Empirical Consideration and Theoretical Development. In Blumberg, R.L. (Ed.), *Gender, Family, and Economy: The Triple Overlap*. Newbury Park, CA: Sage Publications Inc.
Coverman, S. (1985). Explaining Husbands' Participation in Domestic Labor. *Sociological Quarterly*, 26, 81–97.
Cunningham, M. (2001). Parental Influences on the Gendered Division of Housework. *American Sociological Review*, 66, 18–203.
Czapanskiy, K. (1991). Volunteers and Draftees: The Struggle for Parental Equality. *University of California-Los Angeles Law Review*, 38, 1415–82.
Duncan, B. and Duncan, O.D. (1978). *Sex Typing and Social Roles: A Research Report*. New York: Academic Press.
Engel, M. (1999). Pockets of Poverty: The Second Wives Club – Examining the Financial [In]Security of Women in Remarriages. *William and Mary Journal of Women and the Law*, 5, 309–82.
England, P. and Farkas, G. (1986). *Households, Employment and Gender: A Social, Economic and Demographic View*. New York: Aldine de Gruyter.
Erickson, R.J. (2005). Why Emotion Work Matters: Sex, Gender, and the Division of Household Labor. *Journal of Marriage and Family*, 67, 337–51.

Ferree, M.M. (1991). The Gender Division of Labor in Two-Earner Marriages. *Journal of Family Issues*, 12,158–80.
Fineman, M.A. (1991). *The Illusion of Equality: The Rhetoric and Reality of Divorce Reform*. Chicago: University of Chicago Press.
Glendon, M.A. (1985). *The New Family and the New Property*. New York: Butterworth's.
Goldscheider, F.K. and Waite, L.J. (1991). *New Families, No Families? The Transformation of the American Home*. Berkeley: University of California Press.
Gronau, R. (1980). Home Production – A Forgotten Industry. *Review of Economics and Statistics*, 62, 408–16.
Grossbard-Shechtman, S. (1993). *On the Economics of Marriage: A Theory of Marriage, Labor, and Divorce*. Boulder, CO: Westview Press.
Gupta, S. (1999). The Effects of Transitions in Marital Status on Men's Performance of Housework. *Journal of Marriage and Family*, 61, 700–11.
Haas, L. (1980). Role-Sharing Couples: A Study of Egalitarian Marriages. *Family Relations*, 29, 289–96.
Hadfield, G.K. (1999). A Coordination Model of Sexual Division of Labor. *Journal of Economic Behavior and Organization*, 40, 125–53.
Hartmann, H.I. (1981). The Family as the Locus of Gender, Class, and Political Struggle: The Example of Housework. *Journal of Women, Culture and Society*, 6, 366–94.
Hood, J.C. (1983). *Becoming a Two-Job Family*. New York: Praeger.
Knudson, K. and Waerness, K. (2008). National Context and Spouses' Housework in 34 Countries. *European Sociological Review*, 24, 97–113.
Kurdek, L.A. (2007). The Allocation of Household Labor by Partners in Gay and Lesbian Couples. *Journal of Family Issues*, 28, 132–48.
Lachance-Grzela, M. and Bouchard, G. (2010). Why Do Women Do the Lion's Share of Housework? A Decade of Research. *Sex Roles*, 63, 767–80.
Landes, E.M. (1978). The Economics of Alimony. *Journal of Legal Studies*, 7, 35–63.
Lewis, S. and Smithson, J. (2007). *Gender, Parenthood and the Changing European Workplace: Young Adults Negotiating the Work-Family Boundary*. European Commission Community Research, EUR 22086, Luxembourg: Office for Official Publications of the European Communities, available online at http://cordis.europa.eu/documents/documentlibrary/90882381EN6.pdf.
Lundberg, S.J. and Pollak, R.A. (1984). Noncooperative Bargaining Models of Marriage. *American Economic Review*, 84, 132–37.
Lundberg, S.J. and Pollak, R.A. (1993). Separate Spheres Bargaining and the Marriage Market. *Journal of Political Economy*, 101, 988–1010.
Mankiw, N.G. (2008). *Principles of Economics* 4th ed. Florence, KY: South-Western College Publishers.
Mannino, C.A. and Deutsch, F.M. (2007). Changing the Division of Household Labor: A Negotiated Process between Partners. *Sex Roles*, 56, 309–24.
Mather, M. and Adams, D. (2007). *The Crossover in Female-Male College Enrollment Rates*. Population Reference Bureau, available at http://www.prb.org/Articles/2007/CrossoverinFemaleMaleCollegeEnrollmentRates.aspx.
Model, S. (1982). Housework by Husbands: Determinants and Implications. In Aldous, J. (Ed.), *Two Paychecks: Life in Dual-Earner Families* 193–206. Newbury Park, CA: Sage Publications.
Nock, S.L. (1999). *Marriage in Men's Lives*. Oxford: Oxford University Press.
Nock, S.L. (2000). Time and Gender in Marriage. *Virginia Law Review*, 86, 1971–87.

Nock, S.L. and Brinig, M.F. (2002). "Weak Men and Disorderly Women": Divorce and the Division of Labor. In Dnes, A.W. and Rowthorn, R. (Eds.), *The Law and Economics of Marriage and Divorce* 171–90. Cambridge: Cambridge University Press.

Nock, S.L., Sanchez, L.A., and Wright, J.D. (2008). *Covenant Marriage: The Movement to Reclaim Tradition in America*. New Brunswick, NJ: Rutgers University Press.

Parkman, A.M. (1992). *No-fault Divorce: What Went Wrong?* Boulder, CO: Westview Press.

Parkman, A.M. (1999). Bringing Consistency to the Financial Arrangements at Divorce. *Kentucky Law Journal*. 87, 51–94.

Peters, H.E. (1986). Marriage and Divorce: Informational Constraints and Private Contracting. *American Economic Review*, 76, 437–54.

Ricardo, D. (1817). *On the Principles of Political Economy and Taxation*. London: John Murray.

Ross, C.E. (1987). The Division of Labor at Home. *Social Forces*, 65, 816–33.

Rossi, A. (1977). A Biosocial Perspective on Parenting. *Daedalus*, 106, 1–31.

Sayer, L.C., Bianchi, S.M., and Robinson, J.P. (2004). Are Parents Investing Less in Children? Trends in Mothers' and Fathers' Time with Children. *American Journal of Sociology*, 110, 1–43.

Schultz, V. and Yarbrough, M. (2011). Will Marriage Make Gay and Lesbian Couples Less Egalitarian? A Cautionary Tale. University of Southern California Law School, available at http://weblaw.usc.edu/who/faculty/workshops/documents/Schultz.pdf.

Sessums, M.A. (1989). What Are Wives' Contributions Worth upon Divorce?: Toward Fully Incorporating Partnership into Equitable Distribution. *University of Florida Law Review*, 41, 987–1030.

Shelton, B.A. (1992). *Women, Men and Time: Gender Differences in Paid Work, Housework and Leisure*. Santa Barbara, CA: Greenwood Press.

Shelton, B.A. and John, D. (1993). Does Marital Status Make a Difference? Housework Among Married and Cohabiting Men and Women. *Journal of Family Issues*, 14, 401–20.

Smith, B. (1990). The Partnership Theory of Marriage: A Borrowed Solution Fails. *Texas Law Review*, 68, 689–744.

South, S.J. and Spitze, G. (1994). Housework in Marital and Nonmarital Households. *American Sociological Review*, 59, 327–47.

Spain, D.G. and Bianchi, S.M. (1996). *Balancing Act: Motherhood, Marriage and Employment among American Women*. New York: Russell Sage Foundation.

Starnes, C.L. (1993). Divorce and the Displaced Homemaker: A Discourse on Playing with Dolls, Partnership Buyouts and Dissociation Under No-Fault. *University of Chicago Law Review*, 60, 67–140.

Sweet, J.A. and Bumpass, L.L. (2002). *The National Survey of Families and Households – Waves 1, 2, and 3: Data Description and Documentation*. Center for Demography and Ecology, University of Wisconsin-Madison, available at http://www.ssc.wisc.edu/nsfh/home.htm.

United States Bureau of the Census (2010). Marriage and Cohabitation in the United States: A Statistical Portrait Based on Cycle 6 (2002) of the National Survey of Family Growth, Vital and Health Statistics, Series 23, No. 28 (February). Hyattsville, MD.

Vanek, J. (1980). Household Work, Wage Work, and Sexual Equality. In Berk, S.F. (Ed.), *Women and Household Labor* 275–291. Newbury Park, CA: Sage Publications.

Wax, A.L. (1992). Bargaining in the Shadow of the Market: Is There a Future for Egalitarian Marriage? *Virginia Law Review*, 84, 509–672.

Weiss, Y. and Willis, R.J. (1985). Children as Collective Goods and Divorce Settlements. *Journal of Labor Economics* 3, 268–92.
Wilcox, W.B. (2004). *Soft Patriarchs, New Men: How Christianity Shapes Fathers and Husbands*. Chicago: University of Chicago Press.
Williams, J.C. (1991). Gender Wars: Selfless Women in the Republic of Choice. *New York University Law Review*, 66, 1559–1625.
Williams, J.C. (1996). Restructuring Work and Family Entitlements Around Family Values. *Harvard Journal of Law and Public Policy*, 19, 753–58.
Williams, J.C. (1998).Toward a Reconstructive Feminism: Reconstructing the Relationship of Market Work and Family Work. *Northern Illinois University Law Review*, 19, 89–172.
Williams, J.C. (2000). *UnBending Gender: Why Family and Work Conflict and What to Do About It*. Oxford: Oxford University Press.
Williams, J.C. (2001). From Difference to Dominance to Domesticity: Care as Work, Gender as Tradition. *Chicago-Kent Law Review*, 76, 1441–94.
Yogev, S. (1981). Do Professional Women Have Egalitarian Marital Relationships? *Journal of Marriage and Family*, 43, 865–71.
Yu, B. and Borzel, Y. (1984). Effect of the Utilization Rate on the Division of Labor. *Economic Inquiry*, 22, 18–27.
Zelder, M. (1993). Inefficient Dissolutions as a Consequence of Public Goods: The Case of No-Fault Divorce. *Journal of Legal Studies*, 22, 503–20.

4

Marriage at the Crossroads in England and Wales

Rebecca Probert

The dilemmas facing policy makers in England and Wales are familiar ones. Should cohabiting couples be obliged to share their assets or support one another upon separation in the same way that married couples are? Should divorce become a simple matter of administrative compliance, with an increased role for personal choice and agreement in determining its consequences? Should England and Wales follow the lead set by a number of European countries and allow same-sex couples to marry or allow heterosexual couples to enter into an alternative form of union? Or should the government try to promote marriage?

Although the questions are the same, the answers of UK policy makers might differ from those of policy makers in other countries. Developments in Europe have considerable influence on family law in England and Wales, particularly through the jurisprudence of the European Court of Human Rights and, to a lesser extent, the European Court of Justice. However, there is no European-wide consensus on the correct answers to these questions and, while convergence in some areas can be observed, reforms are also opening up new areas of divergence (Antokolskaia 2006; Bradley 1999). Across Europe, marriage policy appears to range from Sweden's "neutrality" stance toward different types of family relationships to the constitutional protection conferred on marriage in countries such as Germany and Ireland (Antokolskaia 2006). Yet, as Harding has observed with regard to the latter, such protection "no longer ensures that marriage is protected from modern influences" and is, in practice, of little effect (Harding 2011). Similarly, the Federal Constitutional Court in Germany has held that "a mere reference to the constitutional protection of marriage . . . does not suffice as a justification" for differences in treatment between registered partners and spouses (Dethloff and Maschwitz 2011). However, the legal consequences of marriage and cohabitation have not been completely aligned even in Sweden (Perelli-Harris and Sánchez Gassen). The differences between jurisdictions are, therefore, not as striking as they might at first appear, and efforts are being made to bring about further convergence. The Commission on European Family

Law, an international group of scholars, is engaged in an ambitious project to harmonize family law across Europe, seeking to identify a "common core" where this is possible and to formulate "better law" where it is not (Boele-Woelki et al. 2004). The Commission's proposals provide possible solutions to at least some of the questions posed earlier.

The aim of this chapter is not, however, to advocate particular solutions, but instead to set out the range of options currently under discussion and the factors that might influence the future direction of reform. The first section sketches the demographic context in which UK policies have been formulated and shows how the demographic statistics are often presented in a way that highlights family change instead of equally significant continuities. It then goes on to examine the different approaches of policy makers and the factors inhibiting the implementation of clear policies. The focus then shifts to the four key questions outlined above: each is set in its historical context (although some have a longer history than others) and in the context of developments across Europe as a whole before the nature of the arguments currently being advanced is evaluated. The chapter closes with a reflection on the limitations of current debates and a plea for a deeper consideration of what marriage means today.

DEMOGRAPHIC TRENDS IN MARRIAGE, DIVORCE, AND COHABITATION

The demographic trends observable in England and Wales are similar to those evident elsewhere in Europe (Perelli-Harris and Sánchez Gassen 2010; Sobotka and Toulemon 2008). The number of marriages has fallen since peaking in the early 1970s, and the number of couples living together before marriage, as an alternative to marriage, or after divorce has increased dramatically (Beaumont 2011; Kiernan, McLanahan, Holmes, and Wright 2011). The divorce rate began to rise steeply in the 1960s and increased still faster in the wake of the Divorce Reform Act 1969, which widened the circumstances in which a divorce could be obtained. Cohabitation before marriage has become almost universal. Fifty years ago, barely 1 percent of couples lived together before marrying (Dunnell 1979); today, around 90 percent of those who marry in a civil ceremony give identical addresses when they marry (Centre for Social Justice 2009). Cohabiting families now account for more than 15 percent of all families (Beaumont 2011), or around 2.3 million couples. Based on current trends, it is predicted that the number of cohabiting couples will rise to 3.8 million by 2033 (Office for National Statistics 2010b).

Yet a different story could also be told. Although these statistics are all accurate, they emphasize change instead of continuity: it is rare to be reminded either that most couples who live together in England and Wales are married or that most of them stay married. Indeed, the divorce rate has actually fallen in recent years and, in 2009, stood at 10.5 divorcing persons per 1,000 married persons. Too many commentators assume that this decline can be explained by the falling number of marriages, overlooking how the divorce rate is calculated, or they confuse the duration of marriages that end in divorce with the average duration of all marriages. Some commentators have also interpreted the data in highly misleading ways. For example, a leading family law textbook for law students claims on its first page that the "stereotypical . . . ideal" family consisting of two parents and children "is not the family form that most people will have experienced," relying on the fact that only a minority of households took this form in 2009 (Herring 2011). But this statement ignores the difference between households and individuals and, more importantly, between a particular "snapshot" in time and an individual's experiences over his or her lifetime. In fact, the vast majority of UK children are born into two-parent households, and single parents do not necessarily remain single. Those who have *never* experienced living in a two-parent family are rare indeed.

At the same time, the movement away from formal marriage is assumed to be predictable, even inevitable. But those who believe that marriage is on track to wither away altogether might do well to study trends in Scandinavia. In Sweden, often seen as being in the vanguard of family trends, marriage is undergoing something of a revival, with the marriage rate increasing since 1998 (Ohlsson-Wijk 2011), and there are signs that the same may be happening elsewhere (Sobotka and Toulemon 2008). This is not to deny the very real changes that have occurred, but simply to point out that the data could be presented in a way that focuses on continuity rather than change. The fact that a particular narrative about the family has dominated public discussion is also an important factor shaping the policies that have been adopted by successive governments.

POLITICS AND MARRIAGE POLICY

Over the last thirty years, the major political parties in England and Wales have vied with each other to present themselves as family-friendly. What is perhaps more surprising is the extent to which, despite this shared rhetoric, no party has adopted any clear policy on marriage and cohabitation. This is not to suggest that pronouncements on these issues have been lacking, and many politicians have clear preferences as to what form the family should take. But if one judges politicians by their actions instead of their oratory, the picture that emerges is very mixed.

Thus, the New Labour government (1997–2010) began its first administration by suggesting that "[w]e want to strengthen the institution of marriage to help more marriages to succeed" (Home Office 1998) and ended its last administration by articulating the view that marriage is "a personal and private decision for responsible adults, with which politicians should not interfere" (Department for Children, Schools and Families 2010). The first statement was, however, prefaced by language assuring the electorate that other family forms were also valued, and the second by an acknowledgment that marriage remained "an important and well-established institution that plays a fundamental role in family life in our society." Between these two points in time, the "marriage allowance," which reduced the amount of income tax payable, was taken from married couples to finance tax credits for families with children (Salter 2007), resources were shifted from marriage education to more general relationship support (van Acker 2008), and various initiatives encouraged the "normalisation" of cohabitation (Finch 2004). Yet no action was taken to implement proposals for the extension of enhanced rights to cohabitants who suffer economic disadvantage as a result of their relationships, despite numerous criticisms of current law (Law Commission 2007).

This gap between rhetoric and action can also be seen in the stance taken by the current Coalition government. Before the 2010 election, the Conservative party pledged to provide further fiscal benefits to married couples, a pledge that has since been repeated on a number of occasions with more enthusiasm than detail. However, the Coalition government has thus far done nothing to fulfill this pledge, largely because of the difficulties in devising a scheme that offers a real incentive to married couples at a time of austerity measures. The problem, as previous Conservative administrations have found (Smart 1987), is that promoting one family form disadvantages others. In the allocation of resources, it is the most needy who tend to have priority; the ideal of promoting marriage has thus been seen as conflicting with the imperative of reducing child poverty. Thus, despite the "stark differentiation . . . between right-wing moral panic about marriage and left-wing celebration and tolerance of diversity" (van Acker 2008), differences in party rhetoric have become blurred in practice. It was, after all, a previous Conservative government that presided over the extension of rights to unmarried fathers in the Children Act 1989 (as well as the imposition of parental responsibilities in the Child Support Act 1991) and which passed legislation that would have made divorce available without the need to establish fault (which the subsequent New Labour government decided not to implement).

Indeed, even at the level of rhetoric, the divisions between different parties are more muted than some accounts suggest. The virtual disappearance of moral and religious arguments from debates about marriage is a striking feature of the modern European cultural landscape. Even the Church of England has held that "living in sin" is no longer sinful (Melkie 1995), relaxed its rules on remarriage after divorce, and accepted its ministers entering into civil partnerships as long as they abstain from sex (House of Bishops 2005).

In the United Kingdom at present, the main influence on family law and policy is arguably economic: the recent Legal Aid, Sentencing and Punishment of Offenders Act 2012 restricts state-funded "legal aid" for legal advice and representation in private family law cases (i.e., divorce, division of assets and disputes over residence and contact) (Family Justice Review 2011; Miles 2011). Strenuous attempts are being made to encourage agreement, to divert warring couples into mediation or therapy, and to obtain early neutral evaluation from a judge without a full trial of the issues.

Although couples diverted from litigation will, in theory, bargain in the shadow of the law, the outcomes may differ depending on whether the result was reached through mediation, negotiation, or adjudication. This background is crucial to understanding current constraints on the formulation of family policy: anything that might cost the state more is unlikely to win government support.

OPTING OUT OF MARRIAGE

Given recent inaccurate claims about the prevalence of cohabitation in past times (Thane 2010), it is worth reiterating that the incidence of cohabitation in England and Wales was statistically insignificant prior to the 1970s (Murphy 2000). Moreover, contrary to popular belief, English law has never recognized the concept of "common-law marriage." The idea that, prior to 1754, it was possible to enter into marriage simply by exchanging vows of consent derives from the mistaken interpretation of English authorities by a New York court in 1809. Nor, during this early period, did the law infer that two people who were living together were married: indeed, such a couple might be brought before the church courts and punished for fornication or the more specific offense of "living scandalously and suspiciously together without lawful marriage" (Probert 2008, 2009).

By the late eighteenth century, however, the church courts had effectively ceased to punish the laity for moral offenses. Thereafter, the few couples who cohabited without marriage occupied an ambiguous position under English law. The nineteenth-century emphasis on precedent ensured that individuals could use the law of contracts, wills, and trusts to provide for a cohabitant, but there was no positive obligation to do so. With a few exceptions – the pragmatic extension of wartime separation allowances and emergency provision for the dependents of the unemployed being the key examples – legislative recognition of cohabiting couples was also limited.

Beginning in the 1970s, however, cohabitation became more visible socially, culturally, and legally. Between 1975 and 1979, cohabitants gained a number of important statutory rights, including the right to exclude a violent partner from the family home regardless of its ownership and the right to claim provision from the estate of a deceased partner. During this period, judges also became increasingly willing to accept cohabitants as members of each other's families and fashioned new doctrines that permitted claims to the family home by the partner without legal title (Probert 2010).

Unfortunately, the manner in which the media presented these new rights to the public gave rise to the impression that they were far more extensive than they were, laying the foundations for the "common-law marriage" myth (Probert 2008, 2012). Whether this myth encouraged more couples to cohabit in the mistaken belief that they would be protected by the law is difficult to assess, although it is perhaps significant that the major increase in child-rearing within cohabiting relationships took place only after these developments. What is clear, however, is that a large proportion of the UK population – and an even larger proportion of cohabiting couples – does now believe that living together gives rise to a "common-law marriage." Few cohabitants attempt to regulate their situation by means of a trust, contract, or will, and attempts to dispel current misunderstandings by means of a public information campaign have had only limited effect (Barlow, Burgoyne, Clery, and Smithson 2008).

Whether cohabitants *should* enjoy the same, or similar, rights as those who have formalized their relationships through marriage has been a contested issue for many years now. Within Europe, there are currently no jurisdictions in which the rights of married and cohabiting couples are identical, although the legal consequences of cohabitation and the extent of the "rights gap" between married and cohabiting couples varies considerably from country to country (Barlow and Probert 2000; Perelli-Harris and Sánchez Gassen 2010). Sweden is often thought of as a pioneer in assimilating cohabitation to marriage, but Antokolskaia includes it alongside Norway and Yugoslavia as examples of countries that specifically regulate cohabitation but provide only minimal protection for cohabitants (Antokolskaia 2006). The conflation of demands for protection of cohabitants with the recognition of same-sex unions has also meant that a number of jurisdictions (including France, Belgium, and some Spanish and Italian regions) have chosen to channel cohabitant rights through registration, but the need to opt in and the limited rights accorded mean that such schemes satisfy neither cohabitants nor same-sex partners (Antokolskaia 2006).

With the virtual eradication from the debate of abstract moral arguments, the focus in England and Wales has tended to be on the expectations of cohabitants who would be affected by reform and on the extent to which cohabiting relationships resemble marital relationships – all points, it should be noted, that are heavily disputed (Crawford, Goodman, Greaves, and Joyce 2011; Miles, Pleasence, and Balmer 2009; Probert 2010). Recent research has demonstrated that U.S. and UK cohabitants differ in a number of important ways; for example, in terms of union stability and socioeconomic status, cohabitants are more like married couples in the United Kingdom than they are in the United States (Kiernan, McLanahan, Holmes, and Wright 2011). Insofar as differences between married and cohabiting couples are observable, it is clear that selection plays an important part: research carried out by the Institute for Fiscal Studies, for example, has demonstrated that the lower cognitive development of children of cohabiting parents "is largely accounted for by the fact that cohabiting parents have lower education qualifications than married parents"; most of the gap in their socioemotional development could also be explained by factors such as education and income (Crawford, Goodman, Greaves, and Joyce 2011). Yet questions still remain about the influence of relationship quality, and whether this is something that is itself influenced by marriage. One study found that marriage remained more stable than cohabitation even after controlling for such factors as education, employment, and class, but noted that those social factors "which are known to be associated with marital stability... are also associated with cohabitation stability," and hypothesized that there might be a potential selection effect if those with more stable relationships chose to marry (Wilson and Stuchbury 2010). However, even after controlling for a wide range of variables, researchers continue to find that cohabitation is less stable than marriage and that the greater stability afforded by marriage is associated with various advantages for children (McLanahan and Garfinkel, Chapter 8).

Standing back from such debates, what is perhaps most striking is the difficulty in divining from the accumulated evidence how the law should treat cohabiting couples. The greater stability of marital relationships could be seen as a reason for promoting marriage, but the fact that cohabiting relationships are more likely to break down could equally be interpreted as indicating a greater need for legal regulation. Similarly, research data showing that cohabitants are less likely to share assets during their relationships might, on the one hand, be taken as a reason why cohabitants should not be required to share assets after separation but, on the other, as a reason why the financially weaker cohabiting partner needs the legal protection that asset reallocation upon separation would provide (Vogler 2009). The problem in attempting to determine policy according to the characteristics of different family relationships, then, is that the evidence is not always clear-cut and can be used to justify a variety of different policy approaches.

In 2007, the UK Law Commission put forward a set of painstakingly researched – if complex – reform proposals, but the New Labour government then in power announced that it intended to evaluate similar reforms in Scotland before deciding whether to implement the Commission's plan, and the current government has recently announced that it does not intend to introduce legislation before the next election. Yet the fact that both Scotland and Ireland have enacted legislation giving economically disadvantaged (Family Law (Scotland) Act s. 28) or dependent (Civil Partnership and Certain Rights and Obligations of Cohabitants Act 2010, s. 173) cohabitants a claim in the event of separation does raise questions as to whether England and Wales can continue to justify the lack of *any* protection for such couples.

ENDING MARRIAGE

The terms on which the state permits exit from marriage tells us much about the way in which marriage is regarded. The conditions that need to be satisfied before a divorce can be obtained vary considerably between countries across Europe (Örücü and Mair 2007). Many legal systems "still cling to a multiplicity of grounds"; although no country's divorce laws are based exclusively on fault today, in some jurisdictions "fault is still one ground for divorce among many others" (Boele-Woelki et al. 2004). Even within the United Kingdom, divorce laws vary. In Scotland, divorce was available from the mid-sixteenth century on the basis of adultery and "malicious desertion," while in Ireland it was only available by a private Act of Parliament before 1922 and then banned altogether until 1996 (Harding 2011). In England and Wales, legislation replacing the old system of parliamentary divorce was passed in 1857 but, until 1937, the only accepted ground for divorce was adultery. Current law, enacted in 1969, represents a compromise between fault and no-fault principles. Under the 1969 legislation, divorce is, in theory, obtainable only when the court has determined that the parties' marriage has broken down irretrievably. To establish irretrievable breakdown, the divorce applicant may either present evidence of spousal fault (i.e., adultery, desertion, or unreasonable behavior) or show that the couple has lived apart for five years (a period that may be reduced to two years if the other spouse consents). There is, in short, no means by which a divorce may be obtained without either making fault allegations or waiting a significant period of time.

The legislation passed in 1969 continues to govern this area forty years on, despite attempts at reform. In practice, of course, spouses may agree that one of them will apply for divorce without making hurtful fault allegations, and commentators have noted that the threshold for unreasonable behavior has been set by the courts at a fairly low level. Moreover, the fact that undefended applications are dealt with by judges in chambers without the parties being present and with minimal scrutiny means that the allegations need not even be true, and the misleadingly named "special procedure" for undefended divorces is now used by over 99 percent of divorcing couples. A divorce will, therefore, be available sooner or later – and rather sooner if the parties are not too scrupulous about the content of the petition – a fact which has tended to mute any demand for reform.

However, there is evidence that making fault allegations may itself exacerbate hostilities between the parties (Wright 2006). Given the current sense that it is important for couples to make their own arrangements on separation wherever possible and, if they have children, to maintain an amicable relationship for the future, it seems perverse that these vestiges of the old fault-based system still remain part of the law. The argument that the retention of fault grounds sends a message that a marriage cannot be ended without good reason cannot be sustained in the light of the widespread perception of the availability of "quickie" divorces.

This is perhaps one context where the usual chronology of reform, whereby changes in the grounds for divorce are swiftly followed by procedural reforms necessitated by unexpected demand, may be reversed. The Family Justice Review has recently proposed making divorce a purely administrative procedure. The change would, in practice, be minimal: individuals would send their divorce petitions to a centralized processing center instead of a court, respondent spouses would be contacted by an administrator and, if the divorce is uncontested, both would be served with notice of divorce, which would perform the same function as the current decree *nisi*. The divorce would become final six weeks later, unless appealed. The few contested divorces would continue to be heard by the courts, as at present. This proposal is likely to attract support because it requires fewer court resources than the current model and it does not necessitate any reform of the substantive law of divorce. Yet the transfer of responsibility from judges to administrators might well lead to concern about the evaluative decisions that need to be made, and thus pave the way for a simpler law of divorce as a result.

Just such a simple law is contained in the *Principles of European Family Law* drafted by the Commission on European Family Law. The proposed law would make divorce available immediately if both parties consent or after separation for one year if they do not (Boele-Woelki et al. 2004). Unfortunately, as I have noted elsewhere, the very fact that these proposals are inspired by the desire to harmonize family law within Europe is likely to generate opposition from conservative sections of the UK press and to make the process of divorce reform even more contentious (Probert 2007).

OPENING MARRIAGE TO SAME-SEX COUPLES

Same-sex couples may now marry in a number of jurisdictions, including Argentina, Belgium, Canada, Iceland, the Netherlands, Norway, Portugal, Spain, Sweden, and some American states. In other jurisdictions, including Andorra, Austria, the Czech Republic, Denmark, Finland, France, Germany, Hungary, Iceland, Ireland, Lichtenstein, Luxembourg, Slovenia, Switzerland, the United Kingdom, and some American states, same-sex couples may enter into a registered partnership.

The extent to which registered-partnership regimes are modeled on marriage does, however, vary considerably between jurisdictions. In France, for example, the *pacte civil de solidarité* offers a genuine alternative to marriage for both same-sex and opposite-sex couples. The parties may write their own *pacte*, setting out the terms of their relationship and how assets will be divided if it breaks down; once registered, they are entitled to certain legal advantages immediately and to others after a period of years has elapsed. De-registration is far simpler than divorce, and marriage to another has the effect of terminating a *pacte* immediately.The *pacsé* alternative has been extremely popular, although there is some evidence to suggest that many *pacsé* couples hope that the institution will evolve to give them the same rights and obligations enjoyed by married couples (Ignasse 2002).

By contrast, in England and Wales, only same-sex couples may register as "civil partners," and such a partnership produces virtually the same rights and responsibilities as marriage. A few minor differences remain, but even in the relatively short period since the Civil Partnership Act was enacted in 2004, these have been reduced. In 2010, the Equality Act provided that religious groups could (but would not be obliged to) host civil partnership ceremonies. The Adoption and Children Act 2002 permitted same-sex couples to adopt a child together even before enactment of the Civil Partnership Act, and the Human Fertilization and Embryology Act 2008 put same-sex partners of women undergoing fertility treatment in the same position as their heterosexual counterparts and allowed same-sex couples to obtain parental orders in cases of surrogacy. The fact that a civil partnership cannot be annulled on the basis of one partner's inability or willful refusal to consummate may be seen by some as implying that such relationships do not have a sexual dimension, but has little relevance in practice given that a refusal to engage in a sexual relationship would no doubt be accepted by a court as behavior with which the other partner could not reasonably be expected to live, and so provide a basis for a dissolution. The unfaithfulness of one partner would also be regarded as unreasonable behavior and justify the dissolution of the relationship despite the fact that a civil partner is not technically regarded as having committed adultery.

More than 40,000 civil partnerships have been registered since 2005 (Beaumont 2011). Yet, despite the fact that both the UK media and the public now regularly use the term "marriage" when referring to civil partnerships, there is still a vocal campaign to allow same-sex couples to marry. In 2006, a lesbian couple filed a lawsuit seeking recognition of their same-sex marriage contracted in Canada, but the High Court (Family Division) upheld section 215 of the Civil Partnership Act, under which a same-sex marriage contracted in another nation has the status of a civil partnership in the United Kingdom. The court's justification for the distinction between marriage and civil partnership was based essentially on a nineteenth-century judicial pronouncement that "[m]arriage as understood in Christendom, may . . . be defined as the union for life of one man and one woman to the exclusion of all others" (*Wilkinson v. Kitzinger* [2006] EWHC 2022 (Fam)), quoting *Hyde v. Hyde & Woodmansee* (1865) 69 L.R. 1 P. & D. 13).

In late 2010, the Equal Love campaign publicly challenged the current law by sending both same-sex couples seeking permission to marry and heterosexual couples seeking permission to enter into civil partnerships to their local register offices. All applications were, of course, refused, but Equal Love plans to challenge the Civil Partnership Act under the European Convention on Human Rights. However, the European Court of Human Rights held only last year that Article 12 of the Convention, which guarantees "men and women" the right "to marry and found a family", does not impose "an obligation on the respondent Government to grant a same-sex couple . . . access to marriage" (*Schalk and Kopf v. Austria* [2010] 29 B.H.R.C. 396, para 63).

Of course, the Court may ultimately change its mind (Bamforth 2011). On previous occasions, the Court has taken account of international developments; when the issue comes before the Court again, it may take account of the increasing number of jurisdictions that allow same-sex marriage. Even without a shift in the Court's view, England and Wales may soon permit same-sex marriage. As this volume was going to press, the government announced strong support for legalization of same-sex marriage and had begun a consultation to consider such a shift. Not all, however, have welcomed this development: the most vigorous discussion of what marriage means is to be found in the vehement arguments voiced by those who feel that same-sex couples should not want to enter into an institution perceived as heterosexual and patriarchal (Auchmuty 2008; Norrie 2000).

PROMOTING MARRIAGE

Until the late twentieth century, marriage was such an integral part of adult life that no one imagined that it required promotion. Today, by contrast, there tends to be skepticism as to whether it is even possible for government policy to lure the public toward marriage. The possibility of special tax allowances for married couples has attracted considerable – and largely unfavorable – commentary in the UK media. Moreover, research carried out by the Institute for Fiscal Studies showed very clearly that such a marriage incentive was unlikely to yield dividends in terms of child development.

But are such incentives actually necessary? The decline in the number of marriages is not quite as precipitous as official statistics suggest. UK residents who marry in another country are not required to notify the authorities of their marriages. And estimates based on the International Passenger Survey suggest that, in 2009, more than 90,000 UK residents traveled abroad to marry (Office for National Statistics 2010a). Some were couples traveling together; others – since twice as many men as women go overseas to marry – were individuals marrying someone from another jurisdiction. There is interesting research to be done on why overseas marriages are proving so popular, but what is clear is that the marriage statistics would look very different were these weddings added to those celebrated in England and Wales. Whether emphasizing the continuing popularity of marriage instead of its decline would have any effect on marriage behavior is unclear, but it would certainly be less costly than tax incentives, the impact of which is also speculative.

CONCLUSION

Marriage may well be at a crossroads in England and Wales, but – to expand the metaphor – the crossroads is not necessarily where we think it is. Although the decision whether or not to marry is now heavily influenced by socioeconomic factors, religion, and ethnic background (Crawford, Goodman, Greaves, and Joyce 2011; Eekelaar and Maclean 2004; Miles, Pleasence, and Balmer 2009), there are still many more married than cohabiting couples. Marriage, contrary to the views of some of its critics, is unlikely to wither away any time soon. The evidence suggests that the public still perceives marriage as having something to offer that goes beyond the sharing of a bed and a bank balance: The answer to the question posed by Baroness Hale more than thirty years ago – "whether the legal institution of marriage continues to serve any useful purpose" – would seem to be "yes."

As to the direction that marriage regulation should take, the answer is still unclear. Stereotypes of marriage continue to abound in public discussion. Baleful effects are willingly attributed to the impact of the legal tie (Auchmuty 2008), while positive effects are perceived to be the result of selection alone. Debates about the desirability of conferring rights on cohabitants commonly contrast "form" with "function." But discussion typically focuses on whether cohabitants fulfill the same functions as married couples (Probert 2010), neglecting the equally crucial questions of whether public marriage commitments have any meaning to the couples that make them and whether the marriage ceremony should be legally reduced to a mere "form" without any substance. While the growing literature on new family forms offers many valuable insights, more empirical research into the values, expectations, and experiences of modern couples, married and unmarried, is necessary to move beyond assumptions and stereotypes. We need, in short, a better informed and more nuanced debate on what marriage means to people today before we can decide where it should go next.

REFERENCES

Antokolskaia, M. (2006). *Harmonisation of Family Law in Europe: A Historical Perspective: A Tale of Two Millennia*. Antwerp: Intersentia.

Auchmuty, R. (2008). What's So Special about Marriage? The Impact of *Wilkinson v Kitzinger*. *Child and Family Law Quarterly*, *20*, 475–498.

Bamforth, N. (2011). Families But Not (Yet) Marriages? Same-Sex Partners and the Developing European Convention "Margin of Appreciation." *Child and Family Law Quarterly*, *23*, 128–143.

Barlow, A. and Probert, R. (2000). Displacing Marriage: Diversification and Harmonisation within Europe. *Child and Family Law Quarterly*, *12*, 153–165.

Barlow, A., Burgoyne, C., Clery E., and Smithson, J. (2008). Cohabitation and the Law: Myths, Money and the Media. In Park, A. et al. (Eds.), *British Social Attitudes: The 24th Report*. London: Ashgate.

Beaumont, J. (2011). Households and Families. In *Social Trends 41*. London: Office for National Statistics.

Boele-Woelki, K. et al. (2004). *Principles of European Family Law Regarding Divorce and Maintenance between Former Spouses*. Antwerp: Intersentia.

Bradley, D. (1999). Convergence in Family Law: Mirrors, Transplants and Political Economy. *Maastricht Journal of European and Comparative Law*, *6*, 127–150.

Centre for Social Justice (2009). *Every Family Matters: An In-Depth Review of Family Law in Britain*. London: Centre for Social Justice.

Crawford, C., Goodman, A., Greaves, E. and Joyce, R. (2011). *Cohabitation, Marriage, Relationship Stability and Child Outcomes: An Update*. London: Institute for Fiscal Studies.

Department for Children, Schools and Families (2010). *Support for All*. London: The Stationery Office.

Dethloff, N. and Maschwitz, A. (2011). Courts Strengthening Equality and New Ways in Cross-Border Matrimonial Property Questions. In Atkin, B. (Ed.), *The International Survey of Family Law 2011*. Bristol: Jordan Publishing.

Dunnell, K. (1979). *Family Formation 1976*. London: Office of Population Censuses and Surveys.

Eekelaar, J. and Maclean, M. (2004). Marriage and the Moral Bases of Personal Relationships. *Journal of Law and Society*, 31, 510–538.

Family Justice Review (2011). *Interim Report*. Available at http://www.justice.gov.uk/about/moj/independent-reviews/family-justice-review/.

Finch, J. (2004). Family Policy and Civil Registration in England and Wales: An Analysis of the White Paper *Civil Registration: Vital Change*. *Journal of Social Policy*, 33, 249–266.

Harding, M. (2011). Religion and Family Law in Ireland: From a Catholic Protection of Marriage to a "Catholic" Approach to Nullity. In Mair, J. and Örücü, E. (Eds.), *The Place of Religion in Family Law: A Comparative Search*. Antwerp: Intersentia.

Herring, J. (2011). *Family Law*. Harlow: Pearson.

Home Office (1998). *Supporting Families: A Consultation Document*. London: The Stationery Office.

House of Bishops (2005). Civil Partnerships – A Pastoral Statement from the House of Bishops of the Church of England.

Ignasse, G. (2002). *Les pacsé-e-s: Enquête sur les signataires d'un pacte civil de solidarité*. Paris: L'Hamilton.

Kiernan, K., McLanahan, S., Holmes J., and Wright, M. (2011). Fragile Families in the US and UK. Available at http://crcw.princeton.edu/workingpapers/WP11-04-FF.pdf.

Law Commission (2007). *Cohabitation: The Financial Consequences of Relationship Breakdown*. London: The Stationery Office.

Melkie, J. (1995). Out with Traditional Sin as Church Embraces Modern Values. *The Guardian*, June 7.

Miles, J. (2011). Legal Aid, Article 6 and "Exceptional Funding" under the Legal Aid (etc.) Bill 2011. *Family Law*, 41, 1003–1009.

Miles, J., Pleasence, P., and Balmer, N. (2009). The Experience of Relationship Breakdown and Civil Law Problems by People in Different Forms of Relationship. *Child and Family Law Quarterly*, 21, 47–64.

Murphy, M. (2000). The Evolution of Cohabitation in Britain, 1960–95. *Population Studies*, 54, 43–56.

Norrie, K. McK. (2000). Marriage Is for Heterosexuals – May the Rest of Us Be Saved from It. *Child and Family Law Quarterly*, 12, 363–369.

Office for National Statistics (2010a). Population Estimates by Marital Status: Methodology Paper. Available at http://www.statistics.gov.uk/about/data/methodology/specific/population/ downloads/Marital_Status_Estimation_Methodology_Feb_2010.pdf.

Office for National Statistics (2010b). Marital Status Population Projections, 2008-Based. Available at http://www.statistics.gov.uk/pdfdir/marr0610.pdf.

Ohlsson-Wijk, S. (2011). Sweden's Marriage Revival: An Analysis of the New-Millenium Switch from Long-Term Decline to Increasing Popularity. *Population Studies*, 65, 183–200.

Örücü, E. and Mair, J. (Eds.) (2007). *Juxtaposing Legal Systems and the Principles of European Family Law on Divorce and Maintenance*. Antwerp: Intersentia.

Perelli-Harris, B. and Sánchez Gassen, N. (2010). The Reciprocal Relationship between the State and Union Formation across Western Europe: Policy Dimensions and Theoretical Considerations. MPIDR Working Paper WP-2010-034.

Probert, R. (2007). England and Wales Juxtaposed to the European Principles of Family Law. In Örücü, E. and Mair, J. (Eds.), *Juxtaposing Legal Systems and the Principles of European Family Law on Divorce and Maintenance*. Antwerp: Intersentia.

Probert, R. (2008). Common Law Marriage: Myths and Misunderstandings. *Child and Family Law Quarterly*, 20, 1–22.

Probert, R. (2009). *Marriage Law and Practice in the Long Eighteenth Century: A Reassessment*. Cambridge: Cambridge University Press.
Probert, R. (2010). Cohabitation: Current Legal Solutions. In O'Cinneide, C. (Ed.), *Current Legal Problems: Volume 62*. Oxford: Oxford University Press.
Probert, R. (2012). *The Legal Regulation of Cohabitation, 1600–2010: From Fornicators to Family*. Cambridge: Cambridge University Press.
Salter, D. (2007). Income Tax and Family Life. In Probert, R. (Ed.), *Family Life and the Law: Under One Roof*. Aldershot: Ashgate.
Smart, C. (1987). Securing the Family: Rhetoric and Policy in the Field of Social Security. In Loney, M. et al. (Eds.), *The State or the Market: Politics and Welfare in Contemporary Britain*. London: Sage.
Sobotka, T. and Toulemon, L. (2008). Changing Family and Partnership Behaviour: Common Trends and Persistent Diversity across Europe. *Demographic Research*, 19, 85–138.
Thane, P. (2010). *Happy Families?* London: British Academy.
van Acker, E. (2008). *Governments and Marriage Education Policy: Perspectives from the UK, Australia and the US*. Basingstoke: Palgrave Macmillan.
Vogler, C. (2009). Managing Money in Intimate Relationships: Similarities and Differences between Cohabiting and Married Couples. In Miles, J. and Probert, R. (Eds.), *Sharing Lives, Dividing Assets*. Oxford: Hart.
Wilson, B. and Stuchbury, R. (2010). Do Partnerships Last? Comparing Marriage and Cohabitation Using Longitudinal Census Data. *Population Trends*, 139, 37–62.
Wright, K. (2006). The Divorce Process: A View from the Other Side of the Desk. *Child and Family Law Quarterly*, 18, 93–111.

5

The Curious Relationship of Marriage and Freedom

Katherine Franke

Marriage is surely at a crossroad, as the chapters in this volume so richly attest. In fact, marriage may be at more than one crossroad, some pointing toward new, uncharted terrain, others amounting to intersections we have visited before. My principal interest in exploring this dynamic moment in the evolution of the institution of marriage is to better understand why and how today's marriage equality movement for same-sex couples might benefit from lessons learned by African Americans when they too were allowed to marry for the first time in the immediate post–Civil War era. I find it curious that the right to marry rather than, say, employment rights, educational opportunity, or political participation has emerged as the preeminent vehicle by and through which the freedom, equality, and dignity of gay men and lesbians is being fought in the present moment. Why marriage? In what ways are the values, aspirations, and even identity of an oppressed community shaped when they are articulated in and through the institution of marriage? What kind of freedom and what kind of equality does the capacity to marry bring forth?

I write this chapter just as same-sex couples have won the right to legally marry in the state of New York. While there is much to celebrate in this victory, I am concerned that this new form of legal recognition for some members of the lesbian and gay community may come at a cost of rendering more marginalized and vulnerable other forms of family, kinship, and care (Franke 2011). Now that same-sex couples *can* marry, many employers have announced that they *must* do so in order to retain benefits to which they had previously been entitled without the legal sanction of the state (Bernard 2011:10–11). "We can now treat you just as we treat heterosexual couples," they say. "Heterosexuals must marry to gain benefits for their spouses and children, you must now as well."

In important ways, what we are witnessing today with same-sex couples echoes the experience of another group of new rights-holders almost 150 years ago. To better understand how the gay rights movement today has collapsed into a marriage rights movement, and what the costs of such a strategy might be, I will look backward in history to another time when marriage rights intersected with the rights of freedom, equality, and dignity of a marginalized population: newly emancipated black people in the mid-nineteenth century. The experiences of formerly enslaved people in the 1860s with newly won rights to marry hold lessons for the gay rights/marriage movement today.

Since the birth of the same-sex marriage movement, advocates have argued that if miscegenation laws (laws prohibiting interracial marriage) were an unconstitutional form of race discrimination, then laws prohibiting same-sex marriage should amount to unconstitutional sex discrimination. Andrew Koppelman (1998) has made this argument earliest and most often. Indeed, this reasoning formed the basis of the first victory for the same-sex marriage movement in 1999 (Baehr 1996), when the Supreme Court of Hawaii found that same-sex couples should have the same marriage rights as different-sex couples.

This analogy never sat well with me. I have long felt that before the gay and lesbian community committed to a civil rights strategy based on "if-they've-got-it-we-want-it," we ought to undertake a little better due diligence about what "they" have before "we" insist on getting it too. Don't get me wrong, I am the first to admit that what motivates most opponents of same-sex marriage is a hatred or intolerance of gay and lesbian people, otherwise known as homophobia. So too, I understand that many gay and lesbian couples want to get married. Who can deny the pull of an institution that is so religiously, socially, legally and financially privileged, particularly as compared with the alternatives? Even as domestic partnership and civil union laws increasingly equalize the financial and legal benefits that same-sex couples can get in lieu of marriage, they cannot match the respect, dignity, and social meanings of being married full stop.

While I recognize why marriage matters so much to some members of the gay and lesbian community, I would have preferred if we, as a community, had paused before we invested so heavily in a politics of recognition – that is, in the blessing that the state can confer on relationships that meet its requirements for legitimacy. A recognition-based project of this sort provides few tools with which to transform or render more just the fundamental underlying norms by which some forms of life are valued more highly than others. As Judith Butler (2009:6) has observed in another context: "The problem is not merely how to include more people within existing norms, but to consider how existing norms allocate recognition differentially. What new norms are possible, and how are they wrought? What might be done to produce a more egalitarian set of conditions for recognizability?"

It strikes me that in the present moment we could learn something from the struggle for racial justice, not by analogizing today's marriage movement to the fight against miscegenation laws, but by looking at what happened last time a previously reviled and disadvantaged group won the right to marry for the first time. That is what leads me to look into the immediate post–Civil War regulation of freed peoples' marriages. I suspected that that period might hold out some cautionary tales for us today. And indeed it does.

Even as I urge this analogy, I won't argue that the racism experienced by the freedmen was the same as the homophobia or heterosexism gay and lesbian people experience today. Nor could I even suggest that the institution of marriage is the same now as it was then. That said, I think we can learn from the comparison of what it means to elaborate a new conception of freedom and equality through a form of state licensure. Like same-sex couples today, the freed men and women experienced moving from outlaws to inlaws, from living outside the law to finding their private lives organized in both wonderful and perilous ways by and within law. Being subject to legal regulation is always something to think carefully about. The experiences of the freedmen suggest some caution with respect to whether, and if so how, rights – and specifically a right to marriage – will set you free. Of course rights are something we cannot not want. But our desire for rights is something we should indulge with an awareness that they come at a cost.

In what follows I highlight three principal concerns I have about the moral hazards associated with a civil rights struggle that prioritizes marriage rights. Each of these concerns – marriage as a civilizing institution, the potential collapse of the right to marry into an obligation, and the disciplinary effects of marriage meted out through criminal enforcement of adultery laws – was borne out in the experiences of newly emancipated former slaves when they won the right to marry in the nineteenth century, and is in play in the contemporary same-sex marriage movement.

As early as 1774, enslaved people identified the inhumanity of slavery as lying, in significant part, in the inability to marry. In a petition to the new government of Massachusetts, a group of enslaved men wrote: "[W]e are deprived of every thing that hath a tendency to make life even tolerable, the endearing ties of husband and wife we are strangers to for we are no longer man and wife than our masters or mistresses thinkes proper marred or onmarred" (Davis 1997:109). Abolitionist Angelina Grimké (1837) argued that both positive and natural legal principles required that the United States "[n]o longer deny [African Americans] the right of marriage, but let every man have his own wife, and let every woman have her own husband" (Grimké 1837:61–63; Richards 1998). In 1850, Henry Bibb, an enslaved man, observed: "I presume that there are no class of people in the United States who so highly appreciate the legality of marriage as those persons who have been held and treated as property" (Bibb 1969:192). Arguing in favor of the 1866 Civil Rights Act, Illinois Senator Lyman Trumbull specifically identified the right to marry as a necessary aspect of citizenship (*Protection of Civil Rights* 1866).

Echoing contemporary arguments in favor of same-sex marriage, the right to marry figured prominently in the bundle of rights understood to have been denied to enslaved people, and was considered necessary to any robust conception of liberty

(Davis 1997; Foner 1988; Grossberg 1985; Gutman 1979; Malone 1992). Marriage "provided a way to establish the integrity of their relationships, to bring a new security to their family lives, and, to affirm their freedom.... If the prohibition on marriage had underscored their dependent position and the precariousness of their family ties in slavery, the act of marriage now symbolized the rejection of their slave status" (Edwards 1996:101). Formerly enslaved people and abolitionists generally deemed the right to marry one of the most important ramifications of emancipation.

In countless ways, the role of marriage as part of what it meant for newly emancipated people to be free parallels the struggles of lesbian and gay people today. Then as now the inability to marry inflicted a stinging badge of inferiority on couples whose love, care, and interdependence otherwise mirrored that of the couples who could legally marry. In important ways for both groups, the incapacity to marry produced and reinforced their identity as a lower caste, and the struggle to win marriage rights figured at the top of the civil rights agenda to expand their equality and freedom as full citizens in society.

That said, the prominence of marriage as the lever by which both formerly enslaved people and lesbian and gay people might be elevated from their subordinate status has entailed noteworthy hazards that are worthy of better understanding. Marriage, then as now, has been a curious and complicated vehicle through which to address the injustice of racism and homophobia.

MARRIAGE HAS ITS OWN AGENDA

Unlike other fora that have provided the setting for important civil rights struggles, such as lunch counters or public transportation, marriage is a particularly value-laden institution within which to lodge claims for full citizenship. The same might be said of military service and even equal educational opportunity. But for present purposes, when claims for full citizenship are articulated through a demand for marriage rights, the disenfranchised group's interest in equality and freedom must contend with the values of dignity, discipline, respectability, and security entailed in the institution of marriage itself. Surely, exclusion from the institution of marriage inflicts a subordinating harm on those excluded. Yet a demand that the exclusion be lifted in the name of equality and freedom must take account of the fact that marriage has its own well-entrenched agenda.

The role of marriage in the lives of formerly enslaved people in the 1860s illustrates just what it means to elaborate a notion of freedom through the values and commitments of marriage.

In its reports to the Secretary of War in the early 1860s, the American Freedmen's Inquiry Commission reflected the view dominant among whites at the time that black people were uncivilized, degraded, and undisciplined and lived in wholly un-Christian ways, and that the rule of law as well as patient guidance from whites would tame and civilize them. Thus the Commission observed that "[t]he law, in the shape of military rule, takes for him the place of his master, with this difference – that he submits to it more heartily and cheerfully, without any sense of degradation" (American Freedmen's Inquiry Commission 1863:12). Urging an active role for the federal government in the moral cultivation of black character, the Commission's Final Report concluded on an optimistic note: "[T]hey will learn much and gain much from us. They will gain in force of character, in mental cultivation, in self-reliance, in enterprise, in breadth of views and habits of generalization. Our influence over them, if we treat them well, will be powerful for good" (American Freedmen's Inquiry Commission 1864). In support of this claim, the Commission referred to a Canadian high school principal who maintained that proximity to whites could even "whiten" black people's "unattractive" physical features: "Colored people brought up among whites look better than others. Their rougher, harsher features disappear. I think that colored children brought up among white people look better than their parents" (American Freedmen's Inquiry Commission 1864:107 n.1).

Thus, federal officials acted as the guardians of the moral practices of black people in order to qualify them for freedom and citizenship. The enforcement of marriage laws was widely regarded as the best tool to accomplish these ends. As Michael Grossberg (1985) notes:

> Although their response to most black demands for legal rights was negative, southern whites readily granted the matrimonial request of their former charges. The prevailing belief that marriage civilized and controlled the brutish nature of all people encouraged the use of formal matrimony as a remedy for the widespread immorality and promiscuity that whites believed to prevail among blacks (Grossberg 1985:133).

Much of the rhetoric of the time related to the need to civilize the freed men and women. Herbert Gutman summarized these beliefs as follows: "As slaves, after all, their marriages had not been sanctioned by the civil law and therefore 'the sexual passion' went unrestrained." White officials informed the freed people that "[t]he loose ideas which have prevailed among you on this subject must cease" (Edwards 1996: 93),[1] and that "no race of mankind can be expected to become exalted in the scale of humanity, whose sexes, without any binding obligation, cohabit promiscuously together" (Edwards 1996: 93).[2]

Many African-American people were acutely aware of the symbolic role that marriage played in the transformation of their status from slave to citizen. Northern black elites were often as judgmental as whites when it came to the practices of poor blacks. Laura Edwards (1997) notes that

[1] Quoting Alfred M. Waddell, a Confederate army officer and newspaper editor.

[2] Quoting a member of the Commission that designed the North Carolina Black Codes. See also Stampp 1956:12.

> [m]any African-American leaders were quite aware that white northerners and southerners alike used marriage as a barometer of their people's fitness for freedom, and they urged poor blacks to adopt the domestic patterns common among elite whites. This, they argued, would help convince the nation that ex-slaves deserved the rights and privileges of freedom.
>
> In support of this effort, one African American leader, James H. Harris, argued, "[L]et us do nothing to re-kindle the slumbering fires of prejudice between the two races. Remember, we are on trial before the tribunal of the nation and of the world, that it may be known . . . whether we are worthy to be a free, self-governing people" (Edwards 1997: 56).[3]

As such, the work of transforming formerly enslaved people into citizens may not have been left to the state alone. The task of discipline and punishment for those who kept up the old ways was taken up by black people themselves. Dan Johnson, it appears, did not consider marrying the woman with whom he had lived for many years until he sought to become a member of the St. John's Lodge of Odd Fellows in 1868. After his death, his widow applied for a war widow's pension, and one witness testified that "they were living together in adultery at the time he petitioned to become a member. . . . [T]he Lodge would not let him join until he married" (Pension File of Dan Johnson, 15).

Colored newspapers also played a role in encouraging African-American people to understand their responsibilities relative to the marriage relation. *The Savannah Tribune*, formerly *The Colored Tribune*, printed an editorial in November 1876 strongly counseling black women against "Marrying in Haste":

> Do not place yourself habitually in the society of any suitor until you have decided the question of marriage; human wills are weak, and people often become bewildered and do not know their error until it is too late. . . . A promise may be made in a moment of sympathy, or even half delirious ecstasy, which must be redeemed through years of sorrow and pain ("Marrying in Haste," p. 4).

In like fashion, the *Semi-Weekly Louisianan* cautioned its readers to consider the sanctity and magnitude of the marital obligation so as to avoid a wedding being

[3] Immediately after the war, Federal Freedmen's Bureau officers also compiled lists of exemplary African-American men who might be appointed to various political offices in the military governments set up by the Bureau after Congress passed the first Reconstruction Act. See Lowe 1993:989. Lowe (1993) argues that the "black men who, in [the Bureau's] opinion, had demonstrated some ability and capacity for leadership in the two years since the end of slavery," were more than likely light-skinned (Lowe 1993: 992). Bureau agents explicitly disfavored "black men who had already established a reputation for alienating the native white community" (Lowe 1993:995). Thus, Lowe concludes, the "black leaders" listed by Bureau officers were not, in many cases, the people whom the black community would have identified had they been asked. Here, as elsewhere, the freedmen who won the praises of white military and civilian authorities served as examples against which "bad blacks" were unfavorably compared for refusing to play within the bounds of white supremacy and Victorian ideology (Lowe 1993).

a "sudden and unconsidered thing – the freak or the passion of an excited hour" ("Hasty Marriages and Divorces," p. 1).

These examples show that by the mid-1870s some African Americans were performing within and serving Victorian cultural institutions, at once evidencing their own successful domestication and regulating those who did not conform to larger cultural norms relating to sex, gender, and sexuality. For some, conformity to these norms was a price paid instrumentally for the respect they believed it would buy. For others, no doubt, this was what it meant to be a freed, if not free, person. Freedom and citizenship entailed a wide range of self-discipline.

Do we have reason to worry that marriage will operate as a civilizing institution for lesbians and gay men today as it did for newly emancipated people in the nineteenth century? Are the Victorian values that structured marriage rights then no longer with us today? Well, there may be some reason for concern today as same-sex couples make the case that they have a right to marry. After the devastating loss that was the Supreme Court's *Bowers v. Hardwick* decision in 1986, the lesbian and gay community understood that it had work to do. It had not made itself recognizable to the public and to legal authorities as a community worthy of full constitutional protection and the dignity that recognition would confer.

So that work began. On school boards, on Little League fields, at parent-teacher association (PTA) meetings, in churches, workplaces, grocery stores – everywhere. Lesbians and gay men set out to demonstrate in fora both quotidian and extraordinary that they were not a perverse Other, but rather that they were respectable citizens, that they were just like everyone else. It is important to understand the turn this work took. The project was not one of sexual liberation, as had been the approach of the early Stonewall activists, of "live and let live," or "keep your laws off our bodies." This was not a politics of neutrality or sexual liberty, nor did it echo the kind of liberal arguments made by H. L. A. Hart in his debates with Lord Patrick Devlin about the legitimacy of criminalizing sodomy.[4] Rather the gay politics of the 1990s took a decidedly normative turn in favor of demonstrating to a skeptical American public that gay men and lesbians were normal, respectable, and responsible citizens, not the perverts that Chief Justice Burger had described in *Bowers*. In short, the shame of *Bowers* was met with a politics of redemption.

This work paid off in the Supreme Court's reversal of *Bowers* in the *Lawrence v. Texas* decision, wherein Justice Kennedy, writing for a slim majority, wrote that the Texas sodomy statute "demeans the lives of homosexual persons," who "are entitled to respect for their private lives. The State cannot demean their existence or control their destiny by making their private sexual conduct a crime" (*Lawrence v. Texas* 2003:574). He then repeated the soaring language that had been used in an earlier abortion rights case: "At the heart of liberty is the right to define one's own concept of

4 Hart's view turned on the application of the harm principle: if no one is harmed by the practice, the state has no legitimate reason to regulate or criminalize it (Hart 1959; Devlin, 1965).

existence, of meaning, of the universe, and of the mystery of human life."[5] (*Planned Parenthood of Southeastern Pa. v. Casey*, 505 U.S. 833, 851 (1992)).

The moralizing of *Bowers* that left a homosexual minority vulnerable to the disgust and judgment of the majority was not replaced in *Lawrence* with a rule respecting sexual freedom or even sexual-orientation-based equality; rather Justice Kennedy gave the boot to the *Bowers'* Court's strong negative moral visions by substituting his own moral reasoning grounded in an almost spiritual reverence for the dignity of the human and a call that the law respect the most intimate choices each person makes about the meaning of their lives.

This turn to morality, respectability, and dignity of the person as the core value that now animates gay rights litigation set the stage for the marriage cases to come. *Perry v. Schwarzenegger*, the case challenging the California proposition that amended the state's constitution to limit marriage to one man and one woman (Proposition 8), perhaps best illustrates the degree to which gay men and lesbians' right to marry is now being articulated through the values and vernacular of interests that marriage holds dear, more so than the values that the gay community has traditionally treasured, such as sexual liberty, diversity, autonomy, and freedom. The testimony by the four plaintiffs in the Proposition 8 trial, two men and two women, focused primarily on their desire for respectability, their longing for the sacred blessing and societal recognition that marriage confers, on the fact that being married would be better for raising children, and finally on the disgrace of exile from the sacred domain of marriage. On top of that, they argued that the state should play a vital role in promoting the institution of marriage, and that including same-sex couples in the institution would be good for marriage more generally.

When asked by Ted Olson, one the of the gay couples' lawyers: "Have you encountered instances where because you are not married you were placed in embarrassing or awkward situations?", Jeff Zarrillo, one of the plaintiffs, testified: "One example is when Paul and I travel, it's always an awkward situation at the front desk at the hotel. The individual working at the desk will look at us with a perplexed look on his face and say, 'You ordered a king-size bed. Is that really what you want?'" Or "It is always an awkward situation walking to the bank and saying, 'My partner and I want to open a joint bank account,' hearing, you know, 'Is it a business account?' It would be a lot easier to be able to say: 'My husband and I are here to check into a room. My husband and I are here to open a bank account.'"

When asked by Olson about why they have had no children, Zarrillo said: "Paul and I believe that in order to have children it would be important for us to be married. It would make it easier for – for us, for our children, to explain our relationship, for our children to be able to explain our relationship."

[5] *Lawrence v. Texas*, 539 U.S. 558, at 574 (2003) (citing *Planned Parenthood of Southeastern Pa. v. Casey*, 505 U.S. 833, 851 (1992)).

Olsen then asked Zarrillo why he and his partner were not domestic partners – the California domestic partnership law confers on same-sex couples all of the legal and economic benefits of marriage, just under a different legal name. Zarrillo answered: "[W]e hold marriage in such high regard. . . . Domestic partnership would not give due respect to the relationship that we have had for almost nine years. Only a marriage could do that."

That the values that motivate much of today's same-sex marriage movement share common ground with the efforts to secure marriage rights for newly freed people in the nineteenth century is perhaps no better illustrated than by a short piece Ted Olson wrote to explain why he was joining the Proposition 8 challenge as co-counsel with David Boies. In "The Conservative Case for Gay Marriage," Olson wrote:

> Many of my fellow conservatives have an almost knee-jerk hostility toward gay marriage. This does not make sense, because same-sex unions promote the values conservatives prize. Marriage is one of the basic building blocks of our neighborhoods and our nation. At its best, it is a stable bond between two individuals who work to create a loving household and a social and economic partnership. We encourage couples to marry because the commitments they make to one another provide benefits not only to themselves but also to their families and communities. Marriage requires thinking beyond one's own needs. It transforms two individuals into a union based on shared aspirations, and in doing so establishes a formal investment in the well-being of society. The fact that individuals who happen to be gay want to share in this vital social institution is evidence that conservative ideals enjoy widespread acceptance. Conservatives should celebrate this, rather than lament it (Olson 2010).

In important ways the success of today's marriage rights movement is premised on a promise of discipline, respectability, and obeisance to a set of civilizing norms that portray those who fall short of those norms as an embarrassment, or worse, undeserving of the full and equal blessings of civic belonging. The African-American community has paid dearly for the "failure" of many of its members to form respectable families, the Moynihan Report being only one salient example thereof (U.S. Department of Labor 1965). I worry that we will witness an increasing divide in the gay community as well, between those who bend their lives toward marriage's expectations and are rewarded therefore, and those who do not or cannot and suffer a price as a result.

A RIGHT TO MARRY COLLAPSING INTO AN OBLIGATION TO DO SO

Without question the right to marry figured prominently in the minds of newly emancipated black people in the U.S. South as they imagined what it meant to be free. The ability to order their private lives with spouses of their own choice, and to protect their families from the wrenching separation created by their sale and other forms of exploitation by hostile outsiders, was among the first aspects of freedom on which the freed people insisted. As such, the right to marry not only signaled the new capacity of black people to enter into civil contracts which were binding on themselves and others, but it also held out a form of security that newly freed people imagined would erect legal pickets around their families to protect them from the malevolent interference of white people.

Many freed people naively thought that the freedom to marry meant a freedom to marry according to their own rules and customs and in family formations of their own choosing free from white interference (Franke 1999). What they quickly found, however, was that with this new right the freedom to marry collapsed in short order into an obligation to do so according to an inflexible definition set out in existing laws. For some time prior to the establishment of the Freedmen's Bureau in 1865, federal officers played a significant role in the promotion of marriage among black people. In 1862, John Eaton was appointed by General Grant to set up what were termed "contraband camps," settlements that housed black fugitives in Tennessee and northern Mississippi. In April 1863, Eaton reported that "all entering our camps who have been living or desire to live together as husband and wife are required to be married in the proper manner.... This regulation has done much to promote the good order of the camp" (Eaton 1863:89–90). In March 1864, the Secretary of War made Eaton's regulation official U.S. policy and ordered Freedmen's Bureau agents to "solemnize the rite of marriage among Freedmen" (Order from Edwin Stanton 1864; Gutman 1979). Thereafter, superintendents of the contraband camps uniformly observed that "the introduction of the rite of Christian marriage and requiring its strict observance, exerted a most wholesome influence upon the order of the camps and the conduct of the people" (Report by Chaplain Warren 1864). Recall that the people seeking entrance to these camps, which today we would call refugee camps, were in many cases suffering from starvation, illness, and the other effects of abuse by their "owners." That the officers administering the camps saw the ennobling influence of marriage as the most pressing need of the immiserated fleeing slaves is quite remarkable.

After emancipation, formerly enslaved people traveled great distances and endured enormous hardships in order to reunite families that had been separated under slavery. Shortly after the end of the war, southern states acted quickly to amend their constitutions or enact statutes validating marriages begun under slavery. Laws that simply legitimized slave marriages if the couple were cohabiting as husband and wife when the law went into effect were quite common. Mississippi's 1865 civil rights law was typical: "All freedmen, free negroes and mulattoes, who do now and have heretofore lived and cohabited together as husband and wife shall be taken and held in law as legally married" (Civil Rights Act of Nov. 25 1865, Ch. 4, § 2, 1865 Miss. Laws 82, 82).[6]

[6] Georgia, North Carolina, South Carolina, and Virginia passed similar laws during this period. See, e.g., Act of Mar. 9, 1866, tit. 31, § 5, 1866 Ga. Laws 239, 240 (prescribing and regulating the relation

Some states took a different approach to the marriage of former slaves, giving "all colored inhabitants of this State claiming to be living together in the relation of husband and wife . . . and who shall mutually desire to continue in that relation" nine months to formally remarry one another before a minister or civil authority (Act of Jan. 11, 1866:31). These laws further required newly married couples to file a marriage license with the county circuit court – a bureaucratic detail that carried a prohibitively high price for many freed people. In every state with such laws, failure to comply with these requirements while continuing to cohabit would render the offenders subject to criminal prosecution for adultery and fornication. North Carolina gave the freed people just under six months to register their marriages with the county clerk. Each month they failed to do so constituted a distinct and separately prosecutable criminal offense.

While many formerly enslaved people merely allowed the law to operate upon them, automatically legitimizing their marriages, others "swamped public officials with demands to validate old and new unions" (Grossberg 1985:134). Mass wedding ceremonies in the postwar South sometimes involved 70 couples; in 17 North Carolina counties in 1866, 9,000 marriages were registered (Litwak 1979). Thus, the right to marry for African Americans in the immediate postbellum period had both symbolic and practical significance – symbolic in the sense that enjoyment of the right signaled acceptance into the moral community of civil society, and practical to the extent that social and economic benefits flowed from being legally married.

However, the right to marry was not merely an unconstrained liberty enjoyed by African Americans independent of state interest or control. Even prior to the end of the war, state and federal officials played an active role in impressing upon black people the responsibilities, rather than the rights, that marriage imposed.

This posed challenges for individuals who earlier had had more than one partner. After emancipation, when formerly enslaved people struggled to reunify relationships shattered by slavery, the first husband might reappear and expect his wife, now in a new relationship, to live with him as his spouse. So too, many women had had children with more than one man and, after emancipation, sought to unify these complex family formations. Thus, many formerly enslaved people found themselves with two or more spouses and with complex, blended families at the end of the war (Gutman 1979).[7] Given that bigamy was a crime in every state, persons with multiple

of husband and wife between persons of color); Act of Mar. 10, 1866, ch. 40, §§ 1–5, 1866 N.C. Sess. Laws 99–101 (concerning Negroes and persons of color or of mixed blood); Act of 1865, 1865 S.C. Acts 291, 292 (establishing and regulating the domestic relations of persons of color, and amending the law in relation to paupers and vagrancy); Act of Feb. 27, 1865, ch. 18, § 2, 1865 Va. Acts 85 (legalizing marriages of colored persons now cohabitating as husband and wife), in Guild 1996:33; see also Howard 1866:179 (a collection of Black Laws assembled by the head of the Freedman's Bureau and submitted to Congress in 1866–67).

7 Gutman (1979) describes how in some cases women who emerged from slavery with more than one husband would choose a legal husband based on a number of different factors, such as the man's wealth, or the man's willingness to provide for all of her children, even those fathered by other men (Gutman 1979:423–425). Litwack (1979) describes how some women chose to reunite with their first

spouses were forced to choose one and only one legal spouse and to cease intimate relations and/or cohabitation with others (Bernard 1996:10–11). Georgia's 1866 law relating to "Persons of Color" set forth the following:

> [P]ersons of color, now living together as husband and wife, are hereby declared to sustain that legal relation to each other, unless a man shall have two or more reputed wives, or a woman two or more reputed husbands. In such an event, the man, immediately after the passage of this Act by the General Assembly, shall select one of his reputed wives, with her consent; or the woman one of her reputed husbands, with his consent; and the ceremony of marriage between these two shall be performed (1866 Ga. Laws:239, 240).

The statute then instructed that persons who fail or refuse to comply with these requirements were to be prosecuted for fornication, adultery, or both. South Carolina imposed a similar statutory duty of election (1865 S.C. Acts 291, 292). Even though some state laws were silent on the question of multiple spouses, state and federal officials forced freed men and women to choose one and only one spouse. In some cases where a freed man or woman was unwilling or unable to choose, Bureau agents felt free to do so for them. An agent in North Carolina reported that "[w]henever a negro appears before me with two or three wives who have equal claim upon him . . . I marry him to the woman who had the greatest number of helpless children who otherwise would become a charge on the Bureau" (Litwack 1979:242; Gutman 1979).

The manner in which newly emancipated black people in the United States managed the right to marry offers several lessons for today with respect to the risk that a right to marry can collapse into an obligation to do so for lesbians and gay men. Just as newly freed people expected that the right to marry would include a recognition of the complex families they had formed outside of legal marriage, so too lesbian and gay people have been surprised to discover the ways in which winning the right to marry has diminished the rights they had enjoyed as domestic partners, cohabiting partners, or in other nonmarital family forms. Consider the following:

> When the state of Connecticut amended its marriage law in 2009 to allow same-sex couples to marry, the law automatically married all of the same-sex couples who had entered into civil unions in Connecticut or in neighboring states, such as Vermont, without providing those couples adequate notice or giving them an option to remain in a civil union (Public Act No. 09–13 Sec. 12(a), 2009). While this provision of the new law was likely intended to be a benevolent blessing on same-sex couples by conferring full marital status upon those couples who had entered into civil unions during a period when they could not marry, it presumed i) that civil unions are an

husbands, to whom they felt a special moral connection because their marriages had ended as a result of the forced separation of the couple. Ex-slave Jane Ferguson chose to reunite with her first husband, Martin Barnwell, even though she had married a man named Ferguson after her master had sold away Barnwell: "I told [Ferguson] I never 'spects Martin could come back, but if he did he would be my husband above all others."

inferior civil status, ii) that all of the couples in civil unions *wanted* to be married, and iii) that they wanted to be governed by the state's rules of divorce and equitable distribution in the event that their relationship ended. It seemed unthinkable to the drafters of the Connecticut marriage equality law that some couples might prefer a civil union over a marriage, or worse, might object to the possibility of facing divorce, having never been married. Thus, in some cases, same-sex couples have found themselves to be automatically married in circumstances very similar to that of freed people in the nineteenth century. As a woman recently wrote me in response to an Op-ed I had published in the New York Times (Franke 2011):

> "I purposely did NOT get a civil union in Connecticut when they recognized civil unions, and didn't even know that my Vermont civil union turned into a marriage when Connecticut then recognized those civil unions as marriages. The VT CU was largely to support the general movement. I knew it expressly did not mean anything in Connecticut. I find myself in the unfortunate and unanticipated position of going through divorce proceedings having never been married."

What is more, same-sex couples are finding that they must marry in order to retain rights they had previously enjoyed without being married, such as employment-related health insurance coverage for one's partner. Immediately on the heels of the New York State legislature amending the state's marriage law to include same-sex couples, several large employers announced that their gay and lesbian employees would have to marry to continue coverage for their partners. Never mind that New York City has a domestic partnership law (which covers both same-sex and different-sex couples) and that many public and private employers had deemed domestic partnership registration a sufficient bureaucratic filter for benefits eligibility. Here, as in other ways, the right to marry has rendered alternatives to marriage less viable and less secure. A right to marry has collapsed into an obligation to do so.

DISCIPLINARY EFFECTS OF MARRIAGE, REAL AND ANTICIPATED

Marriage laws provide a form of economic and legal security for those who qualify, but they also include a set of expectations that are enforced through both civil and criminal laws. Exclusivity, sexual fidelity, and duties of support are some of the most important, but not the only, rules of marriage that one's spouse and public prosecutors are empowered to enforce. Newly freed people learned quickly that the right to marry brought with it the risk of severe sanction in the event that marriage rules were not followed. Indeed, these rules offered both racist public officials and judgmental members of the African-American community itself a tool with which to punish anyone who got caught violating marriage rules. For a significant number of former slaves – mostly men – legal marriage was experienced not as a source of validation and empowerment, but as discipline and punishment when the rigid rules of legal marriage were transgressed, often unintentionally. Recall that in most states the automatic marriage statutes were accompanied by a provision requiring the freed people to choose one and only one spouse if the reunion of formerly fractured families left an individual married to more than one person. If a man, for instance, failed to make such a selection and continued to cohabit with two women, he would be considered married to neither, while at the same time vulnerable to a fornication prosecution. This is exactly what happened to Sam Means. A Georgia jury convicted him of fornication upon a finding that Means, "a negro man, was living with two women as his reputed wives, and had never selected either and made her his lawful wife, as required by the [1866] act" (*Means* 1896).

Southern judges stepped in after a period to rectify this unhappy situation, and, as the following cases demonstrate, the technical requirements of marriage laws were enforced uncompromisingly against African Americans, regardless of whether they were shown to have understood the details or implications of this new regulatory regime. In *Williams v. Georgia* (1881), the male defendant, whose first name is never mentioned by the court, was shown to have been married to Elizabeth Williams when they were both enslaved. They were separated by their master and sold to different owners, but were reunited on December 21, 1864, two months after General Sherman marched to the sea. Thereafter, Elizabeth "associated immorally with another, and the defendant quit her and married another woman." Since Williams had reunited with Elizabeth before March 9, 1866 (the effective date of the act legitimizing preexisting slave marriages) and did not "quit" her until after that date, he was determined to have been legally married to Elizabeth when he married his second wife. The court rejected the defendant's argument that he did not intend his cohabitation with Elizabeth in 1866 to amount to a legal marriage. Instead the court ruled that the 1866 Act married the couple and that "[h]is wife was unfaithful; he got mad and married again without divorce. Being a free citizen, he must act like one, carrying the burdens, if he so considers them, as well as enjoying the privileges of his new condition."

Other freed men and women found themselves in legal jeopardy when they knowingly complied with the legal requirements pertaining to the creation of a marriage, but persisted in the old ways by refusing to dissolve their marriages according to the technical requirements of divorce. In 1867, Celia McConico married David Hartwell. After two and a half years of marriage, they "mutually agreed to separate and did then separate from each other as husband and wife" (*McConico* 1873). A year later McConico married Edom Jacobs and was thereafter prosecuted for bigamy. At trial McConico argued that since Alabama's 1867 law automatically solemnized preexisting slave marriages without legal formalities, she assumed she was able to dissolve her marriage without legal formality. An Alabama jury convicted her of bigamy and the court sentenced her to two years in the state penitentiary. Her conviction and sentence were affirmed by the Alabama Supreme Court.

Living as marriage rights-holders was thus a complicated matter for African Americans in the second half of the nineteenth century. Marriage held out both security and danger, as they found themselves in a new regulatory relationship with the state. These regulations both secured their families and provided opportunity for public officials, scorned lovers, and judgmental members of the community to invoke the laws of fornication, adultery, and bigamy to discipline and punish those who transgressed the rules of marriage. Conviction under these laws carried a heavy penalty, usually a felony, thereby disenfranchising those men found guilty and often subjecting them to the crushingly harsh, sometimes deadly, convict leasing system (Franke 1999:305–307).

I have no evidence to suggest that public prosecutors in New York are about to ramp up adultery prosecutions against married gay men or lesbians who are unable to live up to their vows of monogamy.[8] But I can imagine a scenario in, say, upstate New York where a local official who opposes the marriage rights of same-sex couples decides to take the seldom enforced criminal statute prohibiting adultery very seriously, and initiates a prosecution against a married lesbian or gay man who has had sex with someone not their legal spouse, just as we saw in the postbellum period with African Americans. After all, Dan Savage, a prominent gay journalist and political activist, has argued in the *New York Times Magazine*, to the outrage of many, that marital infidelity is a virtue (Oppenheimer 2011). So, too, it is not unthinkable that a cuckolded spouse, acting out of hurt or revenge, might find a willing partner in the local district attorney's office. This is exactly the scenario that launched the prosecution in *Lawrence v. Texas*, the 2006 Supreme Court case that invalidated laws criminalizing consensual sex between two adult persons of the same sex in private (Carpenter 2004).[9]

Some commentators have resisted the analogy between the civil rights movement today for lesbian and gay people and that of African Americans in the United States. To some degree they are no doubt right. Homophobia and racism are not equivalent forms of social, legal, and political disadvantage. Their sources and their consequences are quite different. So too, the disadvantage and hatred that gay and lesbian people have suffered cannot in any way be analogized to "the badges and incidents of slavery." Our histories of oppression are in so many ways incommensurable.

That incommensurability does not, however, disable us from gaining lessons from one another's experience of oppression and of expanded equality and freedom.

[8] Adultery remains a misdemeanor in New York State, although it is rarely enforced. See New York State Penal Law Art. 255.17, "A person is guilty of adultery when he engages in sexual intercourse with another person at a time when he has a living spouse, or the other person has a living spouse."

[9] Carpenter's description of Lawrence and Garner's "relationship" is quite different from that portrayed by Kennedy's opinion. The two men, Lawrence white and Garner black, were not in a relationship, but were more likely occasional sex partners. The night of the arrest, another sex partner of Garner's called the police to report that "a black man was going crazy" in Lawrence's apartment "and he was armed with a gun." (Carpenter notes that a racial epithet rather than "black man" was probably the term used.) The police arrived at the apartment and found Lawrence and Garner having sex.

For both African Americans and gay people,[10] the right to marry has figured prominently in ongoing struggles for full rights as citizens. Given the prominence of marriage in both public and private civil life, it makes sense that exclusion from civil marriage has been understood as a significant form of social disadvantage, both materially and symbolically. Yet using marriage as the primary container for the advancement of a community's claims for full equality and citizenship brings with it significant moral hazards. Those hazards, to my mind, have not been sufficiently addressed in today's movement to secure marriage rights for same-sex couples. Those hazards might be better confronted and ameliorated were we to take seriously the lessons to be learned from the experiences of African Americans when first able to marry in the immediate post–Civil War period. For them, as for us today, we ought to tread carefully in securing the right to marry. Surely it is a right we want and should have, but without critically engaging that desire we risk rendering more vulnerable significant sectors of our community who cannot or will not conform to marriage's rules and discipline.

REFERENCES

Act of 1865, 1865 S. C. Acts 291, 292.
Act of Dec. 14, 1866, ch. 1552, § 1, 1866 Fla. Laws 22.
Act of Feb. 27, 1865, ch. 18, § 2, 1865 Va. Acts 85.
Act of Jan. 11, 1866, ch. 1469, § 1, 1865 Fla. Laws 31
Act of Mar. 9, 1866, tit. 31, § 5, 1866 Ga. Laws 239, 240.
Act of Mar. 10, 1866, ch. 40, §§ 1–5, 1866 N.C. Sess. Laws 99–101.
American Freedmen's Inquiry Commission. (1863). *Preliminary Report Touching the Condition and Management of Emancipated Refugees* (S. Exec. Doc. No. 38–53).
American Freedmen's Inquiry Commission. (1864). *Final Report of the American Freedmen's Inquiry Commission to the Secretary of War* (S. Exec. Doc. No. 38–53). (p. 107 n.1).
Authors unknown (1774). Petition to the Governor, the Council, and the House of Representatives of Massachusetts. In Davis, P.C. (1997). *Neglected Stories: The Constitution and Family Values* 109. New York: Hill and Wang.
Baehr v. Miike, 1996 WL 694235 (Haw. Cir. Ct. Dec. 3, 1996) aff'd, 950 P.2d 1234 (Haw. 1997).
Bernard, J. (1996). *Marriage and Family among Negroes*. Englewood Cliffs, NJ: Prentice-Hall.
Bernard, S. (2011). As Same-Sex Marriage Becomes Legal, Some Choices May Be Lost. *New York Times*, p. B1. Retrieved from http://www.nytimes.com/2011/07/09/business/some-companies-want-gays-to- wed-to-get-health-benefits.html.
Bibb, H. (1969). *Narrative of the Life and Adventures of Henry Bibb, an American Slave, Written by Himself* (3d ed.). New York: Negro Universities Press. (Original work published 1849).
Butler, J. (2009). *Frames of War: When Is Life Grievable?* New York: Verso.

[10] By this phrasing I do not mean to imply that all African Americans are heterosexual or that no gay people are African-American. Rather I am referring to the movements on behalf of these communities that, for better or worse, tend to isolate one aspect of identity as the animating subject of their civil rights struggles.

Carpenter, D. (2004). The Unknown Past of *Lawrence v. Texas*. *Michigan Law Review*, *102*, 1464–1527.
Civil Rights Act of Nov. 25, 1865, Ch. 4, § 2, 1865 Miss. Laws 82, 82.
Davis, P.C. (1997). *Neglected Stories: The Constitution and Family Values*. New York: Hill and Wang.
Devlin, P. (1965). *The Enforcement of Morals*. London: Oxford University Press.
Eaton, J. (1863). Report of John Eaton, General Superintendent of Freedmen, Department of Tennessee (April 29). N.A.R.G. 94, M619, roll 200 (pp. 89–90).
Edwards, L. (1996). "The Marriage Covenant is at the Foundation of All Our Rights": The Politics of Slave Marriages in North Carolina after Emancipation. *Law & History Review*, *14*, 81, 101.
Edwards, L. (1997). *Gendered Strife and Confusion: The Political Culture of Reconstruction*. Champaign: University of Illinois Press.
Foner, E. (1988). *Reconstruction: America's Unfinished Revolution, 1863–1877*. New York: Harper & Row.
Franke, K. (1999). Becoming a Citizen: Construction Era Regulation of African American Marriages. *Yale Journal of Law & the Humanities*, *14*, 251–301.
Franke, K. (2011). Marriage Is a Mixed Blessing. *New York Times*, June 23, p. A25. Retrieved from http://www.nytimes.com/2011/06/24/opinion/24franke.html.
Frankel, N. (1999). *Freedom's Women: Black Women and Families in Civil War Era Mississippi*. Bloomington: University of Indiana Press.
Grimké, A. (1837). Letter to Catharine E. Beecher. In Hawkins, H. (Ed.), *The Abolitionists: Means, Ends, and Motivations* (1972). Boston: Houghton Mifflin.
Grossberg, M. (1985). *Governing the Hearth: Law and the Family in Nineteenth-Century America* . Chapel Hill: University of North Carolina Press.
Guild, J.P. (1996). *Black Laws of Virginia: A Summary of the Legislative Acts of Virginia Concerning Negroes from Earliest Times to the Present*. Westminster, MD: Willow Bend Books.
Gutman, H.G. (1979). *The Black Family in Slavery and Freedom, 1750–1925*. New York: Random House.
Hart, H.L.A. (1959). Immorality and Treason, *The Listener*, July 30, pp. 162–163.
Hasty Marriages and Divorces (1871). *Semi-Weekly Louisianan*, May 28, p. 1.
Howard, O.O. (1866). Commissioner, Bureau of Refugees, Freedmen and Abandoned Lands. *Laws Relating to Freedmen* (S. Exec. Doc. No. 39–6) (p. 179).
Koppelman, A. (1998). Same-Sex Marriage, Choice of Law, and Public Policy. *Texas Law Review*, *76*, 921–1001.
Lawrence v. Texas, 539 U.S. 558, 574 (2003).
Litwack, L. (1979). *Been in the Storm So Long: The Aftermath of Slavery*. New York: Knopf.
Lowe, R. (1993). The Freedmen's Bureau and Local Black Leadership. *Journal of American History*, *14*, 989–995.
Malone, A.P. (1992). *Sweet Chariot: Slave Family and Household Structure in Nineteenth-Century Louisiana*. Chapel Hill: University of North Carolina Press.
Marrying in Haste (1876). *Savannah Tribune*, November 13, p. 4.
McConico v. State, 49 Ala. 6, 6 (1873).
Means v. State, 25 S. E. 682, 682 (Ga. 1896).
New York State Penal Law Art. 255.17.
Olson, T. (2010). The Conservative Case for Gay Marriage. *Newsweek*, January 8. Retrieved from http://www.thedailybeast.com/newsweek/2010/01/08/the-conservative-case-for-gay-marriage.html.

Oppenheimer, M. (2011). Marriage, With Infidelities. *New York Times*, p. MM22. Retrieved from http://www.nytimes.com/2011/07/03/magazine/infidelity-will- keep-us-together.html?pagewanted=all.

Order from Edwin Stanton, Secretary of War, Special Orders, No. 15. (1864, March 28). In Eaton, J. Report of John Eaton, General Superintendent of Freedmen, Department of Tennessee. (1863, April 29). N.A.R.G. 94, M619, roll 200 (pp. 89–90).

Pension File of Dan Johnson (application 429,023), N.A.R.G. 15.

Protection of Civil Rights: Congressional Debate (Cong. Globe), 39th Cong., 1st Sess. 474 (1866) (statement of Sen. Lyman Trumbull, Republican from Illinois).

Public Act No. 09–13 Sec. 12(a), An Act Implementing the Guarantee of Equal Protection Under the Constitution of the State for Same Sex Couples (2009).

Report by Chaplain Warren (May 18, 1864). In Eaton, J. Report of John Eaton, General Superintendent of Freedmen, Department of Tennessee. (1863, April 29). N.A.R.G. 94, M619, roll 200. (pp. 89–90).

Richards, D.A.J. (1998). *Women, Gays, and the Constitution: The Grounds for Feminism and Gay Rights in Culture and Law*. Chicago: University of Chicago Press.

Stampp, K.M. (1956). *The Peculiar Institution: Slavery in the Antebellum South*. New York: Vintage.

U. S. Department of Labor, Office of Planning and Research. (1965). *The Negro Family: The Case for National Action*. Retrieved from http://www.dol.gov/oasam/programs/history/webid-meynihan.htm.

Williams v. Georgia, 67 Ga. 260 (1881).

PART II

Empirical Research on Family Change

6

Institutional, Companionate, and Individualistic Marriages

Change over Time and Implications for Marital Quality

Paul R. Amato

The institution of marriage has changed more during the last fifty years than in any comparable period in American history. With respect to demographic trends, age at first marriage increased, cohabitation became common as a prelude to marriage, the divorce rate rose, and the percentage of marriages in which one or both spouses had been married previously increased. Changes also occurred in spousal relationships: wives increasingly entered the labor force and became co-providers, husbands took on a larger share of household chores and child-rearing responsibilities, and decision-making equality between spouses became common. Corresponding to changes in behavior were shifts in attitudes toward marriage and family issues, with people becoming more accepting of alternatives to the traditional two-parent, heterosexual family. As these changes unfolded, a society-wide debate emerged about whether these trends have had positive or negative implications for adults and children (e.g., Popenoe 1993; Stacy 1996).

Most scholars have described, explained, and considered the implications of these changes by focusing on one variable at a time. In contrast to a single-variable approach, a typological (or person-centered) approach considers how multiple marital characteristics cluster into naturally occurring types. In this approach, marriages rather than variables serve as the focus of analysis. In this chapter, I adopt such a marriage-focused perspective. Specifically, I use cluster analysis to group marriages into institutional, companionate, and individualistic types. I then show how the frequency of these three types of marriages in the U.S. population changed between 1980 and 2000. My analysis also reveals how marital quality and stability vary across these groups. As I hope to show, a typological approach provides a useful supplement to conventional approaches that focus on types of variables rather than types of marriages. The conclusion of this chapter addresses some policy implications of this research.

BACKGROUND

Family scholars working from a historical perspective have described three types of marriage. Ernest Burgess, a sociologist who wrote on marriage and family life around the middle of the twentieth century, argued that marriage was transforming from a social institution to a private relationship based primarily on companionship (Burgess and Cottrell 1939; Burgess, Locke, and Thomes 1963; Burgess and Wallin 1953). By *institutional marriage*, Burgess meant a formal union that was strictly regulated by law, social norms, and religion. In contrast, the emerging form of marriage, which he referred to as *companionate marriage*, was based primarily on the emotional bonds between spouses.

In his earlier work, Burgess made the mistake of assuming that families in the United States had developed in a manner comparable to that of families in agrarian societies in southern Europe and Asia (Thornton 2005). In later publications, however, he focused more strictly (and appropriately) on historical developments in the United States. According to Burgess, farm families dominated the marital landscape prior to the last few decades of the nineteenth century. In early America, strong and stable marriages were essential to the welfare of family members and the larger community. Family members relied on one another to meet basic needs, including economic production, child care, education, and elder care. Marriage also created bonds between families that facilitated the sharing of resources. Because cohesive, stable, and interconnected families were necessary for survival, society had an interest in regulating marriage and the behavior of individual spouses.

In an institutional system of marriage, the stability of the family is seen as being more important than the needs of individual family members. Although the United States did not have a system of arranged marriages (as in China or India), sons and daughters were expected to obtain their parents' approval prior to marriage. And although many marriages involved strong ties of affection, a "good match" was based more on practical considerations than on romantic love. Once married, community norms and legal restrictions made divorce difficult unless it was absolutely necessary, as in cases of serious physical abuse or abandonment. In general, spouses in institutional marriage were expected not only to conform to traditional standards of behavior, but also to sacrifice their personal needs, if necessary, for the sake of their marriages. Because these marriages were patriarchal, wives presumably sacrificed more than did husbands.

By the beginning of the twentieth century, the United States had become an industrialized nation, and urban two-parent, breadwinner-homemaker families replaced farm families as the dominant family form (Hernandez 1993). During this time, several factors allowed individuals to have greater control over their marriages, including the geographical mobility of young adults (which freed them from the control of parents and the kin group) and a decline in religious control (which resulted in more freedom to adopt unconventional views and behaviors). Moreover, during the twentieth century, the growth of economic opportunities for women gave adult daughters more economic independence from their parents and gave wives more economic independence from their husbands. Spouses continued to value marital stability, but they also recognized that divorce was sometimes a necessary (although unfortunate) solution to a troubled relationship.

As the rules surrounding marriage relaxed, a new idea gained prominence: rather than being based on a code of obligations to society and religion, marriage should be based on ties of affection and companionship between spouses. Of course, many unions, even during the colonial era, involved strong emotional bonds. For example, the letters of John and Abigail Adams (married in 1764) reveal that they had a strikingly close and loving relationship (McCullough 2001). Nevertheless, the notion that marriage should be based *primarily* on love is relatively recent in American history (Coontz 2005). This vision of marriage reached its zenith with the homemaker-breadwinner marriages of the 1950s – a time when most Americans, irrespective of social class, accepted the companionate model of marriage as the cultural ideal (Mintz and Kellogg 1988).

Although these marriages were held together by bonds of love and companionship, it would be a mistake to think that spouses jettisoned the institutional moorings that characterized earlier marriages. Most spouses continued to believe that marriage was bound up with religious ideals and community norms of stability. Nevertheless, these new unions prioritized the notion that husbands and wives should work together to achieve common goals, such as owning a home, attaining a decent standard of living, raising children, and maintaining mutually supportive unions. Spouses also obtained satisfaction from the fulfillment of complementary marital roles such as breadwinning, homemaking, and parenting. Gender roles within marriage were not as distinct as in previous eras, however, and many wives entered the labor force, at least part time. (In low-income families, many wives were employed full time rather than part time, but this usually occurred because of economic necessity rather than preference.) Although companionate marriages were less patriarchal than institutional marriages, husbands retained the role of "senior partner" in the relationship. Despite the continuation of gender inequality, successful teamwork was the hallmark of a good marriage.

Andrew Cherlin (2004) has argued that the shift from institutional to companionate marriage reflected a *deinstitutionalization* of marriage – a trend that continued throughout the second half of the twentieth century. In recent years, a third type of marriage, *individualistic marriage*, began to emerge. During the 1960s and 1970s, American culture shifted toward an ethic of "expressive individualism" (Bellah et al. 1985). This perspective assumes that people have an intrinsic need to express their innermost feelings and that close relationships exist primarily to enhance individual happiness and maximize psychological growth. These ideas were popularized in the Human Potential Movement, as reflected in the writings of psychologists such as Carl Rogers (1961) and Abraham Maslow (1962). As this view became more influential, self-development and personal fulfillment came to replace companionship and team effort as the basis of marriage for many people.

In individualistic marriage, love is absolutely necessary to form a union, but these unions are successful only to the extent that they continue to meet each partner's innermost psychological needs. In this sense, marriage came to have a new "therapeutic" function in which personal growth became the *raison d'être* for forming and maintaining a union. The earlier notion of a spouse as a supportive partner with whom one cooperates to achieve common goals was replaced with the notion of a spouse as "soul mate" who fulfills one's deepest wishes. Because it is difficult to attain a deep level of intimacy and foster self-development in an unequal relationship, individualistic unions tend to be egalitarian with respect to gender. Unfortunately, individualistic unions also tend to be unstable. As Nock (1995) argued, love and personal fulfillment, although important, can be problematic given that emotional closeness is likely to ebb and flow during the course of marriage. Consequently, if one or both spouses fall out of love, or if the union fails to meet one or both spouses' innermost needs, then people view divorce as a necessary – and even positive – outcome.[1]

Corresponding to the rise of individualistic marriage was a tendency for married couples to value privacy and to disengage from other social groups and networks. Robert Putnam (2000) has documented a trend during the last several decades toward less involvement in community organizations, including civic associations, political parties, recreational groups (e.g., bowling teams), and church social groups. Consistent with this trend, a recent study found that, between 1980 and 2000, married individuals reported having fewer close friends and belonging to fewer organizations; more importantly, they reported having fewer close friends and group memberships *in common with their spouses* (Amato et al. 2007). This study also found that spouses were less likely than in the past to eat dinner together, go out for recreation or leisure activities together, shop together, work on projects around the home together, or visit friends together. These trends are consistent with the notion that American culture in general – and marriage in particular – has become increasingly individualistic in recent decades.

Although these marriage types are assumed to represent a rough historical progression, not all marriages during a given era fit the dominant model. In the early nineteenth century, when most marriages were institutional in nature, some

[1] The term "soul-mate marriage" has become popular in recent years. A recent Google search revealed literally thousands of Web sites that describe soul-mate marriages or offer advice on how to have a soul-mate marriage. This term is used in varied and sometimes contradictory ways, however. Some people use it in a religious sense, as when two individuals are united by God. Others note that spouses in soul-mate marriages have extremely strong bonds of companionship, trust, and affection. Yet others claim that these unions meet people's deepest needs for intimacy and personal growth. Overall, this variability in usage suggests that this term may be difficult to incorporate into scholarly thinking about marriage.

people married primarily for love. Similarly, it would be a mistake to assume that all spouses currently hold individualistic views on marriage. Some contemporary couples (especially those who are highly religious) continue to believe both that the marriage contract is sacred and inviolable and that maintaining a stable marriage is more important than pursuing personal happiness. Similarly, many contemporary couples have companionate marriages much like those of the 1950s. No study, however, has been able to estimate the frequency of institutional, companionate, and individualistic marriages in the United States today or how these frequencies have changed over time.[2]

A STUDY OF MARRIAGE TYPES

Perhaps the major distinction between the three marriage types involves the values and beliefs that form the foundation of marital stability. Institutional marriages are held together because marriage is viewed as a valuable status in its own right, and divorce is seen as violating the commitment that spouses made to one another and to their families, communities, and religion. From this perspective, a good marriage is a stable marriage even if the relationship is less than happy because it allows the couple to fulfill their obligations to others, promotes social stability, and produces a secure home environment in which to raise children. Companionate marriages, by contrast, are held together through bonds of affection and mutual support as well as by opportunities to work together to achieve valuable goals. Individualistic marriages are held together to the extent that spouses are passionately in love with one another and the union facilitates the psychological growth and well-being of each spouse. With respect to this progression, one might say that marriage is (or has been) valued primarily because it meets the needs of (1) the larger society, (2) the couple, or (3) the individual spouses, respectively.

Despite the centrality of this typology to our understanding of marriage, no existing data set contains appropriate items to assess spouses' values and beliefs about the basis of marital stability. Nevertheless, one can consider other variables that may serve as indirect indicators of these marriage types. Based on the earlier discussion, spouses in institutional marriages are likely to have a traditional breadwinner-homemaker division of labor with decision-making power invested primarily in husbands rather than wives. These spouses are likely to express strong support for the norm of lifelong marriage. They are likely to be religious because religion provides an important institutional foundation for these unions. They are also likely to have relatively large

[2] Other family scholars have suggested similar typologies of marriage. Wilcox and Nock (2006) distinguished between several models of marriage, including institutional and companionate models. Their description of institutional marriage corresponds to some aspects of my description of institutional and companionate marriage; their description of companionate marriage corresponds to some aspects of my description of companionate and individualistic marriage. Future work will be necessary to determine the optimal way of classifying contemporary marriages.

families because raising children is a fundamental function of institutional marriage. Finally, one might expect these spouses to interact frequently with one another because couple activities are valued more highly than are individual pursuits.

One would expect individualistic marriages to differ markedly from institutional marriages in most of these respects. For example, wives in individualistic marriages are likely to be employed full time and, hence, economically independent of their husbands. Given wives' substantial financial contributions to the household, husbands are likely to do a relatively large proportion of family work and share decision-making power equally. Individualistic spouses are likely to express relatively weak support for the norm of lifelong marriage. Because religion plays only a minor role in individualistic marriages, these spouses are likely to be low in religiosity and to attend religious services infrequently. Children are not central to individualistic marriages, so one would expect to see many childless couples in this group. And because individualistic spouses value and pursue their own individual interests, these couples should interact together less frequently than others.

Companionate marriages are likely to share some characteristics with each of the other two types. With respect to the division of labor, one would anticipate most wives to be in the labor force, although they may not work as many hours as do wives in individualistic marriages. Support for the norm of lifelong marriages is likely to follow a similar pattern, with spouses in companionate marriages falling between spouses in the other two groups. It is also likely that these spouses fall between those in the other two groups with respect to traits such as religiosity and attendance at religious services. That is, spouses in companionate marriages are likely to be more religious than spouses in individualistic marriages and less religious than spouses in institutional marriages. Finally, because of the centrality of mutual support and teamwork, spouses in companionate marriage should report especially high levels of shared interaction and having friends in common.

These distinctions make it possible to produce a rough categorization of marriages into the three types. As is often the case with social research, it is necessary to work with less-than-ideal data. The current study uses cluster analysis to create a typology of institutional, companionate, and individualistic marriages. I used data from two time periods (1980 and 2000) to determine whether some types of marriages became more or less common during this period. I then determined whether two central indicators of marital quality – marital happiness and divorce proneness – differed across these marriage types.

Data Sets

Two data sets, one collected in 1980 and the other in 2000, provided information for the current study. The first was the original wave of a longitudinal investigation: the study of Marital Instability over the Life Course. The second was the 2000 Survey of Marriage and Family Life. (Details on both studies are available in Amato et al. 2007.) Both surveys were based on telephone interviews with married individuals from randomly selected households in the United States (excluding Hawaii and Alaska). The sample sizes for the two surveys were 2,034 and 2,100, and response rates were 65 percent and 63 percent, respectively. The two samples closely matched many demographic characteristics of the married population in each survey year. Nevertheless, to ensure a closer fit of the samples to their target populations, I weighted each survey to be nationally representative (in each year) with respect to gender, age, race, ethnicity, and education. These two data sets are useful because they contain a large number of identically worded survey questions, which makes it possible to pool the two samples and compare trends over time.

Survey Items

I used a variety of questions from the 1980 and 2000 surveys to measure marital characteristics. Several questions asked about the number of hours the wife spent in the labor force each week, the wife's earnings, the wife's earned income as a percentage of the couple's total earned income, and the number of children born into the marriage. Other questions referred to the husband's share of household chores (1 = *none*, 2 = *some but less than half*, 3 = *about half*, 4 = *more than half*, and 5 = *all*), which spouse made most of the important decisions (0 = *the husband*, 1 = *both spouses equally*), and the frequency of attendance at religious services (1 = *less than once per year or never*, 2 = *once a year or more but less than monthly*, 3 = *once a month or more but less than weekly*, and 4 = *weekly or more often*).

The interviewed spouse also responded to seven items designed to measure gender attitudes, such as "A woman's most important task in life should be taking care of her children," and "If his wife works full-time, a husband should share equally in household tasks, such as cooking, cleaning, and washing" (1 = *disagree strongly*, 2 = *disagree*, 3 = *agree*, 4 = *agree strongly*). Items were scored in the direction of traditional gender attitudes, and a summary score based on all items yielded a reliability coefficient (alpha) of .65. Support for the norm of lifelong marriage was assessed with six items, including "Marriage is for life, even if couples are unhappy," and "Couples are able to get divorced too easily these days" (1 = *disagree strongly*, 2 = *disagree*, 3 = *agree*, 4 = *agree strongly*). Items were scored in the direction of support for lifelong marriage, and a summary score based on all items yielded a reliability coefficient (alpha) of .61.

Respondents also were asked about the number of people they considered to be good friends (excluding relatives), and how many of these people also were good friends of their spouses. These questions made it possible to calculate the percentage of shared friends. The extent to which spouses engaged in everyday activities together was based on questions that inquired about how frequently they ate the main meal of the day together, went shopping together, visited friends together, worked on projects around the house together, and went out for recreational activities together (1 = *never*, 2 = *occasionally*, 3 = *usually*, and 4 = *almost always*). The sum of

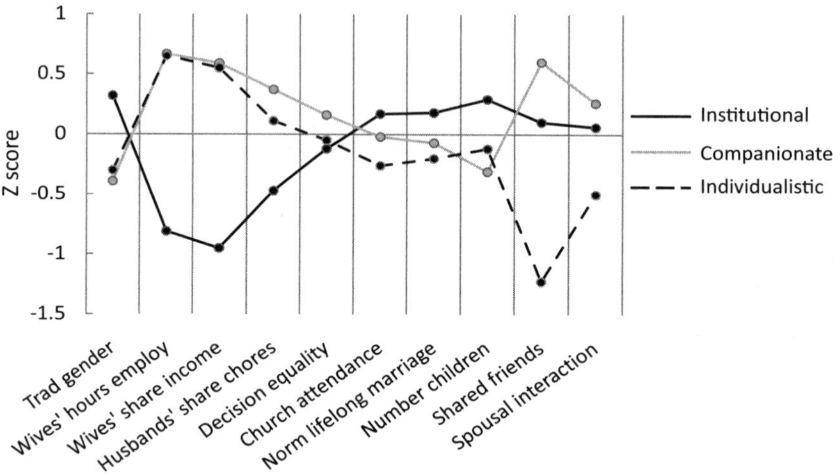

FIGURE 6.1. Cluster Analysis of Three Marriage Types.

the items produced a total score with an alpha reliability coefficient of .65. (The complete wording of all questions is available in Amato et. al. 2007).

Cluster Analysis

The Two-Step Clustering procedure, as implemented in SPSS 17, was used for the analysis. All variables were standardized prior to analysis to ensure that variables with larger variances did not dominate the solution. To include as many cases as possible, missing values were replaced with estimates based on a single imputation. The Two-Step Clustering algorithm calculates the Bayesian Information Criterion (BIC) for a variety of solutions and uses this value to find an initial estimate of the optimal number of clusters. This estimate is then refined by examining the largest increase in the distance between cluster centers at each step. In the current analysis, the algorithm determined that a three-cluster solution provided an optimal fit to the data. That is, the three-cluster solution yielded a low BIC value (which is desirable) and a high level of separation between clusters.[3]

The results of the cluster analysis are summarized in Figure 6.1. This figure shows group differences on all of the variables used to define the clusters, with the

[3] In preliminary analyses, I also relied on a second statistical method: latent class analysis (LCA). LCA yielded a three-group solution with an interpretation similar to that of the cluster analysis. I present the results from the cluster analysis for two reasons. First, cluster analysis is more straightforward than LCA because it does require the assumption of latent (unobserved) categories. Second, LCA requires the assumption that latent marriage classes *produce* the observed scores on the indicators (such as wives' share of earned income). In contrast, cluster analysis assumes that the observed indicators *define* membership in the marriage clusters. In the present case, cluster analysis may be more appropriate theoretically. (For a discussion, see Kline 2011.)

differences represented in standard deviation units. The largest cluster (40 percent of all marriages) was distinctive in the following ways: spouses had the most traditional attitudes about gender arrangements in marriage, wives were employed the smallest number of hours (or not at all), wives earned the lowest share of family income, husbands did the smallest share of household chores, spouses were the most likely to attend religious services regularly, spouses expressed the strongest support for the norm of lifelong marriage, and couples had the largest number of children. Taken together, these relatively traditional unions had many of the characteristics of institutional marriages.

The second largest cluster, 37 percent of all marriages, appeared to represent companionate marriages. These marriages were distinctive in the following ways: husbands performed the largest share of household chores, spouses had the highest level of decision-making equality, spouses had the largest percentage of shared friends, and spouses shared everyday activities most frequently.

The third cluster (23 percent) appeared to represent individualistic marriages. These marriages were distinctive in having the lowest level of attendance at religious services, the weakest support for the norm of lifelong marriage, the smallest percentage of friends shared with spouses, and the lowest frequency of everyday interaction between spouses. But these marriages were similar to companionate marriages in that spouses held relatively nontraditional attitudes toward gender roles in marriage, wives worked a comparatively large number of hours, and wives contributed a relatively large share of household income.

In evaluating the cluster solution, it is important to note that all of the variables in the analysis distinguished significantly between the marriage clusters. The only pairs of clusters that did not differ significantly from one another ($p < .05$) were companionate and individualistic marriages (with respect to traditional gender attitudes, wives' hours of employment, and wives' share of income) and institutional and individualistic marriages (with respect to decision-making equality). These results indicate that all of the input variables made important contributions to the distinctiveness of the clusters.

The three groups did not conform perfectly to the expectations outlined earlier. For example, I expected wives in individualistic marriages to be employed for the longest hours and earn the greatest share of income. Instead, companionate and individualistic marriages were nearly identical in these two respects. I also anticipated that individualistic marriages would score highest in husbands' share of housework and decision-making equality, but these variables attained their highest levels in companionate marriages. Nevertheless, although the results of the cluster analysis did not conform perfectly to expectations, the clusters reflected most of the anticipated patterns for the three groups. And although the surveys did not contain all of the questions that one might wish for, the results of the analysis were clear and consistent enough to justify further investigation.

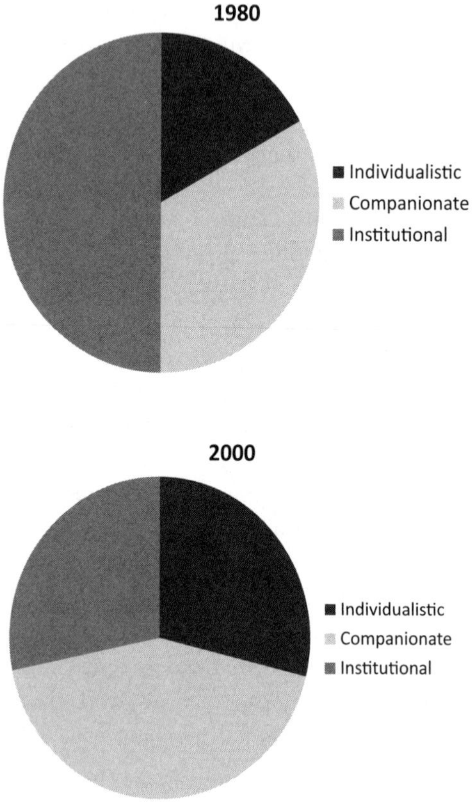

FIGURE 6.2. Percentage of Respondents in Three Types of Marriage: 1980 and 2000.

Differences between Marriage Clusters across Time

The next step in the analysis considered whether the percentage of marriages in each cluster changed between 1980 and 2000. These results are summarized in Figure 6.2. Between 1980 and 2000, the percentage of institutional marriages decreased from 50 percent to 29 percent. By contrast, the percentage of companionate marriages increased from 33 percent to 42.5 percent, and the percentage of individualistic marriages increased from 17 percent to 28.5 percent. These results suggest that institutional marriages (as defined by the variables in the current analysis) were still common in 1980 but that, by 2000, these marriages had become a minority and had been replaced by individualistic and companionate marriages.

Further investigation revealed that the three marriage clusters differed only modestly across a range of demographic variables. For example, spouses in institutional marriages had fewer years of education than did spouses in companionate or individualistic marriages ($p < .01$), although these differences amounted to only one-half of a year. Compared with white respondents, black respondents were more likely to be in companionate marriages and less likely to be in institutional marriages ($p < .01$). The percentage of Hispanics did not vary across the three types of marriages. Similarly, husbands and wives were equally likely to be in the three marriage groups.

Differences in Marital Quality

I used two measures of marital quality to assess differences across marriage clusters. Marital happiness was based on ten items, including "How happy are you with the amount of understanding received from your spouse?" "How happy are you with the amount of love and affection received from your spouse?" and "How happy are you with your spouse's faithfulness?" (1 = *not too happy*, 2 = *somewhat happy*, 3 = *very happy*). A factor analysis revealed that the items formed a single, unidimensional scale. Responses were summed to provide a total score, and the alpha reliability was .88. To facilitate interpretation, the scale was standardized to have a mean of 0 and a standard deviation of 1.

Divorce proneness is the propensity to divorce and includes both a cognitive component (thinking that one would like to live apart from one's spouse, thinking that one's marriage is in trouble, considering the possibility of getting a divorce) and actions (talking with one's spouse about divorce, consulting with an attorney about divorce). The scale consisted of thirteen items that tapped both the frequency and the timing of indicators of relationship instability. For example, a question on thinking about divorce was scored 0 = *never have thought about divorce*, 1 = *have thought about divorce but not within the last three years*, 2 = *have thought about divorce within the last three years but not recently*, and 3 = *thinking about divorce now*. This scoring is based on the assumption that marriages in which spouses are currently thinking about divorce are the most unstable, marriage in which spouses have thought about divorce in the past are moderately unstable, and marriages in which spouses have never thought about divorce are the most stable. (The same reasoning also applies to the other items on this scale.) Additional items included thinking that the marriage is in trouble, talking with one's spouse about divorce, talking with other people about problems in one's marriage, consulting an attorney about divorce, and having a trial separation. A factor analysis revealed one underlying factor, and the alpha reliability coefficient for the scale was .92. To facilitate interpretation, this scale was standardized to have a mean of 0 and a standard deviation of 1. This scale is an excellent predictor of future divorce. One study that used this measure found that the odds of divorcing within the next three years were nine times higher for individuals who scored one standard deviation above the mean than for individuals who scored one standard deviation below the mean (Booth et al. 1985).

Regression analysis was used to estimate the mean levels of marital happiness and divorce proneness for the three groups. To ensure that marital quality differences reflected marriage types rather than demographic variables correlated with marriage

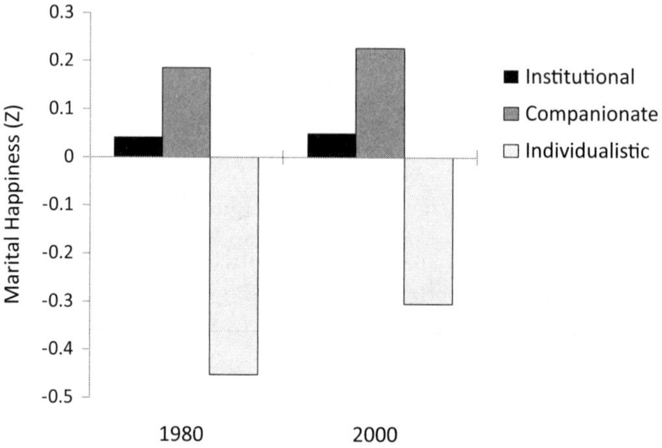

FIGURE 6.3. Marital Happiness and Marriage Type: 1980 and 2000.

types, the analysis controlled for the following variables: the respondent's gender, the respondent's racial and ethnic status, whether this was a first marriage or a second (or higher order) marriage for the respondent, whether the couple cohabited prior to marriage, whether either spouse experienced parental divorce as a child, the number of years married, and the mean of the husband's and wife's years of education.

Figure 6.3 shows the mean levels of marital happiness for the three marriage clusters separately for 1980 and 2000. The results were similar in each decade. In both years, spouses in companionate marriages reported the highest level of marital happiness and spouses in individualistic marriages reported the lowest level. Moreover, in both years, all of the differences between groups were statistically significant. That is, spouses in companionate marriages reported significantly more happiness than did spouses in institutional marriages, and spouses in institutional marriages, in turn, reported significantly more happiness than did spouses in individualistic marriages. Although the level of marital happiness for spouses in individualistic marriages increased significantly between 1980 and 2000, the overall interaction between marriage type and decade was not significant. These findings suggest that companionate marriages are the most likely to involve a high level of marital happiness, whereas individualistic marriages are the least likely.

Figure 6.4 shows the results for divorce proneness. In both decades, spouses in companionate and institutional marriages reported the lowest level of divorce proneness, and spouses in individualistic marriages reported the highest levels. The analysis revealed, however, that the level of divorce proneness in individualistic marriages decreased between 1980 and 2000, and the overall interaction between decade and family type was statistically significant ($p < .05$). This finding suggests that individualistic unions became less divorce prone between 1980 and 2000. Nevertheless, in both decades, spouses in individualistic marriages were the most likely

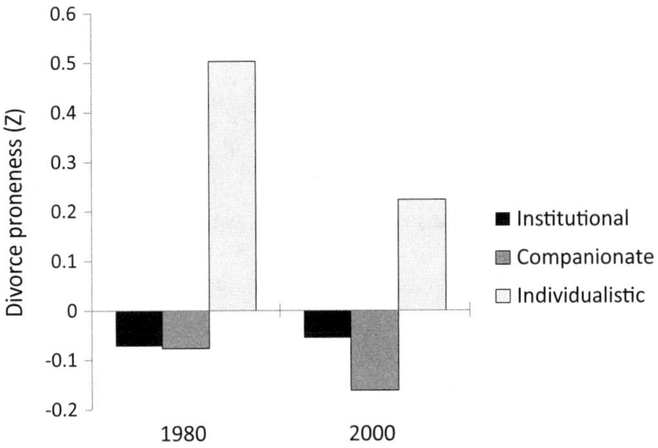

FIGURE 6.4. Divorce Proneness and Marriage Type: 1980 and 2000.

to think that their relationships were in trouble, to think about divorce, to discuss divorce with their spouses, and so on.

Discussion

Although many scholars have suggested a general historic progression from institutional to companionate to individualistic marriage, it is likely that all three types of marriage have existed throughout American history. It has not been possible to determine how many contemporary marriages fall into each of these categories, or how marital quality varies across these groups, because of the absence of appropriate data. The present study represents an initial attempt to gain some traction on these issues. Although this investigation lacked the ideal variables that would allow unambiguous operational definitions of these categories, the cluster analysis produced three distinct groups of marriages with many of the characteristics commonly associated with institutional, companionate, and individualistic marriages.[4]

Based on the variables used in the present analysis, it appears that institutional marriages (involving a clear household division of labor based on gender, frequent church attendance, strong support for the norm of lifelong marriage, and a comparatively large number of children) were common as recent as 1980. Of course,

4 A recent study by Wilcox and Dew (2010) used latent class analysis to produce a similar typology of married couples. Their analysis, based on several attitude scales, produced four groups. The authors classified two groups as "soul mate marriages," which are similar to the individualistic marriages as described in this chapter. These two groups differed in that one had a much higher level of social support than did the other. The authors referred to the other two groups as "religious companionate" and "secular institutional." Wilcox and Dew's results differ from those of the current study because different input variables were used in the two analyses.

the institutional marriages identified in the current study almost certainly differ from institutional marriages in nineteenth-century United States in many respects. Early institutional marriages were more strongly governed by social norms, community standards, and religious strictures than were their counterparts in the 1980s and 2000s. Nevertheless, these more recent institutional marriages can be thought of as being *relatively* institutional, compared with their companionate and individualistic counterparts. These marriages also can be viewed as the "descendants" of their more strongly institutionalized ancestors.

The current analysis indicates that institutional marriages became less common between 1980 and 2000 – declining from 50 percent to 29 percent of all marriages. Correspondingly, the percentage of companionate and individualistic marriages increased during this period. This suggests that companionate as well as individualistic patterns are serving as contemporary alternatives to traditional institutional marriage. Because both marriage types increased at about the same rate between 1980 and 2000, it does not appear to be the case that individualistic marriages are "replacing" companionate marriages in the American population. It is clear, however, that people are turning away from the traditional institutional model.

Today, there is no general consensus on the ideal form of marriage. A positive aspect of the current social climate is that spouses are free to adopt the marital arrangements with which they are most comfortable. Some spouses prefer a traditional division of labor and a stable marriage grounded in religious convictions. Other spouses prefer a companionate or individualistic arrangement. It is unlikely that any one form of marriage will best meet the needs of all people. Nevertheless, it is of interest to know if different types of marriage vary in marital quality, on average. The current study found that spouses in companionate marriages reported the greatest marital happiness and the lowest level of divorce proneness. Correspondingly, spouses in individualistic marriages reported the least marital happiness and the highest level of divorce proneness.

What factors might account for these differences? The work of Scott Stanley and his colleagues on relationship commitment may be relevant (Stanley and Markman 1992; Stanley, Rhoades, and Whitton 2010). This work distinguishes dedication commitment (in which spouses want the relationship to continue because it is intrinsically rewarding and valued) from constraint commitment (in which spouses stay in the marriage because they have made investments in the relationship, there are no good alternatives, and spouses hold strong moral or religious beliefs about lifelong marriage). A central component of dedication commitment is the adoption of a long-term perspective, which provides a necessary corrective to the inevitable short-term ups and downs of relationships. All relationships go through periods of dissatisfaction or conflict, but a spouse with a long-term perspective is motivated to endure short-term difficulties to maintain the long-term viability of the relationship. Another aspect of dedication commitment is a willingness to sacrifice for one's partner. Committed spouses do not view marriage as a zero-sum game in which one partner "loses" if the other partner "wins." Instead, committed spouses sacrifice willingly because they realize that the long-term success of the union benefits both of them.

Dedication commitment may be common in companionate marriage and less so in individualistic marriage. The strong emphasis on teamwork in companionate marriage, and the broad sharing of friends and activities, promotes dedication and stability, even during periods when the relationship is strained. This tendency is probably reinforced by decision-making equality – a companionate characteristic associated with higher marital quality among husbands as well as wives (Amato et al. 2007). By contrast, spouses in institutional relationships rely mainly on constraint commitment to keep their marriages together during difficult times. Although this form of commitment strengthens stability, it does not necessarily lead to greater happiness.

A second relevant (and related) perspective involves theoretical work on communal and exchange relationships (Beck and Clark 2010; Clark and Reis 1988). According to this perspective, spouses in communal relationships do not expect to be "repaid" when they have provided a benefit to their partners. In contrast, spouses in exchange relationships monitor the contributions of each partner and expect to be repaid for sacrifices they have made. Research indicates that partners who adopt a communal norm tend to be more satisfied with their relationships than are partners who adopt an exchange norm. Correspondingly, communal relationships tend to be more stable over time than are exchange relationships. Overall, spouses who are noncontingently responsive to their partners tend to experience more positive and rewarding relationships in the long run. In contrast, spouses who are willing to support a spouse only if the spouse can reciprocate that support tend to experience more negative relationship outcomes in the long run.

This perspective suggests that companionate marriage generally involves a communal model. Presumably, spouses who work closely together to achieve common goals do not mind making occasional sacrifices "for the team." Moreover, these spouses are unlikely to have strict expectations for short-term reciprocation. In contrast, spouses in individualistic marriages are likely to adopt an exchange perspective in which they closely monitor their relationships to ensure that their outcomes are proportional to their inputs. If spouses discover that their outcomes are not as high as expected, they can try to negotiate more favorable terms. They may not invest much time and energy in this process, however, because it is often easier to leave the relationship and seek better outcomes with alternative partners. Ironically, by focusing on the maximization of individual needs, individualistic marriages may lead to less happiness and greater union instability in the long run.

Although this line of reasoning is plausible, readers should consider the limitations of the present study. As noted earlier, the data sets did not contain items that measure people's fundamental values about the purpose of marriage and the basis of marital stability. Moreover, because the study is cross-sectional, it is not possible to determine the direction of causation. It is possible that spouses with high levels of marital quality drift toward a companionate model, and spouses with low levels of marital quality drift toward an individualistic model. Future research with longitudinal data will be necessary to unravel the direction of influence between marriages types and marital quality. Moreover, the data for the current analysis extend only as far as 2000, and it is not possible to determine how trends in marriage and marital quality have changed since then. For the time being, the current results should be treated as suggestive rather than confirmatory.

POLICY ISSUES

The analysis presented in this chapter suggests that marriages in the United States are moving in two divergent directions, with companionate and individualistic forms gradually replacing the earlier institutional model. Curiously, because companionate marriages tend to have a comparatively high level of marital happiness, and because both types of marriage are increasing at about the same rate, the overall level of marital happiness in the population has not changed (Amato et al. 2007). The same conclusion also holds for divorce proneness. Nevertheless, the current results suggest that U.S. marriages could be strengthened by gently "nudging" new unions away from the individualistic model and toward the companionate model.

During the last few decades, policy makers and members of the general public have become concerned about continuing high levels of marital instability and nonmarital childbearing. The federal government became involved with marriage with the 1996 Personal Responsibility and Work Opportunities Reform Act (PRWORA). This act replaced the older Assistance to Families with Dependent Children (AFDC) program with Temporary Assistance to Needy Families (TANF). Although most of the media attention at the time focused on the new rules for single mothers on public assistance (stringent work requirements and time limits for public assistance), the Act also had much to say about marriage. In particular, the Act allowed states to spend some of their TANF funds on programs to promote marriage, reduce the incidence of nonmarital births, and encourage the formation and maintenance of two-parent families (Ooms 2001). A decade later, the Deficit Reduction Act of 2005 (signed in 2006) reauthorized TANF. The new Act also allocated \$100 million a year for five years for programs to strengthen healthy marriage and another \$50 million a year for programs to promote responsible fatherhood.

The Obama administration shifted the federal government's focus away from marriage and more strongly toward responsible fatherhood. Funding for marriage programs was reduced (but not eliminated) and funding for responsible fatherhood programs was increased in 2010 (National Responsible Fatherhood Clearinghouse

2011). Although many responsible fatherhood programs contain a marriage or relationship component, the main focus of these programs is helping low-income fathers maintain their child support obligations, obtain employment, and remain involved in their children's lives in positive ways. Despite this shift, many state governments, such as that of Oklahoma, are maintaining (and continuing to develop) large-scale programs to strengthen marriage (Oklahoma Marriage Initiative 2011).

Most government-funded programs have focused on teaching specific communication and conflict-resolution skills to couples and high school students (Ooms, Bouchet, and Parke 2004). Many curricula also discuss healthy and reasonable expectations for partners, the value of commitment, and the roles of self-sacrifice and forgiveness in relationships. (All government-funded programs have zero tolerance for relationship violence.) Although program personnel would not use this chapter's terminology, many elements of marriage education can be viewed as implicit attempts to shift couples toward more companionate relationships. Teaching relationship skills would appear to be a good idea – at least it is difficult to see how it could do harm. From a general perspective, however, changing the cultural understanding of marriage – away from a model based on meeting individual needs and toward a model based on cooperative teamwork to accomplish mutually desired goals – may prove to be even more useful.

Many people are skeptical about the value of policies to improve marriage (Cherlin 2003; Furstenburg 2007; Huston and Melz 2004). Some observers are opposed to these measures because they fear that people will become trapped in unhappy marriages. Others argue that these programs are likely to be ineffective and a waste of money. Still others believe that marriage is a private rather than a public matter – a perspective consistent with an individualistic view of marriage. Finally, some fear that pro-marriage policies imply a return to a patriarchal authority structure and a traditional gender division of labor.

Despite the thoughtful concerns of critics, improving marital quality and stability may prove to be an appropriate focus of public policy. It is true that some conservative religious groups want to return to the patriarchal (institutional) marriages of the past. The current study, however, suggests that adopting a companionate model of marriage is a more desirable goal for most couples. Spouses in companionate marriages maintain many of the institutional moorings of earlier marriages, such as attendance at religious services, a belief in the norm of lifelong marriage, and frequent spousal interaction. Spouses in companionate and individualistic marriages also have some elements in common, such as holding nontraditional views about gender and sharing the provider role. Indeed, one can view companionate marriage as combining positive elements from the other two models in a manner consistent with contemporary values. Encouraging a shift toward companionate marriage is consistent with the goals of gender equity and equality and does not "turn back the clock" on women's rights.

CONCLUSION

We live in a time in which the culture of marriage is contested, and a general consensus does not exist about the ideal form of marriage. The research described in this chapter suggests that American marriages are indeed at a "crossroads," with some spouses shifting in the direction of individualistic unions and others shifting in the direction of companionate unions. This chapter also suggests that moving from an individualistic model of marriage and toward a companionate model would benefit many couples – and perhaps society more generally. Current marriage education programs and other efforts (whether directed at high school students, engaged couples, married couples, or the general public) should emphasize the value of union-centered marriage. Ironically, the current belief that one's spouse should be one's soul mate, and that marriage should continuously facilitate one's personal growth and satisfaction, is likely to be detrimental to the long-term stability of many unions, as well as to people's basic desire for happiness and emotional security.

REFERENCES

Amato, P.R., Booth, A., Johnson, D., and Rogers, S.J. (2007). *Alone Together: How Marriage in America Is Changing*. Cambridge, MA: Harvard University Press.

Amato, P.R. and Rogers, S. (1999). Do Attitudes toward Divorce Affect Marital Quality? *Journal of Family Issues*, *20*, 69–86.

Beck, L.A. and Clark, M.S. (2010). What Constitutes a Healthy Communal Marriage and Why Relationship State Matters. *Journal of Family Theory and Review*, *2*, 299–315.

Bellah, R.N. et al. (1985). *Habits of the Heart: Individualism and Commitment in American Life*. Berkeley: University of California Press.

Booth, A., Johnson, D.R., White, L.K., and Edwards, J.N. (1985). Predicting Divorce and Permanent Separation. *Journal of Family Issues*, *6*, 331–346.

Burgess, E.W., and Cottrell, L.S. (1939). *Predicting Success or Failure in Marriage*. New York: Prentice-Hall.

Burgess, E.W., Locke, H.J., and Thomes, M.M. (1963). *The Family: From Institution to Companionship*. New York: American Book Company.

Burgess, E.W. and Wallin, P. (1953). *Engagement and Marriage*. Chicago: J. B. Lippincott Company.

Cherlin, A.J. (2003). Should the Government Promote Marriage? *Contexts*, *2*, 22–29.

Cherlin, A.J. (2004). The Deinstitutionalization of American Marriage. *Journal of Marriage and Family*, *66*, 848–861.

Clark, M.A. and Reis, H.T. (1988). Interpersonal Processes in Close Relationships. *Annual Review of Psychology*, *39*, 609–672.

Coontz, S. (2005). *Marriage, a History*. New York: Viking.

Furstenberg, F.F. (2007). Should Government Promote Marriage? *Journal of Policy Analysis and Management*, *26*, 956–961.

Hernandez, D.J. (1993). *America's Children: Resources from Family, Government, and the Economy*. New York: Russell Sage Foundation.

Huston, T.L. and Melz, H. (2004). The Case for (Promoting) Marriage: The Devil Is in the Details. *Journal of Marriage and Family*, *66*, 943–958.

Kline, R.B. (2011). *Principles and Practice of Structural Equation Modeling*. New York: Guilford.

Maslow, A. (1962). *Toward a Psychology of Being*. Princeton, NJ: Van Nostrand.

McCullough, D. (2001). *John Adams*. New York: Simon & Schuster.

Mintz, S. and Kellogg, S. (1988). *Domestic Revolutions: A Social History of American Family Life*. New York: Free Press.

National Responsible Fatherhood Clearinghouse (2011). Available at kttp://www.fatherhood.gov/policy-research/policy.

Nock, S.L. (1995). Commitment and Dependency in Marriage. *Journal of Marriage and the Family*, 57, 503–514.

Oklahoma Marriage Initiative (2011). Available at http://okmarriage.org/.

Ooms, T. (2001). The Role of the Federal Government in Strengthening Marriage. *Virginia Journal of Social Policy & Law*, 9, 163–191.

Ooms, T., Bouchet, S., and Parke, M. (2004). *Beyond Marriage Licenses: Efforts in States to Strengthen Marriage and Two-Parent Families*. Washington, DC: Center for Law and Social Policy.

Popenoe, D. (1993). American Family Decline: 1960–1990: A Review and Appraisal. *Journal of Marriage and the Family*, 55, 527–556.

Putnam, R.D. (2000). *Bowling Alone: The Collapse and Revival of American Community*. New York: Simon & Schuster.

Rogers, C. (1961). *On Becoming a Person*. Boston: Houghton Mifflin.

Stacey, J. (1996). *In the Name of the Family: Rethinking Family Values in the Postmodern Age*. Boston: Beacon Press.

Stanley, M.S. and Markman, H.J. (1992). Assessing Commitment in Personal Relationships. *Journal of Marriage and the Family*, 54, 595–608.

Stanley, M.S., Rhoades, G.K., and Whitton, S. (2010). Commitment: Functions, Formation, and the Securing of Romantic Attachment. *Journal of Family Theory and Review*, 2, 243–257.

Thornton, A. (2005). *Reading History Sideways: The Fallacy and Enduring Impact of the Developmental Paradigm on Family Life*. Chicago: University of Chicago Press.

Wilcox, W.B. and Dew, J. (2010). Is Love a Flimsy Foundation? Soulmate versus Institutional Models of Marriage. *Social Science Research*, 39, 687–699.

Wilcox, W.B. and Nock, S.L. (2006). What's Love Got to Do with It? Equality, Equity, Commitment and Women's Marital Quality. *Social Forces*, 84, 1321–1345.

7

Marriage and Improved Well-Being

Using Twins to Parse the Correlation, Asking How Marriage Helps, and Wondering Why More People Don't Buy a Bargain

Robert E. Emery, Erin E. Horn, and Christopher R. Beam

Married adults are better adjusted than never married, remarried, and – especially – separated/divorced adults as indexed by a wide variety of measures including: (1) *psychological adjustment*, notably greater happiness/subjective well-being (Gove et al. 1983; Johnson & Wu 2002), less depression (Pearlin & Johnson 1977; Wade & Pevalin 2004), and less substance use (Power et al. 1999); (2) *social relationships*, for example, more frequent sex (Laumann et al. 1994; Pedersen & Blekesaune 2003), experiencing less violence inside or outside of the relationship (Waite & Gallagher 2000), and having better-adjusted children (Emery 1999); (3) *finances*, as evident in higher family income (Duncan & Hoffman 1985) and lower perceived economic stress (Pearlin & Johnson 1977); and (4) *physical health*, as indexed by markers, such as better self-ratings of health (Hughes & Waite 2009), less chronic disease (Dupre & Meadows 2007), and greater longevity (Sbarra & Nietert 2009). The descriptive benefits of marriage are so pervasive, in fact, that many commentators and policies encourage marriage as a prescriptive solution for improving individual – and societal – well-being (McLanahan et al. 2005; Waite & Gallagher 2000). Most notable in this regard is the federal government's $1.5 billion campaign to promote marriage initiated under the George W. Bush administration.

Marriage promotion typically, but by no means universally, is linked to the political right. Still, the potential benefits of marriage are of widespread, popular interest. For example, a recent *New York Times Magazine* (April 18, 2010) article posed the question, "Is Marriage Good for Your Health?" Hundreds of studies suggest that the answer to this question is "yes." The so-called marriage benefit is a reliable empirical finding, one replicated by many independent research groups, that generally remains consistent across time and cultures. In fact, a major, recent scholarly review concluded that future research should move from asking "whether" marriage benefits mental and physical health to outlining "when" and "how" the benefits of marriage accrue (Carr & Springer 2010).

SELECTION OR CAUSATION?

We agree with this position, provided that the first "when" for researchers to address is when selection is controlled. Our concern about selection was echoed provocatively in a recent essay, "What If Marriage Is Bad for Us?" As the authors of this article stated, "To say marriage creates wealth is to confuse correlation with causation. If there is more wealth in Manhattan than in Brooklyn, that does not mean that moving to Manhattan will make you wealthier" (*Chronicle of Higher Education Review* 2009). These essayists remind us that one reason wealthier people live in Manhattan is because they can afford the city. Wealthier people *select* Manhattan as their home.

Does living in Manhattan also *cause* an increase in wealth? We suspect it does. Salaries and hourly wages are higher in Manhattan. (Yes, we are ignoring the cost of living.) People's social-reference groups earn more money in Manhattan, too, which probably encourages individuals to work harder, demand even better pay, and take other steps to elevate their status to approach or exceed their peers. Consider, for example, the starting salaries, expected future salaries, and the work hours of investment bankers or first-year associates at major law firms.

The same confounding of selection and causation undoubtedly is true of the marriage benefit. Happier, healthier, wealthier, and sexier people surely are more attractive mates and, as a result, they "select" into marriage. Yet marriage also likely causes improved health and well-being whether as a result of "settling down" and working harder toward a shared future; "nagging" each other to eat better, drink less, and exercise more; or sharing economic and human capital, not the least benefit of which is taking advantage of economies of scale (and other direct economic benefits of marriage, such as health insurance).

These confounded explanations of the marriage benefit are widely termed *social selection* and *social causation*, and the two alternatives are raised in virtually every contemporary study of marriage and adult well-being (Carr & Springer 2010). Nearly every scholarly paper also yearns to better untangle these connected, yet competing, explanations. One goal of the present chapter is to describe and illustrate our unique method for doing so: comparing twins. Twin studies offer powerful controls for social selection which, in turn, allow us to (largely) identify social causation.

A second goal of this chapter is to raise the question: How might marriage promote mental and physical health? In this chapter, we briefly raise a number of possible answers to this question; we have already hinted at several. But we also seek more ideas on this topic. Our objective in doing so is both conceptual and ultimately empirical: We want to encourage and refine theorizing so we can develop clear hypotheses and test them empirically in several ways, including twin studies using national data not only from the United States, but also from Sweden and Australia.

Our third and final goal also is conceptual and, in many ways, it may be our most perplexing and interesting task. We raise this question: If marriage is such a bargain, why aren't more people buying it? We believe that the marriage benefit is mostly real – that is, marriage *does* cause many of the benefits correlated with it (although certainly not all of them). Yet, in the United States and throughout much of the industrialized world, rates of cohabitation have skyrocketed, entry into marriage is delayed (often dramatically), increasing numbers of adults remain single, and rates of separation/divorce have stabilized at extremely high levels by historical standards (Emery, Beam, & Rowen 2011). All of these trends document that far fewer people today are "buying" marriage. Obviously, this must mean that something is missing from the simple economic calculation:

$$\text{Marriage} = \text{more good things}$$

We raise several ideas about what this equation is omitting, including various hidden costs of marriage (including lost opportunity costs), an attempt to avoid divorce risk, foreshortened time horizons, and increased state assumption of traditional family functions that undermine marriage (such as protecting, rearing, and educating children). Our hope in complicating the marriage-benefit formula is twofold. Again, we are searching for hypotheses to test in our research studies. We also hope to contribute to thinking about policies that will be more successful in promoting marriage or, perhaps, alternatives to marriage that achieve social goals equally well.

USING TWINS TO PARSE THE MARRIAGE BENEFIT

The logic and statistical methods we use in analyzing twins can become quite technical. We refer the reader interested in such details to our various published reports using twins and the children of twins (Cruz, Emery, & Turkheimer, 2012; D'Onofrio et al. 2005, 2006, 2007; Harden et al. 2007a,b); Mendle et al. 2006, 2009). In this forum, we think it is more appropriate to offer a conceptual introduction to the method and present some illustrative statistics in a straightforward manner.

To put it simply, our concern about social selection is that we are comparing apples and oranges, not apples and apples, when looking at outcomes associated with marriage versus divorce (to pick one of many alternative marital statuses). For example, assume we find that married adults are less depressed than divorced adults. We would be wrong to conclude from this correlation that divorce caused the depression (or that marriage protected against it), for a host of reasons. For one, the depression may have preceded the divorce and perhaps contributed to it. For another, differences that contribute both to divorce and to depression may explain the correlation; for example, being African American, having a lower income, or growing up in a "broken home" may make people more likely to both become depressed and get divorced. In fact, empirical research shows that people nonrandomly "select" into marriage and divorce based on their race, income, parents' marital status, and their own depression (Emery, Waldron, Kitzmann, & Aaron 1999).

Research also demonstrates nonrandom *genetic* selection into divorce (McGue & Lykken 1993).[1] Genetic selection is not only a concern in the case of divorce, but it is also a general process that behavior genetic researchers call the *gene-environment correlation*. Environmental experiences are correlated with genetic makeup, thus correlated genes must be considered as potential "third variables" that may explain any observed correlation between experience and a given index of adjustment. For example, the correlation between marital status and depression might be explained by genes that increase the risk both for depression and for divorce.

THE LOGIC OF THE TWIN METHOD

Let us now turn to the logic of the twin method as a means of controlling for *genetic and environmental* selection. Consider a study in which we obtain a correlation between depression and divorce when comparing identical (monozygotic or MZ) twins where twin pairs are selected such that one twin is married and the other is divorced. This design immediately and obviously eliminates a huge class of potential noncausal explanations for the correlation between marital status and depression. Obtained differences in depression *cannot* be attributable to genetic differences between divorced and married adults because MZ twins are genetically identical. Genetically, we are now comparing apples to apples.

Eliminating genetic selection is a huge advantage, but twin studies have another, often overlooked and perhaps even bigger advantage: Any differences between our married and divorced twins cannot be due to their race, their parents' marital status, or whether they grew up in poverty. Why? Identical twins also share these experiences. In fact, identical twins share a host of experiences that may influence selection into marriage, including variables that we might be able to measure (e.g., religious upbringing), others that we can measure only imperfectly (e.g., parental discipline), and still others that we cannot measure at all (e.g., the entirety of shared childhood experiences, or what behavior geneticists call the *shared environment*). Twin studies compare apples and apples genetically and in terms of shared experience, whether that experience is measured or indeed can be measured.

All of this means that any differences in depression we find between our married and divorced MZ twins must be attributable to what behavior geneticists call the *nonshared environment*. Of course, the twins in our study were selected so that they did not share the experience of divorce. We cannot say unequivocally that divorce caused the depression because some earlier, nonshared experience (e.g., a previous,

[1] Of course, there is no "divorce gene." However, genes influence personality characteristics (e.g., impulsivity) and physical characteristics (e.g., age at menarche) that, in turn, are linked with divorce risk. Thus, genes are correlated with divorce and with many experiences (Scarr & McCartney, 1983).

bad intimate relationship) theoretically might be the cause of both later marital status and depression. However, the twin study allows us to eliminate two huge categories of alternative explanations – genetic selection and shared environmental selection – thus making a strong, and parsimonious, causal case for the argument that marital status *caused* the increased depression among the divorced twins. We believe, in fact, that twin studies are the most powerful, nonexperimental method for determining causality. We often refer to them as *quasicausal studies*.

Of course, we might not find differences between married and divorced MZ twins, and this possibility gets us deeper into the advantages of the twin design. If the married and divorced twins do *not* differ, the design tells us that the correlation found in prior research, which did not use twins, is spurious – that is, *not* the result of causation. We now know that the correlation was produced purely by selection effects.

COMPARING UNRELATED ADULTS, UNRELATED SIBLINGS, DZ TWINS, AND MZ TWINS

The conceptual advantages we have outlined now allow us to introduce the basic logic of one of our approaches to analyzing twin data and to offer some illustrative findings. A straightforward method for estimating selection and quasicausal effects – and to easily *see* them – is to compare married and divorced: (1) unrelated adults in the general population (this sample offers no control for genetic and shared environmental selection); (2) nontwin sibling pairs (siblings share 50 percent of their segregating genes, on average, and grow up in the same family, albeit at different times); (3) dizygotic (DZ) or fraternal twins (who also share 50 percent of their genes, and who grow up in the same family at the same time); and (4) MZ twins (who share 100 percent of their genes and who grow up in the same family at the same time).

Selection effects are increasingly implicated to the extent that our obtained differences in depression between married and divorced adults grow smaller in each successive comparison (see Figure 7.1, first graph). As noted earlier, to the extent that the effect is not wholly due to selection – that is, quasicausal – effect sizes may shrink, but they will not disappear even among MZ twin comparisons.

To complicate things a bit, we might obtain a variety of possible outcomes, each of which implicates different selection effects. If genetic selection accounts for obtained differences, then effect sizes will grow smaller by 50 percent for siblings and DZ twins and disappear in the MZ twin comparison (Figure 7.1, second graph). If shared environmental selection accounts for obtained differences, then effects for siblings will be small, and effect sizes will go to zero for DZ and MZ twins, who will not differ from each other (Figure 7.1, third graph). If there are no genetic or shared environmental selection effects, effect sizes should be the same for all four groups whether related or unrelated (Figure 7.1, fourth graph). Finally, it is possible that true effects may be suppressed by selection. For example, the relation between

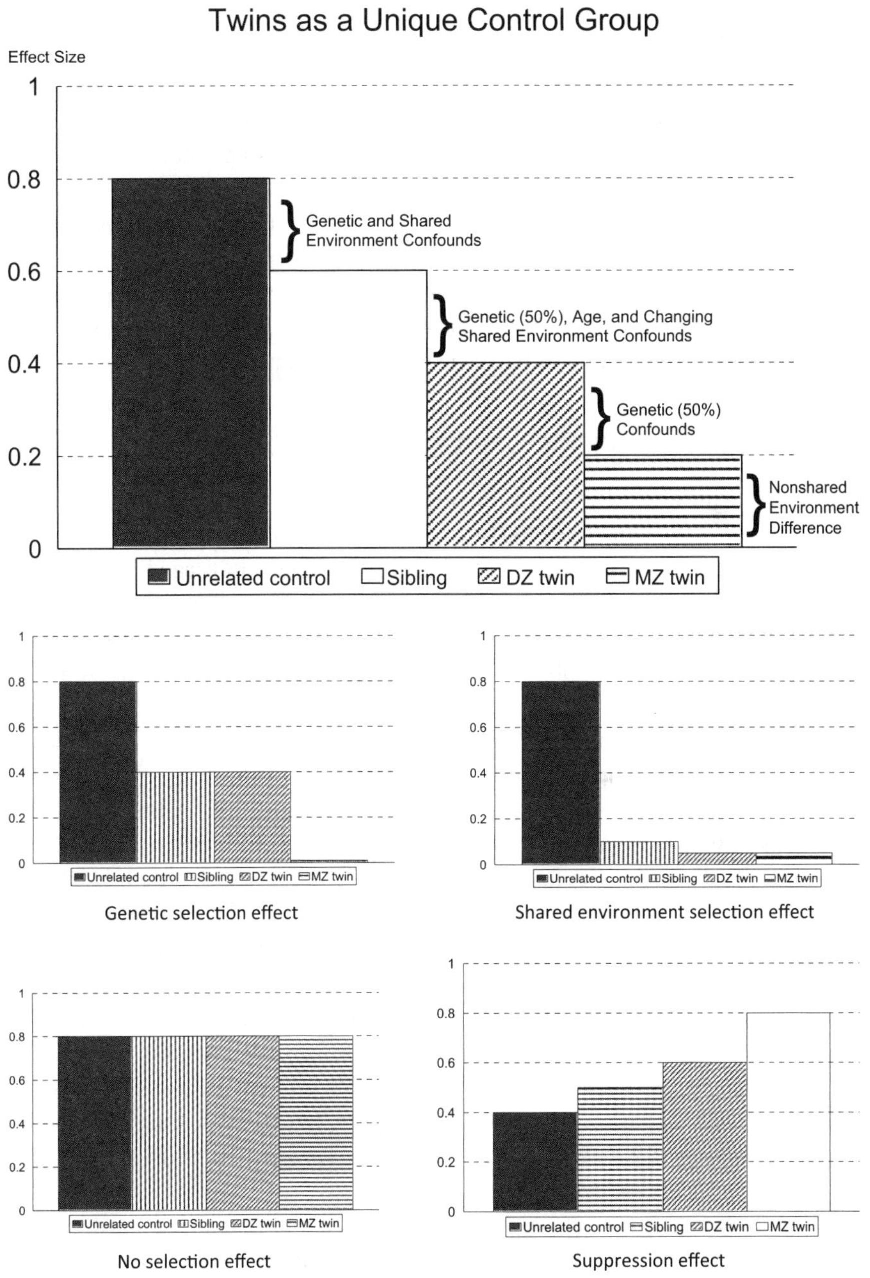

FIGURE 7.1. Using Twins to Control for Selection Effects: Interpreting Theoretical Findings

marriage and mental or physical health would be obscured if marriage benefits women's well-being, but better adjusted women also tend to select *out* of marriage. In this case, effect sizes would grow *larger* for sibling and twin comparisons. The specific differences in these growing effect sizes would depend on whether selection was genetic, shared-environmental, or both (Figure 7.1, fifth graph).

In our scientific reports, we use sophisticated statistical techniques to test the reliability and power of obtained differences. While the statistical methods can become complicated, the logic behind the analyses is the same. We also typically present data in a straightforward manner so readers who are not experts in statistics or twin studies can actually see the results. We turn to an example of this approach, both to show some specific findings and to illustrate the power of the twin method.

MIDUS: A DATA ILLUSTRATION

For the following analyses, we use the first round of the National Survey of Midlife Development in the United States (Brim et al. 2010; MIDUS I 1995–1996), a nationally representative U.S. sample of 7,189 English-speaking adults aged 25 to 74. The MIDUS sample includes oversamples of 952 sibling pairs and 998 twin pairs. This publicly available data set includes measures of mental health (e.g., depression, anxiety, alcohol use, stress), physical health (e.g., smoking, exercise, general health, disease history) (Brim, Ryff, & Kessler 2004), marital status, and marital quality. For present purposes, we focus only on marital status, marital quality, depression (a seven-item DSM-IV symptom count), and a single-item self-rating of overall physical health (widely viewed as a "gold standard" assessment of health) (Ferraro & Farmer 1999; Idler & Benyamini 1997).

The results of our analyses for depression are summarized in Figure 7.2. All comparisons presented in the figure are effect sizes (*d*) calculated as standard deviation unit differences comparing married versus unmarried adults. All effect sizes are in the expected direction, showing that married adults are less depressed than unmarried adults. Several key comparisons are statistically significant. In the comparisons for unrelated adults, the unmarried participants are significantly more depressed in the entire sample, among women and among men. While effect sizes diminish for sibling and twin comparisons, they do not disappear. This indicates that the obtained differences in depression according to marital status are *not* explained by genetic or shared environmental selection.

While many of the comparisons between married and unmarried adults are not statistically significant, we call attention to the smaller Ns and lower statistical power for the sibling and twin groups, particularly when broken down by gender. Also, we do not directly compare various groups where differences appear to be notable. For example, effect sizes are consistently larger for men than for women – a pattern consistent with the existing literature (Waite & Gallagher 2000) – but the present, preliminary analyses do not tell us whether this difference is statistically significant.

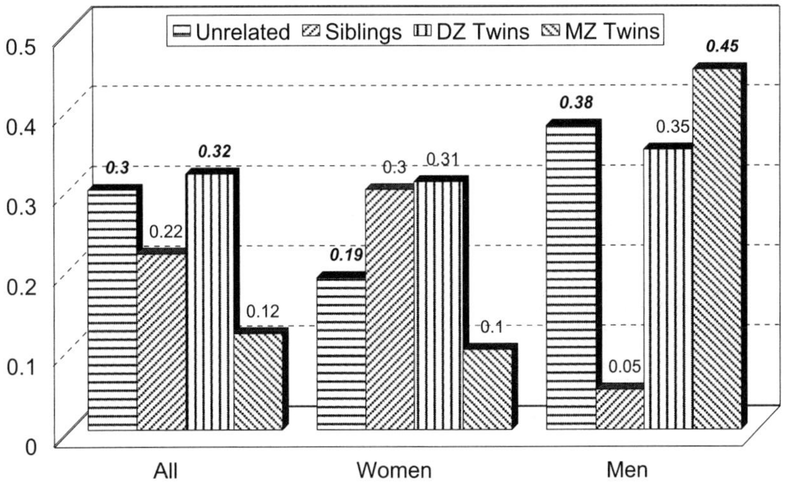

Unrelated, N=2283 married, N=1429 unmarried; Siblings, N=107 pairs; DZ, N=107 pairs; MZ, N=96 pairs.
Statistically significant effect sizes in bold, italics.

FIGURE 7.2. Married versus Unmarried Effect Size Comparisons for Unrelated, Sibling, DZ, and MZ Twin Groups: Depression

We overcome these limitations by using multivariate analyses in our technical reports.

Specifics aside, the overall pattern of findings illustrates the power of the twin method and shows that the marriage benefit for depression is quasicausal. Most notable in this regard is the large and statistically significant difference in depression between married and unmarried MZ male twins, an effect size that is virtually identical to that obtained for the comparison of married and unmarried men who are not related to one another.

Other findings for depression (not shown here) are consistent with the general literature on the marriage benefit. In particular, we find stronger marital-status effects when comparing married and separated/divorced adults (versus the larger unmarried group). This finding is consistent with the view that marital separation causes a period of grieving marked by increased depression that begins before the physical separation and lasts for a year or two afterward (Blekesaune 2008; Emery 2011). We also find (in analyses not shown here) that effect sizes are larger for women when comparing more and less happily married adults. Men's depression appears to be more sensitive to marital status, whereas women's depression is more sensitive to marital quality. We note, however, that *both* marital status and marital quality *are* associated with less depression among *both* women and men. Some writers have wrongly suggested that the different gender patterns mean that men are better off being married irrespective of marital quality while women are better off being single than remaining in an unhappy marriage (Bernard 1972). Our findings, like those

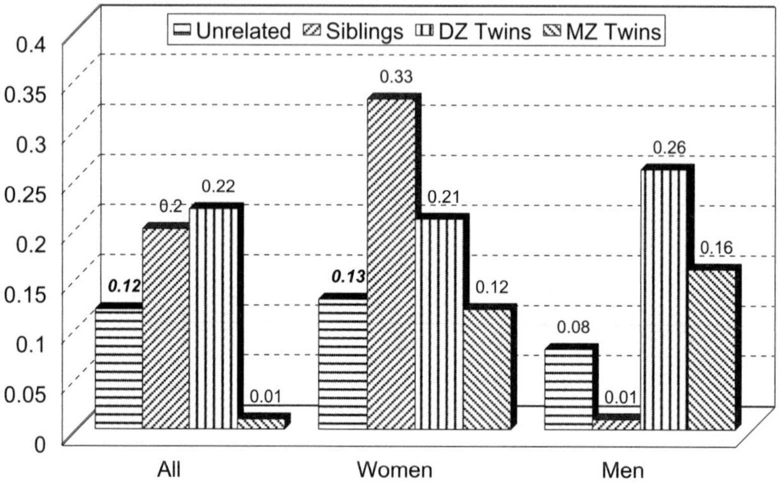

Unrelated, N=2283 married, N=1429 unmarried; Siblings, N=107 pairs; DZ, N=107 pairs; MZ, N=96 pairs.
Statistically significant effect sizes in bold, italics.

FIGURE 7.3. Married versus Unmarried Effect Size Comparisons for Unrelated, Sibling, DZ, and MZ Twin Groups: Physical Health

of others (Waite & Gallagher 2000), indicate that marital status and higher marital quality benefit both genders, even though the former effect is stronger in men and the latter effect is stronger in women.

Figure 7.3 presents the same analyses, using the same sample, but for a different outcome measure, overall rating of physical health. We point briefly to three aspects of these data. First, married adults report significantly better physical health than unmarried adults in the MIDUS general population data. Second, the effect sizes do not disappear in the sibling and twin comparisons, even though few of these differences remain statistically significant. Third, a comparison of effect sizes between our results for physical health and depression shows consistently larger effects for depression.

To summarize, let us return to the first question we raised in this chapter: "Is the correlation between marriage and well-being an artifact of selection?" We conclude that the answer is "no." We find evidence for a marriage benefit even among MZ twins, a powerful method for testing whether the marriage benefit reflects social selection or social causation. While moving into Manhattan may not make you wealthier, moving into marriage does make you healthier. We are pursuing this question in far greater detail than we have presented here, not only with refined multivariate analyses of MIDUS, but also in analyses of two other large U.S. data sets, an Australian data set that includes several thousand twins, and a Swedish data set that includes more than 200,000 twins. We anticipate being able to provide far more complete and detailed answers to questions about the "when" and "how" of the marriage benefit in the next three to four years.

TABLE 7.1. *Causal mechanisms about how marriage may benefit mental and physical health*

	Added Benefits of Marriage	
Direct Partner Support	**Social Support**	**Efficiencies**
Emotional support	"Couples' world"	Economies of scale
Practical/task support	Laws supporting married couples (e.g., health care)	Longer time horizon (more so than cohabitation)
Financial support		Role specialization
Childrearing support		Sexual and emotional availability
		Other practicalities (e.g., "cooking for two")
	Reduced Risks of Marriage	
Avoid single/risky lifestyle	Avoid loss/loneliness	Monitoring/nagging
Safe sex	Not alone	Partner monitors diet, exercise, etc.
Less late-night drinking, smoking, etc.	Grief stemming from separation/divorce	Partner nags about diet, exercise, etc.
Less contact with "bad" same-sex friends (drink too much; antisocial behavior; e.g., *Grease*)		Increased accountability – you know that they know even if they say nothing

HOW DOES MARRIAGE BENEFIT PHYSICAL AND MENTAL HEALTH?

If at least part of the marriage benefit is causal, as our initial evidence suggests, the critical next question to ask is how. That is, specifically what mechanisms within marriage cause the mental and physical benefits that remain after controlling for selection effects?

Speaking most broadly, marriage could cause improved mental and physical health by either by (1) adding benefits relative to other marital statuses or (2) decreasing risks relative to other marital statuses. We have developed a long, yet still incomplete, list of possible causal mechanisms. Rather than expanding on each possibility, we instead have grouped various "added benefit" possibilities into three categories (direct partner support, social support, and efficiencies) and various "decreased risk" possibilities into another three categories (avoiding single/risky life, avoiding loss/loneliness, and nagging/monitoring). These various hypotheses are summarized in Table 7.1. We should clearly note that, although the list is extensive, we do not view it as exhaustive. We also recognize that we could group the hypotheses into completely different categories (e.g., economic, emotional, relationship, and social).

In presenting this initial list of mechanisms/hypotheses, we seek to (1) expand our list, (2) refine both specific hypotheses and a system for categorizing them, and (3) identify hypotheses that apply *uniquely* to marriage. On this last point, we note, for example, that health benefits are not necessarily unique to marriage, although at the present time they are throughout most of the United States. To offer another example, we wonder if commitment time horizons are or ever can be as strong among cohabiting couples as they are for married couples; perhaps longer time horizons are a unique benefit of marriage. We also wonder if married couples' time horizons are shorter today, when divorce is a possibility that cannot be ignored, than they were when divorce was rare. Finally, we suggest that even economic efficiencies that theoretically could be the same for married and cohabiting couples may not be the same in practice. For example, a married couple might readily buy a house together, whereas a cohabiting couple may make that long-term commitment more reluctantly.

MEDIATORS AND MODERATORS

There are two ways to use the twin design to test specific hypotheses about the marriage benefit after accounting for selection effects. First, we can examine potential *mediators* by (1) measuring the hypothesized causal mechanism (e.g., improved health behavior), (2) documenting that the hypothesized mediator is related to marriage (e.g., married twins engage in better health behavior than unmarried twins), (3) documenting that the mediator also is related the outcome of interest (e.g., global physical health), and (4) demonstrating that the mediator statistically accounts for the relationship between marriage and global physical health.

A second approach is to analyze moderators of the relationship between marriage and mental or physical health. In a recent study, for example, we hypothesized that the presence of children under the age of eighteen moderates the relationship between marital quality and depression. Supporting the child-rearing and loneliness hypotheses, we found that the *least* depressed individuals were parents in a happy marriage, while the *most* depressed were nonparents in an unhappy marriage (Beam et al. 2011). This finding suggests that a supportive marriage may protect against the strains of full-time parenting, while parenting may protect against depressive symptoms engendered by an unsupportive marriage.

Other potential moderators of the relationship between marriage and well-being include: social class, income, religious involvement, gender, type/duration of marital status (e.g., cohabitation vs. marriage; time since separation), social acceptance of alternatives to marriage, historical cohort (is marriage as important today as it was for earlier generations?), and societal support for (single) parents (such as the numerous government programs in Sweden). We plan to examine all of these in future research.

THE MARRIAGE PARADOX: WHY AREN'T MORE PEOPLE BUYING THE BARGAIN?

Questions about whether and how marriage actually causes mental and physical health benefits are important for practical, conceptual, and empirical reasons. We have an even more critical and fundamental question to pose: If marriage is such a bargain, why are fewer and fewer people "buying" it? As has been well documented, rates of nonmarital childbearing, cohabitation with or without children, separation, divorce, and choosing to remain single have increased in recent decades throughout the industrialized world (Cherlin 2009). Such behavior is economically irrational if marriage really is a better deal than alternatives to it. We call this the "marriage paradox."

A common policy answer to the marriage paradox is that there is an advertising problem: People just don't know about the many benefits of marriage (Glenn 2001). Bad advertising is the implicit motivator behind the federal government's $1.5 billion dollar investment in marriage promotion. This initiative seeks to encourage marriage by touting its benefits to the public, particularly young people/couples, while also preparing them for the challenges of marriage. But we are unconvinced by the advertising answer to the marriage paradox. Economically, the problem with bargains is disguising them (e.g., using a "loss leader" to encourage people to come into a store and buy more expensive items too), not failing to advertise them. As they should, people quickly discover the best bargain and flock to it. Witness the proliferation of Wal-Mart stores based on the very simple principle of offering lower prices. The benefits of marriage are not newly discovered and widely unrecognized. Government and social groups such as religious organizations, parents, and married peers have long promoted marriage and its benefits. Young people are not turning away from marriage because no one is telling them that marriage is a bargain.

If we want to promote marriage, we need to better understand the hidden motivations behind the growing choice of alternatives to marriage. We briefly raise four alternatives: (1) there are hidden costs to marriage, including opportunity costs such as giving up sexual variety or the possibility of finding a more attractive spouse; (2) avoidance of divorce risk; (3) foreshortened time horizons, specifically that young people are less able to and interested in delaying gratification while many of the costs associated with marriage (e.g., giving up an unhealthy but exciting single lifestyle) are short-term but its benefits (e.g., increased longevity) are often long-term costs; and (4) increased state assumption of traditional family functions (such as protecting, rearing, and educating children) that put comparatively inefficient "mom and pop" operations out of business.

THE HIDDEN COSTS OF MARRIAGE

Clearly, there are hidden costs to marriage, particularly opportunity costs. We have cited a few of the more obvious ones (sexual variety, potentially finding a better mate). The important question, however, is what costs young people considering marriage associate with the married state. Research shows that, across income and ethnic groups, the vast majority of young people report very positive attitudes about and aspirations for marriage (Child Trends 2009) – further evidence against the advertising explanation. Yet, increasing numbers of young people choose to delay marriage, cohabit and have children outside of marriage, or end a marriage. These numbers can be partially explained by a highly competitive "marriage market" (e.g., limited numbers of marriageable African-American men resulting from imprisonment and limited occupational opportunities (Wilson 1987)). But, while the prevalence of marriage alternatives is notably greater among African Americans and low-income individuals, the increase in marriage alternatives is not limited to these groups. What are young people trying to avoid? Commitment? Responsibility? Entrapment? If so, what are the specifics behind these broad categories of explanation? For example, what does "avoidance of commitment" really mean? Can we operationalize it?

Divorce Risk

Divorce risk is one hidden cost of marriage that we suspect young people are attempting to avoid by choosing alternatives to marriage. Divorce, as is well known, is typically associated with large emotional, financial and other costs for both adult partners and their children (Emery 1999). We are frequently asked if a parental divorce increases a child's eventual divorce risk. Our answer is that, while parental divorce clearly increases the risk for divorce based on data from previous cohorts (Wolfinger 2001), the divorce boom seems to have affected an entire generation of young people as much or perhaps more than it affects "children of divorce." In fact, children whose parents have divorced often tell us that their parents' divorce strengthened their own resolve to never divorce themselves. Of course, one's assertions about the future are poor predictors of actual behavior when faced with challenging family circumstances. Still, the vow "I'll never get divorced" perhaps conveys our point: The most certain way to avoid divorce risk is to never get married. Specifically, the vow may translate into an unrealistic search (in today's environment) to find a partner who presents zero divorce risk. Or the resolve to eliminate divorce risk may make one a less attractive mate to potential partners, who may want to enter marriage with an exit strategy.

Time Horizons

A foreshortened time horizon or less ability to delay gratification (two terms for the same concept) is a third possible explanation of the marriage paradox. As we have noted, many of the benefits of marriage are long-term, while many of its costs are short-term. Like today's businesses, widely accused of focusing on quarterly profit statements to the detriment of long-term value, young people today may have foreshortened time horizons about intimate relationships that lead them to discount the greater long-term benefits of potentially lifelong investments in one's own health, in children, and in shared financial goals (e.g., owning a house) relative to the lesser short-term benefits of alternatives to marriage (e.g., "having fun"). Changes in social behavior may also affect a time-horizon analysis. For example, marriage once offered more short-term benefits (e.g., sexual intercourse), but that benefit is now widely available outside of marriage.

The Wal-Mart Family

A final possibility is that marriage and nuclear families no longer are efficient mechanisms for fulfilling traditional functions such as providing economic support and rearing children. Nuclear families may have been necessary "building blocks" of society at one point in history. Today, however, the government fulfills many "family" functions such as educating children, providing children with financial support, and even nurturing and protecting children (e.g., through childcare agencies and child protective services). Of course, the state is an imperfect parent, and the extent of state parenting differs across societies – for example, between the United States and Sweden. (This leads us to note one hypothesis we plan to test: The marriage benefit is smaller in Sweden than in the United States.) Nevertheless, compared to the past, governments today fulfill many traditional family functions. These very large state "families" are more efficient than nuclear families. (Consider the economies of scale of institutionalized childcare versus home care.) From this perspective, government policies designed to support children slowly are putting families out of business – much like Wal-Mart puts mom-and-pop stores out of business. Like small stores, perhaps families just cannot compete effectively with the scale economies of large institutions. And much as we miss the service at the small store around the corner, we still shop at Wal-Mart, all the while bemoaning its impersonal nature and longing for the past. These, of course, are familiar complaints about the disappearance of marriage.

REFERENCES

Beam, C.R. et al. (2011). Revisiting the Effect of Marital Support on Depressive Symptoms in Mothers and Fathers: A Genetically Informed Study. *Journal of Family Psychology*, 25, 336–344.

Bernard, J. (1972). *The Future of Marriage*. New Haven, CT: Yale University Press.

Blekesaune, M. (2008). Partnership Transitions and Mental Distress: Investigating Temporal Order. *Journal of Marriage and Family*, 70, 879–890.

Brim, O.G., et al. (2010). National Survey of Midlife Development in the United States (MIDUS), 1995–1996 [Computer file]. ICPSR02760-v6. Ann Arbor, MI: Inter-University Consortium for Political and Social Research [distributor], 2010-01-06. doi: 10.3886/ICPSR02760.

Brim, O.G., Ryff, C.D., and Kessler, R.C. (2004). The MIDUS National Survey: An Overview. In Brim, O.G., Ryff, C.D., and Kessler, R.C. (Eds.), *How Healthy Are We? A National Study of Well-Being at Midlife* pp. 64–89. Chicago: University of Chicago Press.

Carr, D. and Springer, K.W. (2010). Advances in Families and Health Research in the 21st Century. *Journal of Marriage and Family*, Decade in Review Special Issue, 742–761.

Cherlin, A.J. (2009). *The Marriage-Go-Round: The State of Marriage and Family in America Today*. New York: Knopf.

Child Trends. (2009). *Young Adult Attitudes about Relationships and Marriage: Times May Have Changed, but Expectations Remain High*. Washington, DC: Mindy E. Scott, Erin Schelar, Jennifer Manlove, and Carol Cui. Retrieved from http://www.childtrends.org.

Cruz, J.E., Emery, R.E., and Turkheimer, E. (2012, March 5). Peer Network Drinking Predicts Increased Alcohol Use from Adolescence to Early Adulthood after Controlling for Genetic and Shared Environmental Selection. *Developmental Psychology*. Advance online publication. doi:10.1037/a0027515.

D'Onofrio, B. et al. (2005). A Genetically Informed Study of Marital Instability and Its Association with Offspring Psychopathology. *Journal of Abnormal Psychology, 114*, 1130–1144.

D'Onofrio, B. et al. (2006). A Genetically Informed Study of the Processes Underlying the Association between Parental Marital Instability and Offspring Adjustment. *Developmental Psychology, 42*, 486–499.

D'Onofrio, B. et al. (2007). A Genetically Informed Study of the Intergenerational Transmission of Relationship Instability. *Journal of Marriage and the Family, 69*, 793–809.

Duncan, G.J. and Hoffman, S.D. (1985). Economic Consequences of Marital Instability. In David, M. and Smeeding, T. (Eds.), *Horizontal Equity, Uncertainty and Well-Being* pp. 427–469. Chicago: University of Chicago Press.

Dupre, M.E. and Meadows, S.O. (2007). Disaggregating the Effects of Marital Trajectories on Health. *Journal of Family Issues, 28*, 623–652.

Emery, R.E. (1999). *Marriage, Divorce, and Children's Adjustment* (2d ed.). Thousand Oaks, CA: Sage.

Emery, R.E. (2011). *Renegotiating Family Relationships: Divorce, Child Custody, and Mediation* (2nd ed.). New York: Guilford.

Emery, R.E., Beam, C., and Rowen, J. (2011). Adolescents' Experience of Parental Divorce. In Brown, B. and Prinstein, M. (Eds.), *Encyclopedia of Adolescence*. New York: Academic Press.

Emery, R.E., Waldron, M.C., Kitzmann, K.M., and Aaron, J. (1999). Delinquent Behavior, Future Divorce or Nonmartial Childbearing, and Externalizing Behavior among Offspring: A 14-Year Prospective Study. *Journal of Family Psychology, 13*, 1–12.

Essig, L. and Owens, L. (2009). What If Marriage Is Bad for Us? *The Chronicle of Higher Education: The Chronicle Review* (October 5). Retrieved October 9, 2009 from http://chronicle.com.

Ferraro, K.F. and Farmer, M.M. (1999). Utility of Health Data from Social Surveys: Is There a Gold Standard for Measuring Morbidity? *American Sociological Review, 64*, 303–315.

Glenn, N.D. (2001). Is the Current Concern about American Marriage Warranted? *Virginia Journal of Social Policy and Law, 9*, 5–47.

Gove, W.R., Hughes, M., and Style, C.B. (1983). Does Marriage Have Positive Effects on the Psychological Well-Being of the Individual? *Journal of Health and Human Behavior, 24*, 122–131.

Harden, K.P. et al. (2007a). A Behavior Genetic Investigation of Adolescent Motherhood and Offspring Mental Health Problems. *Journal of Abnormal Psychology, 116*, 667–683.

Harden, K.P. et al. (2007b). Marital Conflict and Conduct Problems in Children-of-Twins. *Child Development, 78*, 1–18.

Harden, K.P. et al. (2008). Rethinking Timing of First Sex and Delinquency. *Journal of Youth and Adolescence, 36*, 141–152.

Hughes, M.E., and Waite, L.J. (2009). Marital Biography and Health at Mid-Life. *Journal of Health and Social Behavior*, 50, 344–358.
Idler, E.L. and Benyamini, Y. (1997). Self-Rated Health and Mortality: A Review of Twenty-Seven Community Studies. *Journal of Health and Social Behavior*, 38, 21–37.
Johnson, D.R. and Wu, J. (2002). An Empirical Test of Crisis, Social Selection, and Role Explanations of the Relationship between Marital Disruption and Psychological Distress: A Pooled Time-Series Analysis of Four-Wave Panel Data. *Journal of Marriage and Family*, 64, 211–224.
Laumann, E.O., Gagnon, J., Michael, R.T., and Michaels, S. (1994). *The Social Organization of Sexuality: Sexual Practices in the United States*. Chicago: University of Chicago Press.
McGue, M. and Lykken, D.T. (1993). Genetic Influence on Risk of Divorce. *Psychological Science*, 3, 368–373.
McLanahan, S., Donahue, E., and Haskins, R. (2005). Introducing Special Issue on Marriage and Child Wellbeing. *The Future of Children*, 15, 3–12.
Mendle, J. et al. (2006). Family Structure and Age at Menarche: A Children-of-Twins Approach. *Developmental Psychology*, 42, 533–542.
Mendle, J. et al. (2009). Associations between Father Absence and Age of First Sexual Intercourse. *Child Development*, 80, 1463–1480.
Pearlin, L.I. and Johnson, J.S. (1977). Marital Status, Life-Strains and Depression. *American Sociological Review*, 42, 704–715.
Pedersen, W. and Blekesaune, M. (2003). Sexual Satisfaction in Young Adulthood: Cohabitation, Committed Dating or Unattached Life? *Acta Sociologica*, 46, 179–193.
Power, C., Rodgers, B., and Hope, S. (1999). Heavy Alcohol Consumption and Marital Status: Disentangling the Relationship in a National Study of Young Adults. *Addiction*, 94, 1477–1487.
Sbarra, D.A. and Nietert, P.J. (2009). Divorce and Death: Forty Years of the Charleston Heart Study. *Psychological Science*, 20, 107–113.
Scarr, S. and McCartney, K. (1983). How People Make Their Own Environments: A Theory of Genotype → Environment Effects. *Developmental Psychology*, 54, 424–435.
Wade, T.J. and Pevalin, D.J. (2004). Marital Transitions and Mental Health. *Journal of Health and Social Behavior*, 45, 155–170.
Waite, L.J. and Gallagher, M. (2000). *The Case for Marriage*. New York: Doubleday.
Wilson, W.J. (1987). *The Truly Disadvantaged: The Inner City, the Underclass, and Public Policy*. Chicago: University of Chicago Press.
Wolfinger, N.H. (2001). The Effects of Family Structure of Origin on Offspring Cohabitation Duration. *Sociological Inquiry*, 71, 293–313.

8

Fragile Families

Debates, Facts, and Solutions

Sara S. McLanahan and Irwin Garfinkel

INTRODUCTION

Nonmarital childbearing increased dramatically in the United States during the latter half of the twentieth century, changing the context in which American children are raised and giving rise to a new family form – *fragile families* – defined as families formed by unmarried parents. As shown in Figure 8.1, the proportion of all children born to unmarried parents grew from about 4 percent in 1940 to nearly 40 percent in 2007, an almost tenfold increase (NCHS). Although the rate of increase was similar for whites and nonwhites, the impact was much more dramatic for nonwhites because they started from a much higher base.

Some analysts argue that the increase in nonmarital childbearing is a sign of progress, reflecting an expansion of individual freedom and the growing economic independence of women (Coontz 1998). To support their claim, they note that similar trends are occurring throughout Western industrialized countries. Other analysts are less sanguine. Pointing to high poverty rates among single mothers in the United States, they argue that the increase in fragile families does not bode well for children and may be contributing to the reproduction of racial and class disparities in future generations (McLanahan and Percheski 2008).

The debate over the consequences of nonmarital childbearing has a long history in the United States, dating back just in the last half-century to 1965 with the release of the well-known and, for some, infamous *Report on the Negro Family*, authored by Daniel Patrick Moynihan (then Assistant Secretary of Labor). According to the report, a "tangle of pathology," consisting of nonmarital childbearing, high male unemployment, and welfare dependence, was weakening the black

The authors thank a consortium of private foundations and the Eunice Kennedy Shriver National Institute of Child Health and Human Development (grants R01 HD369–16) for their support of the Fragile Families and Child Wellbeing Study. We also thank Melanie Wright, Tracy Merone, and Wade Jacobson for their assistance with editing, data analysis, and table preparation.

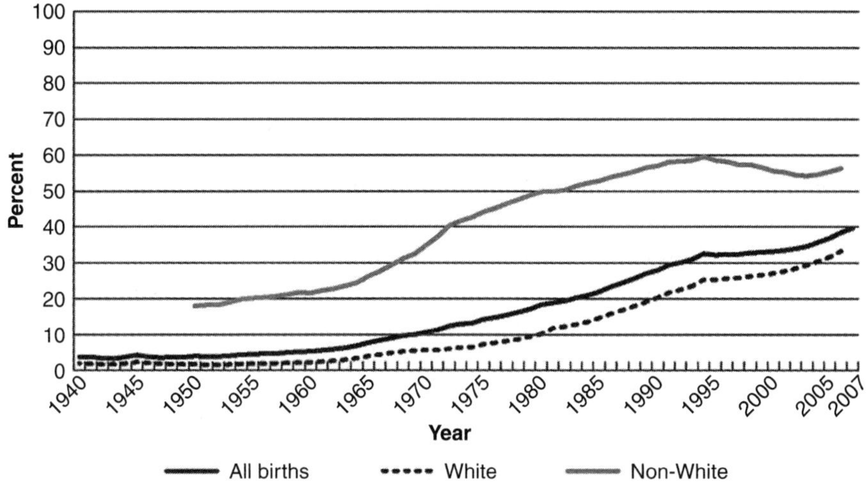

FIGURE 8.1. Percentage of U.S. Births Outside Marriage. *Source*: National Center for Health Statistics.

family and making it difficult for many African Americans to take advantage of their new political rights. Although initially praised by black leaders for focusing national attention on a serious problem, the report soon become the target of harsh and widespread criticism from liberals (and eventually black leaders) for using words like "pathology" and for appearing to attribute the disadvantages of African Americans to family behavior rather than structural factors such as racial discrimination and poverty. In contrast, social conservatives praised the report and used it as evidence for a "culture of poverty" argument that emphasized dysfunctional values and behaviors rather than economic factors as the root cause of poverty among African Americans. In the aftermath of the Moynihan controversy, sociologists and other social scientists avoided the topic of family structure until the 1980s, when William Julius Wilson reopened the debate. In his book on *The Truly Disadvantaged*, Wilson (1988) argued that nonmarital childbearing was contributing to "social disorganization" in low-income communities and undermining the life chances of black children. Like Moynihan, Wilson distinguished between a black middle class, which he saw as moving forward, and a black lower class, which he saw as losing ground.

Today, nonmarital childbearing extends well beyond the lower-class, African-American population. Indeed, the proportion of all births to unmarried mothers was higher among white mothers in 2008 than it was among black mothers in 1965 when the "Moynihan Report" first appeared. Moreover, much of the increase in nonmarital childbearing during the past two decades has been to couples who are cohabiting when their child is born (Cherlin 2005). These changes in the demography of nonmarital childbearing have rekindled old debates while raising new questions about the meaning and potential consequences of these changes in family formation.

THE FRAGILE FAMILY STUDY

Despite the importance of the topic and the intensity of the debate, empirical research on unmarried parents and their children was limited until very recently. Although we knew something from birth records data and census data about the characteristics of women who gave birth outside marriage, information about unmarried fathers was sorely lacking, as was information about the capabilities, values, and relationship quality of unmarried parents. Finally, although we had learned a great deal about the consequences of father absence for mothers and children, most of our knowledge came from studies of divorced parents, who are likely to differ from unmarried parents in important ways (Sigle-Rushton and McLanahan 2007).

To shed some light on these debates and to provide policy makers with better information about the implications of recent trends in nonmarital childbearing, a team of researchers at Columbia and Princeton Universities designed and implemented a large survey of new parents – *The Fragile Families and Child Wellbeing Study*. Between the spring of 1998 and the fall of 2000, interviewers spoke with approximately 5,000 mothers who had recently given birth in hospitals in large U.S. cities, including a large oversample of unmarried mothers. Mothers were interviewed at the hospital soon after giving birth, and fathers were interviewed soon afterward. Parents were asked a series of questions about their economic resources, health, relationship quality, and attitudes toward marriage and parenthood. Both mothers and fathers were reinterviewed when their child was one, three, five, and nine years old. At the three-, five-, and nine-year interviews, the child's primary caregiver (usually the mother) was interviewed in the home, and the child's home environment and cognitive and emotional development were assessed. (A more detailed description of the study design is reported in Appendix A.) In this chapter, we use data from the first five years of the *Fragile Families and Child Wellbeing Study* to address three questions about unmarried parents and their children: first, is nonmarital childbearing a cause for concern; second, if the answer is "yes," what is the source of the problem; and finally, what should be done to solve the problem?

IS NONMARITAL CHILDBEARING A CAUSE FOR CONCERN?

At the time we began our study, there were numerous (and often conflicting) narratives about the nature of parental relationships and capabilities in families formed by unmarried parents (McLanahan 2011). At one extreme were analysts who argued that nonmarital childbearing was not a problem. According to this view, unmarried parents were just like married parents except for a marriage license. Their claim relied heavily on a Scandinavian model where nonmarital childbearing is even more common than it is in the United States, and where most unmarried couples are living

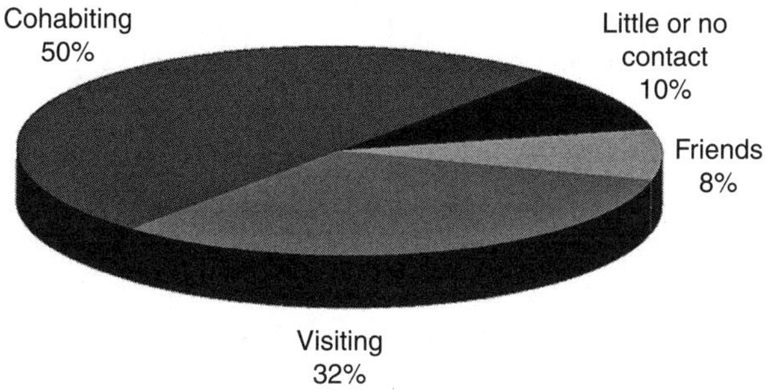

FIGURE 8.2. Unmarried Parents' Relationship Status at Child's Birth. *Source*: The *Fragile Families Study*.

together in stable unions. Other analysts argued that nonmarital childbearing was a cause for concern, although they disagreed sharply over the nature of the problem. One group argued that nonmarital births were the product of casual relationships – "one-night stands" – with minimal commitment on the part of fathers. Another group claimed that couple relationships between unmarried parents were just as committed as relationships in married-parent families, but parents' capabilities and resources were much more limited, hence the title "poor man's marriage." Still others argued that nonmarital childbearing was attributable in large part to the fact that professional women were running up against their "biological time clock" and electing to have children on their own – the Murphy Brown story. The Murphy Brown narrative itself was highly controversial, with some people viewing this behavior as a positive marker of women's independence and others viewing it as morally deviant and setting a bad example (Quayle 1992).

Parental Relationships

Understanding the nature of parental relationships and capabilities in fragile families is a crucial first step toward resolving the debate over whether society should be concerned about the increase in nonmarital births. If unmarried parents are just the same as married parents in terms of their relationships and capabilities, then nonmarital childbearing should probably be viewed as an alternative family form rather than a cause of concern. However, if one or more of the other narratives holds, many people would argue that society should be concerned about the increase in these family forms.

According to the *Fragile Families Study*, a majority of unmarried parents appear to be in committed relationships at the time of their child's birth. As shown in Figure 8.2, fifty percent are living together and another 32 percent are living apart but are romantically involved. In short, more than 80 percent of unmarried parents are in a romantic relationship with one another at the time of their child's birth. Father involvement is also high. More than 95 percent of cohabiting fathers provided financial support or other types of assistance during the pregnancy, and a similar proportion visited the mother and baby at the hospital and planned to be involved in raising the child. Even non-cohabiting fathers show high levels of involvement. Most strikingly, more than 70 percent of fathers that have ended their romantic relationship with the mother say they wanted to help raise their child, and an equally large proportion of mothers say they want the father involved.

In keeping with this picture, unmarried parents are very optimistic about the future of their relationship. More than 90 percent of cohabiting parents, and more than half of non-cohabiting parents, say their chances of marrying the other partner are "fifty/fifty" or better. Parental relationships are mutually supportive, and domestic violence is rare (less than 8 percent).

Capabilities

The Swedish model claims that unmarried parents are just like married parents in terms of their capabilities and resources, whereas the "poor man's marriage" model implies that unmarried parents are much more disadvantaged than married parents. The picture that emerges from the *Fragile Families Study* is consistent with the second narrative. As shown in Table 8.1, unmarried mothers are much younger than married mothers and much more likely to be in their teens. The proportion of teen births is even higher if we focus on mothers having their first child (45 percent). Unwed mothers are less likely to have lived with both of their biological parents growing up and more likely to have had a child by another partner. The prevalence of multi-partnered fertility among unmarried parents, defined as having children by more than one partner, is one of the most significant new findings to have emerged from our study, and we say more about this phenomenon in the next section of the chapter, where we discuss complexity in fragile families.

Most strikingly, unmarried parents are very different from married parents in terms of their human capital and economic status. Less than 3 percent of unmarried parents, compared to 30 percent of married parents, have a college degree – a disparity that translates into lower earnings and high poverty rates. The picture for health and mental health is similar: unmarried parents have more health limitations, more depression, and more drug use than married parents. Moreover, more than 40 percent of unmarried fathers have been incarcerated at some point in their lives.

Finally, we found very little evidence for either the "casual union" or "Murphy Brown" arguments. As noted before, less than 3 percent of unmarried mothers have a college degree, and less than 1 percent meet all of the criteria that are typically associated with the Murphy Brown story: (1) college degree; (2) giving birth for the first time after the age of thirty; and (3) not living with a partner. Casual unions and distant relationships are also rare. At birth, fewer than 10 percent of mothers report having "very little contact" with their child's father.

Thus far, our findings suggest that the "poor man's marriage" narrative comes closest to describing parental relationships in fragile families insofar as half of unmarried

TABLE 8.1. *Parents' demographic characteristics and human capital at birth*

	Mothers			Fathers		
	Married	Cohabiting	Single	Married	Cohabiting	Single
Age (mean)	29.3	24.7	22.6	31.8	27.7	25.6
Teen parent	3.7	17.7	34.3	0.4	17.0	34.2
First birth	35.3	39.4	51.0	34.7	42.7	60.0
Child with another partner	11.7	38.8	34.5	27.1	64.2	76.4
Race						
White, non-Hispanic	48.9	25.9	18.0	50.6	21.1	12.5
Black, non-Hispanic	11.7	29.1	49.1	13.8	33.0	58.4
Hispanic	28.6	41.0	30.1	29.4	43.0	22.5
Other	10.8	4.0	2.8	6.1	2.8	6.6
Immigrant	28.7	22.5	14.1	25.9	21.8	11.9
Two parents growing up	61.9	44.2	35.2	68.1	47.4	36.1
Education						
Less than high school	17.8	41.0	48.8	18.8	40.0	44.9
High school or equivalent	25.5	39.2	34.2	21.4	39.8	34.2
Some college	21.1	17.3	14.3	30.3	17.6	17.2
College or higher	35.7	2.4	2.4	29.5	3.6	3.8
Income						
Earnings (mean)	25,619	11,434	10,764	38,568	20,461	15,893
Worked last year	79.3	83.4	79.40	95.7	91.0	84.3
Poverty status	14.0	32.5	53.1	13.2	33.7	34.1
Not working at birth	–	–	–	5.7	17.0	34.0
Health*						
Poor/fair health	10.4	14.4	17.1	8.1	15.4	12.9
Health limitations	7.1	9.1	11.1	5.4	10.5	14.1
Depression	13.2	16.2	15.7	8.1	9.2	18.0
Heavy drinking	2.0	8.0	7.7	25.1	32.0	21.1
Illegal drugs	0.3	1.7	3.1	1.6	6.0	12.4
Prior incarceration	–	–	–	7.3	34.1	39.3

Source: The *Fragile Families Study*.

parents are living together at birth and most have low human capital. Not all of the evidence is consistent with this story, however. First, half of the parents are *not* living together at birth. Second, a large percentage (more than 80 percent) of unmarried mothers agree with the statement that "a single mother can raise a child just as well as a married mother." The fact that so many mothers view single parenthood as a viable alternative for raising children suggests that these relationships are not just another form of marriage. Finally, and most importantly, despite parents' optimism at the time of their child's birth, most relationships in fragile families do not survive. Only about 35 percent of unmarried couples at birth, compared to 80 percent of married couples, are living together five years after the birth (about half are married and half are cohabiting).

TABLE 8.2. *Mothers' parenting at years 3 and 5*

	Married	Unmarried	Cohabiting	Single
Literacy Activities, Year 3 (0–21)[a]	15.25	14.78	14.70	14.86
Harsh Parenting, Year 3[b]	3.52%	15.05%	13.90%	16.18%
Irregular Bedtimes, Year 5[c]	19.98%	25.16%	23.60%	26.72%

Source: The *Fragile Families Study*.

[a] Mean number of days mother engages in any of three literacy activities in a typical week

[b] Percent of mothers who slapped, spanked, or scolded child during interview

[c] Percent irregular (no regular bedtime or goes to bed at a regular bedtime fewer than four nights a week)

Children's Home Environment

Thus far we have focused on the nature of parental relationships. Relationships are only part of the story, however. To fully assess whether nonmarital childbearing is a concern, we need to know more about the quality of parental investments and the quality of the children's home environments. The most important predictor of a father's investment is whether or not he lives with his child. Thus, the fact that only 35 percent of fathers are living with their child at age five is a worrisome sign. Although in principle a nonresident father could invest as heavily in his child as a resident father, the costs of doing so are much higher (Willis 2000), and such behavior is the exception rather than the rule. Indeed we observe a fairly steep decline in nonresident fathers' involvement over time. Whereas about half of nonresident fathers see their child at least once a month in the first year after the birth, this proportion falls to only 35 percent of nonresident fathers maintaining regular contact by the time the child is five years old. Fathers' financial contributions follow a similar pattern. Whereas nearly a quarter of nonresident fathers make regular cash payments during the first year after birth, this number declines to only 14 percent by year five. Interestingly, whereas the proportion of these men who make regular payments declines over time, the proportion making any payment increases. The increase likely stems from the fact that more of these men are coming under the purview of the formal child support system over time. By the time their child is age five, nearly one-third of fathers who never lived with their child have a formal child support order. (Note that fathers who never lived with their child may be less committed to their child than other fathers.)

As shown in Table 8.2, the quality of mothers' parenting also differs by marital status. Mothers who were unmarried at birth engage in fewer literacy activities with their child, are much more likely to use harsh discipline (yelling and spanking), and are less likely to maintain stable household routines such as having a regular bedtime. All of these behaviors are known to be important predictors of children's health and development.

TABLE 8.3. *Child well-being at year 5*

	Married	Unmarried	Cohabiting	Single
Obesity[a]	12.69%	19.13%	19.42%	18.83%
Asthma[b]	10.22%	18.26%	15.76%	20.72%
Very good or excellent health[c]	91.47%	87.35%	86.83%	87.88%
Vocabulary skills (40–139)[d]	97.39	90.78	91.38	90.18
Internalizing behaviors (0–17)[e]	3.68	3.80	3.80	3.80
Externalizing behaviors (0–34)[f]	5.71	6.94	6.29	7.56

Source: The *Fragile Families Study*.
[a] Percent obese (95th percentile or higher)
[b] Percent of mothers told by a health care professional that child has asthma
[c] Percent of mothers reporting that child is in very good or excellent health
[d] Mean score on vocabulary skills
[e] Mean score on internalizing behaviors (e.g., shy, withdrawn)
[f] Mean score on externalizing behaviors (e.g., aggressive, rule-breaking)

Child Well-Being

Children's health and well-being are the final, and arguably the most important, indicators of whether we should be concerned about the increase in nonmarital childbearing. If the children born to unmarried parents are doing just as well as the children born to married parents, most analysts would agree that society would be much less concerned about the changes in family formation that have occurred during the past four decades. Unfortunately, our data point to fairly large disparities in children's health and development based on parents' marital status at birth. Table 8.3 reports information on five different measures of child well-being: obesity, asthma, overall health, cognitive ability, internalizing behavior (shy, anxious, withdrawn), and externalizing behavior (aggression and poor concentration). These indicators are commonly used to measure children's health and development, and each of them has been found to be associated with long-term health and well-being.

As shown in Table 8.3, children born to unmarried parents are worse off than children born to married parents in many different domains. They are less likely to be in good health, and their rates of obesity and asthma are higher. Asthma rates are especially high among children living with single mothers at age five. Cognitive scores are also much lower among children born to unmarried mothers – nearly 7 percentage points on a 100-point scale. Finally, we find marital status differences in both internalizing and externalizing behaviors, which are associated, respectively, with depression and delinquency in adolescence.

WHAT IS THE SOURCE OF THE PROBLEM?

In the previous section we argued that society should be concerned about families formed by unmarried parents for at least four reasons: (1) parental resources are much lower; (2) parental relationships are less stable; (3) parental investments in children are lower; and (4) child outcomes are poorer. In making our case, we simply compared the conditions and outcomes of children born to unmarried parents with those of children born to married parents in each of these domains. Although these comparisons are useful for documenting the existence of disparities across family types, they do not tell us anything about how these disparities are produced. Specifically, they do not tell us whether a nonmarital birth itself plays a causal role in producing these negative outcomes, or whether the problems we described earlier result entirely from factors that predate the child's birth.

Just as researchers disagree about whether or not nonmarital childbearing is a problem, they also disagree about the source of the problem. One group of researchers argues that the disparities in stability and poor outcomes between married and unmarried parents are a result of differences in parents' material conditions at birth, including differences in education, earnings, and health. In contrast, another group argues that disparities are stemming from differences in culture – that is, differences in the values parents place on marriage and/or differences in behaviors necessary for forming and maintaining stable relationships. The first view is best articulated by W. J. Wilson in his book, *The Truly Disadvantaged* (1988). Wilson argues that the decline in marriage and increase in nonmarital childbearing among African Americans after 1970 were a result of changes in the macro economy that led to a decline in jobs for low-skilled men. According to this view, despite the increase in women's employment, men are still viewed as the primary breadwinners, and their "marriageability" depends heavily on their ability to perform that role. The corrosive effects of men's inability to support their families is documented in several well-known ethnographies, including Bakke's (1940) study of families in the Great Depression and Liebow's (1968) study of street corner life in the 1960s. Furstenberg's (2007) review of the ethnographic literature finds a common pattern described in these ethnographies where male unemployment is followed by marital strain or dissolution and men's retreat from involvement in family life. Recent ethnographies of family life, such as those by Anderson (1990), Edin and Kefalas (2005) and Waller (2002), also find male unemployment and underemployment to be major obstacles to marriage and stable families.

The second view is best articulated by J. Q. Wilson in his book, *The Marriage Problem*. Taking a more cultural (as opposed to a structural or material) position, Wilson argues that Americans are much more individualistic today than they were in the past and less willing to make the compromises and sacrifices necessary to form stable marriages. He also argues that changes in norms about sex outside marriage have made single motherhood more acceptable than it was in the past. Highlighting a different aspect of culture, Orlando Patterson in his book, *Rituals of Blood* (1998), argues that high levels of gender mistrust, which began under slavery and continue to the present day, have made it more difficult for African-American couples to establish stable unions.

The *Fragile Families Study* provides some support for each of these perspectives. The data presented earlier on parents' capabilities, attitudes, and relationships at birth are consistent with W. J. Wilson's argument about the poor economic prospects of unmarried fathers. They also are consistent with J. Q. Wilson's and Orlando Patterson's arguments about the widespread acceptance of single motherhood and high levels of gender mistrust. Regarding marriage attitudes, the data do *not* support the claim that unmarried parents are rejecting marriage. Indeed, in-depth interviews with a subset of parents after their children's birth suggest that most unmarried parents place a high value on marriage and have "high hopes" for marrying the other parent. The major difference in the relationships of these parents and their married counterparts is that unmarried parents express much more uncertainty about the future of their unions, which are better described as "trial marriages."

Not only do we see that that married and unmarried parents differ with respect to their material resources and culture; additional analyses show that each of the previously highlighted factors – fathers' earnings, parents' attitudes toward marriage and single motherhood, and mothers' trust of the opposite sex – are strong predictors of whether or not unmarried parents stay together after the birth (either through marriage or cohabitation).

Our Argument

In this section, we report findings indicating that, net of the economic and cultural factors that predate the birth, the nature of the parents' relationship at birth has an independent, *causal* effect on each of the outcomes we care about – family stability, parental investments, and child well-being. We argue that in the United States, nonmarital childbearing signals a fertility regime in which women have children *while they are searching for a long-term partner*. These mothers are not rejecting marriage, nor do they want to raise their child alone. However, unlike their more educated peers, they are willing to have a child in the context of a "trial marriage." In their book, *Promises I Can Keep*, Edin and Kefalas (2005) argue that low-income women place a high value on children and are confident of their ability to be good mothers. In contrast, these women have serious doubts about their ability to maintain a stable marriage and are reluctant to marry until they are sure their partnership will last. Such a fertility regime inevitably leads to high levels of partnership instability and multi-partnered fertility. Instability, in turn, reduces children's life chances by increasing stress and uncertainty and undermining parental investments. Complexity has a similar effect by creating conflicting loyalties and increasing the transaction costs of managing a family.

Instability and Complexity

As noted in the previous section, nearly two-thirds of unmarried parents' relationships have dissolved by the time the child is age five. Once their romantic relationship

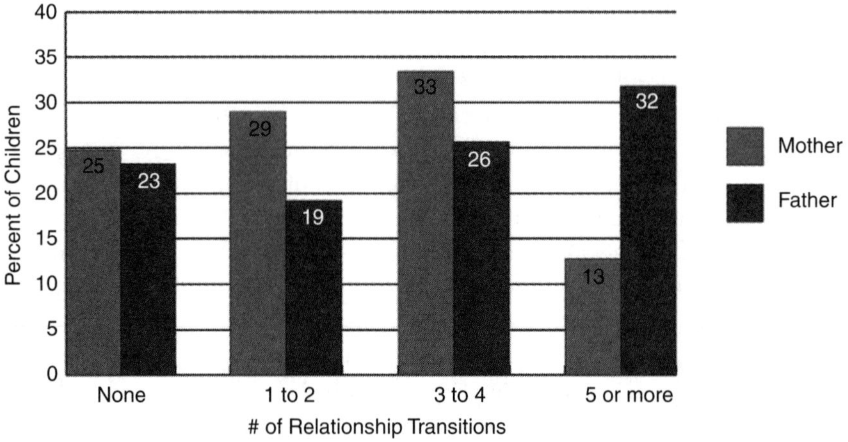

FIGURE 8.3. Children's Exposure to Relationship Stability (birth through age five). *Source*: The *Fragile Families Study*.

ends, most parents go on to form new partnerships and, in many instances, to have children with new partners. The search for new partners results in high levels of instability for many children. As shown in Figure 8.3, more than half of the mothers who are unmarried at their child's birth go on to date or live with a new partner by the time their child is age five. Twenty-four percent of unmarried mothers have one new partner, 18 percent have two new partners, and 10 percent have three or more new partners. Unmarried fathers follow a similar pattern. High rates of partnership instability during mothers' peak fertility years lead to high levels of family complexity, defined as families in which the parents have children by different partners. As shown in Figure 8.4, about 37 percent of unmarried mothers and 40 percent of unmarried fathers have already had a child by another partner at the time of the focal child's birth. These numbers increase to 45 percent and 47 percent, respectively, by the time the child is age five.

The Consequences

A large body of research indicates that family instability is harmful for mothers as well as children (Fomby and Cherlin 2007; Osborne and McLanahan 2007; Wu and Martinson 1993). Whereas most of this research has focused on the negative consequences associated with divorce and remarriage (see Sigle-Rushton and McLanahan 2004 for a review), more recent work has begun to examine instability among unmarried couples. These studies indicate that mothers' partnership changes, including the beginning of new partnerships and the dissolution of existing partnerships, are associated with declines in mothers' physical and mental health (Meadows, McLanahan, and Brooks-Gunn 2008). Although the effect of a single transition on mothers' health

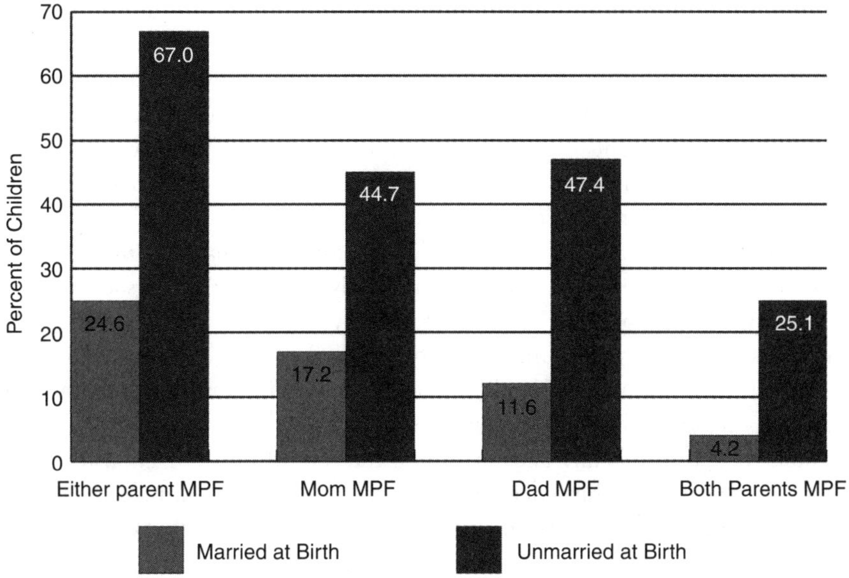

FIGURE 8.4. Children's Exposure to Multiple-Partner Fertility (by age five)

is short-lived, dissipating rapidly over time, mothers who experience multiple transitions do not have an opportunity to recover from these temporary shocks and thus experience ongoing health problems.

Partnership instability also reduces the quality of mothers' parenting, measured as maternal stress, harsh punishment, and engagement in literacy activities (Beck et al. 2010). Both residential changes and changes in dating partners are associated with increases in maternal stress and harsh parenting, with recent transitions showing stronger effects than more distal transitions. Whereas the effects of instability on stress are larger for mothers with low levels of education, the negative effects on literacy activities are larger for mothers with at least some college.

Instability reduces health and increases mental health problems for fathers, just as it does for mothers. However, whereas entrances into new partnerships had negative effects for mothers' health, this is not the case for fathers (Meadows 2009). Instability also reduces the quantity and quality of fathers' investments in children. As noted earlier, nonresident fathers' involvement declines over time as mothers and fathers form new partnerships. Interestingly, mothers' new partnerships have a more negative impact on fathers' involvement than fathers' new partnerships, although both are important. Finally, partnership instability is negatively associated with children's verbal ability and positively associated with behavior problems, especially among boys (Cooper, Osborne, Beck, and McLanahan 2010; Craigie, Brooks-Gunn, and Waldfogel 2010). Instability may also increase asthma and obesity, although the evidence for a health effect is mixed (Bzostek and Beck 2011); Craigie et al. 2010).

Just as research on instability has focused primarily on divorce and remarriage, most of what we know about the negative effects of family complexity comes from studies of parents who remarry after a divorce. The stepfamily literature indicates that blended families have more problems than traditional two-parent families (Hetherington, Cox, and Cox 1985). While only a handful of researchers have examined complexity in families formed by unmarried parents, the evidence to date suggests it plays an important role in reducing children's long-term well-being. We know, for example, that fathers' prior children reduce the quality of mother-father relationships and increase union dissolution (Carlson et al. 2004; Carlson, McLanahan, and Brooks-Gunn 2008). In-depth interviews with parents indicate that jealousy is a serious problem for many unmarried couples, and mothers often object to fathers spending time with children in other households because it means spending time with the children's mothers (Edin and England 2007). Not only do fathers' prior children reduce the quality and stability of the mother-father relationship while parents are together; the birth of a new child with another partner undermines their ability to cooperate once their romantic relationship is over. More generally, contact between the nonresident father and child is very sensitive to the presence of new partners, especially mothers' new partners. When a mother forms a new partnership, the nonresident father's involvement declines; when the new partnership ends, his involvement increases. This pattern of contact is similar when fathers have a new partner, although the association tends to be weaker (Carlson et al. 2008; Tach, Mincy, and Edin 2010). The fact that fathers' involvement declines when either the mother or the father has a new partner may be attributable to the fact that fathers have less time to spend with their nonresident children. It also may stem from the fact that the new partner objects to his spending time with children from a previous relationship. In short, complexity may create a trade-off for fathers between being a good parent and being a good partner.

Mothers' having children with new partners has two notable effects. First, it reduces mothers' access (or perceptions of access) to friends and relatives willing to provide instrumental support, especially financial support (Harknett and Knab 2007). Second, when a mother has a child with a new partner, her other children exhibit more externalizing problems or "acting out." The latter finding is specific to new half-siblings and does not occur with the birth of a full sibling.

WHAT SHOULD BE DONE?

Fragile families are both a consequence and a cause of economic disadvantage. At the time of their child's birth, compared with married couples, couples who have children outside marriage are highly disadvantaged – younger, less healthy, and much less educated. Moreover, although a majority of unmarried parents have "high hopes" for a future together, a nontrivial proportion of these young men and women express distrust of the opposite sex and believe that a single mother can raise a child as well as a married mother can. Together these findings support the claim that nonmarital childbearing is a consequence of disadvantage. They also suggest that both economic and cultural factors have contributed to the rise in fragile families.

Nonmarital childbearing exacerbates preexisting disadvantage by reducing opportunities for children as they grow up, primarily through family instability and complexity. Unmarried couples are much more likely than married couples to end their relationships, and the ongoing search for new partners leads to high levels of instability, periods of single motherhood, and declining fathers' involvement in these families. Moreover, because most unmarried parents in fragile families are in their peak childbearing years, new partnerships frequently lead to new children and ultimately to complex households in which mothers are forced to negotiate with several different fathers over visitation and over child support requirements, which many fathers have a hard time meeting because they have financial obligations to children in other households. Instability and complexity reduce parents' economic resources and increase mental health problems that, in turn, reduce the quantity and quality of the parenting that children receive. Ultimately, inadequate resources and poor parenting undermine children's opportunities, thus reproducing inequality in the next generation.

The challenge for social policy is to reduce the number of fragile families and to invest in the children born into fragile families to ensure they receive the support they need to grow into healthy, productive adults. Investments in children can be made directly by providing health and education services to them and indirectly by making their parents and families more economically and socially secure. For several reasons, investing in the children should be given priority. First, many investments in children, especially children in poor and fragile families, are very productive and more than pay for themselves in terms of reductions in future government and social costs. Second, a large proportion of American children are currently growing up in fragile families, and no matter how successful we are in reducing prevalence, these families will be with us for a long time. Third, investing in these children will not only increase their future productivity and well-being, but also reduce the chances that they will reproduce fragile families themselves. Investing in children is surely an important way and, indeed, may well be the most effective way, to reduce the future prevalence of fragile families. It is also important to reduce the number of children who grow up in fragile families because such children are disadvantaged by the family form. Social policy is unlikely to ever make up fully for the disadvantage.

Good investment opportunities in children – both direct and indirect – abound (Garfinkel et al. 2010; Haskins and Sawhill 2010; Waldfogel 2010; multiple issues of *The Future of Children*). Many of the best investments in children in fragile families are from programs that are targeted at all children rather than limited to fragile families. Universal programs are superior to targeted programs in terms of their effects on the prevalence of fragile families, as well as more generally. Programs that are targeted at fragile families, single-parent families, or poor families alter the relative costs of living in such a family and may therefore lead to increases in fragile families. Programs that limit benefits to the poor reduce benefits as income increases and, thereby, put a tax on both earnings and marriage. Programs that limit benefits to single parents or fragile families tax marriage. One of the many virtues of universal programs such as national health insurance, universal pre-kindergarten, and paid parental leave is that, by virtue of being universal, they do not alter the relative price of being married or single. Safety-net programs for single mothers – Temporary Assistance for Needy Families and, before it, Aid to Families with Dependent Children – but also more general safety-net programs such as public housing, Medicaid, and child care create incentives for couples to avoid marriage and live together informally so that the earnings of fathers will not be reported, resulting in exclusion from the programs. They also discourage legitimate work, encourage underground work, create poverty traps (Atkinson 1999), stigmatize the poor (Rainwater 1982), and undermine social cohesion and trust (Kumlin and Rothstein 2004). In contrast, floors, or universal programs, like universal elementary and secondary public education, Social Security, Medicare, and, in all other rich countries, national health insurance, provide benefits to all citizens. As a consequence, floors prevent poverty, reduce dependence on safety nets, integrate the poor into mainstream society, and increase the productivity and economic security of all citizens. (For a more extended discussion, see Garfinkel et al. 2010.) Thus, our overarching approach is to increase the resources of fragile families primarily through universal programs in order to increase incentives for marriage, work, and upward mobility.

But, even though programs that are based on income or that target broken or fragile families – like TANF and child support assurance, respectively – tax marriage, this negative effect must be weighed against the positive effects of income security on child development and eventually perhaps also on marriage.

Yet, no single investment or approach is a magic bullet. Investments should begin at birth (or before) and continue throughout childhood. Here we focus on just a few particularly promising programs for the first five years of childhood that, taken together, would notably improve the lives and adult outcomes of children in fragile families. We begin with two direct investments in child health and education: universal health insurance for children and universal preschool education. In the following section, we discuss investments in the economic and social security of fragile families, which vary in the degree of targeting.

Direct Investments in Children

There is particularly strong evidence that the benefits exceed the costs for two direct investments in children: health insurance and education. A universal health insurance system for children, including prenatal care, would constitute a very productive investment in all children, including most especially those in fragile families. Past expansions in public insurance produced significant gains in child health outcomes (Currie 2006). Currie and Gruber (1996a, 1996b) find that the 30 percent increase in Medicaid eligibility of pregnant women during the 1980s and early 1990s reduced infant mortality by 8.5 percent and child mortality by 8 percent. More health insurance coverage at young ages is associated with better health status as children become older (Currie, Decker, and Lin 2008). Expansions in coverage are also associated with a 22 percent reduction in preventable hospitalizations (Dafny and Gruber 2000). Benefits from Medicaid expansion are greatest for the lowest income groups because they are the least likely to have private insurance and the most unhealthy and in need of care. They also benefit children in higher income groups. Using conventional economic estimates of the value of a life, the benefits for children in the highest income group still exceeded the costs – just in terms of the lives saved (Currie and Gruber 1996b). Though Medicaid and State Children's Health Insurance Program now cover the vast majority of poor parents and children, 13 percent of fragile families as compared to 8 percent of married families have no health insurance. Twenty percent of unwed mothers, as compared to 12 percent of married mothers, went without early prenatal care. While a universal health insurance system that provides free prenatal, postnatal, and well-baby care might not entirely close the gaps in preventive medical care service use between children in fragile families and children in married families, it would certainly reduce the gaps.

The recent health care legislation takes a huge stride toward universal health insurance. But the stride is slow and, even when completed in a few years following 2014, will still fall short. A truly universal program could build on the current employer-based system, or it could be modeled after Medicare and financed by payroll or income taxes. We prefer the latter because it is a more equitable way of financing a universal public service and because it is a practical method of reducing rampant inequality (Garfinkel et al. 2010).

Another direct investment that is just as important as health is universal preschool for three- and four-year-olds. Seventy percent of children age three to five whose mothers are college-educated attend preschool, compared with only 38 percent of children whose mothers did not complete high school (Karoly and Bigelow 2005). Among children in the *Fragile Families Study*, only 25 percent of children born to unmarried parents attended preschool at age three, as compared with 31 percent of children born to married parents. Children from fragile families have the most to gain from preschool, and the broader society will benefit the most from educating these children in high-quality public schools beginning at age three.

The benefits of high-quality early childhood education exceed the costs, especially for disadvantaged children. James Heckman reports in *Science* (2006) that the present discounted value of the benefits of the Perry preschool program was nearly nine times the costs – or about $144,000! Evaluations of high-quality preschool programs, including Head Start, also find positive effects.[1]

Universal high-quality preschool would produce much smaller benefits for more advantaged children, for two reasons. Many are already enrolled in such programs, and more advantaged children are less at risk for special education, grade retention, dropping out of school, crime, and welfare dependence. That does not mean, however, that the benefits would be zero. A Rand Corporation study by Lynn Karoly and James Bigelow (2005) of a universal preschool program in California found that half of all students who use special education, get held back a grade, or drop out of school are from families in the middle three quintiles of the income distribution. Moreover, there is some direct evidence of positive effects of preschool on more advantaged children. Assuming that the benefits decline gradually from the highest for those most at risk to zero for those least at risk, the study finds that for Californians the benefits of universal preschool exceed costs by 2.6 to 1.

Whereas universal high-quality preschool education would be a good investment for any state and for the nation as a whole, low-quality preschool education may not be a good investment and might even do more harm than good.[2] The Perry preschool experiment suggests that what children need to learn in preschool is to interact well in a group, to sit still at times, and to get excited about and engaged in learning.

Investing in Parents in Fragile Families

Investments in the health, education, and economic security of parents improve their functioning and thereby improve the well-being and development of their children. In this section, we focus on one program that is relevant for all children – paid parental leave – and three that are particularly salient for fragile families: child support assurance, marriage and fatherhood programs, and reducing mass incarceration. Despite evidence that breast-feeding notably increases child health (American Academy of Pediatrics 2005), only half of the children in fragile families are breast-fed, and the average duration of breast-feeding is nineteen weeks. The comparable figures for children in married-parent families are 73 percent and twenty-six weeks.

[1] The only other experiment with high-quality early child education and care directed at very disadvantaged children that was initiated long enough ago to allow for follow-up of the children through adulthood also finds equally impressive long-term benefits. But the Abecedarian program provided high-quality care beginning a few months after birth until the children entered kindergarten. For an outstanding review of the literature on the short-term and long-term effects of early childhood education, see Karoly and Bigelow (2005).

[2] There is evidence that boys who spend substantial time in average child care are more likely to have behavioral problems. On the other hand, boys who are randomly assigned to high-quality child care do no worse or better in terms of behavioral problems (Waldfogel 2006, pp. 56–62).

An increasing body of scientific evidence suggests that children from all income groups would benefit from paid parental leave during their first year of life (Waldfogel 2006). Paid family leave encourages mothers and fathers to take time off from work and care for their newborn infants. Research based on differences in parental leave policies across rich nations and within nations over time finds that longer periods of leave are associated with more and longer breast-feeding and better child health, especially postneonatal mortality (Ruhm 2000; Tanaka 2005). Parents also benefit. Longer periods of paid family leave (across and within rich nations) are associated with lower maternal mortality (Tanaka 2005) and higher maternal mental health (Chatterji and Markowitz 2005).

Because eligibility for paid parental leave is contingent on having work and earnings, such a policy reinforces work even as it releases parents from work for a time-limited period to care for their newborns. Paid parental leave also creates an incentive for women to delay childbirth until they have established a work record that enables them to qualify for the benefit. Universal paid parental leave polices have been adopted in all rich countries except Australia and the United States (Gornick and Meyers 2008). A number of states and employers within the United States have made pioneering efforts. California, Washington, and New Jersey have adopted paid family leave programs as extensions of state unemployment and disability insurance programs. Based on the scientific evidence of its productivity and equity effects, these countries, employers, and states have made wise decisions, which other states and eventually the United States as a whole would do well to imitate. Federal legislation to nationalize the program is desirable. The legislation could create a federal/state program along the lines of unemployment insurance, which allows for great variations across states, or a pure federal program like old age insurance, or something in between.

Another policy that increases parental investments in children is *child support assurance*. Most children in fragile families will live apart from one of their natural parents before reaching adulthood. Indeed, more than half of all American children will do so (Bumpass and Lu 2000). The overwhelming majority will live in a single-mother family. These children are disadvantaged compared with those in two-parent families precisely because there is only one parent. Just as Social Security Survivor's Insurance is a social program designed to ensure that parents who die can support their children, a child support assurance system that both enforces the obligation of living parents to share income with their children and undergirds the system with a public guarantee of a minimum level of support would ensure that parents who live apart from their children nonetheless support them (Garfinkel 1992).

In the United States, states and the federal government have already substantially strengthened enforcement of private child support. Improvements on the collection side are still needed to make the system more equitable and efficient. A particularly salient concern is to end the exceptionally harsh treatment of fathers from low-income and fragile families. Offices of child support enforcement routinely impose much stiffer child support obligations (as a percentage of income) on poor fathers (Huang et al. 2005). Low-income fathers are more likely to be ordered to pay amounts that exceed state guidelines than middle- and upper-income fathers. Frequently the child support obligations imposed on low-income fathers are unreasonably high. A large number of these unrealistic obligations appear to arise because child support agencies or the courts base orders not on fathers' actual earnings, but on presumptive minimum earnings (e.g., the minimum wage for full-time, full-year work) or on how much the father earned in the past. Some fathers are required to pay back the mother's welfare or Medicaid birthing costs. Many fathers who become unemployed or incarcerated build up huge arrearages (debts) during these periods of unemployment. Such onerous child support obligations are rarely paid in full, but they do prompt fathers to avoid legitimate work where their wages are easily attached, and they breed resentment on the part of fathers and mothers toward the system and perhaps toward each other. Imprisonment for nonpayment of support exacerbates this negative dynamic. Evidence from the Fragile Families and Child Wellbeing Study indicates that most unmarried fathers in urban areas face substantial barriers to obtaining stable jobs that would allow them to make regular child support payments. Half of these fathers have a history of incarceration, 40 percent have not completed high school, and more than half have children with more than one woman, indicating multiple child support obligations (Sinkewicz and Garfinkel 2009). Given what we know about the low earnings capacity of most unmarried and virtually all poor fathers, these enforcement practices are not likely to be effective and are likely to have unintended negative consequences.

Equally important, enforcing private support is inherently limited (Nepomnyaschy and Garfinkel 2010). Child support from fathers with low and irregular earnings, at best, will be low and irregular. The Scandinavian countries and a few of the continental European nations have advanced maintenance benefits that guarantee minimum child support payments and thereby create a floor in the child support system (Kahn and Kamerman 1988; Kunz et al. 2001).

Creating a child support floor – a publicly financed minimum child support benefit – that is conditional on being legally entitled to receive private child support reduces the poverty and insecurity of single mothers and their children and increases mothers' incentives to cooperate in identifying the fathers of their children, establishing paternity and securing a child support award (Garfinkel 1992).[3] Assured child

[3] Reducing welfare benefits by one dollar for each dollar of child support paid reduces mothers' incentive to cooperate and fathers' incentive to pay child support. Counting only a portion of support in determining eligibility and benefits would increase cooperation and payments. It would also increase costs, at least in the short run. In the long run, however, if the proportion of fathers paying support increases sufficiently, it might not even increase costs. Rather than restoring the old AFDC $50 set-aside for child support payments, Congress should consider requiring or encouraging states to ignore a substantial portion – say, 50 percent – of child support payments in determining TANF eligibility and payments.

support, like other universal benefits, will further reduce the dependence of single mothers on TANF and other safety net programs.

Minimum benefits are common in social insurance programs. The enforcement features of the American system of assuring child support increasingly resemble social insurance. Nonresident fathers are required to pay a share of their income for child support, and the obligations are deducted from their paychecks. Adding a minimum benefit to the system is consistent with this evolution. An assured child support benefit is a relatively cheap floor that would substantially reduce the poverty and economic insecurity of single mothers and their children and simultaneously strengthen child support enforcement.[4]

Responsible Fatherhood and Healthy Marriage Programs

We lump responsible fatherhood and marriage programs together because they have a common focus on strengthening family relationships. The fatherhood grant program, initiated by President Clinton in 1999, funds around 100 projects that promote responsible fatherhood; they help community-based organizations and others run programs that provide responsible parenting services (including encouraging fathers to make their child support payments) and economic stability services (including employment or skills training assistance). The marriage grant program, initiated by President George W. Bush in 2002, funds 125 community-based marriage projects. Grantees include churches, postsecondary schools, county and state governments, nonprofit and for-profit entities, and faith-based organizations. Most of the programs provide relationship and marriage education for low-income couples, but some conduct marriage education for high school students. Others provide divorce reduction programs, and still others combine educational activities with public advertising campaigns on the value of healthy marriage and the availability of services.

Providing parents with skills to strengthen family relationships has worked with middle-class parents and holds promise of working with lower-class parents (Cowan et al. 2010). If these programs improve relationship skills, they are likely to increase family stability and thereby benefit children. But only a few of the programs for couples, a handful of fatherhood programs, and most recently, one set of marriage programs (Wood 2010) have been systematically evaluated. No research has investigated whether interventions may have different effects when unmarried fathers live with or apart from their child. Furthermore, even though the marriage programs appeared to have positive effects on parent relationships in some sites, the overall effects across all sites and ethnic groups are zero (Wood et al. 2010). Finally,

4 So long as the guaranteed minimum benefit is conditioned on legal entitlement to support, the costs of even a very generous minimum benefit are modest – in 1985, it was less than $5 billion (Meyer et al. 1992). If the benefit is not conditioned on entitlement to private child support, the incentive to obtain legal entitlement is eliminated and costs increase substantially.

although programs for couples or fathers tout the potential benefits for children, they rarely assess child outcomes systematically. Both fatherhood and marriage programs should be pursued and evaluated. Marriage programs could be expanded to include employment and training and mental health components. Fatherhood programs could be expanded to include mothers and could incorporate some elements of the marriage programs. Rigorous evaluations should be conducted to determine what works.

Reducing Mass Incarceration

So far, all of the investments we have discussed would add resources to the child's family. Incarceration reduces family resources. By the time their children are age five, half of the fathers in fragile families have been incarcerated at some point in their lives. Incarceration rates in the United States have grown by more than 500 percent in the past thirty years; today they are five to eight times higher than rates in Canada and Western Europe. By the middle of 2007, an estimated 1.7 million children (2.3 percent of all U.S. children under eighteen) had a parent, most often a father, in state or federal prison (Glaze and Maruschak 2009), and hundreds of thousands of children had a parent in a local jail. Incarceration is far from a universal experience. The prison boom has been concentrated among those already on the periphery of society: black and (to a lesser degree) white men with little schooling – the same segments of society in which fragile families are most likely to be formed (Wacquant 2010; Wildeman and Western 2010).

Imprisonment diminishes the earnings of fathers in fragile families, compromises their health, contributes to family breakup, reduces familial resources, increases material hardships, and adds to the deficits of their vulnerable children (Wildeman and Western 2010; Geller et al. 2011; Schwartz-Soicher et al. 2011). Ending mass imprisonment would, therefore, increase children's resources while reducing the prevalence of fragile families. Providing better support to men and women returning home from prison could also indirectly benefit children by diminishing recidivism rates and improving employment among ex-prisoners.

Mandatory sentencing laws should be revised in accord with the recommendations of the United States Sentencing Commission. Community programs that work with adolescents and their parents are more effective than imprisonment in preventing subsequent offending and also more cost-effective (Greenwood 2008). Policy makers should make every effort to modify federal and state mandatory sentencing laws to keep young offenders out of prison.

Rather than imprisoning drug offenders and parolees who violate the technical conditions of their parole (as opposed to committing new crimes), we should rely instead on inexpensive and effective alternatives such as intensive community supervision, drug treatment, and graduated sanctions that allow parole and probation officers to respond to violations without immediately resorting to prison sentences.

Reducing Prevalence

To the extent that they increase the human capital and the economic and social security of children in fragile families, all of the previously discussed programs are likely to reduce the future prevalence of fragile families. In this section, we first describe how investments in children described earlier – increasing human capital, increasing economic security, continuing strong child support enforcement, and reducing mass incarceration – will affect the prevalence of fragile families. We conclude with a discussion of programs to avoid unintended pregnancies and delay childbearing.

That increases in human capital will lead to increases in marriage and family stability – and therefore to decreases in fragile families – makes sense intuitively. Increased human capital leads to higher earnings, more security, more confidence and trust, and so on. The intuition also has strong empirical support. Educational attainment – a critical element of human capital – is not only a strong predictor of earnings, but is also one of the strongest predictors of marriage and family stability. While part of the association is undoubtedly attributable to unmeasured traits of adults that affect educational attainment, earnings, and marriage, there is a plethora of research that finds evidence of a causal relationship between education and earnings (Goldin and Katz 2008) and some research that finds evidence of a causal relationship between education and teenage nonmarital childbearing (Wolfe, Wilson, and Haveman 2001).

In theory, strong child support enforcement could either reduce or increase nonmarital births. Strong enforcement increases the costs of nonmarital births to fathers, but reduces the costs to mothers. Empirical evidence from cross-state comparisons over time indicates that strong child support enforcement deters nonmarital births (Garfinkel et al 2003). While it is possible that the more equitable and humane treatment of low-income fathers that we recommend in this chapter would weaken the deterrent effect and thereby increase nonmarital childbearing, research on deterrence of crime indicates that certainty and swiftness are more important than severity of punishment (Durlauf and Nagin, 2011). Thus, the collection-side reforms we recommend are not likely to weaken the deterrence effect on men.

Last, mass incarceration undermines marriage. It is hard to imagine that we can make serious headway in reducing the number of fragile families if we continue incarcerating such a large proportion of poorly educated, low-income men.

Programs to Avoid Unintended Pregnancies and Delay Initial Childbearing

Anything that encourages children from poor, near-poor, lower-middle- and even middle-class families to delay childbearing until they have found a partner with whom they can form a stable union will reduce the prevalence of fragile families. Men and women with college degrees – that is, mostly children from upper-middle and upper-income families – are delaying childbearing until they find suitable marriage partners. Their divorce rates are at 1950s levels. As a result, their children are experiencing more stability and security. The challenge to social policy with regards to fragile families is to extend these benefits from top to bottom.

Isabel Sawhill, Adam Thomas, and Emily Monea (2010) find that (1) mass media campaigns that encourage men to use condoms, (2) teen pregnancy prevention programs that discourage sexual activity and educate teens about contraception use, and (3) Medicaid programs that subsidize contraception all reduce pregnancy rates among unmarried couples and save more than enough public dollars to cover their costs. Though most expensive in tax terms, the Medicaid expansion has the highest benefit-cost ratio. A provision in the new health care legislation gives states the option to cover additional women with family-planning services without the need for a waiver, as required under current law. This reform represents a positive step, but how big the step will be depends on state's willingness to adopt such policies, which, given the current fiscal condition of states, is likely to be small in the near future. The Obama administration's plan to expand teen pregnancy programs, now funded by Congress and being aggressively implemented, holds great promise for further reductions in teen pregnancy rates. But nothing has been done to promote media campaigns encouraging men to use condoms. Spending on such a social marketing campaign would be good policy and would pay for itself.

CONCLUSION

Fragile families are both a consequence and a cause of economic disadvantage. Couples who have children outside marriage, as compared to married couples, are highly disadvantaged – younger, less healthy, and much less educated. Nonmarital childbearing exacerbates preexisting disadvantage by reducing opportunities for children, primarily through family instability and complexity. Instability and complexity reduce parents' economic resources and increase mental health problems that, in turn, reduce the quantity and quality of the parenting that children receive, thus reproducing inequality in the next generation.

The challenge for social policy is to reduce the number of fragile families and to invest in the children born into fragile families to ensure they receive the support they need to grow into healthy, productive adults. Reducing the number of children that grow up in fragile families is important because such children are disadvantaged by the family form. Social policy is unlikely to ever make up fully for the disadvantage. Nonetheless, investing in the children should be given priority. A large proportion of American children are currently growing up in fragile families, and no matter how successful we are in reducing prevalence, these families will be with us for a long time. Investing in these children both increases their future productivity and well-being and reduces the chances that they will reproduce fragile families themselves.

Many investments in children, especially those in poor and fragile families, are very productive and more than pay for themselves. Indeed, good investment opportunities in children abound. Many of the best investments in children in fragile families are from programs that are targeted at all children – such as universal health insurance and universal preschool education – rather than limited to fragile families. Investments should begin at birth (or before) and continue throughout childhood.

Finally, incarceration looms large in the lives of fragile families. There is increasing evidence that mass incarceration is having deleterious effects on families and children. It is time to explore alternatives to mass incarceration.

APPENDIX A

Fragile Families and Child Wellbeing Study Design and Content

The Fragile Families and Child Wellbeing Study is a nationally representative, birth cohort study of approximately 5,000 children born in large U.S. cities (population more than 200,000) between 1998 and 2000, including a large oversample of children born to unmarried parents. The study is a joint effort by scholars at Princeton and Columbia universities, with financial support from the National Institute of Child Health and Human Development (NICHD), the National Science Foundation, and several private foundations. Mothers were interviewed in the hospital shortly after the birth of their child; biological fathers were interviewed either in the hospital or by phone as soon as possible after the birth. Telephone interviews were conducted with both parents one, three, five, and nine years after the child's birth. In all waves, parent interviews lasted about an hour and included questions about parents' relationships, attitudes, parenting behaviors, mental and physical health, economic and employment status, demographic and neighborhood characteristics, and program participation. In addition, in-home interviews with the primary caregiver (usually the mother) and assessments of children's cognitive and socioemotional development and health were conducted three, five, and nine years after the birth. Measures overlap with those from the Infant Health and Development Program (IHDP), Early Head Start, the Teenage Parent Demonstration, and the Early Childhood Longitudinal Study – Birth Cohort 2000 (ECLS-B). The nine-year interview collected saliva samples from mothers and children for genetic analysis. For an extended description of the study design, see Reichman, Teitler, Garfinkel, and McLanahan (2001).

The Fragile Families Study is unique in several respects. Because it oversamples nonmarital births, the study includes a large number of low-income parents, which makes it especially useful for studying vulnerable families. The study also provides previously unavailable data on nonresident fathers. By contacting fathers shortly after the child's birth, the study was able to interview the fathers of nearly 80 percent of the focal children. Another unique aspect of the study is the rich data on mother-father and parent-child relationships, including relationships with nonresident parents. Careful attention was given to recording parents' partnership changes, including transitions into and out of residential partnerships (marriage, cohabitation) and transitions into and out of dating partnerships.

Additionally, several collaborative studies funded the collection of new information on mothers' medical records, incarceration histories, religious beliefs and practices, and early childhood education. The TLC3 (England and Edin 2007) and "Fragile Families and Public Policy: Fathers' Ties to Unmarried Mothers and Their Children" (Waller 2002) projects, for example, added in-depth, qualitative interviews with a subset of more than 100 couples living in four cities. The "Childcare and Parental Employment in Fragile Families" project added interviews with childcare providers and kindergarten teachers who worked with children ages three and five, and the "Fragile Families and Child Health" project added geographical data on census track characteristics. More information on the Fragile Families and Child Wellbeing Study and a complete list of collaborative studies can be found on the Fragile Families Web site at http://www.fragilefamilies.princeton.edu/index.asp.

REFERENCES

* *Papers based on data from the Fragile Families Study are indicated by an asterisk.*

American Academy of Pediatrics (2005). Breastfeeding and the Use of Human Milk. *Pediatrics*, 115, 496–506.

Anderson, E. (1990). *Streetwise: Race, Class, and Change in an Urban Community*. Chicago: University of Chicago Press.

Atkinson, A.B. (1998). Social Exclusion, Poverty and Unemployment. In Hills, J. (Ed.), *Exclusion, Employment and Opportunity* pp. 1–20. London: Centre for Analysis of Social Exclusion (CASE), London School of Economics and Political Science.

Atkinson, A.B. (1999). *The Economic Consequences of Rolling Back the Welfare State*. Cambridge, MA: MIT Press.

Bakke, E.W. (1940). *Citizens without Work: A Study of the Effects of Unemployment upon Workers Social Relations and Practices*. New Haven, CT: Yale University Press.

Beck, A., Cooper, C., McLanahan, S. and Brooks-Gunn, J. (2010). Partnership Transitions and Maternal Parenting. *Journal of Marriage and Family*, 72, 219–233.*

Bumpass, L. and Hsien-Hen, L. (2000). Trends in Cohabitation and Implications for Children's Family Contexts in the United States. *Population Studies*, 54, 29–41.

Bzostek, S. and Beck, A. (2011). Familial Instability and Young Children's Physical Health. *Social Science and Medicine*, 73, 282–292.

Carlson, M., McLanahan, S. and England, P. (2004). Union Formation in Fragile Families. *Demography*, 41, 237–262.*

Carlson, M.J., McLanahan, S.S. and Brooks-Gunn, J. 2008. Coparenting and Non-resident Fathers' Involvement with Young Children after a Non-marital Birth. *Demography*, 45, 461–488.*

Chatterji, P. and Markowitz, S. (2005). Does the Length of Maternity Leave Affect Maternal Health? *Southern Economic Journal*, 72, 16–41.

Cherlin, A. (2005). American Marriage in the Twenty First Century. *Future of Children*, 15 (2), 35–55.
Coontz, S. (1998). *The Way We Really Are: Coming to Terms with America's Changing Families*. New York: Basic Books.
Cooper, C., Osborne, C., Beck, A., and McLanahan, S. (2010). Partner Instability, School Readiness, and Gender Disparities. Working Paper #2008–08-FF, Center for Research on Child Wellbeing, Princeton, NJ.*
Cowan, P.A., Cowan, C.P., and Knox, V. (2010). Marriage and Fatherhood Programs. *The Future of Children*, 20, 205–230.
Craigie, T.-A., Brooks-Gunn, J., and Waldfogel, J. (2010). Family Structure, Family Stability and Early Child Wellbeing. Working Paper #2010–14-FF, Center for Research on Child Wellbeing, Princeton, NJ.*
Currie, J. (2006). *The Invisible Safety Net: Protecting the Nation's Poor Children and Families*. Princeton, NJ: Princeton University Press.
Currie, J., Decker, S., and Lin, W. (2008). Has Public Health Insurance for Older Children Reduced Disparities in Access to Care and Health Outcomes? *Journal of Health Economics*, 27, 1407–1652.
Currie, J. and Gruber, J. (1996a). Health Insurance Eligibility, Utilization of Medical Care, and Child Health. *The Quarterly Journal of Economics*, 111, 431–466.
Currie, J. and Gruber, J. (1996b). Saving Babies: The Efficacy and Cost of Recent Expansions of Medicaid Eligibility for Pregnant Women. *The Journal of Political Economy*, 104, 1263–1296.
Dafny, L. and Gruber, J. (2000). Does Public Insurance Improve the Efficiency of Medical Care? Medicaid Expansions and Child Hospitalizations. Mimeograph. MIT.
Durlauf, S.F. and Nagin, D.S. (2011). The Deterrent Effect of Imprisonment. In Cook, P.J., Ludwig, J. and McCrary, J. (Eds.), *Controlling Crime: Strategies and Tradeoffs*. Chicago: University of Chicago Press.
Edin, K. and Kefalas, M.. (2005). *Promises I Can Keep: Why Poor Women Put Motherhood Before Marriage*. Berkeley: University of California Press.
England, P. and Edin, K. (2007). *Unmarried Couples with Children*. New York: Russell Sage Foundation.*
Fomby, P. and Cherlin, A.J. (2007). Family Instability and Child Well-being. *American Sociological Review*, 72, 181–204.
Furstenberg, F.F. (2007). The Making of the Black Family: Race and Class in Qualitative Studies in the Twentieth Century. *Annual Review of Sociology*, 33, 429–448.
Garfinkel, I. (1992). *Assuring Child Support*. New York: Russell Sage.
Garfinkel, I., Meyer, D., and McLanahan, S.S. (1998). A Brief History of Child Support Policies in the United States. In Garfinkel, I., McLanahan, S., Meyer, D., and Seltzer, J. (Eds.), *Fathers under Fire: The Revolution in Child Support Enforcement* pp. 14–30. New York: Russell Sage Foundation.
Garfinkel, I., Miller, C., McLanahan, S., and Hanson, T. (1998). Deadbeat Dads or Inept States? A Comparison of Child Support Enforcement Systems. *Evaluation Review*, 22, 717–750.
Garfinkel, I., Rainwater, L., and Smeeding, T. (2010). *Wealth and Welfare States: Is America a Laggard or Leader?* New York: Oxford University Press.
Garfinkel, I., Huang, C.-C., McLanahan, S., and Gaylin, D. The Roles of Child Support Enforcement and Welfare in Non-Marital Childbearing. *Journal of Population Economics*, 16, 55–70.

Geller, A., Garfinkel, I., and Western, B. (2011). Incarceration and Support for Children in Fragile Families. *Demography*, 48, 25–47.*

Glaze, L. and Maruschak, L.M. (2009). *Parents in Prison and Their Minor Children*. Washington, DC: United States Department of Justice, Bureau of Justice Statistics.

Goldin, C. and Katz, L.F. (2008). *The Race between Education and Technology*. Cambridge, MA: Harvard University Press.

Gornick, J.C. and Meyers, M.K. (2008). Creating Gender Egalitarian Societies: An Agenda for Reform. *Politics and Society*, 36, 313–349.

Greenwood, P. (2008). Prevention and Intervention Programs for Juvenile Offenders. *The Future of Children*, 18(2), 185–210.

Harknett, K. and Knab, J. (2007). More Kin, Less Support: Multipartnered Fertility and Perceived Support among Mothers. *Journal of Marriage and Family*, 69, 237–253.*

Haskins, R. and Sawhill, I. (2010). *Creating an Opportunity Society*. Washington, DC: Brookings Institution Press.

Heckman, J.J. (2006). Skill Formation and the Economics of Investing in Disadvantaged Children. *Science*, 312, 1900–1902.

Hetherington, E.M., Cox, M., and Cox, R. (1985). Long-Term Effects of Divorce and Remarriage on the Adjustment of Children. *Journal of the American Academy of Child Psychiatry*, 24, 518–530.

Huang, C.-C., Mincy, R., and Garfinkel, I. (2005). Child Support Obligation of Low Income Fathers. *Journal of Marriage and the Family*, 67, 1213–1225.

Kahn, A. and Kamerman, S. (1988). *Child Support: From Debt Collection to Social Policy*. Newbury Park, CA: Sage.

Karoly, L.A. and Bigelow, J.H. (2005). *The Economics of Investing in Universal Preschool Education in California*. Santa Monica, CA: Rand Corporation.

Kumlin, S. and Rothstein, B. (2004). Making and Breaking Social Capital: The Impact of Welfare-State Institutions. *Comparative Political Studies*, 38, 339–365.

Kunz, J., Villeneuve, P., and Garfinkel, I. (2001). Child Support among Selected OECD Countries: A Comparative Analysis. In Vleminckx, K. and Smeeding, T. (Eds.), *Child Well-being, Child Poverty, and Child Policy in Modern Nations: What Do We Know?* pp. 485–500. Bristol: The Policy Press.

Liebow, E. (1967). *Tally's Corner: A Study of Negro Streetcorner Men*. Boston: Little Brown.

McLanahan, S. (2011). Family Instability and Complexity after a Nonmarital Birth: Outcomes for Children in Fragile Families. In Carlson, M.J. and England, P. (Eds.), *Social Class and Changing Families in an Unequal America*. Stanford, CA: Stanford University Press.*

McLanahan, S. and Percheski, C. (2008). Family Structure and the Reproduction of Inequality. *Annual Review of Sociology*, 34, 257–276.*

Meadows, S., McLanahan, S., and Brooks-Gunn, J. (2008). Family Structure and Maternal Health Trajectories. *American Sociological Review*, 73, 314–334.*

Meadows, S.O. (2009). Family Structure and Fathers' Well-Being: Trajectories of Mental Health and Self-Rated Health. *Journal of Health and Social Behavior*, 50, 115–131.*

Meyer, D.R., Garfinkel, I., Oellerich, D.T., and Robins, P.K. (1992). Who Should Be Eligible for an Assured Child Support Benefit? In Garfinkel, I., McLanahan, S.S. and Robins, P.K. (Eds.), *Child Support Assurance* pp. 159–188. Washington, DC: The Urban Institute Press.

Moynihan, D.P. (1965). *The Negro Family: The Case for National Action*. Washington, DC: U.S. Department of Labor.

Nepomnyaschy, L. and Garfinkel, I. (2010). Child Support Enforcement and Fathers' Contributions to Their Non-marital Children. *Social Service Review*, 84, 341–380.*

Osborne, C. and McLanahan, S.S. (2007). Partnership Instability and Child Wellbeing. *Journal of Marriage and Family*, 69, 1065–1083.*

Patterson, O. 1998. *Rituals of Blood*. New York: Basic Civitas.

Quayle, D. (1992). Address to the Commonwealth Club of California. Speech at Commonwealth Club of California, May 19, San Francisco, CA.

Rainwater, L. (1982). Stigma in Income-Tested Programs. In Garfinkel, I. (Ed.), *Income-Tested Transfer Programs: The Case For and Against* pp. 19-46. London: Academic Press.

Ruhm, C.J. (2000). Parental Leave and Child Health. *Journal of Health Economics*, 19, 931–960.

Sawhill, I., Thomas, A., and Monea, E. (2010). An Ounce of Prevention: Policy Prescriptions to Reduce the Prevalence of Fragile Families. *The Future of Children*, 20(2), 133–155.

Schwartz-Soicher, O., Geller, A., and Garfinkel, I. (2011). The Effect of Paternal Incarceration on Material Hardship. *Social Service Review*, 85(3), 447–493.

Sigle-Rushton, W. and McLanahan, S. (2004). Father Absence and Child Wellbeing: A Critical Review. In Moynihan, D., Rainwater, L., and Smeeding, T. (Eds.), *The Future of the Family* pp. 116–155. New York: Russell Sage Foundation.

Sinkewicz, M. and Garfinkel, I. (2009). Unwed Fathers' Ability to Pay Child Support: New Estimates Accounting for Multiple-Partner Fertility. *Demography*, 46, 247–263.*

Tach, L., Mincy, R., and Edin, K. (2010). Parenting as a Package Deal: Relationships, Fertility, and Non-resident Father Involvement among Unmarried Parents. *Demography*, 47, 181–204.*

Tanaka, S. (2005). Parental Leave and Child Health across OECD Countries. *Economic Journal*, 115(501), F7–F28.

Wacquant, L. (2010). Class, Race & Hyperincarceration in Revanchist America. *Daedalus*, 139(3), 74–90.

Waldfogel, J. (2006). *What Children Need*. Cambridge, MA: Harvard University Press.

Waller, Maureen R. (2002). *My Baby's Father: Unmarried Parents and Paternal Responsibility*. Ithaca, NY: Cornell University Press.

Wildeman, C. and Western, B. (2010). Incarceration in Fragile Families. *The Future of Children*, 20(2), 157–177.

Willis, R. (2000). The Economics of Fatherhood. *American Economic Review*, 90(2), 378–382.

Wilson, J.Q. (2002). *The Marriage Problem: How Our Culture Has Weakened Families*. New York: HarperCollins.

Wilson, W.J. (1988). *The Truly Disadvantaged*. Cambridge, MA: Harvard University Press.

Wolfe, B., Wilson, K., and Haveman, R. (2001). The Role of Economic Incentives in Teenage Non-marital Child-bearing Choices. *Journal of Public Economics*, 81(3), 473–511.

Wood, R.G., et al. (2010). *The Building Strong Families Project: Strengthening Unmarried Parents' Relationship: The Early Impacts of Building Strong Families*. Princeton, NJ: Mathematica Policy Research.

Wu, L.L. and Martinson, B.C. (1993). Family Structure and the Risk of a Premarital Birth. *American Sociological Review*, 58(2), 210–232.

9

Should Marriage Matter?

Ira Mark Ellman and Sanford L. Braver

INTRODUCTION

Since 1970, Americans' median age at first marriage has increased by about five years for both men (23.2 to 28.2) and women (20.8 to 26.1) (U.S. Bureau of the Census 2010). The necessary consequence is a decline in the proportion of men and women who marry by any benchmark age. Whereas 94 percent of women born between 1940 and 1944 had married by age forty, only 86 percent of those born between 1960 and 1964 had (Ellwood & Jenks 2004). The question is whether this decline is an artifact of the increasing age at first marriage or a true decline in the proportion of the population that will ever marry. Researchers are divided on this puzzle (Blau, Ferber, & Winkler 1998:274; Oppenheimer 1994). The current consensus seems to be that the educated continue to marry at the same rate but later in life, while the less educated have experienced a true decline in the proportion who ever marry (Cherlin 2010:404; Goldstein & Kenney 2001).

There have been larger marriage-rate declines in some European countries where an increasing proportion of couples live in long-term, marriage-like relationships without formal marriage. But in the United States, cohabiting relationships remain largely short-term, usually ending with separation or marriage.[1] Yet longer-term cohabiting relationships are perhaps becoming more common here also, even among couples with children.[2] In any event, the possibility invites our consideration of how Americans believe the law should deal with such relationships. The potential legal questions divide between those that involve the couple's treatment by third parties, such as employers and government agencies, and those that involve

[1] A set of comparable surveys in the mid-1990s found that the median duration of cohabiting relationships in the United States was fourteen months, the shortest duration of the eleven countries surveyed. It was forty months in Canada and fifty-one months in France (Heuveline & Timberlake 2004).

[2] About 35% of unmarried parents are living together five years after their child's birth, although half of them have married (McLanahan & Garfinkel, chapter 8).

the couple's rights with respect to one another (their rights *inter se*). Both categories are obviously important. This chapter focuses on the second.

One might imagine that couples who live together without marriage make that choice in order to avoid the legal rules associated with marriage. But that vision may overstate the legal planning the average couple puts into the cohabitation decision. Unmarried unions sometimes develop gradually, the partners slowly increasing the frequency with which one stays over at the other's home, without any discussion of the changing nature of the relationship (Manning & Smock 2005). Those who plan their cohabitation more overtly may discuss immediate practical issues without addressing directly the larger question of whether they should marry or cohabit. And even those who do discuss that larger question may not focus on its *legal* aspects. For example, Edin and Kefalas (2005) found that young unmarried mothers in Philadelphia focused on the emotional and symbolic commitments they associated with marriage, not its legal rules.

If couples do discuss the law, they may be primarily interested in the impact marriage could have on their treatment by third parties, which can be immediate and certain. Marriage may qualify one of them for dependent health insurance, or disqualify one of them from a public benefit they are now receiving; it may raise or lower their joint tax liability. By contrast, marriage rarely has any *immediate* impact on their legal obligations *to one another* because the law does not generally regulate spousal relations *during* marriage. Marital status becomes important when their relationship ends, whether by death or divorce. We know, however, that such temporally distant and contingent consequences are generally less potent in motivating human behavior than are immediate and certain consequences (Gilbert 2007:121–161).

So for all these reasons, one might doubt that many cohabiting couples have in any meaningful sense chosen to avoid marriage as a result of their comparative assessment of the legal rules that govern the dissolution of a marital versus a nonmarital intimate relationship. It seems rather more likely that the weak motivational power of marriage's distant and contingent effects at death or divorce are swamped by other considerations, such as the social, emotional, and religious importance of marriage as a symbolic affirmation of their relationship, or the legal advantages marriage may provide them in their relationships with third parties.

Because few couples will consult a lawyer before they marry, those who do think about marriage's legal consequences will likely rely on their own understanding of the law. Their understanding may be flawed. Under U.S. law, as in England, living together as a couple, no matter how long, does not *alone* create any financial rights or obligations between intimate partners.[3] Yet studies have shown that most British residents believe cohabitation alone *does* establish marriage-like *inter se* obligations,

3 A handful of American states recognize a cohabiting couple as married if they also agree to be married and consistently present themselves to the world ("hold themselves out") as if they were. See Ellman et al. (2010, ch. 10).

and such information as we have about the beliefs of Americans suggests they are the same.[4] So not only may the expectations of cohabiting partners regarding the legal consequences of their relationship be largely unformed, but any expectations they do have may be inconsistent with the legal rules that would in fact apply.

Our studies sought to learn what our respondents think the law *should be*, not what they think it is. The fact that cohabiting partners may not give much thought at the outset of their relationship to their particular legal rights as against one another after the relationship ends does not mean that people in general have no views about what the law *should* provide in that circumstance. And it turns out that knowing what people believe the law should say does tell you something about what they think the law is because people tend to assume that legal rules align with what they believe a fair law would provide (Barlow et al. 2005:45; Kim 1999:45, 447). Intimate partners may well conduct their relationship on the implicit if unexpressed assumption that the law will treat them fairly, as they understand what fairness requires. And even if this were not true, lawmakers should care what the public believes a fair law would provide because lawmaking, especially in the regulation of matters such as personal relationships, should surely take account of any citizen consensus as to what result is fair. The data presented in this chapter tell us there is such a consensus.

The data described in this chapter come from a series of empirical studies that ask a sample of American citizens about the legal obligations intimate partners should have to one another when their relationship ends (Ellman & Braver 2011, 2012; Ellman, Braver, & MacCoun 2009, 2012). The data published until now have focused on child support and claims for post-relationship support (alimony). They use a common methodology and a respondent pool assembled in the same way from study to study. This chapter draws together findings from these earlier studies that bear on the impact of a couple's marital status on our respondents' views. In addition, we report here for the first time data from a study in this series that examined our respondents' views about how a couple's marital status should affect the allocation of their property at the termination of their relationship. Our earlier publications provide methodological and statistical details, for the entire sequence of studies, that we shall only summarize briefly here. Those publications also offer additional context and background, as well as a fuller account of some of the findings described here. The interested reader is referred to that earlier work.

We probe what our respondents think the law should be by giving them a series of vignettes across which key facts are systematically varied. We then ask them to

4 In a national survey conducted in 2000, 56% of respondents said that British law "definitely" or "probably" provided that "unmarried couples who live together for some time have a 'common law marriage' which gives them the same legal rights as married couples." That result led to a concerted effort by the government, with intense media coverage, to educate the public about the actual law, which treats cohabiting and married couples quite differently. When the same question was then put after this campaign, in 2006, the percentage had declined to 51% (Barlow et al. 2008:40–41). For similar, if less definitive, U.S. reports, see Bowman (1996:711).

imagine that they are the judge asked to decide the case presented by each vignette. Here is an example, taken from our child support surveys, of the basic instructions setting up the questions on each form used in that survey:

> We want to know the amount of child support, if any, that you think Dad should be required to pay Mom every month, all things considered. What will change from story to story is how much Mom earns and how much Dad earns. There is no right or wrong answer; just tell us what you think is right. Try to imagine yourself as the judge in each of the following cases. Picture yourself sitting on the bench in a courtroom needing to decide about what should be done about ordering child support in the case and trying to decide correctly. To do so, you might try putting yourself in the shoes of Mom or of Dad, or both, or imagine a loved one in that position.

When respondents resolve a series of such cases in a coherent and consistent pattern, their policy preferences can be inferred from their decisions. The process might be regarded as a statistical equivalent to the familiar common law method by which legal principles are abstracted from the decisions made by judges over time. When we have asked the same respondents directly about principles as well as cases, we have found that their judgments in cases are related to their ratings of proffered principles in ways that are sensible, rational, and nuanced (Ellman, Braver, & MacCoun 2012).

The data we describe here were gathered during 2008 and 2009. Our respondents were Arizona citizens called to jury service in Pima County, where the city of Tucson is located. Citizens are selected for jury service in a random process, and they are rarely excused. State law imposes significant penalties on citizens who fail to respond to a jury summons, and well over 90 percent respond. The Tucson jury pool is thus an excellent cross-section of the county's citizens. Surveys were distributed to members of the jury pool while they sat in the jury assembly room waiting to be called to serve on a particular jury. Our assistant addressed the pool members immediately after the jury commissioner staff welcomed them and oriented them to their jury service. They were told that completion of this "university" survey was voluntary, but the majority chose to accept it and most completed it. Some were unable to complete the survey because the bailiff called them to the courtroom before they finished. Depending on the particular survey form, it might take a respondent from fifteen to thirty minutes to complete. The response rate among those who had the opportunity to complete the survey was always higher than 50 percent and was usually considerably higher. We typically gathered data from a few hundred respondents on any given day. Our surveys included demographic questions that allowed us to determine whether different population subgroups answered our questions in systematically different ways. As we shall see, in most respects they did not.

In our child support surveys, the dependent variable was the amount of child support the law should require. In our alimony surveys, the dependent variables were whether alimony should be ordered and, if so, the amount of alimony that should be ordered. In our property surveys, it was how the property pool identified in each vignette ought to be divided between the partners. The surveys distributed on any given day generally focused on only one particular issue: child support, alimony, or property allocation. Some surveys were administered on only one day, but others were repeated over several weeks in order to increase the number of respondents.

We first present selected findings from our previously published studies of alimony and child support and then present our new findings on property allocation. The final section of the chapter then considers the implications of the overall picture these data present.

FINDINGS

Alimony

Unlike the law of some other English-speaking countries, American law is generally clear that unmarried intimate partners have no continuing claim on one another's earnings after they separate (Bowman 2010). By contrast, married partners may seek post-separation alimony, often relabeled in recent decades as "maintenance" or "spousal support." Although alimony is not an entitlement, in nearly all states it is within the divorce court's equitable authority to allow such a claim, at least where the lower-income spouse will otherwise be unable to maintain a living standard that is adequate in light of the couple's marital living standard.[5]

The duration of the marriage is usually an important factor in a court's decision of whether to allow an alimony claim. Because we did not want our respondents' answers anchored by any particular belief about the legal rules (even if the belief was correct), the lead-in for the alimony questions told them the law on alimony claims varied considerably between courts and judges, even as to issues (such as claims between unmarried cohabitants) where it does not actually vary much. Here is what we said:

> When couples divorce, one of the spouses may make more money than the other. Judges sometimes require the one who earns more to make regular payments (usually once a month) to the one who earns less. Alimony is different than child support. The purpose of alimony is to assist the former spouse, not the children. A judge can require alimony when no child support is required (because the couple never had children, or because their children are grown). If the couple does have children under 18, a judge can order alimony for the spouse in addition to child support for the children.
>
> While judges can order alimony, they don't have to. In fact, judges don't always agree with each other about the kind of case that should include an alimony order,

[5] Ellman & Braver (2012) contains additional sources for statements in this section.

> and the kind that should not. And even when they agree alimony should be ordered in a certain kind of case, they often disagree about the size of each monthly payment, or for how long the payments should continue. Finally, some courts would require alimony when a couple lived together as if they were married, even if they weren't, but other courts would never require alimony unless the couple had married.
>
> Some cases are described below. In each one, a judge must decide whether to require the man to pay alimony to the woman, and if so, how much. We want to know what you think the judge should decide in these cases. There is no right or wrong answer. The facts will vary from case to case, and you may think alimony is appropriate in some cases but not in others. Or, you may think that all the cases should be decided the same way. Either is fine. We just want to know what you think is right.

Respondents were given vignettes in which a couple identified as "Adam" and "Eve" (each forty-five years old) had "agreed to separate" after having decided "their relationship wasn't working for them anymore." Respondents were also told that Adam and Eve will each get one of their two cars, and that they "don't have a lot of other property or savings, but they'll divide what they have equally between them." The vignettes described the husband's "take-home pay" as either $6,000 or $12,000 per month and the wife's take-home pay as either $1,000 or $3,000 per month. There were thus four different combinations of spousal income. There were also six different "Cases" (identified alphabetically as Case A through Case F), and each case was presented with all four income combinations. The six Cases differed on three dimensions: (1) Marital Status: whether the couple was described as married or as cohabiting (while "they never married, they have lived together for the past . . . years just as if they were married"); (2) Relationship Duration: whether the couple had been together (married or cohabiting) for either twenty-two years or six years; and (3) their status with respect to Children: "None" (the vignette specified that "They have no children"), "Grown Children" (the vignette specified that they "have two children who are now 19 and 21 years old"); or "Young Children" (the vignette specified that there were two children now "4 and 6 years old").[6]

For the "young children" condition, respondents were told that Eve took "primary responsibility" for the children, leaving work each day by 4:30 PM to pick them up from child care and taking days off when the children are sick. They were also given

[6] Because there were three child conditions rather than two, there were actually twelve different cases rather than six. (Two versions of marital status [married and cohabiting] times two versions of relationship duration [6 years or 22 years] times three versions of children [none, young, grown] equals twelve different cases.) There were thus forty-eight different vignettes in all (twelve cases times four income combinations), but each respondent considered only 24 vignettes. The reduction from 48 to 24 was achieved by varying marital status between subjects for half of our 330 respondents, while duration varied between subjects for the other half. For a more complete explanation, see Ellman and Braver (2012).

the dollar amount of child support that Adam will pay Eve each month.[7] For the "grown children" condition, respondents were told that "[w]hen the children were younger, Eve took primary responsibility for them."

Our respondents were more likely to give alimony to a married claimant than to one who had cohabited. They were also more likely to award alimony when the couple had been together longer, their incomes were more disparate, and they had young children (as compared to either grown children or no children). These findings are unlikely to surprise most readers. Seventy-four percent of our respondents would award alimony in the case combining all the conditions most favorable to an award (a mother of young children, married twenty-two years, who is taking home $1,000 per month and whose husband is taking home $12,000 per month). By contrast, only 18 percent of respondents would award alimony in the case combining all the facts least favorable to an award (a childless woman, cohabiting for six years, who is taking home $3,000 per month and whose male partner is taking home $6,000 per month).

These basic findings tell us two things. First, our respondents may be willing to allow alimony in a higher proportion of cases than do many courts.[8] Second, marriage matters, but as one of several factors that influence the judgments of our respondents, not as an absolute eligibility requirement. Alimony was awarded in 40 percent of the vignettes involving cohabitants as compared to about 60 percent of the otherwise identical group of cases involving a married couple. Perhaps of even greater interest, 68 percent of our respondents made an alimony award in at least one cohabitation vignette.

The importance of marriage to our respondents' decision on whether to award alimony also depended on whether the couple had children, and especially on whether they had young children. That relationship is seen most easily by examining Figure 9.1, which shows that the difference marriage made in our respondents' inclination to award alimony – the "marriage premium" – shrank considerably for vignettes in which the alimony claimant had custody of the couple's minor children. There was a similar reduction in the "duration premium" for vignettes in which the claimant had custody of the couple's young children, as shown in Figure 9.2.[9] In considering both figures, recall that in vignettes with young children, our respondents were told that Adam was required to pay child support and were given the

7 The child support amount was itself varied in a separate between-subject manipulation described in Ellman and Braver (2012).

8 Our respondents made alimony awards in 60% of the vignettes involving married couples. A Maryland study found that alimony was allowed in 17.4% of divorce petitions filed statewide in 1999; the median marital duration for cases in the study's sample was about ten years. Alimony was allowed in half the cases in which it was requested (Women's Law Center of Maryland 2004).

9 As there was no triple interaction of the marital status, duration, and children conditions, the results in Figure 9.1 are averaged over both relational durations, and the results in Figure 9.2 are averaged over both the married and unmarried conditions (Ellman & Braver 2012).

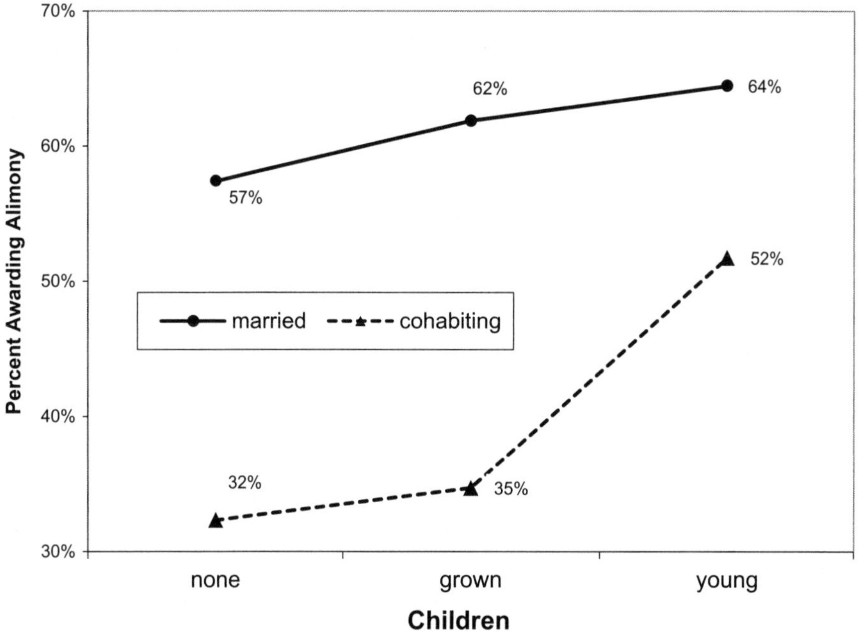

FIGURE 9.1. Percentage of vignettes in which respondents award alimony, by marital status and children condition.

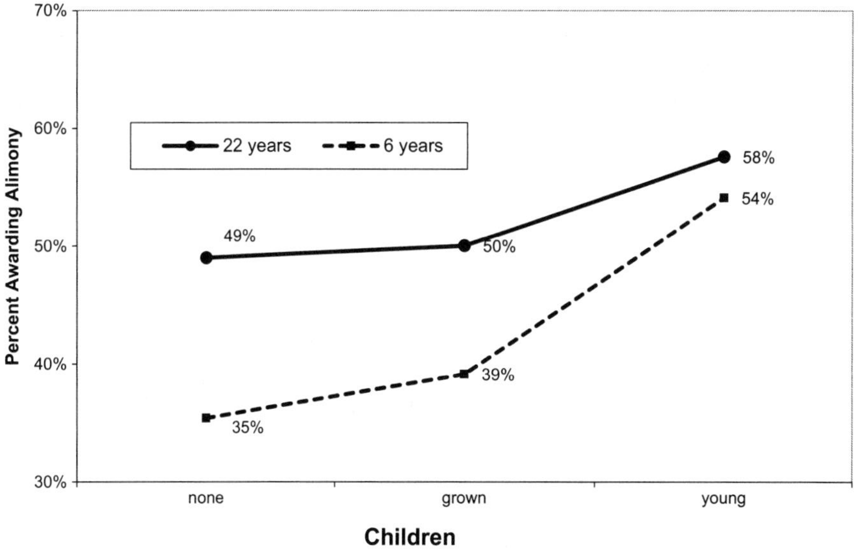

FIGURE 9.2. Percentage of vignettes in which respondents award alimony, by relationship duration and children condition.

precise dollar amount he was required to pay. They were thus *more* inclined to award alimony to the claimant who was also collecting child support than to the claimant with grown children who was not, and this effect is most evident when the couple was unmarried or had a shorter relationship. The mean *amount* of the alimony award, when an award was made, was *not* affected by the presence of a child support award.

These results confirm that marriage was a factor in our respondents' decisions about whether alimony should be allowed, but no more important than other factors such as the disparity in the partners' incomes, the absolute level of each partner's income, the presence of children, and the duration of the parties' relationship. Indeed, one of our more general findings is that our respondents seem to prefer an alimony principle grounded in the partners' income disparity rather than whether the alimony claimant is at risk of falling below a minimally adequate income. For example, when the man earned $12,000 a month in take-home pay, the award rate for middle-class claimants earning $3,000 a month (56 percent) was barely lower than that of poor claimants earning only $1,000 (59 percent). Moreover, the *amount* of the alimony award for cases in which one was made was determined primarily by the man's income, which accounted for 76 percent of the variance in the amount of the award. The woman's income accounted for another 11 percent, while the remaining three factors combined (Children, Marital Status, and Relationship Duration) accounted for only another 3.5 percent. Thus while all five factors influenced *whether* our respondents gave an award, only the partners' incomes had much influence on its *amount*.

Finally, we found little or no relationship between our respondents' demographic characteristics and the effect of marriage on their award rate. For example, although women were somewhat more likely than men to award alimony, marriage had no greater or lesser effect on their award rate than it did on men's. Most other demographic characteristics had no effect on either the overall award rate or on the marriage premium. For example, self-identified conservatives or Republicans did not award alimony at a rate different than self-identified liberals or Democrats; those who had been married (54 percent of our sample) or divorced (34 percent) were no more or less likely than others to allow an alimony award. The one exception to this pattern was education: the marriage premium was greater for the more educated. But the reason was that the more educated had a higher award frequency for married claimants, not a lower one for cohabiting claimants.

Child Support

The marital status of parents was historically important in establishing a child's paternity and thus the legal obligation of the father to support the child. Modern science has combined with social policy to reduce marriage's importance in establishing legal paternity, although there are still circumstances in which a married woman's husband, rather than the child's biological father, is treated as the child's legal father (Ellman 2002). The increased use of new reproductive technologies also complicates the assignment of paternity (Garrison 2000). But in the more common case of unmarried mothers who become pregnant the old-fashioned way, the child's biological father will normally be the legal father, and his obligation to support his child is generally treated as identical to that of a father who was married to the mother. The duration of the parents' relationship is irrelevant in calculating the amount of the child support obligation.

The child-support rule that marriage shouldn't matter is consistent with the modern belief that children should not suffer disabilities just because their parents had not married, while the different alimony rule that marriage does matter has the force of long history and nearly universal acceptance in American law. Yet as plausible as each rule may seem when considered alone, they are unavoidably incoherent when considered together. The law may distinguish transfers of income between households by their label – alimony or child support – but the reality of household economics makes those labels largely meaningless. Households have joint consumption items, such as the bulk of housing and utility expenditures, which comprise a large portion of the total household expenditures. Parents and the children living with them inevitably share a common living standard. The cost of providing comfortable middle-class housing for the child necessarily includes the cost of providing it for the custodial parent. And the custodial parent who uses alimony income for personal expenses, such as clothing or food, then necessarily has more funds left from other sources with which to buy clothes or food for the child.

So the reality is that child support payments will necessarily benefit the custodial parent, and alimony payments will necessarily benefit the children living with that parent. This very point might help explain why many of our respondents were more inclined to grant alimony to a mother with young children than to an otherwise identically situated woman whose children were grown. The difference in treatment might not have been for her sake as much as for her children's. But note that the reverse is also possible. Someone less inclined to provide alimony when the intimate partners have not married might also be inclined to allow less child support to the unmarried mother than to the married one.

Federal law requires all states to establish numerical child support "guidelines" that contain tables or formulas specifying the presumptive amount of the award to be ordered in most cases. Current guideline amounts are determined largely by parental incomes and the number of children.[10] In a series of studies, we sought to learn the principles our respondents would apply to guideline design (Ellman & Braver 2011; Ellman, Braver, & Maccoun 2009, 2012). One of those studies

[10] Adjustments to this basic amount are commonly allowed or required to reflect the custodial arrangement or the cost of child care and health insurance (see Ellman et al. 2010 ch. 5).

(Ellman & Braver 2011) asked about the relevance of marital status. Four respondent groups constituted a 2 × 2 factorial in which the parents were described as having married or cohabited and as having been together for either four years or fifteen years. In a separate "trailer control" condition (Himmelfarb 1975), a fifth group of respondents was given cases in which the parents' relationship was limited to the single act of intercourse that led to the conception of the child whose support order was in question; these parents never lived together or married.[11]

Parental incomes varied within-subjects in each group. The mother's income was $1,000, $3,000, or $5,000 a month in take-home pay, and the father's was $2,000, $4,000, $6,000, $9,000, or $12,000 in take-home pay. Respondents (N = 356) were asked to state the amount of child support they would order if they were the judge, all things considered. Each respondent named support amounts in all fifteen income combinations (three maternal incomes × five paternal incomes), in whichever of the five family configuration cases they were given, effectively creating his or her personal child support guideline for that family configuration. Respondents were also given other facts that were constant across all the vignettes: that there was one child, a three-year-old boy, who "now lives mostly with Mom, but Dad sees him often," and that the boy "frequently" stayed with Dad overnight.

The results averaged across the four family configurations in the 2 × 2 factorial are presented in Figure 9.3. They replicated but also extended our earlier findings as to respondent preferences about the construction of child support guidelines. Each parental income had a significant main effect, and their linear × linear interaction was also highly significant.[12] These three effects can be appreciated most easily by examining the lines displayed in the figure. The main effect of paternal income is seen in the upward slope of all three lines, demonstrating that the support amount increased with paternal income through the highest paternal income we asked about, $12,000 monthly in "take-home pay." This effect tells us that our respondents rejected the view that support should be limited to the amount needed to provide a child a basic or minimum living standard because their preferred support amount would not keep rising across the full range of paternal incomes, had they applied that principle. Our respondents instead favored the principle implicit in most U.S. child support guidelines, i.e., that children should share, at least to some extent, in the living standard enjoyed by the higher-income obligor, even when their basic needs have been met. One might guess that respondents would cease applying this principle when net obligor incomes exceeds some threshold beyond $12,000 monthly, but we know they apply it at least through that relatively high income.

The main effect of maternal income is why three different lines are required for the three different custodial-parent (CP) incomes, and it tells us that our respondents

[11] Our respondents were told that "the woman got pregnant by the man on the night they met, but they have never lived together, nor been in a relationship since."

[12] $F(1,251) = 46.08$, $p < .01$.

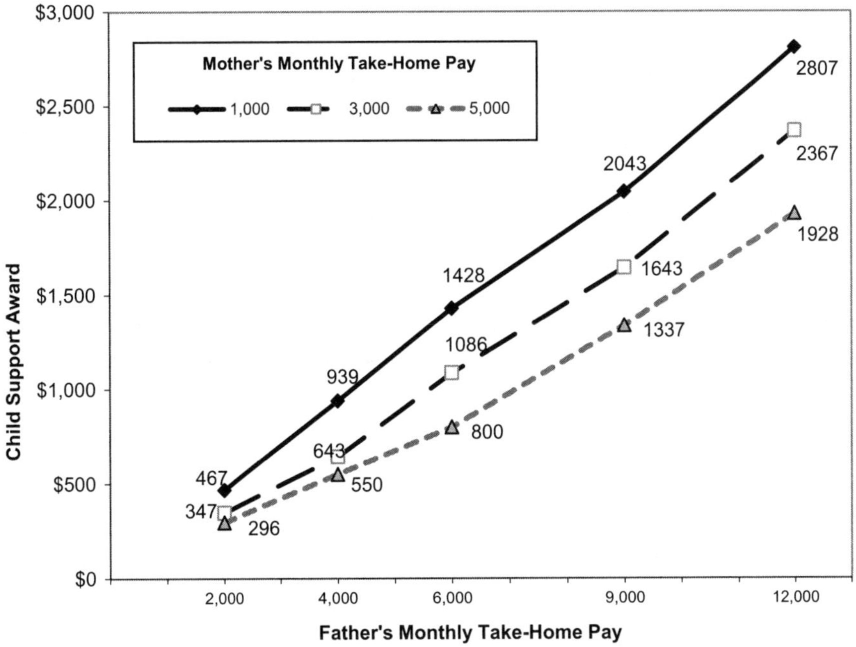

FIGURE 9.3. Mean child support amount named by respondents, by parental incomes

reject the guideline model, used by about ten American states, in which support amounts are a percentage of obligor income without regard to CP income. To the contrary, our respondents believe that, for any given level of noncustodial parent (NCP) income we asked about, the amount of child support should decline as CP income increases. Finally, the significant interaction between the parents' incomes is shown by the fact that the three lines "fan apart" as one moves right – they are not parallel. That means our respondents believe that support amounts should increase more rapidly with NCP income when CP income is lower. American support guidelines do not exhibit such a pattern as consistently as did our respondents.

These three basic patterns persisted whether the vignette parents were married or cohabiting, or together for four years or fifteen years. They were also pervasive across our respondents. That is, while there is considerable dispersion around the *mean* support amount for any given set of parental incomes, there was relatively little dispersion in the *adjustment* to their preferred support amount that our respondents made in response to changes in either parent's income. One can visualize this result by imagining a version of Figure 9.3 that did not present the mean child support amounts for each maternal income, across all respondents, but rather the 356 individual sets of the three regression lines best describing each individual respondent's support amounts. We would see that the three lines for most respondents formed the same pattern as the regression lines for the group means displayed in

Figure 9.3 – three separate, upward-sloping lines that are not parallel but fan out. We would also see that for any given maternal income, the height of these individual lines – their Y-intercepts – varied considerably across respondents, but that the lines' slopes (and thus the regression coefficients for each income term) varied much less.[13] In sum, the three basic patterns we have replicated and extended here are highly robust, arising across individual respondents and across vignettes with an expanded income range and across the variations in parental relationships we presented to our different groups.

That does not mean, however, that marital status did not also affect our respondents' judgments about the appropriate child support amount. It did, both as a significant main effect *and* as a significant interaction with the obligor's income.[14] The overall mean monthly support amount, averaged over all fifteen income combinations for all four family configurations in the 2 × 2 factorial, was $1,245. But the mean support amount for the cases in which the couples were married was $121 more, $1,366, while the mean for cohabiting couples was $121 less, at $1,124. There was thus a "marriage premium" of $242, the difference between the marital and cohabiting means. In addition, the significant interaction between marital status and paternal incomes reveals that the marriage premium results primarily from cases in which paternal income was higher. Figure 9.4 illustrates the pattern by comparing our respondents' mean support amounts for married and cohabiting couples for vignettes in which the mother's take home pay was $3,000. Note how the lines for married and cohabiting partners converge at the left end of the figure when paternal income is lowest, but increasingly diverge as paternal income increases – a visual representation of the fact that the marriage premium increases with paternal income. The same pattern was repeated for the two other maternal incomes we asked about.[15]

This interaction of marital status and paternal income arises *in addition to*, not instead of, the three general effects we previously noted – the effect of paternal income, of maternal income, and of their interaction. So, while child support amounts rose more steeply with paternal income when maternal income was lower, they rose even more steeply when the parents had married, but less steeply when they had cohabited. The fact that support amounts increased with paternal income at all, we previously observed, suggests that our respondents rejected the view that child

[13] However, we previously found that the slope was indeed steeper for women than for men and for those with more education, meaning that the amount of support increased significantly more rapidly with NCP income for women and for the more educated, even though the variance in slope across all respondents was considerably smaller than the variance in Y-intercept (Ellman, Braver, and MacCoun 2009). A subsequent study also found that differences among respondents in both slope and Y-intercept could be predicted from their Likert ratings of statements setting out abstract principles by which child support amounts should be determined (Ellman, Braver, & MacCoun 2012).

[14] For the main effect of marital status, $F(1,355) = 8.38$, $p < .01$; for the interaction of marital status and NCP's income, $F(1,355) = 7.14$, $p < .01$.

[15] Results for all three maternal incomes are in Ellman and Braver (2011).

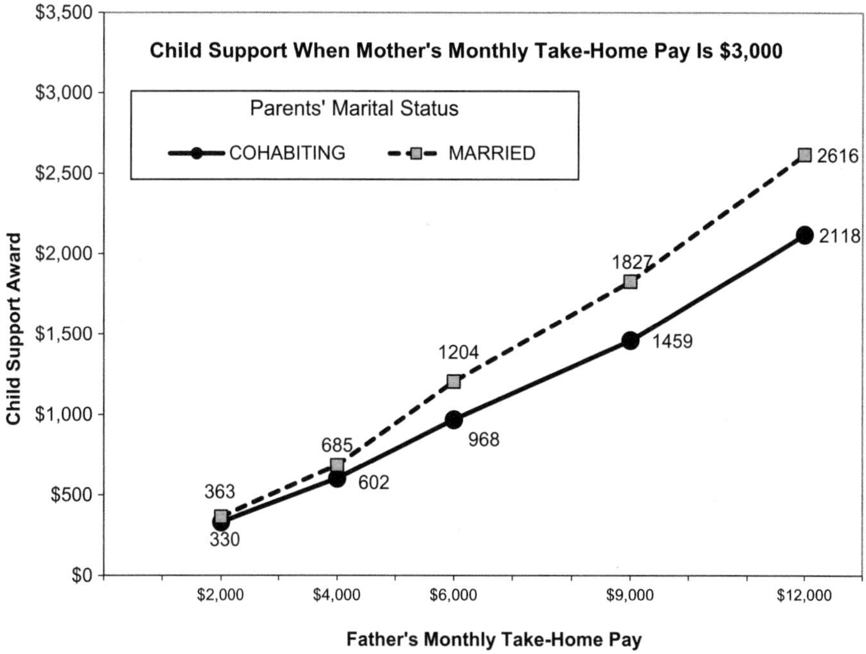

FIGURE 9.4. Mean child support amounts named by respondents for custodial mother earning $3,000 monthly in take-home pay, by father's income and marital status.

support's only purpose is to ensure children some minimally adequate income, and that they instead believe child support should permit the child to share in the better living standard of the father whose income is higher than the custodial mother's (when it is). How close to the paternal living standard a support order brings a child depends on how one trades off the competing interests of the child and the higher-income obligor (who can object to lifting the custodial parent's living standard under the child support rubric). These results show that our respondents make that trade-off move favorably to the child when the parents had married than when they had cohabited.

Critics of existing guidelines have argued that support amounts for low-income mothers are too low because the guidelines' trade-off of these competing claims is skewed too heavily in favor of the support obligor's interests. In our earlier work, we showed that our respondents appear to agree with the guideline critics because they consistently awarded more child support than would the typical American guideline when custodial parent income was low (but made smaller support awards when custodial parent income was high and the child's interests were therefore not at risk). The newer results on marital status show that, while our respondents would also increase support amounts (over amounts in the typical American guideline) for low-income mothers who had cohabited with the child's father, they would increase them by a larger amount if the mother had been married to the father.

TABLE 9.1. *Mean child support amount across all income combinations, for each of three family configurations*

One-night relationship	Cohabiting parents	Married parents
$989	$1,124	$1,366

While marriage mattered to our respondents, it did not matter whether the parents had been together for four years or fifteen years; that durational difference had no overall effect on awards, nor did it have any effect on cohabiting or married parents considered separately. But it did matter if the parents had not been together at all. The mean support amount in our "one night" or no-relationship cases was significantly lower than that in the other cases. Table 9.1 gives the relative values and shows that there is a "relationship premium" of $135 – the difference between the mean amount for the cohabiting parents and for parents with no relationship beyond a single incident of sexual relations.

Again, these two effects, of marriage and relationship, lay on top of the overall pattern of three fanning lines that is produced by the interaction of the two parental incomes. This interaction effect alone, found in all family configurations including the one-night case, results in a larger difference in support amounts between family configurations when NCP incomes are higher and CP incomes are lower. The point is illustrated by comparing that difference in two bookend cases: the case that combines the highest maternal take-home pay ($5,000) with the lowest paternal take-home pay ($2,000), and the case that combines the lowest maternal take-home pay ($1,000) with the highest paternal take-home pay ($12,000). Table 9.2 presents the mean support amount for those two bookend cases for the one-night relationship, cohabiting couples, and married couples.

In the first case (the upper row), involving a low-income father and a high-income mother, our respondents' mean child support amount changes very little across these three family configurations. By contrast, for the case of the high-income father and the low-income mother (the lower row), the mean support amount increases by more than $400 when the couple had lived together, as compared to the one-night relationship, and by an additional $500 higher if the couple had married. In short,

TABLE 9.2. *Mean child support amounts for two "bookend" cases across family configurations*

Father's THP/ Mother's THP	One-night relationship	Cohabiting	Married
$2,000/$5,000	$277	$278	$314
$12,000/$1,000	$2,131	$2,533	$3,080

family configuration hardly mattered at all in the first case, but mattered quite a bit for cases involving wealthy fathers and poor mothers.

So if child support guidelines were based on our respondents' views, a low-income Dad would pay about the same amount of child support no matter whether the parents were together one night, had cohabited for years, or had married, but a high-income Dad would pay more when the parents had cohabited and more yet if they had married, especially when the mother's income was much lower than his. Looking at all our child support data, we conclude that it matters to our respondents whether the parents were married, and if not, whether they had a relationship or just one sexual encounter. At least one important reason it matters, we believe, is that the respondents intuitively appreciated that child support payments confer a benefit on the custodial parent as well as the child, and that they are more tolerant of providing that benefit when the facts of the parental relationship provide more justification for it. At the same time, we must also note that our respondents' support awards rose with paternal income no matter the parental relationship, even if their absolute support levels were lower for unmarried parents and lower yet for those with no relationship. This tells us that, while our respondents' choice of trade-off point (between the child's interest and the father's interest) was more favorable to the father when there was no relationship or the parents had not married, they went beyond a "minimum living standard" approach to child support in all these cases.

Indeed, the low-income *cohabiting* mother would receive more support from our respondents than from a median American support guideline in effect at the same time, except when the father is also poor.[16] (The guideline amount does not vary with marital status.) So our respondents would allow the cohabiting mother more support than does current law, and they would raise support levels by an even greater amount when the parents had been married. They would allow the mother who had

[16] We calculated support amounts from a contemporaneous median guideline (Iowa's) in Ellman, Braver & MacCoun (2009), but only for the three paternal incomes considered in that study (which did not ask about the two highest paternal incomes we examined in the study reported here). The following table shows the Iowa amounts for cases with those three paternal incomes, and the lowest maternal income we asked about, a take-home pay of $1,000 monthly. It also shows our respondents' mean support amounts for married and cohabiting couples in those same three cases:

2,000	4,000	6,000	Paternal income (maternal income 1,000 in all cases)
456	804	1,122	Support Amount in Iowa Guideline
447	862	1,271	Mean respondent amount for cohabiting parents
487	1,016	1,584	Mean respondent amount for married parents

One can see very little difference for the low-income father, although our respondents demand a bit more from him than the median when the parents are married, but essentially the same as the median when they cohabit. But as the paternal income goes up, our respondents clearly raise support amounts above the median guidelines – but more for the married parents than the cohabiting ones.

no relationship with the father a support amount quite similar to that provided in current law. Our data thus suggest that our respondents' adherence to a child support system that considers family configuration arises from the fact that they would give *more* weight than the typical American guideline to protecting the child's living standard, not less weight.

Allocation of Property When the Partners Separate

The law of every American state makes marriage significant in the allocation of property owned by separating intimate partners. In all but a handful of states, the divorce court has authority to make an "equitable" distribution of property acquired during a marriage even if it was purchased with the earnings of one spouse alone and owned solely by that spouse.[17] In many states, either formal rules or customary practice leads courts to presume that in most cases property acquired during the marriage should be divided equally between the spouses. That presumption is particularly well entrenched in the nine community property states, some of which *require* equal division of marital assets, but in virtually all states there is a strong tendency toward equal division of marital assets following a long marriage. On the other hand, in most American states, cohabitation alone, even a long-term cohabitation, confers no equitable authority on the courts to allocate property between separating intimate partners who were not married.[18]

We investigated our respondents' views concerning the allocation of property in a study we describe here for the first time. We assumed our respondents would favor an equal division of property after a long marriage with no special facts that suggested otherwise, but we wondered whether they might move away from equal division in response to certain factual variations. The partners' marital status was one of the variations we were interested in testing, along with others, such as their relative earnings and their division of domestic chores.[19] As in other studies in this project, we presented potential Pima County, Arizona jurors (N > 600) with a series of hypothetical cases to decide. The questions were introduced to them with this language:

> This survey is about how *property is divided* between people when they separate after living together or after a divorce. If they cannot agree on how to divide it, a judge may be asked to decide what to do. What the judge might decide depends on both the law and the facts. The law varies from state to state, and the facts vary

[17] For a more complete description of U.S. marital property law, see Ellman et al. (2010) ch. 4.

[18] Washington is the one state in which courts may allocate property between separating unmarried partners in such a case. Many states will, in principle, enforce contracts between cohabiting partners concerning the allocation of their property if they separate, but formal contracts between cohabitants appear to be uncommon, and efforts to enforce informal or implied contracts are usually unsuccessful (Ellman 2001; Estin 2001; Garrison 2008).

[19] We also examined the possible role of fault in our respondents' evaluations, but we defer reporting that data.

from case to case. In the first two parts of this Survey form, we give *you* some cases to decide. In each case, we tell you some facts, and we ask what *you* think should be done. There is no right or wrong answer. We just want to know what *you* think would be fair in each case.

Try to imagine yourself as the judge in each of the following cases. You might picture yourself sitting on the bench in a courtroom needing to decide how the couple's property should be divided between them. You might try putting yourself in the shoes of each spouse or partner, or imagine a loved one in their position.

Assume the law allows you, as the judge, to make the decision, and does not require you to decide in any particular way. You might decide it is right to divide the property equally in every case, or you might decide it is right to give most of the property, or all the property, to one or the other spouse or partner. Just choose the result that *you* think is right in each case.

All the stories concern a couple we call Adam and Eve, whose union is coming apart. The question is how to divide the money they have accumulated while they were together.

Some facts were the same in all the vignettes: Adam and Eve have been together for twenty-two years; have two sons, nineteen and twenty-one years old, who are now grown and out of the house; some time ago, Adam and Eve bought a house together; when they separated, they both moved out and sold it; they have already divided up their personal possessions and agreed that each would keep the car each drove during the relationship. Most vignettes said that, by the time their house sold, it had gone up a lot in value, so that after paying off their mortgage loan and various fees, they cleared about $250,000 from the sale, which, in addition to the $50,000 they were said to have in savings (for a total of $300,000 in money assets), must now be divided. The vignettes involving unmarried partners said that "Although they never married, Adam and Eve have lived together for the past 22 years just as if they were married." The other vignettes simply described Adam and Eve as married.

Most respondents were asked about eight cases (vignettes) in a within-subjects design.[20] A full set of facts was presented for the first case given; for subsequent cases, respondents were told that "All the facts are the same as in the previous question, except that . . . " In addition to marital status, the series of eight vignettes varied the partners' relative earnings (and therefore their relative contribution to the current wealth) and their contribution to domestic chores. In one "unequal earners" variant, it was said that "*Adam, a college graduate, generally earned more than Eve, who did not graduate from college. At the time of their separation, Adam earned about* $6,000 *each month in a management position, while Eve earned about* $2,000 *each month as a retail clerk*." A second "equal earners" variant stated instead that: "*They usually earned about the same income as one another during most of their*

20 The vignettes were presented in a systematically varying or counterbalanced order, and all results reported here aggregate over these orders.

relationship, and right now they are each earning about $4,000 *a month.*" When their contribution to domestic chores was unequal, the vignette said: "While the children were young, Eve spent more time than Adam taking care of them (although Adam was clearly an involved father), and she also did most of the housework." When their contributions were equal, the vignette said: "They shared parenting duties and housekeeping chores pretty equally during their marriage." Thus, the factors that were varied within subjects constituted a 2 × 2 × 2 factorial: with two values each for marital status (married vs. cohabiting), earning (unequal vs. equal), and caretaking (also unequal vs. equal). This factorial thus produced the eight different vignettes presented to each respondent. When one spouse was portrayed as earning more, either the other spouse did more domestic chores or their division of domestic chores was equal. When one spouse was portrayed as contributing more to domestic chores, either the other spouse earned more or their earnings were equal.

The examples just described portray Adam as the higher earner when the partners' earning were not equal and describe Eve as the primary parent and housekeeper when their domestic contributions were not equal. However, these gender roles were reversed for some respondents. Gender was thus a fourth factor, investigated in a between-subjects design. For example, a separate group of respondents received the same 2 × 2 × 2 factorial of eight questions except that the italicized sentence quoted earlier, which states that Adam was the higher earner, was changed in all the vignettes by replacing "Adam" with "Eve." Similarly, for another group, "Eve" was changed to "Adam" in the sentence stating that Eve spent more time than Adam taking care of their children and doing housework. We varied these gender depictions between subjects, rather than within subjects (as we did other factors), because of the concern that some respondents who were in fact inclined to respond differently when genders were reversed might mask that view in a within-subjects design that asked them about both gender configurations, because it would direct their attention to the fact that we were interested in learning whether gender affected their answers. The concern was that some respondents, if thus made self-conscious about this question, might then conform their answers (but not their true beliefs) to a gender-equality principle they perceived as socially expected (or "politically correct"). But we wanted to know what their true beliefs were, not the beliefs they may have thought they were expected to have.

Each vignette concluded with a single question for the respondent: "What do you believe is a fair division of the $300,000 they have?" Respondents answered by circling a number from 1 (all to Eve) to 7 (all to Adam); 4 indicated equal division. (For vignettes in which Eve was the higher earner, the scale was reversed so that 1 was "all to Adam" and 7 was "all to Eve.")

For the vignette in which Adam and Eve were equal earners, had married, and had taken equal responsibility for their now-grown children, it is difficult to see a basis for choosing any answer other than an equal division of the couple's property when they divorce. Our respondents felt the same way, as 97.1 percent chose "4"–

"equal division." The proportion was virtually the same, however (96.4 percent), if the otherwise identical couple had cohabited but not married. An equal-contributing couple together for twenty-two years and described as living together "just as if they were married" is, of course, about as strong a case as one could construct for treating cohabitants the same way as a married couple. If we aggregate all the equal-earner, equal-child care vignettes, whether married or cohabiting, the mean response is 4.01 – virtually exactly equal. We can take this as our baseline case. The question, then, is whether our respondents moved away from this baseline of equal division if told that the partners' contributions, financial or nonfinancial, were not equal – and whether any such inclination to favor the greater contributor might be stronger when the couple had not married.

Figure 9.5 presents the *mean* response of the indicated group of respondents to each indicated vignette. Our baseline case is the first bar at the far left of Figure 9.5. The additional bars are cases for which statistical significance was found. Numbers higher than 4 indicate a larger share of the property to the partner who earned more: Adam, in the cases with the conventional fact pattern; Eve, in the gender-reversal vignettes.

Notice that, although some bars vary from the baseline result of 4, they do not differ very much. The highest mean response is 4.32; the lowest is 3.92. Our comparatively large N allows the detection of relatively small experimental effects. Because they are statistically significant, we discuss them, but their small size must be kept in mind. A mean response could be close to 4 because almost all respondents chose 4 or because different subgroups departed from equal division, but in opposite directions. The former is generally the case in these data, although the discussion that follows notes an exception for certain vignettes in which male and female respondents answered the questions differently. We found no other demographic characteristics that interacted with our vignette variables, and respondent gender interacted only in the cases we note.

The first group of bars, on the left side of Figure 9.5, show results for the vignettes in which one parent earned more than the other, but they split domestic chores equally. One can see a small shift toward allowing more property to the higher earner, with an overall mean of 4.22. Moving right to the first *pair* of bars, we see that the inclination to award the higher earners more property was significantly[21] greater where the partners were not married (4.28) than when they were (4.17). Put another way, the lower earner was treated a bit better when the partners were married, receiving a small "marriage premium" in the property allocation. The next pair of bars reveals that male respondents were more likely to favor the higher earner than female respondents, as their overall mean for these vignettes, 4.32, was significantly[22] greater than the female respondent mean of 4.13. Finally, we see that the respondents

[21] $F(1, 475) = 15.00, p < .001$.

[22] $F(1,475) = 8.34, p < .01$.

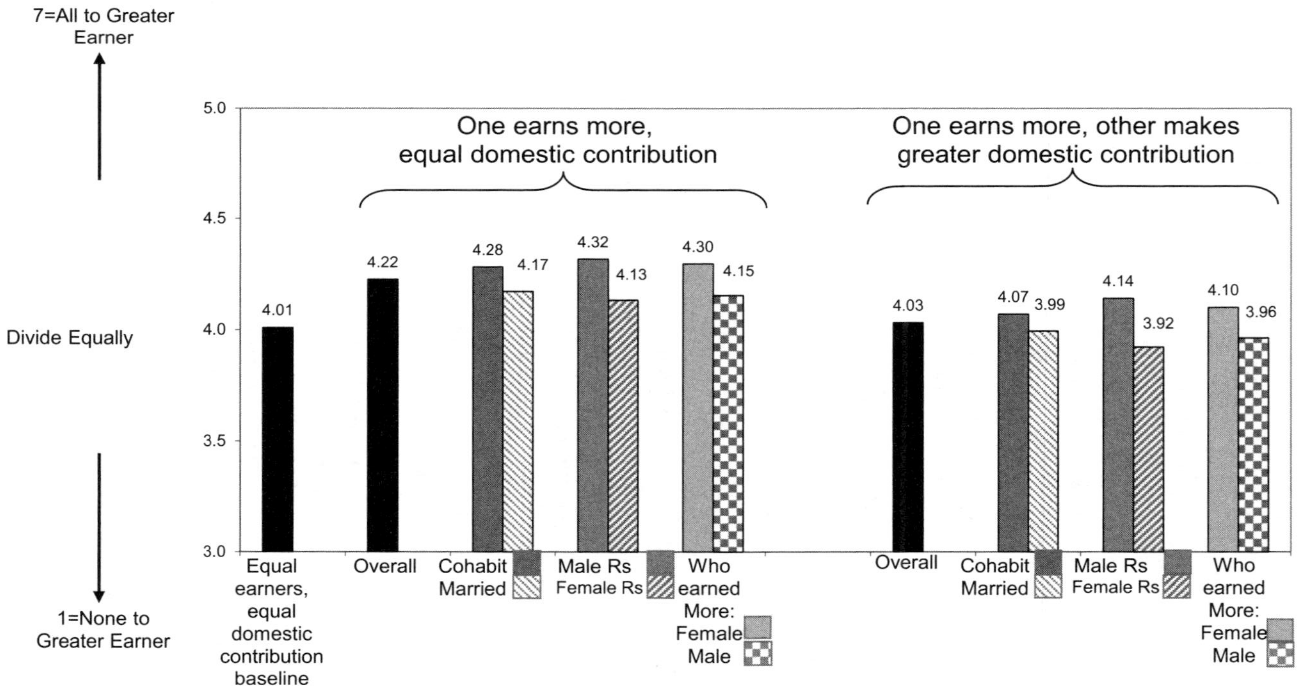

FIGURE 9.5. Division of property, by relative earnings and domestic contributions, marital status, and respondent's gender

overall were more inclined to favor the higher-earning female partner (4.30) than the higher-earning male partner (4.15).[23] Note that while respondent gender mattered for the unequal earnings vignette – as shown, men favored the higher earner more than did women – there was no interaction of respondent gender with marital status. So male and female respondents both averaged a small marriage premium for the lower earner, and the size of their premium did not differ.

The group of bars on the right side of Figure 9.5 show results for the case in which one spouse earns more, but (unlike the group on the left of the figure) the other one performs a larger share of the domestic tasks – what one might call "reciprocal contribution" cases. There is a small marriage premium in these cases as well, as shown in the first pair of bars: the partners were awarded almost exactly equal shares of the property (mean of 3.99) when they were described as married, but the high earner had a small premium when they were not (4.07).[24] Of more general interest, however, is the fact that the means for this group of bars are generally closer to 4 than are the means in the first group; the small premium received by the higher earner is even smaller for cases on the right side of the figure than for cases on the left side. So, it seems our respondents believe that one spouse's greater financial contribution can be offset by the other's greater domestic contribution. Indeed, the overall result for reciprocal contribution cases – a mean of 4.03 – is essentially the same as the overall result for the baseline case in which the parents earned the same amount and also contributed equally to domestic chores (4.01).

Yet these similar overall results were reached through different routes. The percentage of our respondents who actually chose equal division exceeded 96 percent in the baseline case, but fell between 66 percent and 78 percent (depending on other vignette facts) in reciprocal contribution cases. That is, somewhere between about a quarter to a third of our respondents did not believe equal division appropriate in reciprocal contribution cases. The respondents' overall mean nonetheless remained at about 4 because this dissenting group was about evenly divided between those who counted the greater financial contribution more and those who counted the greater domestic contribution more.

Further insight into this phenomenon is gained by looking at the two pairs of bars at the right end of Figure 9.5. The first pair compares female and male respondents; the second pair compares the mean response of *all* respondents in the case in which the man earned more, to the case in which the woman earned more. Male respondents gave higher earners a larger share than did female respondents in reciprocal contribution cases overall (4.14 to 3.92),[25] and respondents overall awarded the female higher earner a larger share (4.10) than they awarded to the male higher

[23] $F(1,475) = 5.00$, $p < .05$.
[24] $F(1.475) = 8.89$, $p < .01$.
[25] $F(1.475) = 11.07$, $p < .001$.

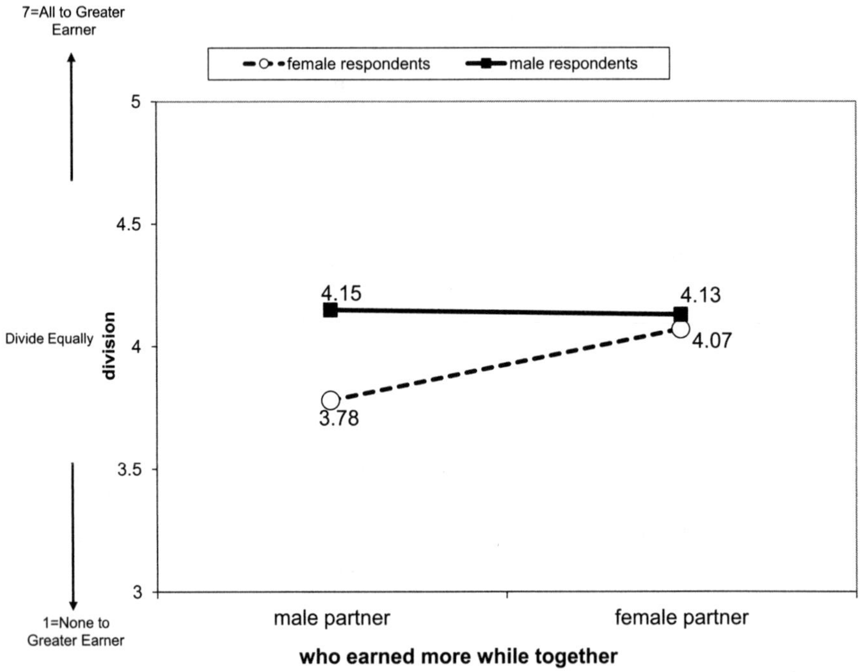

FIGURE 9.6. Division of property, interaction of who earned more with respondent's gender, in reciprocal contribution vignettes

earner (3.96) in reciprocal contribution cases.[26] One might guess that at least some respondents were not inclined to give the lower-earning male partner as much credit for his disproportionate contribution to domestic tasks as they were willing to give the lower-earning female partner, perhaps not accepting at face value the experimenters' description of his contribution (which was of course identical to the description of female partners who were the primary domestic contributor).

Of particular interest, however, is the fact that, unlike in other cases, there was a significant interaction of the two gender effects. As shown in Figure 9.6, male respondents treated the case in which the man was the higher earner essentially the same as the case in which the woman was, slightly favoring the higher earner in both cases (means of 4.15 and 4.13, respectively). Women respondents, however, on average favored the *woman*, whether or not she was the higher earner, in both reciprocal contribution cases: both female higher earners (4.07) and female partners of the male higher earners (3.78) did better than their partners. The mean male response treated the female higher earner (4.13) better than did the mean female response (4.07), as the greater inclination of men to favor the higher earner was gender-neutral.

[26] $F(1.475) = 4.39$, $p < .05$.

In results not shown in Figure 9.5, there was a slight but significant tendency for our respondents to favor the partner who made more domestic contributions while their earnings were equal, and in this case there were no significant differences by either the respondent's gender or the marital status of the couple in the vignette.

Our single most powerful finding is our respondents' general and strong inclination to divide assets equally. Combining the results of all the vignettes considered by all the respondents, they chose equal division 82 percent of the time. Other factual variations we also investigated, but do not report in this chapter (concerning the amount of property and claims of marital misconduct), revealed the same reluctance to depart from equal division.

We may have inadvertently pushed our respondents toward equal division by our choice of the basic fact pattern. One can imagine other cases in which their inclination toward equal division might have been weaker, for example, those involving a shorter relationship or different assets, such as stock shares one of them received from his or her employer that became quite valuable.[27] Perhaps the factors that pushed respondents in our study away from equal division might have had a larger effect against such a different factual background. Marital status, then, might have also mattered more in those cases. On the other hand, it would have to have mattered a lot more to have mattered very much. Nor is there any obvious reason to think that the relative importance of the different factors we investigated would change with such factual changes. For example, marital status mattered less to our respondents than did the gender of the higher earner and had less effect on the results than did the gender of the respondent. In short, these data suggest that our respondents believe marital status is relevant in thinking about the allocation of property when intimate partners separate, but they do not believe it is particularly more important than other factors and would not give it the special emphasis that it currently receives in American law. We note that this also seems to be the case in England, where the law also gives no rights in accumulated property to an unmarried cohabitant, but the public believes it *should*.[28]

[27] The possibility that some of our respondents might have assumed that the partners purchased the home in some form of joint title (even though we did not state that) could also have pushed them in the direction of equal division, although that would not necessarily be the legal result; a co-owner who paid more than half the carrying charges (mortgage, taxes, etc.) is entitled to reimbursement by the other owner in an accounting or partition action when they separate (Dukeminier & Krier 1998:359). Unequal financial contribution can establish a correspondingly unequal ownership interest in property held jointly, but that result is more likely if the parties hold title as tenants in common rather than as joint tenants (for which a stronger presumption of equal ownership will arise). "[T]he court may consider the fact the parties have contributed different amounts to the purchase price in determining whether a true joint tenancy was intended. If a tenancy in common rather than a joint tenancy is found, the court may either order reimbursement or determine the ownership interests in the property in proportion to the amounts contributed." *Milian v. De Leon*, 181 Cal. App. 3d 1185, 1196, 226 Cal. Rptr. 831, 837 (1986). We doubt, however, that many of our respondents would be aware of, much less have considered, such property-law details.

[28] Perhaps remarkably, two-thirds of the British public believes an unmarried woman who has lived with a partner for only two years should have the same financial rights as a married woman to a house they

DISCUSSION

We have offered a sample of results of experiments that seek to learn what facts people believe matter in determining the legal obligations intimate partners have to one another when their relationship ends. Asking respondents to decide cases provides a truer and more nuanced test of their values than can be obtained by asking only general questions about the values themselves. As law teachers know well, people do not often think carefully about a principle until they apply it to decide a case. Asking respondents about cases nonetheless has some unavoidable limitations. On one hand, we did not give our respondents principles to apply because we wanted to learn the principles *they* believe important. On the other hand, what we learned about the principles the respondents used was necessarily affected by the facts we gave them. Had we not systematically varied the marital status of the couples in our vignettes, we could not have investigated whether or how marital status mattered to our respondents' decisions. But it is always possible that factual variations we did not investigate would have interacted with marital status in important ways our current data do not reveal.

The data nonetheless offer some clear messages about our respondents' values. They care a lot about financial inequality and a lot about children. Consider inequality first. Their overarching preference for equal division in the allocation of property is only one example. They also want alimony and child support awards to reduce living-standard disparity between households rather than reserving them to cases where they are needed to ensure that a claimant does not fall below some minimal living standard. And they would reduce living-standard disparity more aggressively than does current U.S. law. While available data do not allow us to make a definitive comparison between our respondents' award rate and the award rate in judicial rulings on alimony claims for cases with comparable facts, they do suggest our respondents would award alimony in more cases than do the courts.

Another one of our studies, not fully described here, compared our respondents' child support awards to the awards called for in current state guidelines and made the same point more clearly. That study (Ellman, Braver, & MacCoun 2009) used vignettes with three different incomes for the mother and father. It found that our respondents favored child support amounts *lower* than the typical guideline result at high maternal income and amounts *higher* than the typical guideline result at low maternal income. This very consistent and systematic pattern would thus reduce living-standard disparity between parental households across all the income combinations we asked about more than do existing guidelines.

Our respondents' approach to child support also reflects their apparent concern for the well-being of children; their approach would increase support amounts for

lived in together but which he had bought in his name alone three years before their relationship began when the partner dies without a will (Barlow 2008: 6).

the cases in which the children's living standard depends on it while reducing them for cases in which it does not. Put another way, our respondents were more inclined than current law to require financially capable fathers to pay support amounts big enough to have a large impact on their children, but less inclined to order low-income fathers to pay amounts burdensome to them but too small to be important to their children. Similarly, our respondents were most inclined to award alimony when the claimant was also the primary custodian of the couple's minor children, and they did not make lower awards in those cases even though they were told the dollar amount of the child support award the claimant would receive.

Our inquiry into the importance of marriage to our respondents takes place against these background values; what we learned is that they care about marital status, but they care more about financial inequality and about children. That means that marriage is a brighter line in law than in the intuitions of lay respondents as to what a fair law would provide. So, for example, a small minority of our respondents gave the married lower-earning partner a slightly larger property share than they would give the cohabiting one, but this tendency was swamped by the much more widely shared commitment to treat the two types of intimate partners equally. And while more of our respondents were willing to favor the married partner over the unmarried one with respect to alimony claims, most of that marriage premium disappeared when the claimants had young children, which is of course quite different than current law. When our respondents did make an alimony award, its *amount* was not much affected by marital status or anything else beside the partners' incomes (which provide the main measure of their financial inequality). The mean child support amounts that our respondents set for married claimants were higher than their means for the unmarried – further evidence that they believe marriage matters. But the fact that their entire child support schedule is elevated, so that low-income unmarried claimants would receive higher child support awards than current law allows married claimants, shows their focus is at least as much on children and equality as on marriage.[29] While marriage seems to have mattered to our respondents, the presence or absence of a relationship also mattered, as shown by the higher support awards they allow cohabiting couples as compared to those with no relationship beyond a brief sexual liaison.

Our overall conclusion, then, is that while our respondents certainly give marriage weight in thinking about obligations between adult partners, they do not give it the overarching weight it often receives in American law. They believe intimate partners can acquire legal obligations to one another without marriage as well as from marriage. They see marriage as a relevant factor but not as a qualifying condition.

So how would the law change if it were revised to be more consistent with our respondents' values? Given all the variables we necessarily could not test, we cannot

[29] Compare the support amounts, e.g., in Figure 9.4 with the support amounts for the same parental incomes found in the Iowa guidelines and set out in Ellman, Braver, and MacCoun (2009) at table 3.

give a definite answer to that question. But we can make a pretty good guess. There would be a strong presumption that property acquired during any long relationship that produced children should be divided equally between the partners, whether or not they were married. We would guess that they would favor the same result even if there were no children, but our data do not directly address that variation. The fact that, when there is financial disparity between the separating partners, more than a third of our respondents would allow alimony after relationships of only six years' duration, married or unmarried, leads us also to guess that most would also divide accumulated property equally at the end of relationships considerably shorter than the twenty-two years we asked about. As for alimony itself, most of our respondents would likely be comfortable with a rule that presumed it should be allowed when (1) there is a substantial financial disparity between the partners, *and* (2) the claimant had primary responsibility for the couple's minor children *or* the couple had been together for some minimum period of time that might be longer if they had not married than if they had. They would base the award amount primarily on the size of the income disparity. Finally, the revised law would require higher-income obligors to pay more child support than they now do, whether they were married to the mother or not, but it would not raise the child support amount as much if they were not married, and might not raise it at all if the parents had no relationship beyond a short sexual liaison.[30]

Marriage would matter in such a revised set of rules, but differently than it does now. Something similar might be said more generally about the relationships of young people today: formal marriage (as distinct from living together) matters to them, but perhaps not quite so much as it did for their parents or grandparents. In that sense, the legal changes our respondents seem to support are not only (we would say) interesting and thoughtful, but perhaps also more compatible than current law with how people live their lives today.

REFERENCES

Baker, L. and Emery, R. (1993). When Every Relationship Is Above Average: Perceptions and Expectations of Divorce at the Time of Marriage. *Law and Human Behavior*, 17, 439–450.

Barlow, A., Burgoyne, C., Clery, E. and Smithson, J. (2008). Cohabitation and the Law: Myths, Money and the Media. In Park, A., et al. (Eds.), *British Social Attitudes: The 24th Report* pp. 29–52. London: Sage Publications.

Barlow, A., Duncan, S., James, G. and Park, A. (2005). *Cohabitation, Marriage and the Law: Social Change and Legal Reform in the 21st Century*. Oxford: Hart.

Blau, F., Ferber, M. and Winkler, A. (1998). *The Economics of Women, Men and Work* (3rd ed.). Upper Saddle River, NJ: Prentice Hall.

Bowman, C.G. (1996). A Feminist Proposal to Bring Back Common Law Marriage. *Oregon Law Review*, 75, 709–780.

[30] Oddly, while raising the amount of child support significantly reduced the alimony award rate for married couples, it did not have the same pervasive effect for unmarried couples (Ellman & Braver 2012, at table 1).

Bowman, C.G. (2010). *Unmarried Couples, Law, and Public Policy*. New York: Oxford University Press.

Bramlett, M.D., and Mosher, W.D. (2002). *Cohabitation, Marriage, Divorce and Remarriage in the United States* (Series 23, No 22). Retrieved July 20, 2011, from http://www.cdc.gov/nchs/data/series/sr_23/sr23_022.pdf.

Braver, S., Ellman, I.M., Votruba, A., and Fabricius, W. (2011). Lay Judgments about Child Custody after Divorce. *Psychology, Public Policy, and Law*, 17, 212–240.

Cherlin, A.J. (2010). Demographic Trends in the United States: A Review of Research in the 2000s. *Journal of Marriage and Family*, 72, 403–419.

Dukeminier, J. and Krier, J.E. (1998). *Property* (4th ed.). New York: Aspen Publishers.

Edin, K. and Kefalas, M. (2005). *Promises I Can Keep: Why Poor Women Put Motherhood Before Marriage*. Berkeley: University of California Press.

Ellman, I.M. (2001). "Contract Thinking" Was *Marvin*'s Fatal Flaw. *Notre Dame Law Review*, 76, 1365–1380.

Ellman, I.M. (2002). Thinking about Custody and Support in Ambiguous-Father Families. *Family Law Quarterly*, 36, 49–78.

Ellman, I.M. and Braver S. (2011). Lay Intuitions About Family Obligations: The Relationship Between Alimony and Child Support. *Children and Family Law Quarterly*, 23, 465–489.

Ellman, I.M., and Braver S. (2012). Lay Intuitions about Family Obligations: The Case of Alimony. *Theoretical Inquiries in Law*, 13(1), 209–240.

Ellman, I.M., Braver, S., and MacCoun, R.J. (2009). Intuitive Lawmaking: The Example of Child Support. *Journal of Empirical Legal Studies*, 6, 69–109.

Ellman, I.M., Braver, S., and MacCoun, R.J. (2012). Abstract Principles and Concrete Cases in Intuitive Lawmaking. *Law and Human Behavior* 36, 96–108.

Ellman, I.M., et al. (2010). *Family Law: Cases, Text, Problems* (5th ed.). San Francisco: Lexis-Nexis.

Ellwood, D. and Jenks, C. (2004). The Spread of Single Parent Families in the United States Since 1960. In Moynihan, D., Smeedling, T., and Rainwater, L. (Eds.), *The Future of the Family* pp. 25–65. New York: Russell Sage Foundation.

Estin, A. (2001). Unmarried Partners and the Legacy of *Marvin v. Marvin*: Ordinary Cohabitation. *Notre Dame Law Review*, 76, 1381–1408.

Garrison, M. (2000). Law Making for Baby Making: An Interpretive Approach to the Determination of Legal Parentage. *Harvard Law Review*, 113, 835–923.

Garrison, M. (2008). Nonmarital Cohabitation: Social Revolution and Legal Regulation. *Family Law Quarterly*, 42, 309–332.

Gilbert, Daniel. (2007). *Stumbling on Happiness*. New York: Vintage Books/Random House.

Goldstein, J.R. and Kenney, C.T. (2001). Marriage Delayed or Marriage Forgone? New Cohort Forecasts of First Marriage for U.S. Women. *American Sociological Review, 66*, 506–519.

Goodwin, P.Y, Mosher, W.D., and Chandra, A. (2010). *Marriage and Cohabitation in the United States: A Statistical Portrait Based on Cycle 6 (2002) of the National Survey of Family Growth*. National Center for Health Statistics. Vital Health Stat 23(28). Retrieved July 20, 2011 from http://www.cdc.gov/nchs/data/series/sr_23/sr23_028.pdf.

Heuveline, P. and Timberlake, J.M. (2004). The Role of Cohabitation in Family Formation: The United States in Comparative Perspective. *Journal of Marriage and Family, 66*, 1214–1230.

Himmelfarb, S. (1975). What Do You Do When the Control Group Doesn't Fit into the Factorial Design? *Psychological Bulletin*, 82, 363–368.

Kim, P.T. (1999). Norms, Learning, and Law: Exploring the Influences on Workers' Legal Knowledge. *University of Illinois Law Review*, 1999, 447–515.

Manning, W.D. and Smock, P.J. (2005). Measuring and Modeling Cohabitation: New Perspectives from Qualitative Data. *Journal of Marriage and Family*, 67, 989–1002.

Oppenheimer, V. (1994). Women's Rising Employment and the Future of the Family in Industrial Societies. *Population and Development Review*, 20, 293–342.

Pleasence, P. and. Balmer, N. (2011). Ignorance in Bliss: Modeling Knowledge of Rights in Marriage and Cohabitation. Unpublished manuscript.

The Women's Law Center of Maryland, Inc. (2004). *Custody and Financial Distribution in Maryland*. Retrieved August 15, 2011, from http://www.wlcmd.org/pdf/publications/CustodyFinancialDistributionInMD.pdf.

U.S. Bureau of the Census. 2010. Table MS–2. Estimated median age at first marriage, by sex: 1890 to the present. *Families and Living Arrangements*. Retrieved July 20, 2010, from http://www.census.gov/population/socdemo/hh-fam/ms2.xls.

Wasoff, F. and Martin, C. (2005). *Scottish Social Attitudes Survey 2004 Family Module Report*. Edinburgh: Scottish Executive.

PART III

Family Policy and Law for the Twenty-First Century

10

Forsaking No Others

Coming to Terms with Family Diversity

Judith Stacey

When I came of age in the 1950s, Frank Sinatra was crooning that love and marriage go together like a horse and carriage, and my girlfriends and I jumped rope on the schoolyard chanting, "First comes love, then comes marriage, then comes [Judy] with a baby carriage." That was a time when such platitudes were uncontroversial and almost as empirically accurate as they were morally prescriptive, a time when, in the eyes of many voters, divorce rendered presidential candidate Adlai Stevenson unfit for office, and marital infidelity turned Hollywood heartthrob Ingrid Bergman, the Swedish star of *Casablanca*, into a pariah denounced on the floor of the U.S. Senate as "Hollywood's apostle of degradation" (http://www.ingridbergman.com). Those were the days, of course, when any sort of love other than heterosexual monogamy dared not yet whisper its name, and nobody would have thought to specify the sexual orientation of the imaginary blissful couple that the song and the jump-rope jingle celebrated.

No 1950s rope jumper, 1970s feminist, or family sociologist, like me, could possibly have imagined a world in which an unwed pregnant teenager and her boyfriend would mount the dais at a Republican presidential convention to join the proud family tableau as her mother, a right-wing governor, accepted the party's nomination for vice president of the United States. But that, of course, was what happened when Sarah Palin became Republican John McCain's running mate in 2008. Clearly, the intervening decades had unsettled long taken-for-granted assumptions about the links between love, marriage, and babies. Lots of horses and carriages had come unhitched.

And yet, despite mind-bending changes in family patterns and practices, the word *family* continues to conjure an image of a married, monogamous, heterosexual pair and their progeny. This is still the model of a "normal family," not only in the world of soccer moms and Joe six-packs and among politicians across the ideological spectrum who bid to win their votes, but even among some family researchers. As the popular rubric "alternative families" makes clear, this "normal family" remains the standard against which all other forms of intimacy and kinship are compared, and frequently found lacking. Citizens and numerous scholars alike generally take it for granted that the "normal family" is not only superior to all others but close to universal historically and cross-culturally, a quasi-natural institution, virtually the core definition of family. Few doubt that marriage is a culturally universal and necessary institution or that the ideal family structure for raising children is a married couple and their biological or adopted children.

Of course, the United States and many other societies are now deeply divided over the gay rights movement's powerful challenge to the conventional gender composition of a marital couple. If contemporary marriage is at a crossroads, the traffic lights monitoring the intersection signal the road to same-sex marriage. Yet, despite potent cultural polarization, activists on both sides of this issue largely share the dominant cultural perspective on normal family life. Advocates and opponents of same-sex marriage alike celebrate the institution of marriage and fail to question the weighty privileges that married couple-families receive compared with everyone else. Same-sex marriage suitors also endorse the same ideals of romantic love, monogamy, and gender equality that the U.S. state has always used to justify prohibiting polygamy.

This essay summarizes my recent book, *Unhitched: Love, Marriage and Family Values from West Hollywood to Western China* (Stacey 2011), that directly challenges these popular views. Drawing from ethnographic research projects on family diversity at home and abroad, the book demonstrates that the normal family is not normal. My research on intimacy, kinship, and parenthood among gay men in the greater Los Angeles area, polygynous families in South Africa, and maternal extended families who raise children "without husbands or fathers" among the Mosuo minority culture in Southwestern China attests to the irrepressible variety of intimacy and kinship in the modern, as well as the premodern, world. Family diversity, I demonstrate, has always been normal, and it is here to stay. I believe that societies, as well as social scientists, must come to terms with this reality.

WE ARE *ALL* NEGRO FAMILIES NOW

If the normal married-couple family that was so taken for granted in my youth no longer describes the intimate lives of even many of the most conservative Christian Republicans in the United States, and if family diversity is both the historical norm and its irreversible current course, why does the ideology of the normal family remain so potent? Why haven't our beliefs about happy and unhappy families morphed along with our behaviors? In part, this is because of the ways in which the personal became so politicized during the last half-century. Since the 1960s, every time the U.S. Census Bureau released new data that indicated slippage from Ozzie-and-Harriet ideals, it provoked fractious finger-pointing over the social culprits and casualties of family changes. From soaring rates of single mothers (first among black women, later among whites), the "divorce revolution," "deadbeat dads," working moms, day care, the "mommy track," and the "second shift," to dwindling percentages of couples who exchange vows and rings and to the mounting masses who live alone, with their lovers, roommates, or "child-free," or most controversially during the past decade, to the escalating ranks of lesbian and gay couples and parents insistently demanding equal rights – moralistic clashes over personal life offer tempting wedge issues to politicians hungry for motivated voters. They have become routine features of the political landscape.

With rearview vision, I would anoint the late senator Daniel Patrick Moynihan the great-granddaddy of the modern politics of family values. His 1965 report, *The Negro Family: The Case for National Action*, written for the Johnson administration's War on Poverty, branded the burgeoning number of black single-mother families a matriarchal "tangle of pathology" and blamed it for a host of social ills. Penned (when writers still used pens) in a turbulent decade of racial combat and cultural upheaval, those were fighting words. Black leaders promptly condemned what came to be called *The Moynihan Report* as racist (Staples 1978), and a reborn feminist movement soon pilloried it for sexism as well (Stack 1997). During the 1960s, Western family verities began to take it on the chin from all sides. *The Feminine Mystique*, Betty Friedan's (1964) incendiary critique of the gender conventions of the *Father Knows Best* family of my youth, had been published just one year before Moynihan's report. Grassroots movements for women's and gay liberation were about to explode. And, of course, those were the years when the Age of Aquarius dawned, thanks in part to the Pill – a countercultural youth rebellion swept up in sex, drugs, and rock 'n' roll. To criticize waning rates of marriage and waxing rates of fatherlessness, particularly among black victims of searing racism, sexism, and poverty, as Moynihan had done, seemed politically tone-deaf, if not unforgivably retrograde, then.

Well, that was then. Since the late 1970s, Moynihan's diagnosis of black family failures has enjoyed a stunning reversal of fortune. Its shift in cultural stature from inflammatory to mainstream common sense, among even leading black scholars (Murray 2005; Patterson 1999), celebrities (Cosby 2004), and politicians in the United States, including President Obama, serves as a handy litmus test of the gains that pro-marriage ideology has been scoring ever since. Moynihan's analysis of black family disarray proved to be a harbinger of the culture wars over mainstream family values that were about to erupt, not to speak of offering an object lesson in the perverse Law of Unintended Consequences. *The Negro Family*, despite its liberal origins in the Great Society and its commitment to the War on Poverty, anticipated arguments that later became pivotal to the startling ascent of the religious New Right and the ultimate dismantling of the U.S. welfare state.

When Moynihan tolled the alarm bells for black fatherless families in 1965, 22 percent of black children were born to unwed women (and girls). By the early 1980s, the percentage of unmarried white mothers broached that level (Garfinkel and McLanahan 1986), and what Moynihan had bemoaned as the pathology of an underclass took on the stature of a national catastrophe for his intellectual heirs. Welding the links that he had drawn between marriage, morality, and social pathology into an ironclad Christian gospel, the New Right propelled the Reagan revolution and ushered in nearly three decades of conservative Republican dominance.

Since the late 1970s, New Right culture warriors have battled, with startling success, to rescue 1950s, *Father Knows Best* family *ideals* (behavior is quite another matter, of course) from ravages of what they construe to have been the narcissistic, irresponsible, Aquarian culture of the 1960s and 1970s. They scuttled President Carter's attempt to convene a national White House Conference on the Family in 1979. Furious battles over the legitimate definition of family broke out when the administration appointed Patsy Fleming, a divorced, black, single mother of three, as executive secretary (Ribuffo 2006). The planned national event fractured into three contentious regional conferences on *families*. Waving the banner of family values, the New Right also seized defeat of the Equal Rights Amendment from the jaws of a feminist near-victory.[1] Conservative family values composed a core platform of the Moral Majority, a key constituency behind Reagan's presidential landslide in 1980, and of the Contract with America that Newt Gingrich designed to engineer the triumphant Republican congressional takeover in 1994.[2]

The New Right wielded religious and cultural authority to support its brand of family values. Armed with Holy Scriptures, Moral Majority's founder, the late Jerry Falwell, and James Dobson, of Focus on the Family, crusaded against abortion, premarital sex, infidelity, divorce, and homosexuality (Giloff 2007; Reyes 2007). In one of the more surreal episodes in the U.S. family wars, 1992 Republican vice presidential candidate Dan Quayle lambasted the unwed pregnancy of a fictional TV sitcom anchorwoman, Murphy Brown. As if summoning the ghost of the 1950s film star Ingrid Bergman, Quayle railed against Hollywood and the popular-culture industry for undermining family values by glamorizing single motherhood ("Dan Quayle v. Murphy Brown" 1992).

In the early 1990s, however, Moynihan's views of family pathology attracted new political converts. They, too, appealed to social science to give heft to their arguments. A centrist, secular marriage promotion campaign emerged that replenished the right-wing, religious troops doing battle to resist the winds of family change. In the early 1990s, Senator Moynihan himself repeatedly reprised his old argument. A 1994 campaign fundraising letter of his, for example, reprinted famous lines from his

1 Phyllis Schlafly warned that the ERA would cause women to lose preferential child custody and support after divorce and would lead to gay rights, unisex toilets, and women in combat. Although such arguments stirred sufficient fears to defeat the ERA, most of these predictions have come to pass nonetheless. See Schlafly, *Feminist Fantasies*, Spence Publishing, 2003; Schlafly, "Stop ERA," at http://www.smithsoniansource.org/display/primarysource/viewdetails.aspx?PrimarySourceId=1159.

2 "Republican Contract with America," http://www.house.gov/house/Contract/CONTRACT.html. For a critique, see Borosage, "A *Real* Contract with America," at http://www.thenation.com/doc/20051024/borosage.

1965 report and lamented that they had come to describe the sorry state of American family life as a whole:

> From the wild Irish slums of the 19th-century Eastern seaboard to the riot-torn suburbs of Los Angeles, there is one unmistakable lesson in American history: a community that allows a large number of young men to grow up in broken families, dominated by women, never acquiring any stable relationship to male authority, never acquiring any set of rational expectations about the future – that community asks for and gets chaos. Crime, violence, unrest, unrestrained lashing out at the whole social structure – that is not only to be expected; it is very near to inevitable.[3]

The contemporary secular marriage movement owes Moynihan a direct intellectual debt. It too blames most social problems on marital decline and the spread of fatherlessness. It too brandishes social science research rather than scriptures or cultural tradition as authority. The opening lines of *Fatherless America* by David Blankenhorn, founder of the Institute for American Values and a leading figure in this campaign, typify the genre: "Fatherlessness is the most harmful demographic trend of this generation. It is the leading cause of declining child well-being in our society. It is also the engine driving our most urgent social problems from crime to adolescent pregnancy to child sexual abuse to domestic violence against women" (Blankenhorn 1995, 1).

Despite its self-description, the secular "Marriage Movement" is not a grassroots social movement. It is an ideological campaign coordinated by public intellectuals like Blankenhorn, Maggie Gallagher, and David Popenoe, who have set up independent think tanks and councils, like the Institute for American Values, the Institute for Marriage and Public Policy, and the National Marriage Project.[4] With financial backing from private foundations and intellectual support from a smattering of sympathetic social scientists, they pursue a form of cultural politics that they inappropriately liken to the antismoking campaign.[5] Of course, when antismoking forces warn that inhaling tobacco laced with nicotine risks lethal effects on our lungs and lives, they are accurately reporting an overwhelming scientific consensus based on published, peer-reviewed, research evidence. Marriage promotion advocates, in contrast, dispense a steady stream of what I have described as

[3] I personally received one of these campaign fundraising letters. The same quote appears in Moynihan, "Defining Deviancy Down," 26.

[4] The personnel and boards of many of these institutes are interlocking, with David Blankenhorn, David Popenoe, and Maggie Gallagher playing central roles in most of them. Related institutes and advocacy projects include the late sociologist Steven Nock's Marriage Matters at the University of Virginia, Gallagher's National Organization for Marriage, and Don Browning's Religion, Family and Culture Project at the University of Chicago.

[5] "Don't glamorize unwed motherhood, marital infidelity, alternative lifestyles and sexual promiscuity. Imagine depicting divorce and unwed childbearing as frequently and as approvingly as you currently depict smoking and littering." Popenoe, Elshtain, and Blankenhorn, *Promises to Keep*, 313.

"virtual social science" (Stacey 1996) that touts the benefits of heterosexual marriage for adults, children, and society and warns that dire social consequences attend its decline.

Whether or not the secular marriage campaign has nudged many repentant, confirmed bachelors and bachelorettes down the aisle or stemmed the stampede of feckless spouses to the divorce courts is impossible to say, but there is no denying the campaign's potent influence on U.S. political rhetoric and public policy. What had been the credo of a right-wing religious minority became bipartisan mainstream orthodoxy during Clinton's presidency. In 1992, Murphy Brown seemed to have won her prime-time debate with Dan Quayle, and successful Democratic candidate Clinton defended pluralist family values. However, less than a year after Clinton took office, even the liberal wing of the mainstream media reversed course on family values. Early in 1993, for example, the *Atlantic Monthly* published a wildly popular cover story, "Dan Quayle Was Right," by Barbara Dafoe Whitehead, who was then Blankenhorn's codirector at the Institute for American Values. Clinton speedily caught the new current: "Remember the Dan Quayle speech?" he soon mused in a *Newsweek* interview. "There were a lot of very good things in that speech. . . . Would we be a better-off society if babies were born to married couples? You bet we would" (Kranish 2009, 17).

With unsettling haste, and considerable political irony, the only Democrat to occupy the White House between 1981 and 2009 (and the son of a divorced mother, to boot) was the one who signed into law two weighty, and in my view wrongheaded, public policies rooted in marriage promotion ideology – the 1996 Personal Responsibility and Work Opportunity Reconciliation Act (popularly known as the Welfare Reform Act) and the Defense of Marriage Act (DOMA). The former, more consequential of these, opens with a textbook illustration of virtual social science. "The Congress makes the following *findings* [my emphasis]," the act's preamble begins, and then it proceeds to itemize them:

(1) Marriage is the foundation of a successful society.
(2) Marriage is an essential institution of a successful society which promotes the interests of children.
(3) Promotion of responsible fatherhood and motherhood is integral to successful child rearing and the well-being of children. . . .
(7) The negative consequences of an out-of-wedlock birth on the mother, the child, the family and society are *well documented* as follows . . .

And what follows is a list of misleading correlations, including claims that out-of-wedlock children are more likely to suffer child abuse, low cognitive attainment, lower educational aspirations, and so on.

The 1996 Welfare Reform Act poured the political concrete for a profound shift in the priorities of national poverty policy from promoting welfare to promoting marriage. In another poignant irony, Moynihan proved to be the most prominent and eloquent senator to oppose the law in the end. He denounced the decision to drop children born to unmarried women from "federal life-support" as the most "regressive and brutal act of social policy since Reconstruction" (DeWitt 2005). The entire edifice of the subsequent George W. Bush administration's faith-based Federal Marriage Initiative rested on this foundation.

A second, competing marriage movement also congealed in the 1990s, of course – the international drive to legalize same-sex marriage. A favorable ruling by the Hawaiian Supreme Court in 1993 aroused national hopes and fears that the island state would be the first to make same-sex marriage legal. The issue swiftly became the central focus of the gay rights movement, and opposing it began to usurp abortion as the favorite wedge issue for New Right cultural warriors. Almost overnight, presidential candidates felt politically obliged to oppose gay marriage. That explains why during President Clinton's reelection campaign in 1996, he signed into law the Orwellian-named Defense of Marriage Act, which passed with overwhelming bipartisan support.[6] DOMA authorized states to refuse to recognize, let alone to defend, the marriages of same-sex couples who wed in states where it was legal. There were no such states then. But of course, that was then. As of this writing, there are six states and the nation's capital city, Washington, D.C., and of course the high-visibility, high-stakes court battle over Proposition 8 under way in California that is designed to reach the U.S. Supreme Court.

The presidential victory of Barack Obama in 2008 seemed to signify a generational shift in American politics that would spell the end of cultural combat between loyalists of white-bread 1950s values and the aging Aquarian remnants of the rebellious 1960s and 1970s. Although Obama hewed to the obligatory, bipartisan line that marriage is for a woman and a man, he made a daring campaign promise to work to repeal DOMA (as well as the "Don't Ask, Don't Tell" military policy). With the electorate facing economic meltdown and military quagmire, the politics of family values failed, for the first time since 1980, to influence the outcome of a national election in the United States. Despite Obama's stance against DOMA, he won even in two big states, California and Florida, whose voters passed ballot measures against same-sex marriage on the same day.

Nonetheless, President Obama himself seems to subscribe to core principles of marriage promotion ideology. It is refreshing and to his considerable credit that Obama appears actually to practice the family values of commitment to monogamous marriage and responsible fatherhood that he preaches, unlike so many of the prominent Republican Scarlet Lettermen, like Newt Gingrich, Larry Craig, and Mark Sanford, who were the main architects and advocates of the political ideology. However, Obama too has bought into the inaccurate, virtual social science claims that marriage promotion advocates disseminate. In fact, Moynihan, Blankenhorn,

[6] The bill passed by a vote of 85–14 in the Senate and 342–67 in the House and was signed into law by President Clinton on September 21, 1996.

or even the author of Dan Quayle's Murphy Brown speech could have written lines from the major Father's Day sermon that candidate Obama delivered to a black church in Chicago during his 2008 presidential campaign:

> Of all the rocks upon which we build our lives, we are reminded today that family is the most important. And we are called to recognize and honor how critical every father is to that foundation. They are teachers and coaches. They are mentors and role models. They are examples of success and the men who constantly push us toward it. We know the statistics – that children who grow up without a father are five times more likely to live in poverty and commit crime; nine times more likely to drop out of schools and twenty times more likely to end up in prison. They are more likely to have behavioral problems, or run away from home, or become teenage parents themselves ("Obama's Fathers Day Speech" 2008).

President Obama reprised this theme the following year on his first Father's Day in office in June 2009 (Obama 2009). One could be forgiven for expecting that having grown up with a single mother who divorced twice during his childhood, Obama's own stupendous achievements would have served as sufficient rebuke to this doomsday message about the critical need for fathers to achieve successful child outcomes. At the very least, it should have aroused the president's skeptical curiosity about the source and validity of that litany of alarming statistics that he asserted "we know." Instead, the ideological claims of the marriage promotion campaign seem to have trumped both President Obama's life experience and his propensity for critical reflection. Like a preponderance of contemporary citizens, policy makers, and even some scholars, the president appears to have been persuaded that research supports the main popular beliefs about love, marriage, and family values that my research dispels. I can think of no more unsettling testimony than this to the unwarranted ideological success of the marriage promotion campaign whose lineage dates back to the publication of Moynihan's *The Negro Family* in 1965.

UNTYING THE KNOT

Drawing from my research on contemporary family life among gay men in Los Angeles, polygamy in South Africa, and the non-marrying Mosuo of Lugu Lake in China, I pose four challenges to the bipartisan hegemony of the normal family ideology: (1) Marriage is *not* a universal, necessary, or intrinsically superior institution for sustaining children and families. (2) Extending marriage rights to same-sex couples, however humane and just on civil rights grounds, is more likely to increase than to reduce social inequality. Disestablishing marriage would promote a far more equitable family policy. (3) Laws that criminalize polygamy foster hypocrisy and yield perverse effects that are more harmful than helpful to women, children, and society. (4) Fidelity should be redefined to signify integrity rather than sexual exclusivity.

Marriage Is Not Universal or Necessary for Child Welfare

The family system of the Mosuo people, an ethnic minority culture in the remote mountainous borderlands of China's Yunnan and Sichuan provinces, provides the most dramatic empirical challenge to claims about the cultural universality of the married-couple (and particularly the one father-one mother) family. Approximately two millennia ago, Tibeto-Burman ancestors of the 30,000–50,000 surviving members of this ancient Buddhist culture devised a remarkably durable family system that is not based on marriage or a heterosexual union. Mosuo kinship, in startling contrast with traditional Chinese patriarchy, is primarily matrilineal and matrilocal. Instead of marrying and sharing family life with spouses and genetic offspring, adult children remain in their natal, extended, multigenerational households with their mothers and maternal kin. Together family members rear all children born to the women of the household, care for aged and dependent members, and share property and labor. The culture does not assign social responsibility or status to male genitors.

Traditional Mosuo family values radically separate sexuality and romance from domesticity, parenting, and economic bonds. Sex life is strictly voluntary and nocturnal, while family life is obligatory and diurnal. The Mosuo practice "tisese," a system of night visiting, which the Chinese misleadingly translate as walking marriage. The Mosuo term, however, literally means that a man "goes back and forth." Men live, eat, work, and parent with their maternal families by day, but after dinner, they can seek entry into a woman's "flower chamber" for the night. Mutual desire alone governs romantic and sexual union for women and men alike. Because men generally do not live with or co-parent their biological progeny, their sexual behavior has no implications for their own parenting careers or family size. Parents and kin do not meddle or concern themselves with the love lives of their daughters or sons, because mate choice carries almost no implications for the family or society.

To assure its economic and social survival, a Mosuo household needs each generation of women to bear at least one daughter and to produce a gender mix of children. The collective childbearing of their sisters, rather than their own procreative activity, determines men's parental roles. Mosuo men become social fathers to their nieces and nephews. Likewise, sisters jointly mother their collective issue, irrespective of individual fertility. In fact, Naru, the native language, does not distinguish between a mother and a maternal aunt, but employs the same word, "emi," for both (Shih 2009). Although biological paternity carries no inherent implications for Mosuo kinship, male genitors of children born within exclusive tisese relationships generally acknowledge their offspring, give them occasional gifts, and develop avuncular relationships with them. In a sense, one could say that Mosuo kinship rules reverse the social expectations that the West assigns to fathers and uncles.

Although Mosuo kinship is not rooted in marriage, it has been a flexible system open to pragmatic adaptations that helped families survive. One strategy devised to redress gender imbalances allowed exceptions to the cultural rule against couples living together. Households short of males or of females might invite a lover of the underrepresented gender to move in with them. Nonetheless, traditional Mosuo culture did not employ the idiom of marriage to depict such relationships, and the categories of husband and father did not apply. Contemporary Mosuo informants regard tisese rather than marriage as their practice "since time immemorial," which, according to some scholars, extends back earlier than 200 BC (Shih 2001). Although there have been substantial changes in Mosuo family practices since then, particularly upheavals since the Communists came to power, tisese remains the primary institution for sexual union and reproduction. It coexists with secondary forms of contemporary marriage and cohabitation.

With the surgical stroke of excising marriage, Mosuo kinship circumvented a plethora of familiar Western family traumas associated with what feminist family law scholar Martha Fineman (1995) terms "the sexual family."[7] A society without marriage is one with no divorce and with no spinsters or bachelors, widows or widowers, or unmarried, solitary individuals of any sort. Nobody's social status or fate hinges on the success or failure of their love life or marriage. In a family system without marriage, no children are illegitimate, fatherless, or motherless, and few are orphaned. No marriage or divorce means no remarriage as well, and thus no wicked (or benevolent) stepmothers, stepfathers, or Cinderellas. Rarely need anyone become a single parent, and even children with no direct siblings seldom grow up without playmates in their households.

Contemporary advanced industrial societies cannot directly transplant the Mosuo's historic family system, of course, which itself is now threatened by the impact of the global market. We can, however, draw significant lessons from the Mosuo approach to love and parenting. Indeed, I found creative resonances of some of their family values and practices among some of the families formed by gay men that I studied in California. Between 1999 and 2003, I conducted field research on intimacy, kinship, and parenthood among fifty gay men and their families in the Los Angeles area. Twenty-four of the men were parenting children they had sired or adopted in a broad array of family forms. Several were single adoptive parents, others were co-parenting couples who adopted children or became parents through different forms of surrogacy. However, several of the gay men in my study had created successful poly-parenting families formed around a shared desire for parenthood rather than through romantic love, sex, or marriage.

After thirteen years of close friendship, Paul, a gay man, and Nancy, a lesbian, decided to become parents together through alternative insemination. After two years spent carefully discussing their familial values, expectations, anxieties, and limits, they wrote and signed a co-parenting agreement. They understood that the document would lack legal force but believed that going through the process of devising it would

[7] Martha Albertson Fineman, *The Neutered Mother, the Sexual Family, and other Twentieth-Century Tragedies* (New York: Routledge, 1995).

lay a crucial foundation for co-parenting. Their agreement could serve as a model of ethical, sensitive planning for egalitarian, responsible co-parenting.[8] In fact, it has already done so for several friends of Paul's and Nancy's, and for two of mine.

Nancy and Paul became the biological and legal co-parents of two children, but they are not the children's only parents. Before Nancy became pregnant with their first child, she fell in love with Liza, a woman who long had wanted to have children. Paul lived up to the commitment in their agreement to incorporate a new committed partner into the co-parenting alliance. And so their two children were born into a three-parent family. Nancy and Paul honored all of the pertinent terms in their shared parenting plan. They jointly purchased a duplex residential property. Nancy and Liza live together in the front house, Paul inhabits the back house, and their children migrate freely between the two. Paul and Nancy, the two primary parents, fully shared the major responsibilities and expenses along with the joys of parenthood. When their first child was born, both reduced their weekly work schedules to three days so that each could devote two days weekly to full-time parenting while the children were young. A hired nanny cared for the children on the fifth day. Liza, who was employed full time, did early evening child care on the days that Nancy and Paul worked late, and she fully co-parented with them on weekends and holidays.

This three-parent family enjoyed the support of a thick community of kin. One of Paul's former lovers was godfather to the children, and he visited frequently. The three-parent family celebrated holidays with extended formal and chosen kin, including another gay-parent family. Paul had been one of the core members of the gay Pop Luck Club in Los Angeles and of its subgroup of at-home dads. On Fridays, Paul brought the children to the group's weekly play date in the West Hollywood playground where they played with children of other gay dads and where the dads swapped child-rearing tales and tips. Their three-parent, dual-household structure was still intact when I contacted the parents again in 2008.

A second planned poly-parent family in my study included two moms, two dads, two kids, and two homes. Lisa and Kat, a white lesbian couple, initiated this family when after fifteen years together they asked their dear friend and former housemate Michael to serve as the sperm donor and an acknowledged father to the children they wished to rear. Michael, a white gay man who was single at that time, took five years of serious reflection and discussions before he finally agreed to do so. Gradually Michael had realized that he did not wish to become a parent unless he too had a committed mate. Fortuitously, just when his lesbian friends were reaching the end of their patience, he fell in love with Joaquín, a Chicano gay man who had always wanted children. The new lovers asked Lisa and Kat to give them a year to solidify their union before embarking on co-parenthood. Both couples reported that they spent that year in a four-way parental courtship.

[8] I reprint this co-parenting agreement in the appendix to *Unhitched*.

The two couples never sought to equalize parental rights and responsibilities, as Paul and Nancy had done. Although Lisa and Michael are the children's biological and legal parents, because both their names are on the birth certificates, the children have always lived with Lisa and Kat, who are their primary, daily caretakers and chief providers. Michael and Joaquín lived 75 miles away and visited their children every weekend and occasional weeknights. They also conferred with the co-moms and spoke, sang, read, or sent e-mails to their children almost daily. In addition, the adults consciously sustained, monitored, and nurtured their co-parenting alliance and friendship by scheduling periodic "parent time" for the four adults to spend together while the children slept.

Like Nancy, Paul, and Liza, the four parents regularly shared holidays and social occasions with a wide array of legal and chosen kin. They too were immersed in a large local community of lesbian- and gay-parent families, a community Lisa had taken the initiative to organize. Three sets of doting grandparents vied for visits, photos, and contact with their grandchildren. In painful contrast, Kat's parents had rejected her when she came out and refused to incorporate, or even to recognize, her children as their grandchildren or any of their lesbian daughter's family members within their more rigid, ideological understanding of family.

Legal Same-Sex Marriage Will Not Reduce Social Inequality

Same-sex marriage advocates claim that legalizing same-sex marriage will promote social equality. To be sure, it would eliminate one galling and, in my view, indefensible form of discrimination against lesbians and gay men. But the upshot of opening the exclusionary gates of the marital country club to same-sex couples would be to shift more of the onus of discrimination from sex orientation to marital status, and thereby to exacerbate the latter. Marriage never has been and never will be an equal-opportunity institution. In both the United States and South Africa, for example, access to marriage skews heavily against people from subordinate racial and class backgrounds. Making the membership rules gender inclusive will deepen the class and race disparities.

All of the gay and lesbian parents from my original study whom I was able to locate again in the fall of 2008 were actively supporting the (unsuccessful) campaign to defeat Proposition 8. Five of eight co-parenting couples from the original study, including Lisa and Kat, had rushed to hold gay "shotgun" weddings during California's brief window of legal opportunity. Legal marriage held potent symbolic and emotional meaning for them and for most of their children well beyond the significant material benefits it bestowed.

Legal marital status, however, would do nothing to recognize or protect the impressive parenting and kin relationships in the poly-parenting families. It would not have conferred parental status on Liza, who has shared parenting of two children since their birth with Paul and Nancy. Not would Kat or Joaquín gain parental legitimacy with Lisa and Michael in their four-parent family. It will not legitimate the deep family bonds that another gay couple and their three children have forged with the children's gestational surrogate, her husband, and their two children, or the social relationships that developed between their egg donor's two youngsters and the three genetic half-siblings she helped create for the gay couple.

Likewise, legal marriage offers no benefits to the gay single adoptive parents and their children I studied (or to any single-parent family). It also would have been utterly irrelevant to the mutually sustaining intergenerational bonds that "Mother Randolph," an iconoclastic sixty-something disabled gay man in my study, had formed with his multicultural array of younger gay caregivers, among them two undocumented Latin American immigrants and two formerly indigent HIV-positive men. In fact, legalizing same-sex marriage would exacerbate the invisibility of parents and kin in these families. As Nancy Polikoff (2008) methodically documents in *Beyond (Straight and Gay) Marriage*, it would also reinforce pervasive discrimination against all unmarried adults and the people they nurture.

Criminalizing Polygamy Does More Harm Than Good

Ever since the new Republican Party targeted polygamy along with slavery as the "twin relics of barbarism" in the mid-nineteenth century, hostility to polygamy has been one of the few genuinely popular, time-honored, bipartisan family values in the United States. Public antipathy to polygamy is so entrenched that same-sex marriage advocates fear guilt by association whenever opponents exploit this national prejudice by mounting slippery-slope arguments against legalizing same-sex marriage. Political anxiety, however, is not the only source of gay disavowals of any logical link between same-sex and plural marriage. Most of the gay men I studied who wished to marry shared the popular aversion. The battle for same-sex marriage is a white-bread – and in fact an overwhelmingly white, assimilationist – agenda, rather than a subversive one, as queer theorists and activists long have complained (Warner 1999; Duggan 2004; Polikoff 2008). Distancing itself from the taint of promiscuity that is popularly associated with gay sexual culture, the same-sex marriage drive aspires to tame gay desire in the interests of domesticity and social respectability.

However, my research on polygamy in South Africa and the United States shows that some contemporary polygamists in both nations legitimately draw on the same love-makes-a-family ideology that same-sex marriage fans embrace. They also offer resonant arguments about the propriety of their brand of family values, particularly when compared with the endless parade of hypocritical married, "monogamist" Scarlet Lettermen in the United States, like recent inductees, former California Governor Arnold Schwarzenegger and former Democratic presidential candidate John Edwards. I differ, therefore, with gay marriage advocates who deny that there are any legal parallels between bids for same-sex and for plural marriage rights.

Gays and lesbians have now achieved too much cultural confidence and clout to consider a return to the closet. Political attempts to suppress gay varieties of love, marriage, and baby carriages, such as California's Prop 8 and state bans on gay adoption, are powerless to increase the ranks of heterosexual marriages or the percentage of children who will be raised in "normal" mom-and-pop families. During the season in 2000 when California voters approved Proposition 22, the state's first initiative against same-sex marriage, Paul and Nancy and Liza were moving into their front-house and back-house property with their first baby; Lisa and Kat and Michael and Joaquín were consummating their four-parent courtship; a gay male couple in my study were searching for an egg donor and another woman willing to be a gestational surrogate mother for their first child; two gay single men were adopting children on their own; and the Pop Luck Club in Los Angeles was growing by leaps and bounds.

What once was true for closeted gays, however, remains true for underground polygamists in the United States. Perversely, criminalizing polygamy not only shoos such families into the closet or, worse, encourages them to join outlaw compounds, but it actually increases fatherlessness and divorce. In South Africa, polygynist President Jacob Zuma continues to court and impregnate multiple women, but then to marry them publicly (well, most of them!) and to bestow on his many children access to his paternal name, attention, and property (Hughes 2010). Zuma's co-wives were welcome to jointly mount the official inaugural viewing platform and hold their heads high (or drop them in slumber) as he took the oath of office.[9] But by driving polygamy underground, the United States enabled now-imprisoned FLDS patriarch Warren Jeffs to appropriate more than sixty women and underage girls as his brides and to sire literally countless children, all of whom lack legal protection or the ability to choose to enter or exit his dominion.[10] Perversely, too, after open polygynist Tom Green served his six-year prison sentence for a bigamy conviction, he was forbidden to reside with more than one of the four wives who still claimed to love him or to resume paternal responsibility for all of his children, as he wished to do.

In the United States, the clandestine "love children" who some Scarlet Lettermen, like John Edwards and Arnold Schwarzenegger, sire also usually become fatherless children. When their existence comes to light, it spells political downfall for their "fathers" and visits on the men's legal wives and children a torrent of public humiliation, pain, and family upheaval. Some of the aggrieved wives feel social pressure to

9 In *Unhitched* I reprint a popular photograph that depicts Zuma's three co-wives sitting side by side and dozing during his presidential inauguration ceremony (Stacey 2011).

10 Estimates of the number of Jeffs' wives and children vary greatly, ranging from 40 to 80 wives and as many as 250 children. See, for example, Wade Goodwyn, Howard Berkes, and Amy Walters, "Warren Jeffs and the FLDS," NPR, May 3, 2005, http://www.npr.org/templates/story/story.php?storyId=4629320; and Jamie Colby, FOX Online w/ Jamie Colby, "FOX Facts: Warren Jeffs" August 31, 2006, http://www.foxnews.com/story/0,2933,210959,00.html.

divorce their husbands, even when they might prefer to attempt to reconcile.[11] If they do decide to split, their offspring swell the ranks of what the Marriage Movement disparagingly, and inappropriately, calls "children of divorce."[12]

In South Africa, in contrast, I interviewed co-wives who preferred to share their husbands rather than cope with their philandering or, worse, risk desertion or divorce. Likewise, one rural Zulu woman whose four children all had died in infancy agreed to share her husband with a single mother who agreed to share her children. They lived in neighboring cabins as co-wives and co-mothers without social disapproval and without fear that the state might decide to take their children into protective custody, as Texas authorities did when they raided the YFZ ranch.

A Case for Redefining Fidelity

My research underscores the need to jettison the traditional marital pledge to forsake all others, which does less to foster fidelity than bad faith, bad behavior, and bad public policy. A singular focus on monogamous heterosexual marriage justifies discrimination and disrespect for everyone who lives outside the charmed family circle, whether by design or by destiny. It generates infidelity, deception, desertion, divorce, and family instability. It also underwrites the malignant levels of hypocrisy that erupt in our chronic political sex scandals. Too often these personal transgressions yield weighty political consequences, such as the impeachment of Clinton and the political demise of public figures, like former New York Governor Elliot Spitzer.

Many of the gay men I studied negotiated the basic tension between desire and domesticity more creatively and honestly than mainstream heterosexual culture encourages people to do. Because they had been compelled to create their relationships outside the prescribed template of "the sexual family," they devised a variety of ways to unhitch and recombine love, lust, commitment, nurturance, residence, and parenthood.

Partly due to necessity and perhaps partly due to gender, gay men do seem to manage sexual jealousy and to turn former lovers into friends and kin more easily than most heterosexuals tend to do. These are useful skills in a divorce-prone culture. As some of my gay research subjects quipped, pursuing eros exclusively among men

[11] In the wake of the Tiger Woods ultra-Scarlet Letterman expose, for example, it became newsworthy when his wife had second thoughts about divorcing him. As one typical news story began, "Ever since the news broke of Tiger Woods' viral infidelities, it's been kind of a common assumption that his wife Elin Nordegren would soon file for divorce. But she apparently has other ideas." McMullen, "People: Hold Everything, Tiger Woods' Wife Doesn't Want a Divorce," http://www.mercurynews.com/ci_14272676?source=most_viewed.

[12] Note that when a marriage with young children ends because one or both parents die, we do not refer to their offspring as "children of death." In the news story about Tiger Woods, his wife was reported to want to protect her children from being "child[ren] of divorce" who felt slighted by their father as she had.

allows gay men more opportunities to enjoy sex, if they so desire. Better yet, in my view, accepting a stigmatized sexual identity seems to allow gay men to be more forthright and less defensive about acknowledging whatever their erotic desires may be. Whether or not the rest of us want more sex in our lives, we and our societies could certainly benefit from more forthrightness and less shame or hypocrisy about our sexual yearnings. Gay men could inspire us to redefine fidelity and sexual ethics in ways more compatible with the principles and social conditions of liberal democracy.

My cross-cultural research on love, sex, and family led me to wonder how and why the concept of "infidelity" ever came to acquire its contemporary reference to sexual adultery. When the concept arose in the fifteenth century, an infidel was a religious rather than a sexual sinner, someone who was living outside the (Christian) faith. I was writing the chapters about gay men in *Unhitched* during the summer of 2008 in the wake of what seemed like a record-breaking season of political sex scandals and exposés in the United States – most prominently those involving presidential candidate John Edwards and, in my own state of New York, Governor Eliot Spitzer, and then capped off by the unwed teen pregnancy of Bristol Palin, the daughter of the 2008 Republican vice presidential nominee, Sarah Palin. The sexual escapades of staunch right-wing, family-values warriors South Carolina governor Mark Sanford and Nevada senator John Ensign, a Capitol Hill Christian Fellowship resident, had usurped the media limelight when I wrote the book's conclusion during the summer of 2009. And the strictly virtual sexual escapades of the New York Congressman dubbed "Weinergate" have displaced Schwarzenegger's exposé as I revise this chapter in the summer of 2011. It is increasingly difficult to fathom how these perennial breaches of private marital vows can remain matters of great public import, or why a sexual ethics for the twenty-first century should be wedded to a monolithic erotic standard, particularly one that is so regularly honored in the breach.

My research on gay intimacy led to me to favor an ethic of sexual integrity, responsibility, and respect over a uniform insistence on sexual exclusivity. The most impressive relationships I studied modeled a mature willingness to acknowledge the variety, complexity, fluidity, and sheer mystery of individual sexual longings, limits, aesthetics, and meanings. Some were unequivocally exclusive, but others allowed for outside and even asymmetrical sexual encounters under a variety of rules and principles. After their initial sexual fires faded, for example, one formerly monogamous couple opened their relationship to allow especially the younger, more frustrated partner to enjoy casual sexual encounters so long as he always informed his partner and returned home to sleep with him. Conversely, a once sexually open couple closed the door to outside sex play after they both fell in love with a third man and invited him to join their bed, home, and lives. All were faithful to their beloveds, and all of their relationships were still enduring when I contacted them again in 2008. Infidelity did dissolve one of the gay unions in my study, however, because it violated the presumptively shared monogamous credo. In my view and theirs, the infidelity was not a sexual but an ethical breach of trust. Inspired by such examples, we might cease promoting monogamy for all and castigating those who lapse. Instead we might redefine fidelity to signify faithfulness to the particular sexual, emotional, and social commitments that intimates mutually arrive at through honest negotiation and renegotiation. Sexual integrity should trump exclusivity.

TOWARD A CORNUCOPIA OF CIVIL UNIONS

The normal-family ideology serves to rationalize discriminatory, hurtful policies, like the Federal Marriage Initiative, DOMA, and bans on gay adoption, that in turn stoke the exaggerated emphasis the gay rights movement places on winning the legal right to marry. However, as I argued earlier, expanding access to civil marriage to same-sex couples represents far too meager a vision of intimate equality or justice. I believe that a democratic society should encourage dignity, respect, and success for all of the honest, consensual, and responsible modes of living, loving, and caretaking its citizens devise. The state should be trying to ensure that citizens can freely enter and sustain supportive relationships and freely exit abusive ones. It has a legitimate interest in promoting responsible, committed care and protection for children and other dependents. These are goals that can be and are being met or shirked by people who are chaste, infertile, sexually impotent, adventurous, polyamorous, or just plain randy. They are within the reach of people who live in love-match or arranged marriages, whether these are monogamous, open, celibate, or polygamous. And they beckon as well to folks who live outside of matrimony in intergenerational, dual-household, or single-parent families or who reside with their lovers, housemates, beloved pets, or all alone.

A democratic state has no business dictating or even favoring any particular brand of intimacy or family life. It should value the quality and substance of relationships over their form. This demands a move beyond straight, gay, or even plural marriage, the sort of vision that was proposed in a statement of principles, "Beyond Same-Sex Marriage: A New Strategic Vision for All Our Families and Relationships," authored by a group of activists, artists, scholars, and educators who want to nudge struggles for gay family rights in a more creative, inclusive direction (www.beyondmarriage.org). Like many of the statement's other supporters, I would like the state to get out of the marriage business entirely and return oversight of marital rituals, requisites, rewards, and sanctions to the provenance of religious and cultural communities. I agree with those political and legal theorists, as well as with a handful of politicians across the political spectrum, who favor the "disestablishment" of marriage as a civil status (Culbertson 2007; Garrett, 2009; Metz, 2010). However marginal such an approach might appear, it has the capacity to bridge the usual ideological divides in the family wars. During the Massachusetts legislature's debate over same-sex marriage, Republican assemblyman Paul Loscocco, who opposed same-sex marriage, proposed eliminating the term "marriage" and providing equal civil union benefits to all couples. Deborah Glick, a lesbian Democratic state senator in New York, made a similar proposal (Stacey 2004, 8). Likewise, in the spring of 2011, a group of conservative Republican representatives introduced a bill in the New Hampshire legislature to phase out state marriage licenses in favor of domestic partnerships (http://www.care2.com/causes/civil-rights/blog/new-hampshire-to-phase-out-marriage).

Civil rights, benefits, and duties should be tied to citizenship, parenthood, and guardianship, in my view. The state's mandate should be to facilitate – or at the very least not to thwart – individual commitments to give love, care, and support in however many guises they appear. Rather than policing access to and from the marital gates, the state should enable a cornucopia of truly civil unions, and these need not be exclusively dyadic or rooted in sexual intimacies.

Learning from the lives, loves, and losses I encountered in my field research on gay men in Los Angeles, polygamy in South Africa, and the non-marrying Mosuo minority in China as well as from my own untidy, intimate history – and likely some of yours too – should convince us that our erotic and domestic yearnings, abilities, and aversions are irrepressibly varied and complex. We cannot will our desires or funnel them into a single, culturally prescribed domestic norm. But we can and should acknowledge that our needs for both eros and domesticity are often at odds. How many more times can we possibly be "shocked, *shocked!*" when another Scarlet Letterman (or more rarely, a Letterwoman) is caught forsaking his or her marital vows? How much more evidence from the natural and social sciences do we need to convince us that human desires and relational capacities differ? Monogamy is not natural or even possible for everyone. But then, too, neither is "promiscuity" natural or pleasurable for everyone. Not everyone can, or wishes to, become a parent, let alone a good one. Human sexual and emotional variation, on the other hand, *is* natural, and this should be no cause for distress. That is why happy families will never be all alike.

Making our peace with sexual and family diversity does not commit us to a laissez-faire ethics of pure cultural relativism. Some family systems are clearly patriarchal, authoritarian, and even brutal, whereas others are more egalitarian, democratic, and humane. Some are more permissive and others are more prescriptive. Different family forms can be more or less child-centered, more or less cooperative, and more or less resilient. Most cultures in the world create families that favor domesticity over desire, but their ways of doing so differ. Some allot eros a much wider berth than others, typically where men's urges are concerned, but in rare instances, like the Mosuo, for women's as well.

The modern, romantic, companionate union that both U.S. marriage movements take to be normal represents a quixotic effort to plant durable domestic turf in desire's rocky soil. History teaches that this is a utopian, or perhaps just a naive, strategy for trying to have one's cake and eat it too. If a lucky few gay male couples I studied, and perhaps President Barack Obama and his wife Michelle, seem able to grasp hold of this brass ring, too many others suffer needlessly from repeated, failed rotations astride what sociologist Andrew Cherlin (2010) terms the "marriage-go-round." The normal, horse-and-carriage, family ideology can make it seem embarrassing, inauthentic, and even cowardly to remain in a passionless marriage. It can lead a sexually frustrated spouse to abandon domesticity in order to pursue desire, either by "cheating" or by fleeing the corral. The sole alternative it permits is to forfeit desire altogether.

Revising Our Vows

Coming to terms with the irrepressible variety of intimacy and families in our modern world demands tough ideological concessions and political compromises from all combatants in the family wars. As in South Africa, religious and cultural conservatives must learn to tolerate equal family rights and benefits for lesbian, gay, and transgender people whose desires and practices they find sinful, repugnant, or threatening. Same-sex marriage advocates must come to grips with the unavoidable race and class inequities that are intertwined with marriage as a legal institution and that are tellingly reflected in the social makeup of their core political constituency. Rather than fighting merely to open membership in the exclusive conjugal clubhouse to comparatively privileged lesbians and gay men, they should pitch a big family tent agenda, such as the frameworks proposed in a report, *Beyond Conjugality*, issued by the Law Commission of Canada in 2001 or in the 2006 "Beyond Same-Sex Marriage" statement in the United States. There should be enough room in that tent to shelter not only "sex pigs" and monogamous couples but also single dads and moms, poly-parenting families, child-free individuals, and members of plural unions.

Feminists, for our part, must come to grips with unwelcome evidence that our quest for intimate equality will never speak to or for all women. We need to respond to women's myriad desires and compromises with greater empathy and nuance. Without whitewashing the painful patriarchal history of polygamy, for example, we should resist knee-jerk opposition to it. We might concede that polygamy is not *inherently* more harmful or oppressive to women than monogamous marriage or remaining unhitched. To be sure, plural marriage systems (whether polygynous or polyandrous) derive from patriarchal interests in controlling women's bodies and babies. They were designed to serve masculine erotic, domestic, and political agendas. However, the same can be said about the history of monogamous marriage. Assuring paternity and transmitting property to men's heirs were central motives for "the origins of the family, private property and the state," as the title of Engels's classic nineteenth-century book (1952; originally published 1884) put it. At the time that book was published, monogamously married women could not vote or own property in most of the Western world. Meanwhile, patriarchal Mormon polygamists granted women the right to vote in the Utah territory, but women lost the suffrage when the LDS Church reluctantly repudiated polygamy in order to enter the Union.

Feminists need to respect the preferences of heterosexual women who, facing acute shortages of eligible men in their communities, would rather share a husband, children, and family than resign themselves to a life of single motherhood or of childlessness, or having to forsake their desire for family. A dearth of marriageable black men is one of the toxic legacies of racial apartheid in both the United States and South Africa, the factor that served as catalyst for Moynihan's incendiary report. Some black Muslim women in the United States, like some rural women in Kwa-Zulu Natal, consider polygyny to be far the less evil option, as black feminist legal critic Adrien Wing (2003) also points out. And although a Johannesburg polygynist I interviewed was an unapologetic patriarch, he was not wrong to claim that a woman married to a man like him might find polygyny a less threatening expression of his roving libido than his philandering. In fact, some plural wives count it a blessing not to bear sole responsibility to satisfy their husband's sexual desires. Gary Tuchman interviewed fundamentalist Mormon co-wives on CNN's *Anderson Cooper 360°* in 2006 and asked the predictable question, "How is it decided which wife the husband sleeps with on a given night?" "We draw straws," one wife parried, "and the one with the short straw has to."

Still, some of my feminist colleagues worry that by advocating tolerance of polygyny and of other unequal varietals of intimacy, I forfeit the crucial feminist insistence that the personal is political. I believe, however, that respecting the intimate choices of women who do not share feminist desires is a way to honor, rather than betray, this value. A feminist commitment to gender justice should mandate promoting social conditions that make it possible for women (and men) to imagine and achieve intimate equality, if that is what they desire. It does not entitle feminists to dictate or disparage whatever else other women actually do desire. Under social conditions that enable genuine consent, women and men should be free to opt for polygyny, polyandry, or monogamy, for arranged or love-match unions, for celibacy or polyamory, or for whatever domestic arrangements sustain them and those they love.

Finally, coming to terms with our species' unruly panoply of desires and domestic arrangements would liberate us from some of the destructive burdens of bad faith and hypocrisy that we presently suffer. We could spare ourselves, for example, those political disruptions that follow each time another public figure earns his (or, less often, her) Scarlet Letter for infidelity. I favor a concept of fidelity defined to strengthen diverse family bonds rather than to impose a uniform code of sexual behavior on everyone that is unattainable and, in my view, uninspiring. If we take our lead from the Mosuo, from Nancy, Liza, and Paul, from the gay trio that I studied, from the Zulu plural marriages described earlier, as well as from many strictly monogamous couples, whether gay, straight, or undefined, we would encourage people to pledge vows of fidelity to whatever principles of intimacy and commitment they choose to negotiate and renegotiate among themselves – freely, honestly, and openly. Public policy should aim to create conditions than enable such fidelity.

This includes taking measures to end discrimination against all minority forms of intimacy, to ensure consent, to prevent and prosecute abuses, and to protect the rights of "the faithful" and their dependents.

No family system is ideal, and no family form can be best for everyone. In part this is because of the irresoluble tension between our needs for both eros and domesticity, in part because people (and cultures) are not and never will be all alike. Each family regime displays characteristic strengths and weaknesses; each offers distinctive satisfactions and sorrows, challenges and constraints. Every brand of family values has its fans and foes, and these are not as predictable as we so often suppose. In a liberal democracy, especially, we cannot possibly prevent all spouses from forsaking their vows. But we can, and should, prevent our society from forsaking all of our other families.

REFERENCES

Beyondmarriage.org. (2006). Beyond Same-Sex Marriage: A New Strategic Vision for All Our Families and Relationships.

Blankenhorn, D. (1995). *Fatherless America: Confronting Our Most Urgent Social Problem*. New York: Basic Books.

Cherlin, A.J. (2010). *The Marriage-Go-Round: The State of Marriage and Family in America Today*. New York: Knopf.

Colby, J. (2006). FOX Facts: Warren Jeffs. *FOX Online w/ Jamie Colby*, August 31. http://www.foxnews.com/story/0,2933,210981,00.html.

Cooper, A. (2006). Hiding in Plain Sight. *Anderson Cooper 360°*. CNN. Aired May 10. http://transcripts.cnn.com/TRANSCRIPTS/0605/10/acd.02.html.

Cosby, B. (2004). Dr. Cosby Speaks at the 50th Anniversary Commemoration of Brown v. Topeka Board of Education. http://www.eightcitiesmap.com/transcript_bc.htm.

Culbertson, T. (2007). Arguments against Marriage Equality: Commemorating and Reconstructing *Loving v. Virginia*. *Washington University Law Review* 85, 575–609.

Dan Quayle v. Murphy Brown. (1992). *Time*, June 1. http://www.time.com/time/magazine/article/0,9171,975627,00.html.

DeWitt, L. (2005). Moynihan, Welfare Reform and the Myth of 'Benign Neglect.' *Larry DeWitt's personal website*, October. http://www.larrydewitt.net/Essays/Moynihan.htm.

DOMAwatch.org. (2009). Marriage Amendment Summary. October 15. http://www.domawatch.org/amendments/amendmentsummary.html.

Duggan, L. (2004). Holy Matrimony. *The Nation*, February 26. http://www.thenation.com/doc/20040315/duggan.

Engels, F. (1952). *The Origin of the Family, Private Property, and the State*. Moscow: Foreign Languages Publishing House. Originally published 1884.

Fineman, M.A. (1995). *The Neutered Mother, the Sexual Family, and Other Twentieth-Century Tragedies*. New York: Routledge.

Friedan, B. (1997). *The Feminine Mystique*. New York: Norton. Originally published 1963.

Garfinkel, I., and McLanahan, S.S. (1986). *Single Mothers and Their Children: A New American Dilemma*. Washington, DC: Urban Institute Press.

Garrett, J. (2009). Marriage Unhitched from the State: A Defense. *Public Affairs Quarterly*, 23(2) (April), 161–180.

Giloff, D. (2007). *The Jesus Machine: How James Dobson, Focus on the Family and Evangelical America Are Winning the Culture War*. New York: St. Martin's Griffin.
Goodwyn, W., Berkes, H., and Walters, A. (2005). Warren Jeffs and the FLDS. *NPR.org*, May 3. http://www.npr.org/templates/story/story.php?storyId=4629320
H.R.3734–Personal Responsibility and Work Opportunity Reconciliation Act of 1996. U.S. Library of Congress. http://thomas.loc.gov/cgi-bin/query/z?c104:H.R.3734.ENR
Hughes, D. (2010). Zuma's Woes: 3 Wives, 1 Fiancée and an Out-of-Wedlock Child. ABCNews.com, February 8. http://abcnews.go.com/International/south-african-president-jacob-zumas-sex-scandal/story?id=9781141.
Ingrid Bergman's Official Web Site, http://www.ingridbergman.com/.
Kranish, M. (2009). In Bully Pulpit, Preaching Values. *Boston Globe*, December 10.
Law Commission of Canada. (2001). *Beyond Conjugality: Recognizing and Supporting Close, Personal Adult Relationships*. http://www.lcc.gc.ca.
McMullen, R. (2010). People: Hold Everything, Tiger Woods' Wife Doesn't Want a Divorce. *Mercury News*, January 26.
Metz, T. (2010). *Untying the Knot: Marriage, the State, and the Case for Their Divorce*. Princeton, NJ: Princeton University Press.
Moynihan, D.P. (1993). Defining Deviancy Down. *American Scholar* (Winter), 17–30.
Moynihan, D.P. (1965). *The Negro Family: The Case for National Action (The Moynihan Report)*.
Murray, C. (2005). Rediscovering the Underclass. American Enterprise Institute for Public Policy Research, October 7. http://www.aei.org/issue/23313
Obama, B. (2009). We Need Fathers to Step Up. *Parade*, June 21. http://www.parade.com/export/sites/default/news/2009/06/barack-obama-we-need-fathers-to-step-up.html.
Patterson, O. (1999). *Rituals of Blood: Consequences of Slavery in Two American Centuries*. New York: Basic Books.
Polikoff, N. (2008). *Beyond (Straight and Gay) Marriage: Valuing All Families under the Law*. Boston: Beacon.
Popenoe, D., Elshtain, J.B., and Blankenhorn, D. (Eds.) (1996). *Promises to Keep: Decline and Renewal of Marriage in America*. New York: Rowman & Littlefield.
"Republican Contract with America," House of Representatives Web site. http://www.house.gov/house/Contract/CONTRACT.html.
Reyes, R.P. (2007). Jerry Falwell Is Gone, but James Dobson Still Preaching Intolerance. *American Chronicle*, May 18. http://www.americanchronicle.com/articles/view/27498.Reyes2007.
Ribuffo, L.P. (2006). Family Policy Past as Prologue: Jimmy Carter, the White House Conference on Families, and the Mobilization of the New Christian Right. *Review of Policy Research*, 23, 311–338.
Schlafly, P. (2003). *Feminist Fantasies*. Dallas: Spence.
Schlafly, P. (1978). Stop ERA. *Smithsonian Source*, December 6. http://www.smithsoniansource.org/display/primarysource/viewdetails.aspx?PrimarySourceId=1159.
Shih, C.-K. (2001). Genesis of Marriage among the Moso and Empire-Building in Late Imperial China. *Journal of Asian Studies*, 60(2), 381–412.
Shih, C-K. (2009). *Quest for Harmony: The Moso Traditions of Sexual Union and Family*. Palo Alto, CA: Stanford University Press.
Shih, C-K. (2000). *Tisese* and Its Anthropological Significance: Issues around the Visiting Sexual System among the Moso. *L'Homme* 154–155, 697–704.
Stacey, J. (2004). Can Marriage Be Saved? A Forum. *The Nation*, July 5. http://www.thenation.com/doc/20040705/forum2/8.

Stacey, J. (2011). *Unhitched: Love, Marriage and Family Values from West Hollywood to Western China*. New York: New York University Press.

Stacey, J. (1997). Virtual Social Science and the Politics of Family Values. In Marcus, G. (Ed.), *New Locations: The Remaking of Fieldwork and the Critical Imperative at Century's End*. Santa Fe: School of American Research.

Stack, C.B. (1997). *All Our Kin: Strategies for Survival in a Black Community*. New York: Basic Books.

Staples, R. (1978). *The Black Family*. Belmont, CA: Wadsworth.

Warner, M. (1999). *The Trouble with Normal: Sex, Politics, and the Ethics of Queer Life*. New York: Free Press.

Whitehead, B.D. (1993). Dan Quayle Was Right. *Atlantic*, April, 47ff.

Wing, A.K. (2003). Polygamy in Black America. In Wing, A.K. (Ed.), *Critical Race Feminism: A Reader*, 2nd ed., pp. 186–194. New York: NYU Press.

11

Why Marriage?

Suzanne B. Goldberg

In a well-known *New Yorker* cartoon, a man and a woman sit together on a couch, clearly in the midst of a conversation about marriage for gay and lesbian couples. "Haven't they suffered enough?" one of them asks. Although the cartoon characters jest, the question of why gay people are fighting so hard for the right to marry is a serious one. After all, marriage rates have been dropping steadily in the United States and in much of the world, and divorce rates remain high. Why, then, are lesbians and gay men fighting so hard to join an institution that appears, by most indicators, to be on the decline?

There is no single answer to this question, of course. Political ideology and social experiences are important determinants of any given person's position, and individuals' positions are often complex, with overlapping justifications. From among the many possible reasons, this chapter looks closely at several leading responses to the "Why bother with marriage?" question. Building on these responses, the chapter also offers an analytic framework for understanding contemporary marriage debates and a foundation for thinking about how marriage might fare as we move beyond the current crossroads.

Note that the inquiry here is not about why a particular gay or lesbian couple might want to get married. That question, for most couples, is answered by reference to love rather than rights; by desires for binding familial commitments rather than concerns about the signaling effects of legally recognized marital status. At an individualized level, one could answer the "why bother with marriage" question simply by saying that marriage has traditionally been, and continues to be, what adult couples seek when they want state sanctification of their relationships, and that same-sex couples are simply asking for what different-sex couples already have.

But to accept that as our answer is to stay on the surface of the question. Even assuming that same-sex couples seek marriage because it is still the primary means for couples to announce and protect their relationships, we need to know more about why marriage, as opposed to some other form of relationship recognition, seems to matter so much. After all, while gay and lesbian individuals and advocacy groups pursue a range of efforts to obtain recognition and protection for their families, marriage remains a prominent and leading priority. Indeed, some marriage equality advocates have gone so far as to reject proposals for quasi-marital statuses such as civil unions, saying they "establish a second-class citizenry" (Goodnough 2011).

One preliminary point about language is in order before turning to our inquiry. I avoid the phrase "gay marriage" in this chapter because, although it is concise and widely used, it is also misleading. When same-sex couples seek marriage rights, they are seeking to marry, not to "gay marry." Likewise, when different-sex couples marry, they do not have a "straight" marriage; instead, they have a marriage. Therefore, to talk about "gay marriage" plays into the idea, with which I disagree, that marriage for gay people is something different from marriage for nongay people.

INTRODUCING THE THREE INTERESTS IN MARRIAGE

The interests motivating the movement for marriage that I explore in this chapter fall roughly into three sets. The first is an interest in accessing the material protections and benefits accorded to those who are married. These goods are the ones that same-sex couples often cite to courts and legislatures when they claim a right to marriage equality, pointing out, for example, that their married neighbors and coworkers receive valuable tax, employment, and other benefits solely by virtue of being married, and that the absence of marriage renders same-sex couples painfully vulnerable in emergency settings. For purposes here, I describe this as the "tangible goods" interest.

The second grows out of a desire for equal status. By this, I mean the recognition, in both formal and social settings, that the committed partnerships of same- and different-sex couples are on par with one another. While this status interest often dovetails with the interest in tangible goods, in that equal status frequently brings status-related goods along with it, my focus here is on the social and political connotations of marriage equality. That is, the recognition of equal status says something more about same-sex couples than that they are entitled to the goods associated with marriage. It says that same-sex couples are a fully equal part of the citizenry and are as critical to the nation's present and future as the different-sex married couples, who have long been recognized for their foundational social and political role. Even the U.S. Supreme Court has reinforced this sense of marriage as essential to the state, describing marriage, in 1888, as "the foundation of the family and of society, without which there would be neither civilization nor progress" (*Maynard v. Hill* 1888:205, 211), and again, in 1942, as "fundamental to the very existence and survival of the race" (*Skinner v. Oklahoma ex rel. Williamson* 1942:541).

If the first two interests are in accessing marriage "as is," the third interest focuses on the transformative potential of including same-sex couples in marriage. The focus here is less on what marriage equality will do for gay people than on what gay people getting married will do for marriage or for society more generally. To be sure, this is less an "interest" in marriage than a set of observations about the meaning of marriage. Still, the "interest" label aims to capture something more about why, in addition to the equalization of goods and status, gay people are seeking marriage rights and about what will happen when they marry. It focuses on some of the most contentious questions about what agendas might underlie support for, or opposition to, marriage rights for same-sex couples and what consequences those agendas might have as the legal and social terrain shifts. This interest in the transformation of marriage and society is not typically articulated in court filings or in mainstream debates because it does not respond directly to the central legal and social questions presented by same-sex couples' exclusion from marriage. But, because it implicates primal and often inchoate concerns about the meaning of marriage, it may have the most to tell us about where marriage is likely to head as gay couples' inclusion in it becomes increasingly accepted.

Arguably woven into all of these interests is a related, often unarticulated desire to break down the sorts of primal or first-degree social hostility that exist toward gay people. To the extent the state recognizes same-sex couples as fully equal civic participants, that hostility becomes harder to maintain. Likewise, those who oppose marriage rights for same-sex couples may also believe that allowing for marriage not only validates same-sex couples' relationships but also validates being gay as equivalent to being heterosexual. For some, this shift would cut against a deeply held intuition about societal ordering (Goldberg 2010). Although this chapter will not focus distinctly on this interest, its presence must be noted because it surely accounts for at least some of the tension continually sparked by the issue of marriage for same-sex couples.

SOME CONTEXT FOR THE "WHY MARRIAGE?" QUESTION

Before turning to a discussion of these interests and the insights they offer, two points warrant our attention. The first is whether the reasons gay and lesbian couples have for seeking marriage continue to matter. After all, in many quarters, there remains little meaningful debate regarding whether same-sex couples should be granted marriage rights. Instead, at one end of the spectrum, the question of why gay couples should be able to marry is seen as passé; rather, debates concern why marriage equality is taking so long. At the other, debate centers on how best to counter ongoing marriage demands.

In addition, while political campaigns against marriage equality have moved forcefully to oppose recognition of same-sex couples' relationships, many observers on both sides of the marriage question conclude that it is only a matter of time before the exclusion of same-sex couples from marriage is a thing of the past. Statements from President Obama and Vice President Biden supporting the right of same-sex couples to marry reinforce this trend, as do supportive positions from prominent conservatives, including former Vice President Dick Cheney and former First Lady Laura Bush (Baker 2012; Baker and Calmes 2012). Demographic data likewise consistently show increasing support among younger people for marriage rights (Newport 2011). Indeed, many people in their twenties, regardless of political affiliation, express befuddlement when trying to understand why marriage for same-sex couples remains such a fraught political and social issue. (To be sure, many others, albeit in smaller numbers, hold strong views in opposition to marriage for same-sex couples.)

Still, the marriage question is far from full resolution. Consequently, the arguments that are made – and not made – by same-sex couples and their allies, and by advocacy organizations that represent lesbian, gay, bisexual, and transgender (LGBT) constituencies, can help us not only understand the shape of the public and legal campaigns but also make informed assessments about marriage's future.

The second preliminary point concerns the insights we can glean about marriage's future when we compare the discussion of marriage within LGBT communities historically to today's conversation. It will not surprise most readers that the arguments that gain traction both within a social movement and more publicly vary over time depending on the surrounding political, legal, and social conditions (Anderson 2005). Still, it may be surprising to some that, for much of the 1980s and beyond, fierce disagreement roiled LGBT communities over whether organizations should dedicate their limited resources to seeking marriage rights for lesbian and gay couples.

A (very) short version of this background is this: During the 1980s, lesbian and gay leaders traveled the country debating the virtues of marriage as a movement goal. "*Gay Marriage: A Must or a Bust?*," published in Out/Look magazine in 1989 (Ettelbrick and Stoddard 1989:8–17),[1] contained two essays capturing the poles in the debate at the time. In one, Thomas Stoddard, then Lambda Legal's Executive Director, urged aggressive advocacy for marriage rights on the view that marriage would provide practical benefits and political leverage, and that "enlarging the concept to embrace same-sex couples would necessarily transform [marriage] into something new" (Ettelbrick and Stoddard 1989:13). On the spectrum's other end, and working out of the same organization, was Lambda's Legal Director, Paula Ettelbrick, who titled her essay "Since When Is Marriage a Path to Liberation?" She offered two arguments. First, she wrote, marriage will "constrain us, make us more invisible, force our assimilation into the mainstream, and undermine the goals of gay liberation." And second, she added, "attaining the right to marry will not transform our society from one that makes narrow, but dramatic distinctions between those who are married and those who are not married to one that

[1] The essays have been reprinted in numerous publications, including in Rubenstein, Ball, and Schacter (2008:678) and Eskridge, Jr. and Hunter (2004:1098).

respects and encourages choice of relationships and family" (Ettelbrick and Stoddard 1989:14).[2]

Informed by this debate and the lack of consensus that marriage would be an unequivocal good, marriage advocacy has been more complicated than recent public discourse might suggest. While many have argued strongly for marriage, others continue to proffer a mixed sense of whether marriage, with all of its benefits, might also have some serious and ultimately overwhelming costs (Polikoff 2008).

To be clear, no one within LGBT communities has argued prominently against the idea that same-sex couples should have the same access to marriage as non-gay couples. Even Ettelbrick acknowledged that "[w]hen analyzed from the standpoint of civil rights, certainly lesbians and gay men should have the right to marry." Yet, she continued, "obtaining a right does not always result in justice" (Ettelbrick and Stoddard 1989:14). Thus, an interest in obtaining formal equality is not where the conflict lies. Instead, the tension erupted, as in the Stoddard-Ettelbrick debate, over the prioritization of marriage as a movement goal. We can see the residue of this tension in the "why marriage?" conversation today, particularly when we reconsider, later in this chapter, the link between equal marriage rights for same-sex couples and broader social transformation.

Similar strands have emerged in debates among bisexual and transgender rights advocates about marriage, although those debates will not be our focus here (Yoshino 2000; Flynn 2001; Currah 2006; Arkles, Gehi, and Redfield 2009; Leff 2011). Courts, too, have tended to treat marriage litigation involving transgender people as presenting separate issues (Stirnitzke 2011).

With these contextual points in mind, the chapter now turns to an extended discussion of the three sets of reasons why lesbians and gay men continue to invest tremendous energy in securing marriage rights at a time when marriage, by most other measures, seems to be decreasing in social and legal importance.

TANGIBLE GOODS OF MARRIAGE

The first set of reasons behind marriage advocacy, which focuses on tangible goods, is perhaps the most straightforward. Different-sex couples receive goods by virtue of being married, from both the government and the private sector, that same-sex couples do not. This disparity began to receive national attention as far back as 1997, when the then-General Accounting Office (now the Government Accountability Office, or GAO) released a report identifying 1,049 federal statutory references to "marriage," many of which grant rights, benefits, and privileges wholly or partly based on marriage (General Accounting Office 1997). The research, done prior to

[2] For related arguments in legal scholarship, see, for example, Duclos (1991), Franke (2006), Hunter (1997), Polikoff (1993), Polikoff (2009), Schacter (2009), and Stein (2009).

Congress's passage of the federal Defense of Marriage Act, highlighted that restricting marriage to male-female couples had substantial material as well as social consequences for same-sex couples. By 2004, when the GAO updated its research in the wake of DOMA's being in effect, the number of marriage-linked references had grown to more than 1,100 (General Accounting Office 2004).

These GAO reports limited their study to federal law, but when state and local rights and benefits are added to the mix, the gap between same-sex and different-sex couples widens even further (Vermont Civil Union Review Commission 2001; New Jersey Civil Union Review Commission 2008; New York Civil Liberties Union 2011; "Tax problems for Illinois civil unions" 2011).

Notably, it is not only the rights of adults vis-à-vis each other or the state that marriage affects. Within state law, whether someone is married can dramatically affect his or her legal recognition as a parent, with married parents typically having a significant advantage over non-married parents when seeking custody of or visitation with a child born during the couple's relationship. In one well-known case, the Supreme Court ruled that a child's biological father had no right to maintain a relationship with the child because the mother was married to another man when the child was born (*Michael H. v. Gerald D.* 1989). Lesbian and gay parents likewise have been denied contact with the children they were raising with a former partner on the ground that they and their former partner were not married (*Jones v. Barlow* 2007).

Of course, there are strong arguments that marriage should not be the trigger for establishing parent-child relationships. And there are other methods, including second-parent adoption, to create a legally recognized parent-child relationship. Still, the fact remains that marriage, for different-sex couples, can be a simple and low-cost way to protect familial rights, one that is not currently available to most same-sex couples.

But the disparity does not end there. Just as governments rely on marriage as a means for allocating benefits, so also do private-sector entities. So, for example, many employers provide family health care coverage to employees with spouses but not to employees with nonmarital partners. Car rental companies likewise frequently provide breaks to married renters that they deny to others. As the Alternatives to Marriage Project (2011) laments, "renting cars is one area where discrimination on the basis of marital status is still alive and well." Even health clubs single out married couples for special memberships that they do not offer to unmarried partners (*Monson v. Rochester Athletic Club* 2009).

Considered in light of these kinds of facts, the argument for marriage rights for same-sex couples seems uncomplicated. In simplest form, it observes that marriage is used as a touchstone for distributing benefits in both the public and private sector. To remedy the inequality that results when same-sex couples cannot access marriage-associated benefits, the argument continues, it is only fair that same-sex couples be able to marry and that their marriages be recognized as equal to different-sex couples' marriages. Equal marriage rights, in other words, will put an end to the unjustified inequality in distribution of marital goods.

Yet the goods equalization argument cannot be the full force behind the marriage equality claim. After all, a growing number of states have enacted legal frameworks – typically called either "civil union" or "domestic partnership" – that provide same-sex couples with most of the goods enjoyed by married couples. But even if these frameworks were to provide exactly the same rights and benefits, there is something unsatisfying to many marriage equality advocates about an arrangement that reserves marriage for different-sex couples and a marriage-like regime for same-sex couples. In early 2000, just months after Vermont became the first state to offer civil unions to same-sex couples, and well before marriage first became available to same-sex couples in Massachusetts, one scholar and advocate (Barbara Cox 2000) described the state's new form of relationship recognition as "separate but (un)equal." Others, more charitably, frame civil unions as a step along the path to marriage. Still, few who desire marriage deem civil unions to be a sufficient substitute status. As the California Supreme Court observed, most heterosexual couples would not be pleased if their marriages were to be converted to civil unions (*In re Marriage Cases* 2008:434–435).

To be sure, not everyone takes such a dismal view of domestic partnerships and civil unions. Indeed, for some, their value arises from their role as *non*marital gateways to benefits distribution and status recognition. On this view, by delinking marriage from relationship-related benefits, the status of domestic partnership or civil union has the capacity to expand our recognition of families beyond the borders of marriage. Hawaii, for example, has opened its "reciprocal beneficiaries" status to pairs of adults who are unable to marry (Haw. Rev. Stat. Ann. § 572C 1997). Outside of the United States, France has been a leader in revising adult relationship recognition through its domestic partnership-like status, known as the civil solidarity pact or PACS, which has become a popular alternative to marriage for many different-sex couples (Sayare and De La Baume 2010).

Yet in the United States, in all but a few jurisdictions, these statuses have not lived up to this potential. Instead, they are most commonly offered only to same-sex couples as a substitute for marriage rather than to all couples, including those eligible to marry, as an alternate path to relationship recognition. The private sector has reinforced this view, with many employers and others that previously offered benefits based on nonmarital statuses such as domestic partnership now insisting on marriage in jurisdictions where same-sex couples are eligible to marry (Bernard 2011).

STATUS EQUALITY

This brings us to the second broad motivation behind the marriage equality claim – that excluding same-sex couples from marriage denies access not only to goods but also to marriage's social and political meaning. This argument has two major strands. The first, tied to the tangible goods argument just discussed, maintains that civil unions provide formal, but not functional, equality. That is, even if civil unions are equal on paper, they do not and cannot achieve equality with marriage in reality. The second is that the state's creation of a separate status for same-sex couples itself causes an injury, even if the two statuses could be made to result in equal treatment.

On the first point, New Jersey's experience helps illustrate the substantial difficulties associated with efforts to create a marriage-like status for same-sex couples. In a 2006 decision, the New Jersey Supreme Court held that denying marriage to same-sex couples violated the state constitution's equality guarantee but then let the legislature decide whether to remedy that constitutional injury by providing marriage or a similar status. After vigorous debate, the legislature opted for civil unions; scores of reports soon followed, however, showing that civil unions were not being recognized on the same basis as marriages. The legislature appointed a Civil Union Review Commission to study how civil unions were faring, and the results were dismal from an equal treatment perspective. Couples reported being denied hospital visitation, financial aid, and other services and resources, with the common response to their civil union being either "what's that?" or "that's not the same as marriage" (New Jersey Civil Union Commission 2008). Indeed, the harms were so egregious that Lambda Legal, the organization that had brought the initial marriage lawsuit in New Jersey, brought a new lawsuit challenging the state's ongoing denial of marriage rights (*Garden State Equality v. Dow* 2011).

Conceivably, if a government was committed to maintaining civil unions as the marriage-alternative for same-sex couples, it might launch a massive public education campaign to help overcome the public's lack of familiarity with the new status. One could imagine a training program for government employees and then, in addition, a campaign to familiarize every person in the state with civil unions so that no one, at any age, could claim that they did not know that a civil union is the functional equivalent of marriage.

Yet even sketching this plan highlights the wastefulness of the state's duplicative relationship recognition systems. Having both to create new forms and office signage (to indicate that civil unions are available where marriage licenses are available) and also to dedicate resources to public education about civil unions seems impossible to justify in the face of budget cuts to public health, education, and welfare programs. But, in keeping with the constitutional mandate, the state would arguably be required to do just that if it is to remedy through civil unions the inequality imposed on same-sex couples by the denial of marriage.

Still, even if the state were to create an effective enough campaign to make civil unions as well known as marriage, the separate status is deficient, from the perspective of those who seek marriage, because by creating civil unions, the government is signaling that gay and non-gay couples do not have the same status in the state's eyes. No amount of public education can remedy this problem because the denigration of same-sex couples is inherent in the state's act of differentiation. Here is why: Any time the state differentiates between two groups of people, it must, consistent with the U.S. Constitution's equality guarantee, have at least a legitimate explanation for the line it has drawn. It cannot, in other words, distinguish between groups of people for arbitrary reasons or out of hostility.

Applying this basic doctrinal point here enables two related observations. First, the state's act of giving same-sex couples the same rights as different-sex married couples tells us that the state sees no meaningful difference between the couples. And second, because the state values same-sex and different-sex couples identically, its decision to create a distinct status for same-sex couples must either be arbitrary, meaning that there is no rational explanation for the state's line-drawing, or impermissible because it embodies hostility toward or disapproval of same-sex couples (Goldberg 2008).

Some would respond by saying that if gay and lesbian couples experience a sense of inferiority as a result of being offered civil unions but not marriage, it is not the state's problem because the state has done all it can to treat civil unions and marriages equally. In this view, any sense of stigmatization is in the minds of same-sex couples or of other private parties, and is not the state's responsibility or under the state's control.[3]

Two arguments respond to this point. First, even if the state did not give marriage all of its social meaning, the state does control who is allowed access to this meaning. That is, the state functions as the gatekeeper for marriage. By deciding that some couples cannot get "marriage" and others can, the state is allocating not only government protections and benefits but also access to the social meaning and value of marriage. Therefore, the state can and should be held responsible for injuries experienced by the excluded same-sex couples.

The second point is that the injury inflicted in the exclusion of same-sex couples from marriage does not derive only from lesbian and gay couples' experience of stigmatization. Instead, the problem that needs to be redressed begins at the very moment the state separates its gay and lesbian constituents into a different category for purposes of relationship recognition. Simply put, the state cannot escape responsibility because it is the state's act of line-drawing without a legitimate justification that triggers the injury.

Together with the tangible goods concern, the status equality interest seems to capture all that might motivate same-sex couples to seek marriage. These two interests are certainly the primary reasons articulated in court and in the public debates.

3 This is something like the argument made by the Topeka, Kansas Board of Education in *Brown v. Board of Education* when it maintained that the racial separation of children in public schools was not, in itself, unequal. The Court found that it was the fact of separation that triggered the harm at issue: "To separate the [children] from others of similar age and qualifications solely because of their race generates a feeling of inferiority as to their status in the community that may affect their hearts and minds in a way unlikely ever to be undone" (*Brown v. Board of Education* 1954, p. 494).

But there is an additional reason discussed in the next section that, although far less prominent, may be especially useful in thinking about marriage's future.

CAN MARRIAGE BE TRANSFORMED?

The third broad reason why gay and lesbian couples are seeking to marry, or at least why some believe same-sex couples want to marry, is to transform marriage – to change it in some way from what it is as a status shaped by the coupling of a man and a woman. As this interest is more abstract, and perhaps less familiar, than the others, some historical context will be helpful in understanding its potential implications.

Preliminarily, it bears noting that discussion of this interest is more speculative than descriptive of popular claims like those for equality in status and tangible goods. Most same-sex couples who are interested in marrying today would say that their aim is to be within marriage, not to change it. Indeed, many lesbian and gay couples, like many heterosexual couples, hope that marriage will transform their relationships by deepening and solidifying the commitment they have to each other.

In fact, it is most often opponents of extending marriage to same-sex couples who argue that allowing gay couples to marry will transform marriage from the stable institution it has always been into a new and undesirable relationship recognition structure. For some individuals who hold this view, the end of the male-female eligibility rule for marriage also portends a slippery slope that will flow into recognition of plural marriages, animal-human marriages, and more.

Marriage's Evolution over Time

Yet the position that allowing same-sex couples to marry has the potential to transform marriage, though deeply held by its adherents, is more thought experiment than reflection of reality. It is important to remember that marriage has never been the stable, immutable institution described by those who purport to defend it from change (Goldberg 2006). Indeed, marriage today looks little like marriage of 150 years past or even 50 years ago. After all, it was not until 1967 that the U.S. Supreme Court finally invalidated race-based limits on marriage when it held unconstitutional Virginia's ban on interracial marriage (*Loving v. Virginia* 1967).

Likewise, and even more relevant, is the prolonged evolution of sex roles, and rules, in marriage. Through most of marriage's history, the law was quite specific that a married man headed his household not only in name but also in rights. Throughout the nineteenth century, this doctrine, known as coverture, meant that, upon marriage, a woman's legal identity merged into that of her husband. Married women could not enter into binding contracts, earn independent wages, or engage in many economic transactions. In this way, marriage became "the primary means of protecting and providing for the legal and structurally devised dependency of wives" (Fineman 2001:245). Even as coverture began to unravel, many of its rules remained in place, including restrictions that prevented married women from obtaining credit independent of their husbands or retaining their original surnames (Emens 2007). Notorious, too, were laws that refused to recognize rape if it occurred within marriage (Buckborough 1990). For couples that divorced, the law continued to differentiate between men and women, imposing financial support obligations primarily on men and granting child custody primarily to women (Scott 1992; Selfridge 2007: 174–176).

From a gender perspective, then, marriage today looks like a completely different institution than it did even a few decades ago. Men and women enter as legal individuals, remain that way during marriage, and exit that way as well. While there are some important legal consequences of being married that go beyond the rights and benefits discussed earlier, such as the ability to invoke marital privilege in an evidentiary hearing and to transfer property without tax liability, none of these is tied to gender. Instead, the spouses are treated by law as coequal partners; neither is legally advantaged or disadvantaged by virtue of being male or female.

When considered against this history, the rule that requires marriages to have one male and one female partner arguably made sense in an earlier era; each of the partners had a distinct role and set of responsibilities. Today, however, none of these distinctions exists, and the rule that marriage requires a male and a female is perhaps best understood as an artifact of that earlier time.

Although the demise of race-and sex-based rules are the most widely known changes to marriage over time, the evolution can also be seen in changing eligibility rules regarding age and blood relations (consanguinity). The minimum age at which individuals can marry generally has risen in past decades, and the degree of familial closeness that couples may have before marriage will be permitted has also been altered – to be closer in some jurisdictions and more distant in others. Notably, too, age and consanguinity requirements have always varied across states (Cahill 2005; Cornell Law School Legal Information Institute 2011). In no sense, then, has there been, or is there now, an absolute stability in these marriage rules.

Thus, when we think about transformation of marriage, either as a goal of same-sex couples seeking to enter marriage today or as a reason to oppose those couples' entry into marriage, we cannot take at face value the position that marriage has always been a stable and predictable institution that will be destabilized by abolishing the different-sex eligibility rule. Change, more than stability, is the best way to describe marriage's history, and in that sense, including same-sex couples would be more consistent with marriage's developmental course than maintaining the exclusion that is currently in place in so many jurisdictions.

The Transformation Argument's Evolution

But, some would say, *this* proposed transformation is different. Even if marriage has changed over time, it will still be different to recognize two men or two women as having the same kind of relationships as the male-female couples that traditionally have been permitted to marry. So, in considering transformation as a possible goal of same-sex couples seeking to marry, we ought to ask how exactly gay and lesbian couples might transform marriage.

Here, it is helpful to refer to Tom Stoddard's claim that gay people marrying would have that transformative effect. He wrote: "Marriage may be unattractive and even oppressive as it is currently structured and practiced, but enlarging the concept to embrace same-sex couples would necessarily transform it into something new." Continuing, he added: "If two women can marry, or two men, marriage – even for heterosexuals – need not be a union of a 'husband' and a 'wife.'" Why? He explained: "Extending the right to marry to gay people . . . can be one of the means, perhaps the principal one, through which the institution divests itself of the sexist trappings of the past" (Ettelbrick and Stoddard 1989:13).

Ettelbrick was dubious. "By looking to our sameness and deemphasizing our differences, we don't even place ourselves in a position of power that would allow us to transform marriage from an institution that emphasizes property and state regulation of relationships to an institution which recognizes [marriage as] one of many types of valid and respected relationships," she wrote (Ettelbrick and Stoddard 1989:15). In other words, if gay people prioritize the fight for marriage in an effort to reinforce and establish this sameness, marriage will remain the primary vehicle for allocating state and private benefits, while many nonmarital relationships warrant similar recognition.

Legal scholars have carried the debate further. Some have made the point, consistent with Stoddard, that inclusion of same-sex couples within marriage will necessarily alter marriage by upending, or at least undermining, the social expectations that women have certain responsibilities within marriage and men have others (Hunter 1991). As one author argued, marriage would become "less sexist" (Wriggins 2000:313). Other scholars have expanded on Ettelbrick's position, arguing that marriage advocacy detracts from efforts to obtain broader recognition of family diversity (Polikoff 1993). From a different angle, some scholars have focused on the potential risks associated with having civil unions replace marriage (Scott 2007), while still others have argued that the focus on adult pairings misses the caregiving relationships that are most in need of (and most deserve) legal protection (Fineman 2005).

Yet despite the early preeminence of arguments about transformation, the goal of changing marriage has dropped almost entirely from contemporary discussions about why lesbian and gay couples want to marry. Several developments help explain this shift.

First, as Ettelbrick observed, to claim a legal right to marry, lesbian and gay couples must show that they are like other couples who already can marry. That is, the U.S. Constitution's equality guarantee is understood to require only that likes be treated alike. If same-sex and different-sex couples are not alike, the inequality claim goes away. To suggest that same-sex couples have the capacity to make marriage into something different from what different-sex couples have would be to concede that same-sex couples are different from different-sex couples in some material way.

In addition, in the political sphere, an argument favoring transformation of marriage would likely be perceived as an argument for instability – for change to a deeply rooted social institution. Although most people would agree that marriage in practice is far distant from its idealized version, many still consider marriage to be foundational to a strong society and "the most important relation in life" (*Zablocki v. Redhail* 1978:384). Against this backdrop, an open commitment to transforming marriage could be perceived as a direct threat. (A quick empirical observation here: same-sex couples have been marrying in Massachusetts since 2004. There is no evidence to date suggesting that marriage itself has changed or that the rates at which different-sex couples are marrying [or divorcing] has been influenced by the marriages of their gay and lesbian neighbors [Kurtzleben 2011].)

Why then would Stoddard, an astute political and legal advocate, have been so open about his own interest in seeing the sexist underpinnings of marriage transformed? In part, Stoddard was writing in the late 1980s, when the only major Supreme Court pronouncement on lesbian and gay rights had come three years earlier, in *Bowers v. Hardwick*, where the Court upheld Georgia's sodomy law based on the "presumed moral belief of a majority . . . that homosexual sodomy is immoral and unacceptable" (1986:195). The few lower courts that had taken up the marriage question at that point had similarly hostile responses to the gay rights claim before them, swiftly rejecting arguments that the rights of gay people were violated by their exclusion from marriage.

In other words, Stoddard was not engaged in an external political campaign. He was making an appeal internal to the gay and lesbian community in the context of an intra-community publication. His aim was not to persuade legislators or courts; he sought, instead, to reach those who were committed to gay people's equality but also deeply uncomfortable with marriage's legacy as an institution in which women's interests were subordinated, both legally and socially, to those of men. His point was not that gay people would shake the foundations of marriage, but instead that, by removing the last of the formal gendered restrictions in marriage, lesbian and gay couples would present the next incremental step in marriage's evolution to a non-gendered institution. Understood in this way, Stoddard was not arguing that the prospect of marriage by same-sex couples would open the doors to other intimate unions. His transformation argument might sound surprising, even radical, to those familiar with tightly crafted equality arguments, but it is actually quite limited. In essence, his claim is that gay couples' marrying might strengthen ongoing challenges to dominant social presumptions about the roles of men as husbands and women as wives.

Because the law no longer formally enforces those presumptions, his transformation argument is, thus, not relevant to the law. It does not signal that the inclusion of same-sex couples in marriage will mean anything at all for marriage's other eligibility requirements, including age, consanguinity, and the two-person rule. And it likewise does not present any challenge to the state's privileging of marriage over other relationships.

MARRIAGE AT A CROSSROADS

The ultimate question, then, is whether marriage equality advocacy for gay and lesbian couples has actually transformed marriage in any of the ways hoped for or feared. Considering this question in light of the interests discussed here prompts several observations.[4] First, the two major arguments for marriage – equalization of tangible goods and status – are really much more about bringing gay and lesbian couples into the existing institution of marriage than about changing marriage in any way. Indeed, the very point of these arguments is that same-sex couples want marriage precisely because of what it currently offers rather than for what it might be or offer in the future. Simply put, transformation is not the reason most gay people are seeking marriage.

Second, whatever transformation might occur with the inclusion of same-sex couples is, at most, part of an ongoing shift in the nature of marriage from a deeply gendered institution to one that is no longer that way. Indeed, even if the issue of same-sex couples' marrying had never been raised, it is reasonable to think that the degendering of marriage roles would be continuing apace. As we know, formal legal equality between men and women in marriage is now well settled. The divergent social expectations related to husbands and wives, though still powerful, have likewise dissipated substantially in recent decades and will continue to erode, perhaps even at a heightened speed, given the economic and social conditions that make maintenance of rigid differentiations difficult at best.

Finally, as marriage continues on its own path of transformation, with or without lesbian and gay couples' participation, we are left with the question whether there will be less momentum to recognize nonmarital relationships. Here, my prediction builds on the previous analysis. Just as marriage has continued to evolve, so too has the diversity of American families. Marriage rights for same-sex couples will not change that trend, and the law, however haltingly, will continue to find ways to catch up.

[4] For a contemporary evaluation of the Ettelbrick/Stoddard debate, which concludes that "going forward . . . the LGBT rights movement does not have to choose between a sustained and vigorous focus on marriage equality for same-sex couples, on the one hand, and a more revisionist and pluralist approach," see Stein (2009). For a related discussion, see Kim (2011).

REFERENCES

Alternatives to Marriage Project. (n.d.). Legal & Financial F.A.Q. Retrieved July 27, 2011, from http://www.unmarried.org/legal-financial-f.a.q.html.

Anderson, E. (2005). *Out of the Closets and into the Courts: Legal Opportunity Structure and Gay Rights Litigation*. Ann Arbor: University of Michigan Press.

Arkles, A., Gehi, P., and Redfield, E. (2009–10). The Role of Lawyers in Trans Liberation: Building a Transformative Movement for Social Change. *Seattle Journal of Social Justice*, 8, 579–641.

Baker, P. (2012). Same-Sex Marriage Support Shows Pace of Social Change Accelerating. *The New York Times* (May 11). Retrieved from http://www.nytimes.com/2012/05/11/us/same-sex-marriage-support-shows-pace-of-social-change-accelerating.html.

Bernard, T.S. (2011). As Same-Sex Marriage Becomes Legal, Some Choices May Be Lost. *The New York Times* (July 8). Retrieved from http://www.nytimes.com/2011/07/09/business/some-companies-want-gays-to-wed-to-get-health-benefits.html.

Bowers v. Hardwick, 487 U.S. 186 (1986).

Brown v. Board of Education, 347 U.S. 483 (1954).

Buckborough, A. (1990). Family Law: Recent Developments in the Law of Marital Rape. *Annual Survey of American Law*, 1989, 343–370.

Cahill, C.M. (2005). Same-Sex Marriage, Slippery Slope Rhetoric, and the Politics of Disgust: A Critical Perspective on Contemporary Family Discourse and the Incest Taboo. *Northwestern University Law Review*, 99, 1543–1611.

Calmes, J. and Baker, P. (2012). Obama Says Same-Sex Marriage Should Be Legal. *The New York Times* (May 9). Retrieved from http://www.nytimes.com/2012/05/10/us/politics/obama-says-same-sex-marriage-should-be-legal.html?pagewanted=all.

Cornell Law School Legal Information Institute. (n.d.). Marriage Laws of the Fifty States, the District of Columbia and Puerto Rico. Retrieved July 27, 2011, from http://topics.law.cornell.edu/wex/table_marriage.

Cox, B. (2000). But Why Not Marriage: An Essay on Vermont's Civil Unions Law, Same-Sex Marriage, and Separate but (Un)equal. *Vermont Law Review*, 25, 113–147.

Currah, P. (2006). Gender Pluralisms under the Transgender Umbrella. In Currah, P., Juang, R.M., and Minter, S.P. (Eds.), *Transgender Rights* pp. 3-31. Minneapolis: University of Minnesota Press.

Duclos, N. (1991). Some Complicating Thoughts on Same-Sex Marriage. *Law & Sexuality*, 1, 31–61.

Emens, E. (2007). Changing Name Changing: Framing Rules and the Future of Marital Names. *University of Chicago Law Review*, 74, 761–863.

Eskridge, W.N., Jr., and Hunter, N.D. (2004). *Sexuality, Gender, and the Law* (2d ed.). New York: Foundation Press.

Ettelbrick, P., and Stoddard, T. (1989). Gay Marriage: A Must or a Bust? *Out/Look*, **Autumn**, 8–17.

Fineman, M.A. (2001). Why Marriage? *Virginia Journal of Social Policy & the Law*, 9, 239–271.

Fineman, M.A. (2005). *The Autonomy Myth: A Theory of Dependency*. New York: New Press.

Flynn, T. (2001). Transforming the Debate: Why We Need to Include Transgender Rights in the Struggles for Sex and Sexual Orientation Equality. *Columbia Law Review*, 101, 392–420.

Franke, K.M. (2006). The Politics of Same-Sex Marriage Politics. *Columbia Journal of Gender & Law*, 15, 236–248.

Garden State Equality v. Dow, No. L-001729–11 (Mercer County Ct. filed June 29, 2011).

General Accounting Office. (1997). Defense of Marriage Act (GAO/OGC-97-16). Retrieved from www.gao.gov/archive/1997/og97016.pdf.
General Accounting Office. (2004). Defense of Marriage Act: Update to Prior Report (GAO-04-353R). Retrieved from www.gao.gov/new.items/d04353r.pdf.
Goldberg, S.B. (2006). An Historical Guide to the Future of Marriage. *Columbia Journal of Gender & Law*, 15, 249–272.
Goldberg, S.B. (2009). Marriage as Monopoly. *Connecticut Law Review*, 41, 1397–1423.
Goldberg, S.B. (2010). Sticky Intuitions and the Future of Sexual Orientation Discrimination. *UCLA Law Review*, 57, 1375–1414.
Goodnough, A. (2011). Rhode Island Senate Approves Civil Unions Bill. *The New York Times* (June 30). Retrieved from http://www.nytimes.com/2011/06/30/us/30unions.html.
Goodridge v. Department of Public Health, 798 N.E.2d 941 (Mass. 2003).
Hawaii Revised Statutes Annotated. § 572C. (1997).
Hunter, N. (1991). Marriage Law and Gender: A Feminist Inquiry. *Law & Sexuality*, 1, 9–30.
Hunter, N. (1997). Lawyering for Social Justice. *New York University Law Review*, 72, 1009–1021.
In re Marriage Cases, 43 Cal. 4th 757 (2008).
Jones v. Barlow, 154 P.3d 808 (Utah 2007).
Kim, S.A. (2011). Skeptical Marriage Equality. *Harvard Journal of Law and Gender*, 34, 37–80.
Kurtzleben, D. (2011). Divorce Rates Lower in States with Same-Sex Marriage. *U.S. News & World Report* (July 6). Retrieved from http://www.usnews.com/news/articles/2011/07/06/divorce-rates-lower-in-states-with-same-sex-marriage.
Leff, L. (2011). Bisexuals Work for Recognition in the LGBT Rainbow. *San Jose Mercury News* (May 7). Retrieved from http://www.mercurynews.com/breaking-news/ci_18016284.
Lewis v. Harris, 188 N.J. 415 (2006).
Loving v. Virginia, 388 U.S. 1 (1967).
Maynard v. Hill, 125 U.S. 190 (1888).
Michael H. v. Gerald D., 491 U.S. 110 (1989).
Monson v. Rochester Athletic Club, 759 N.W.2d 60 (Minn. 2009).
New Jersey Civil Union Review Commission. (2008). The Legal, Medical, Economic and Social Consequences of New Jersey's Civil Union Law. Retrieved from http://www.state.nj.us/lps/dcr/downloads/CURC-Final-Report-pdf.
New York Civil Liberties Union. (n.d.). Know your Rights: Frequently Asked Questions about New York's Marriage Equality Act. Retrieved July 27, 2011, from http://www.nyclu.org/marriageFAQ.
Newport, F. (2011). For the First Time, a Majority of Americans Favor Gay Legal Marriage. *Gallup* (May 20). Retrieved from http://www.gallup.com/poll/147662/First-Time-Majority-Americans-Favor-Legal-Gay-Marriage.aspx.
Pearlston, K. (2009). Married Women Bankrupts in the Age of Coverture. *Law & Social Inquiry*, 34, 265–299.
Polikoff, N. (1993). We Will Get What We Ask for: Why Legalizing Gay and Lesbian Marriage Will Not "Dismantle the Legal Structure of Gender in Every Marriage." *Virginia Law Review*, 79, 1535–1549.
Polikoff, N. (2008). *Beyond (Straight and Gay) Marriage*. Boston: Beacon Press.
Polikoff, N. (2009). Equality and Justice for Lesbian and Gay Families and Relationships. *Rutgers Law Review*, 61, 529–560.
Rubenstein, W.B., Ball, C.A., and Schacter, J.S. (2008). *Cases and Materials on Sexual Orientation and the Law* (3rd ed.). New York: Foundation Press.

Sayare, S., and De La Baume, M. (2010). In France, Civil Unions Gain Favor over Marriage. *The New York Times* (December 15). Retrieved from http://www.nytimes.com/2010/12/16/world/europe/16france.html.

Schacter, J.S. (2009). The Other Same-Sex Marriage Debate. *Chicago-Kent Law Review, 84*, 379–402.

Scott, E.S. (1992). Pluralism, Parental Preference, and Child Custody. *California Law Review, 80*, 615–672.

Scott, E.S. (2007). A World without Marriage. *Family Law Quarterly, 41*, 537–566.

Selfridge, A. (2007). Equal Protection and Gender Preference in Divorce Contests over Custody. *Journal of Contemporary Legal Issues, 16*, 165–176.

Skinner v. Oklahoma ex rel. Williamson, 316 U.S. 535 (1942).

Stein, E. (2009). Marriage or Liberation? Reflections on Two Strategies in the Struggle for Lesbian and Gay Rights and Relationship Recognition. *Rutgers Law Review, 61*, 567–593.

Stirnitzke, A.C. (2011). Transsexuality, Marriage, and the Myth of True Sex. *Arizona Law Review, 53*, 285–318.

Tax Problems for Illinois Civil Unions. (2011). *IRN/KROX* (July 5). Retrieved from http://stlouis.cbslocal.com/2011/07/05/tax-problem-for-illinois-civil-unions/.

U.S. Government Accounting Office. (1997). *Defense of Marriage Act* (Publication No. GAO/OGC-97–16) (January 31). Retrieved from http://www.gao.gov/archive/1997/og97016.pdf.

U.S. Government Accounting Office. (2004). *Defense of Marriage Act: Update to Prior Report* (Publication No. GAO-04–353R) (January 23). Retrieved from http://www.gao.gov/new.items/d04353r.pdf.

Vermont Civil Union Review Commission. (2001). Report of the Vermont Civil Union Review Commission. Retrieved from http://www.leg.state.vt.us/baker/cureport.htm.

Wriggins, J. (2000). Marriage Law and Family Law: Autonomy, Interdependence, and Couples of the Same Gender. *Boston College Law Review, 41*, 265–325.

Yoshino, K. (2000). The Epistemic Contract of Bisexual Erasure. *Stanford Law Review, 52*, 353–461.

Zablocki v. Redhail, 434 U.S. 374 (1978).

12

Essential to Virtue?

The Languages of the Law of Marriage

Carl E. Schneider

INTRODUCTION

Now and then it is possible to observe the moral life in process of revising itself, perhaps by reducing the emphasis it formerly placed upon one or another of its elements, perhaps by inventing and adding to itself a new element, some mode of conduct or of feeling which hitherto it had not regarded as essential to virtue.

Lionel Trilling, *Sincerity and Authenticity* (1972)

American moral life is in process of revising itself. Briefly, Americans[1] decreasingly speak in the language of morality. This is *not* to say that American discourse is necessarily less moral, that it necessarily lacks a moral basis, or that there are not moral reasons for eschewing moral discourse. Quite obviously, much of this change can be defended in quite conventional moral terms – as an expression, for instance, of various standard liberal views. My point, rather, is that the terms we use in explaining (and presumably in thinking about) our lives are decreasingly drawn from the vocabulary of morals and are increasingly drawn from the discourse of therapy, economics, psychology, public-policy studies, rights, and assorted other modes of thinking. Thus the language of morals is being displaced by other discourses or even by silence.

Obviously, these alternative discourses may, and even must, have a moral component, if only because each of them has some sort of moral justification ready at hand. But language matters (to recite what is now an idea familiar to the point of cliché). Different discourses use different verbal and conceptual vocabularies, and those different vocabularies affect what we think, say, and do. What is more, they affect how we are understood. By studying our languages, we better see how we reason, how we act, what we seek, and what we find.

[1] This essay must frustratingly ignore the many important differences – particularly the class differences – in the way Americans use moral language. For a discussion of some of these differences and marriage law, see Schneider (2006).

In particular, we better understand the choices that confront us and that we have made as we stand at this crossroads for marriage. Not least, this is because the change in American moral life I describe is especially clear and consequential in family law. First, few areas of law reveal moral attitudes as plainly as family law generally and marriage law particularly. Moral issues are central to family life and family self-governance and central to the context in which family law works. Indeed, "morality" in its narrowest meaning but commonest usage connotes exclusively one aspect of family morality – sexual morality. Moral issues arise especially often in the family, where their effect can be especially momentous and their resolution especially hard. For in marrying we take responsibilities for the welfare and happiness of someone who, trusting our assurances, has confided welfare and happiness to us; and in having children, we take responsibilities for the welfare and happiness – even the existence – of people who must confide that welfare and happiness to us. No morality is learned so early and so compellingly as the morality of family life; no other morality seems as axiomatic, is felt as passionately, so fixes the behavior we exact of ourselves and expect of others. Yet what other morality contends with conflicting impulses and temptations so imperious, so ingenious, so insistent?

Second, while morals and law need not coincide, the moral views of citizens and of lawmakers shape their opinions about the law – once again, especially marriage law. Because people have tenacious and passionate beliefs about family morals, because many people believe that law should vindicate right in matters so vital, moral principles are deliberately and expressly incorporated in statutes and case law. And for similar reasons, moral sentiments influence lawmakers unawares.

Third, moral issues command special attention from marriage law because it typically intervenes in the family precisely when pressing moral problems arise. Furthermore, marriage law is one of the rare areas of law that sometimes tries – in some disputes surrounding divorce, for instance – to take into account people's entire moral personalities. And marriage law, more than most law, encounters crippling problems of enforcement when its rules mismatch popular morals.

THE CHANGING LANGUAGE OF MARRIAGE LAW

The law is the witness and external deposit of our moral life.
Oliver Wendell Holmes, *The Path of the Law*

Today, legal actors decreasingly discuss marriage law in the language of morality. Rather, they have tended to discuss those issues in other than moral terms or to avoid handling some moral issues altogether – often by transferring responsibility for such decisions to the people the law once regulated.

Let me reiterate the stipulations I made about the change in American discourse generally. The diminution in the moral discourse of marriage law does *not* mean that legal decisions are necessarily less moral, that marriage law is necessarily deprived of a moral basis, or that lawmakers necessarily lack moral reasons for avoiding moral discourse. But when legislators, judges, and other legal actors write statutes, opinions, and regulations, they decreasingly deploy the vocabulary of morals and increasingly draw on the discourse of economics, psychology, public policy studies, medicine, or on legal doctrines that speak in other than moral terms. Thus the language of morals is being displaced by other discourses or even by obviating the need to speak at all.

No-fault divorce exemplifies the trend away from moral discourse in marriage law. Before that reform, courts often had to ask whether a petitioner was morally entitled to a divorce, a question often answered in expressly moral terms. After that reform, a petition for divorce might need no discussion in any terms at all. Today, the moral elements of the question whether to seek a divorce, if they are to matter at all, must be addressed by the spouse seeking the divorce. (True, covenant marriage was partly a reaction to this change in divorce law, but it seems to have been conspicuously confined to a few states and a few couples within those few states.)

No-fault divorce has not, of course, eliminated spouses' disputes over property, spousal maintenance, and child support. Here, too, the law's tendency has been to avoid debating such issues in moral terms. Sometimes the adoption of no-fault divorce is taken to have prohibited courts from analyzing the spouses' economic relations in moral language (although this conclusion was often reached with little analysis and apparent relief). Sometimes courts have explicitly or implicitly moved away from moral discourse without that spur. Thus courts treating the spouses' economic relationships have increasingly been unwilling to discuss the factors that fault-based divorce law made relevant. Instead, efforts are made to look, for example, at the economic relations of the parties in economic terms. Attempts are also made to substitute something like rules for the discretion that creates opportunities for moral discourse. And there is increased tolerance for allowing spouses to use contracts that can relieve courts of some of the burden of decision. For example, the permissible scope of prenuptial agreements has expanded, as the Uniform Premarital Agreement Act suggests, and separation agreements encounter less resistance than before. Commentators yearn to press this trend yet further.

Similar developments have altered the ways courts resolve disputes about the custody of the great marital product – children. Some kinds of moral considerations – like the sexual conduct of custodians – are regarded with particular skepticism. The interests of children have increasingly been understood in psychological and therapeutic, not moral, terms. Sustained direct attacks have been mounted against judicial discretion in custody decisions, and rules have been proposed and tried, like primary-caretaker and joint-custody presumptions. Decreasing discretion increasingly closes off discourses of all kinds, including moral discourse.

This quick dash over the legal landscape provides a rough sense of the nature of the trend away from moral discourse in marriage law (Schneider 1985). We can understand the trend yet better by investigating some of its origins. The trend has been powerful and perduring, partly because it has multiple sources, some quite fertile. For example, one of the strongest marriage law traditions for many decades has been the principle of noninterference in the family generally and in marriage particularly, a tradition that narrows the scope for discourse of any kind. That tradition is closely associated with the liberal tradition that the state should be neutral among conceptions of the good so that citizens may follow their own understandings of it. No-fault divorce flows naturally from this view since the state has no legitimate standards for evaluating whether a couple should stay married, while the couple is well-situated both to choose and apply those standards. Seen in this light, the problem with traditional divorce was exactly that it required moral discourse; no-fault divorce was needed exactly to excise moral discourse from the law.

Another force behind the transformation is more practical: legal agencies seek administrable rules, but moral discourse generally requires discretion that impairs administrability. This was a large part of the reason no-fault divorce was proposed and adopted with surprising ease (Jacob 1988). As Lynn Wardle describes them, no-fault laws were primarily intended to, among other things, "reduce the acrimony of divorce proceedings, eliminate a major incentive for perjury . . . [and], close the 'gap' between the written divorce law and the law as actually enforced" (Wardle 1991:80). Thus was an inviting occasion for eliminating moral discourse in order to make courts more easily managed.

Another engine of the transformation away from moral discourse in marital law is the fact that some especially relevant moral ideas have changed in ways that make some kinds of moral discourse less salient and significant. For example, for many people, marriage need not require a moral commitment to permanence. For such people, the moral purpose of marriage has changed. As Lawrence Friedman (1990:176) wrote, "Marriage had a new task; it was becoming a mode of self-fulfillment. It was a freely chosen arrangement, a partnership. Each partner had to satisfy and enrich the life of the other. If a marriage failed to provide this kind of fulfillment, each partner had the moral right to break off and try again."

Another cause of the transformation in discourse comes from the rise to social and legal power of competing discourses. One such discourse – especially prominent in modern legal scholarship – is economic. This discourse provides a robust way of talking about – one gathers – almost anything. It certainly offers a way of talking about the economic relationships within a family without having to analyze or even notice the moral obligations and entitlements that a family's economic relationships are shaped by and shape. The allure of this discourse has been impressively illustrated by the American Law Institute's *Principles of the Law of Family Dissolution* (Schneider 1991).

Another discourse is academically less assertive but culturally more potent. It is a discourse that has shouldered aside much else in the conversation of the law. This we might call therapeutic discourse. The therapeutic view, in its ideal type, holds that life's goal is the search for personal well-being, adjustment, authenticity, and contentment – in short, for "health." As Rieff (1966:8) says mordantly, "[E]vil and immorality are disappearing . . . mainly because our culture is changing its definition of human perfection. No longer the Saint, but the instinctual Everyman, twisting his neck uncomfortably inside the starched collar of culture, is the communal ideal." Therapeutic discourse rarely asks questions about moral duties and is, if anything, hostile to moral discourse.

Therapeutic discourse is not only culturally prepotent. It is also symbiotic with another language that has displaced moral discourse – the language of rights. Their closeness can be inferred from the two premises Friedman finds revealed by the "behavior and language of people in Western societies." First, "the *individual* is the starting point and ending point of life." Second, "a wide zone of free choice is what makes an individual." Therefore, choice is "vital, fundamental: the right to develop oneself, to build up a life suited to oneself uniquely, to realize and aggrandize the self, through free, open selection among forms, models, and ways of living" (Friedman 1990:2). Rights discourse secures for individuals that "wide zone of free choice." The language of rights displaces moral discourse because it removes issues from the law's purview and transfers the assessment of them to the right-holder. If a problem is to be examined in moral terms, the right-holder must do it.

Legal agencies are also propelled away from moral discourse by changes in the way we think about morality itself. These changes were most forcefully brought home to me in discussions with a number of classes over a number of years, and I will use those discussions as my vehicle here. I devised a parable that imagined a marriage of thirty years. During those years, Mrs. Appleby had become economically, emotionally, and socially dependent on Mr. Appleby. He wanted a divorce to marry his nineteen-year-old secretary; she was vehemently opposed for religious reasons and because she feared economic, emotional, and social misery. (He earned so little that Mrs. Appleby could expect no support.) I asked whether Mr. Appleby was *morally* – not legally – entitled to a divorce.

The class conversation was always the same. The first response was invariably that Mr. Appleby was *legally* entitled to a divorce. I reiterated my request for a moral evaluation of his choice. This led many students to deny that there is such a thing as "morality." Some people just believe one thing, some another. As James Q. Wilson (1993:6) comments, "Ask college students to make and defend a moral judgment about people or places with which they are personally unfamiliar. Many will act as if they really believed that all cultural practices were equally valid, all moral claims were equally suspect." In short, to invite a moral discussion is to invite an exchange of happenstantial and undebatable preferences rather like the discussion of oysters in *Spartacus*.

Some of my students would go further and say that thinking morally was actively dangerous. Not least, moral thinking meant intolerant thinking. As Wilson (1993:7) reports, "In my classes, college students asked to judge a distant people, practice, or event will warn one another and me not to be judgmental or to impose your values on other people." My students, like Wilson's, saw morality as a mask for and an incitement to callousness, narrow-mindedness, hypocrisy, prudery, and prejudice. Relatedly, moral systems are not just regimes of prohibitions and duties; they also import blame, shame, and stigma, all of which are always destructive. Even when people "make an error in judgment," guilt is dysfunctional. It rests on misapprehensions about the extent to which people can control their own conduct, it makes people unhappy, and it interferes with the therapies people might recruit to improve their lives and psychological health. Guilt is an injury people do themselves, stigma an injury people do others, in the grip of morality.

Some students went further and said Mr. Appleby was actually entitled to divorce Mrs. Appleby because she was wrong to oppose him. She was wrong for several reasons. First, it was not in her own interest to stay married to someone who did not want to be married to her. Even if Mr. Appleby forced himself to stay married, he could hardly offer her love. Worse, he must resent being trapped in his marriage, and this resentment would immiserate his wife.

This led to a disquisition about marriage. Marriage exists only when both spouses truly love each other. Thus the Appleby marriage – *nolens, volens* – had ended when Mr. Appleby stopped loving Mrs. Appleby. Further, marriage is intended to promote the personal growth of the spouses. Where one spouse wishes not to be married, such growth becomes impossible, and the marriage has ended. As Karl Marx (1967:141) wrote, "Divorce is nothing but the declaration that a marriage is *dead* and that its existence is only pretense and deception. It is obvious that neither the arbitrariness of the legislator nor that of private persons can decide whether or not a marriage is dead." To insist that the Applebys stay married would be to insist that they live in something other than marriage, which would be unfair to both spouses and inconsistent with true marriage.

Mr. Appleby, some argued, was morally entitled to a divorce for another reason – he had never committed himself to stay married, or even if he had, he had gradually been absolved by the changing meaning of marriage. Marriage may once have been lifelong. But *autre temps, autre moeurs*. As divorce rates have climbed, as religious ideas of marriage have waned and secular ones have waxed, marriage has become a "nonbinding commitment." Promises like "for better or for worse, for richer for poorer, in sickness and in health, to love and to cherish, till death us do part," if they are articulated at all, are expressions of hope, romantic effusions, purely precatory.

But Mr. Appleby was morally free to divorce his wife for a yet stronger reason than that he had not promised – and should not have been asked to promise – to stay married. He was free because he, like anyone else, was entitled to seek personal growth, self-fulfillment, and human happiness. He might have a moral duty to himself to do so. If Mrs. Appleby truly loved her husband, she would not want to stop him. Nor should we expect Mr. Appleby to find the happiness that is everyone's right except by obeying the commands of his preferences. He could not help falling in love with his secretary. He could not help falling out of love with his wife. He could not persuade himself out of the former love or back into the latter.

Some students also felt that to deny Mr. Appleby, or even for Mr. Appleby to deny himself, a divorce would be "punitive." If something was punitive it was impermissible, although it is not altogether clear why. "Punitive" often meant nothing more than that unpleasant consequences attached, not that punishment was intended. But I think these students associated punishment with morality. Binding Mr. Appleby was a moral idea, and because the consequences of being bound are painful, they are punitive. In addition, these students associated punitiveness with harshness and argued that binding Mr. Appleby to his wife for the rest of her life was harsh, and thus, again, punitive.

Yet another reason Mrs. Appleby could not oppose Mr. Appleby's divorce was that Mrs. Appleby was herself responsible for many of the ills she would suffer after a divorce. She was vulnerable because of decisions she had made during the marriage: she did not develop saleable skills; she did not make friends of her own; she did not develop a life of her own; she depended on her husband for purpose, prosperity, and happiness. Mrs. Appleby had violated a primary duty, the duty to maintain one's independence, to be one's own person, and not to rely for well-being, worth, and identity on someone else. Even if Mrs. Appleby expected to be married all her life, did she not see how vulnerable her dependence made her, and how much less than a whole person? Why should Mr. Appleby now be held responsible for his wife's weakness, lack of unwisdom, and improvidence (Schneider 1998)?

Significantly, the one argument that students thought might limit Mr. Appleby's freedom to divorce Mrs. Appleby was a contractual argument. If Mr. Appleby had insisted that Mrs. Appleby not work outside the house, if he had isolated her from her friends, if, in short, he was in some direct way responsible for the distress she would feel on divorce, then he might have entered into a contract of some sort. He was not bound by moral constraints; he was bound because he had entered into an agreement with someone else by which he voluntarily limited his freedom in exchange for promises from his wife.

But how bound was he? Only to pay money damages. He could not be asked for anything like specific performance. It did not matter that Mrs. Appleby thought she had bargained for marriage, not money. It did not matter that Mr. Appleby could not support two families and thus could not in fact pay damages. So if Mr. Appleby would breach a contract by divorcing his wife, it would be a wrong without a remedy.

The Appleby conversations teach one more lesson. I've often asked both law and medical students whether they had a moral duty to give blood or to donate a kidney to a dying sibling. No. No, I don't have a duty to do that. No one should make me do that. Like Mr. Appleby, they should not be made to do something. This, I think, suggests that, when asked about moral issues, my students do not imagine themselves having an internal conversation in which they decide whether they are morally obliged to behave in some way. Rather, they imagine themselves being bound by something external (like the law). And that they resent and resist.

Nevertheless, these responses give a false impression of my students and Americans generally. However passionately they reject any duty to behave well, they are quite capable of *doing* good. Tocqueville (1960:122) said that Americans "frequently fail to do themselves justice," for they "are sometimes seen to give way to those disinterested and spontaneous impulses that are natural to man; but the Americans seldom admit that they yield to emotions of this kind; they are more anxious to do honor to their philosophy than to themselves." And like Tocqueville, the authors of *Habits of the Heart* thought that Americans generally act more altruistically and circumspectly than their language would suggest or require. Americans "are responsible and, in many ways, admirable adults. Yet when each of them uses the moral discourse they share, what we call the first language of individualism, they have difficulty articulating the richness of their commitments. In the language they use, their lives sound more isolated and arbitrary than, as we observed them, they actually are" (Bellah et al. 1996:20–21). Similarly, Wilson (1991:4) finds that, "[a]s with self-interest, so with individual rights: we assert large claims to freedom, spontaneity, and self-expression but act in ways that for the most part respect constraints, moderate excesses, and reveal our capacity for self-control."

Tocqueville, Bellah, and Wilson found an American discourse in which individualism flourished but in which other moral strains had withered (Bellah et al. 1996). The Appleby conversations resonate with that finding. They also suggest that many strains of moral discourse have not only withered; they have become tainted. Americans may act as though they were bound by the very discourse they reject professedly. But – to bring ourselves back to the law – that oddity is hard for legal agencies to emulate. Their discourse is part of the way they govern, and legal discourse must account for the law's acts.

Our review of the sources of the diminution of moral discourse in American marital law describes changes with considerable appeal, at least in considerable parts of American society. Each source has roots deep in American thought. Each source has desirable elements. The change in discourse has eliminated some ideas few people want to retain or think it practical to preserve. But as Dr. Johnson perhaps said, when you walk toward one blessing, you walk away from another. Therefore, we next turn to the costs of the trend.

THE COSTS OF THE TREND

The first requirement of a sound body of law is that it should correspond with the actual feelings and demands of the community, whether right or wrong.
Oliver Wendell Holmes, *The Common Law*

I have been describing the nature of the diminution in moral discourse in American marital law, and I have reviewed some of the reasons for it and advantages of it. Now I want to consider some of the trend's costs.

The diminution in moral discourse and some of its costs are aptly illustrated by the Supreme Court's struggles with the constitutional right to have an abortion. I particularly consider *Roe v. Wade* because I have found that it continues to remain at the moral center of the way so many influential Americans think about the moral aspects of family issues; any principle that cannot be reconciled with *Roe* has an almost insuperable burden of justification. At the heart of that case are two moral questions. First, what is the moral status of the fetus? Second, what is the woman's moral claim to abort the fetus? As our theory predicts, the Court attempted to decide the case without addressing either question in any serious way.

The Court knew its authority to infer constitutional rights is one of the most momentous questions of constitutional law since the Civil War. Nevertheless, the Court's attempt to identify the origin of the woman's moral claim seems casual:

> In a line of decisions . . . going back *perhaps* as far as . . . [1891], the Court has recognized that a right of personal privacy, *or* a guarantee of certain areas *or* zones of privacy, does exist under the Constitution. In varying contexts, the Court *or* individual Justices have, indeed, found at *least* the roots of that right in the First Amendment . . . ; in the Fourth and Fifth Amendments . . . ; in the penumbras of the Bill of Rights . . . ; in the Ninth Amendment . . . ; *or* in the concept of liberty guaranteed by the first section of the Fourteenth Amendment. (*Roe*:152)

After this disjunctive jumble of precedent (which may establish no more than "the roots of that right"), and after saying mysteriously that the right has "some extension to activities relating to" various marriage law issues, the Court surrenders its attempt to define and defend the right, having established neither the principle that justifies nor the principle that limits it. Nevertheless, the Court next says, "This right of privacy . . . is broad enough to encompass a woman's decision whether or not to terminate her pregnancy" (*Roe*:153). *Why* that right is "broad enough" the Court does not say and cannot, since it hardly knows what the right is.

Apparently, the Court is so offhand because it does not see the case's principal moral issues. When the Court reflects on the decision whether to have an abortion, the "factors the woman and her responsible physician necessarily will consider in consultation" (*Roe*:153) turn out to be largely "therapeutic," having almost exclusively to do with the woman's medical and psychological health. But the central question of the morality of abortion itself and any moral questions about the extent to which the woman's conduct and situation influence the morality of her particular abortion are all conspicuously absent.

The Court's therapeutic viewpoint is similarly apparent in the central role it sees for the doctor. So powerful is that viewpoint that at one point the Court actually attributes primary responsibility for the decision to the doctor: "[T]he attending physician, in consultation with his patient, is free to determine, without regulation by the State, that, in his medical judgment, the patient's pregnancy should be terminated" (*Roe*:163). Nevertheless, the Court stresses that the doctor will be consulted – will be worth consulting and available for consultation – on the psychological, social, and moral issues the Court believes determine the decision. But as significant as the doctor's central role in the decision is the absence of any role for the father, of any indication that the father has any interest in the decision, or about how the father's relationship with the mother might affect the way the decision is to be made.

When the *Roe* Court turns to the state's interests, it feints toward dealing with the other central moral question the case presents – whether abortion destroys something we value in the way we value human life. But the Court immediately veers off to ask whether the fetus is a "person" within the meaning of the Fourteenth Amendment (on the theory that, if it were, "of course . . . the fetus' right to life would . . . be guaranteed specifically by the Amendment" (*Roe*:156–157). The Court then embarks on a weird inquiry into whether the Constitution ever says "person" when it also means a fetus. Oddly enough, no constitutional use of the former word "indicates, with any assurance, that it has any possible pre-natal application"[2] (*Roe*:157).

The Court then again feints toward the central moral problem but again swerves away: "We need not resolve the difficult question of when life begins. When those trained in the respective disciplines of medicine, philosophy, and theology are unable to arrive at any consensus, the judiciary, at this point in the development of man's knowledge, is not in a position to speculate as to the answer" (*Roe*:159). Thus relying on its own incapacity to decide when life begins, and again without explaining its reasoning, the Court announces that "by adopting one theory of life, Texas may [not] override the rights of the pregnant woman that are at stake" (*Roe*:162).

Why not? If all those disciplines disagree, why is the legislature's "theory of life" illegitimate? The Court seems not to realize that this is a question that deserves an answer. Does the Court even mean what it says? Although the Court had denied that Texas could, by defining "life," deprive a woman of her right to decide whether to have an abortion, the Court next declares that Texas has an "important and legitimate interest in protecting the potentiality of human life" and that that interest "grows in substantiality as the woman approaches term, and at a point during pregnancy . . . becomes 'compelling'" (*Roe*:162–163). That point is reached at "viability." This is so "because the fetus then presumably has the capability of meaningful life outside the mother's womb" (*Roe*:163). The Court does not say why its definition of "meaningful life" (which deprives a woman of a constitutional right to an abortion in the last trimester) is reasonable when the legislature's is not. Nor does the Court say why the "potentiality of life" that the Court concedes exists through the second trimester is not something the state may protect.

[2] Ironically, corporations are "persons" within the meaning of the Fourteenth Amendment. If a fetus could incorporate under state law, would it be a person, within the meaning of the Fourteenth Amendment? The Court's discussion reminds one of *Punch*'s railroad conductor, who says, "Cats is dogs and rabbits is dogs, but tortoises is hinsects and goes free."

All this is not to show yet again that the opinion in *Roe* is sadly unpersuasive. Rather it is to propose that a principal reason for that unpersuasiveness is the Court's inability to address – perhaps to recognize the presence of – critical moral issues that it lacked the equipment to discuss. And there is more. *Roe* provoked enormous hostility, a hostility that has poisoned American politics for decades. This hostility seems to have astonished the Court, probably because it did not recognize that the moral issues it treated so elusively mattered so much to a segment of the American population. In *Planned Parenthood of Southeastern Pennsylvania v. Casey*, the Court worried greatly about its perceived legitimacy. That perception is not improved by the Court's distance from the thinking of the people it regulates.

Having examined in detail how the trend away from moral discourse is exemplified by a case that continues to mold the way that many people think about family law and how that case exemplifies some of the costs of that trend, we move on to other kinds of costs. I said that one reason for the trend was that moral analysis could present practical difficulties in administering the law. Some of the trend's costs also grow out of such practical difficulties. This is because the change in the language available to the law affects the way the law speaks to and understands the people whose attitudes it seeks to shape, whose behavior it seeks to regulate, and whose disputes it seeks to adjudicate.

For example, the law cannot easily escape the need to adopt and apply a moral theory of marriage. Perhaps the law does not need such a theory to decide whether a couple should be allowed to divorce, for it may say – as it has said – that the morality of a divorce is for the couple (or, more accurately, the spouse seeking a divorce) to determine (although even this says something about the law's understanding of marriage and its moral obligations). But this solution fails when the law deals with the disputes that frequently accompany divorce. Not least, it needs such a theory where the question is whether one spouse owes the other maintenance or how the spouses' property should be divided. The riddle of maintenance is why one former spouse should have to support the other when no-fault divorce seems to establish the principle that marriage need not be for life and when governmental regulation of intimate relationships is conventionally condemned. That riddle cannot, I think, be answered without a way to discuss the moral nature of marriage (Schneider 1991).

In some ways, division of marital property is even more difficult. During a marriage, the spouses' economic relationships are inextricably tied into an elaborate spousal web of moral debts, duties, and claims. When the law tries to divide the spouses' property, it needs some language for interpreting those moral relations. That language is needed because, if the moral aspects of the dispute are not expressly brought to notice – either through legal rules or through an analysis of a case's facts – they sneak in unexamined, often in indefensible forms. The rise of the doctrine requiring the "equitable distribution" of marital property seems on its face to invite a judicial examination of the parties' moral relations. The cases, however, do not seem to indicate that this is what is happening. And even were it happening, it would be uninformed by a satisfactorily developed and articulated moral understanding of marriage.

Even when courts resolve child-custody disputes, they would benefit from some better-understood and better-articulated theory of marriage. The law in books treats custody issues as purely matters of the child's interest. It is hard to believe that the law in action is always blind to the parents' interests, and especially their relationship, when it actually makes decisions. Similarly, various proposals to treat "functional families" in the same way legally created families are treated are best formulated and evaluated in light of a theory of the moral nature of a family.

This leads us to another cost of a law with little way to address the moral issues in the disputes it encounters. If the law is to operate predictably and fairly, it needs to understand the assumptions and beliefs on which people base their lives. Although moral discourse has lost an important part of its status, many people think seriously about their moral relationships (even if they lack the vocabulary for analyzing them fluently). A law that tries to understand people's descriptions and explanations of their marriages with an ear deaf to their moral language will misconstrue what they are saying. Furthermore, married people will, to some extent, expect the law to take their moral relations into account in a divorce, and they will base decisions on that assumption, however mistaken it may be. A law that is out of touch with common social practices and beliefs will thus lead too often to situations in which people misunderstand the law and the law misunderstands people.

A striking illustration of this danger comes from research into the way clients speak to divorce lawyers. Sarat and Felstiner (1995) tell us that "divorce clients consider marriage and marital conduct a highly moralized domain where judgments of right and wrong still seem both necessary and appropriate. . . . The meaning of marriage remains tied to ideas of loyalty, commitment, and personal responsibility." In talking with their lawyers, "clients keep the question of marriage failure very much alive in their minds. They talk about the marriage in terms of guilt (their spouse's) and innocence (their own)" (Sarat and Felstiner 1995:37). The lawyers (the interpreters of the law to their clients) "avoid responding to these interpretations because they do not consider that who did what to whom in the marriage is relevant to the legal task of dissolving it" (Sarat and Felstiner 1995:30).

The inhibition of moral discourse may also help us understand a perverse feature of marriage law. There is evidence that reforms of divorce law have much less effect on the way judges resolve the disputes associated with divorce than reformers intended. For example, although Congress adopted a numerical-guidelines requirement for awarding child support "with the aim of significantly increasing award levels and decreasing award variability, available evidence suggests that these goals have not been met. Awards calculated under existing guidelines do not appear to differ dramatically from those produced under earlier discretionary standards" (Garrison 1998:44). Similarly, equitable distribution was introduced in New York largely to produce awards more favorable to women. However, Marsha Garrison reports, "there was little change in the percentage distribution of marital property." Worse, over a shortish period, "the proportion of cases in which alimony was awarded in the three research counties declined by fully 43%." Garrison found it particularly "ironic that the equitable distribution law has diminished the alimony prospects of long-married, economically disadvantaged wives – the consensus case for long-term alimony – more than those of any other group" (Garrison 1991:735).

Both these failures to achieve legislative goals have many causes. But one of them may well be that the moral purposes of the statutes were not clearly stated and that the judges who decided the cases did not understand (and perhaps did not accept) the moral principles they brought to their decisions or the moral understandings of the people they were judging. And when moral discourse is inhibited, all these kinds of understanding will be diminished.

Another cost of the trend is less concrete but perhaps no less important. A marriage law from which moral discourse is suppressed is a law that invites moral shallowness. It is the kind of moral shallowness John Maynard Keynes celebrated in his youth and rejected in his grey hairs. When young, he and his friends "repudiated all versions of the doctrine of original sin, of there being insane and irrational springs of wickedness in most men. We were not aware that civilization was a thin and precarious crust . . . only maintained by rules and conventions skillfully put across and guilefully preserved" (Keynes 1956). The law needs to be able to acknowledge the "insane and irrational springs of wickedness" and to treat appropriately what flows from those springs. It cannot do so without an adequate moral language.

This is not to say that the law *can* have an adequate moral language. As I once wrote, "courts and legislatures speak a language shaped by the special exigencies of a legal system of social regulation" (Schneider 1994), and moral language is often incompatible with those exigencies. Unfortunately, as Tocqueville observed, "Scarcely any political question arises in the United States that is not resolved, sooner or later, into a judicial question. Hence all parties are obliged to borrow, in their daily controversies, the ideas, and even the language, peculiar to judicial proceedings" (1994 vol. 1:280). If the language of the law cannot practically address the range of moral problems and ideas that should shape social policy, and if that language also becomes the language the populace finds itself speaking, we pay a considerable price for the law's impoverished vocabulary.

This leads me to a final cost of losing a moral language for discussing family life and marriage law. That language plays a central part in shaping and sustaining marriage as a social institution. A social institution is "a pattern of expected action of individuals or groups enforced by social sanctions" (Bellah et al. 1991:10). Social institutions shape human behavior by rewarding virtue and penalizing vice, by making virtue natural and vice unthinkable. As James Fitzjames Stephen neatly put it, "The life of the great mass of men, to a great extent the life of all men, is like a watercourse guided this way or that by a system of dams, sluices, weirs, and embankments.... [I]t is by these works, that is to say, by their various customs and institutions – that men's lives are regulated" (1882:19).

Nowhere are we more vulnerable to human weakness or more inclined to it than in family life. In family life, we are buffeted by emotions and drives we do not understand and cannot acknowledge. In family life, we deal with those who mean the most to us and can do the most for us. In family life, harsh words, blows, betrayal, and desertion hurt most keenly. In family life, we can injure each other in ways we cannot elsewhere. In family life, the most vulnerable people – children – live at the mercy of their parents. And in family life, success demands a lifetime of labor and love, compromise, concession, and commitment.

Social institutions are a classic response to such situations – where legal intervention is practically and normatively implausible but where the social costs of destructive behavior is high. The preeminent institution of family life is marriage. It has traditionally been seen as a way of inhibiting people from abandoning each other, from betraying each other, from destroying their children's home. In marriage, people give hostages to destiny. In marriage, people cede freedom. Marriage proffers rich rewards, its yoke can be easy and its burden light; but in marriage begins responsibility, and responsibility chains liberty.

Social institutions can perhaps exist without moral language, but it is hard to see how *this* social institution can. Moral language gives us a way of shaping the institution and its public role. It gives us a way of understanding the institution and why we might want to conform ourselves to it. And it gives us a way of criticizing and changing it. To see all these things in action, we now turn to a contemporary crossroad in the law of marriage.

MORAL LANGUAGE AND SOCIAL INSTITUTIONS

> *Marriage is the beginning and the end of all culture. It makes the savage mild; and the most cultivated has no better opportunity for displaying his gentleness.... The condition of man is pitched so high, in its joys and in its sorrows, that the sum which two married people owe to one another defies calculation. It is an infinite debt, which can only be discharged through all eternity.*
>
> Johann von Goethe, *Elective Affinities*

The role of marriage as a social institution and of the moral language that can give this institution meaning is instructively illuminated by the movement toward same-sex marriage. One of the most intriguing arguments for same-sex marriage has rested on marriage's socializing function. Quite early such an argument was advanced by two proponents of same-sex marriage – William Eskridge and Andrew Sullivan. Sullivan put the argument in virtually classic form: "Marriage provides an anchor, if an arbitrary and often weak one, in the maelstrom of sex and relationships to which we are all prone. It provides a mechanism for emotional stability and economic security. We rig the law in its favor not because we disparage all forms of relationship other than the nuclear family, but because we recognize that not to promote marriage would be to ask too much of human virtue" (Sullivan 1995:183. More succinctly, Eskridge titled his book *The Case for Same-Sex Marriage: From Sexual Liberty to Civilized Commitment*.

Eskridge and Sullivan, in other words, suggested that if you exclude a group from marriage, it will have been deprived of a force that constrains sexual behavior and shelters commitment. Invite the excluded group to marry, and its members are brought within the social institution, find their preferences shaped by it, respond to its incentives and disincentives, and can be safer in their vulnerability and dependence. Marriage, Sullivan thought, would "be an unqualified social good for homosexuals. It provides role models for young gay people, who, after the exhilaration of coming out, can easily lapse into short-term relationships and insecurity with no tangible goal in sight" (Sullivan 1995:183).

This argument suggests several questions about marriage as a particular kind of social institution and the moral language that might promote that social institution. For example, how well would marriage perform the socializing function Sullivan imagined? What effect would same-sex marriage have on the socializing function of heterosexual marriage? The answer to these questions depends on much beside the law. Such institutions arise out of social attitudes and practices. Law can only operate at the margin (for example, through divorce laws) to affirm, to assist, to adjust institutions.

How are same-sex couples likely to understand marriage as a social institution? Even heterosexuals are now marrying less reliably than they used to (as several of the chapters in this volume strikingly show), and when they do, it is often because they have decided to have children. And while arguments for same-sex marriage dwell on the advantages of marriage, it must have its burdens if it is to mean anything. Thus leaving marriage is not easy, marital property relations can be problematic, spouses have economic responsibilities for each other, and marriage turns inconstancy into adultery. On balance, marriage may not seem as alluring as cohabitation.

How would same-sex marriage change marriage as a socializing institution? In answering this question, it may help to look at some of the other arguments for broadening the definition of marriage. Prominent among these is the sense that same-sex marriage would be the most telling social statement of approval of same-sex relationships: "In a law-drenched country such as ours, permission for same-sex couples to marry under the law would signify the acceptance of lesbians and gay men as equal citizens more profoundly than any other nondiscrimination laws that might be adopted. Most proponents of same-sex marriage, within and outside gay and lesbian communities, want marriage first and foremost for this recognition" (Chambers 1996:450). Is the price of this symbol of acceptance that same-sex marriages are subjected to the same institutional constraints as heterosexual marriages perhaps are? Or will it require changing those institutional constraints to accommodate the new marriages?

This question gains significance from the fact that same-sex marriage proposals may be part of a general movement toward *loosening* marriage's constraints. That is, they may be part of a movement that is opposed diametrically to the socializing argument. That movement reflects a more sanguine view of human nature and makes the discovery and expression of one's authentic nature life's linchpin. That movement is animated by a belief that law should free people from any social force that promotes inauthenticity. As Sullivan wrote of what he called the liberationist view espoused by some homosexual writers, "the full end of human fruition is to be free of all social constructs, to be liberated from the condition of homosexuality into a fully chosen form of identity, which is a repository of individual acts of freedom" (Sullivan 1995:57). This movement sees law as facilitative, not socializing; as liberating, not repressing. Thus Chambers believed that "the rules bearing on marriage offer significant advantages to those to whom they apply.... [M]ost of the rules may be seen as facilitative, in the sense that they enable a couple to live a life that they define as satisfactory to themselves" (Chambers 1996:485).

More broadly, we may be witnessing a deinstitutionalization of marriage. Divorce proliferates; out-of-wedlock births burgeon; family forms multiply. "Deinstitutionalization is even celebrated, on the grounds that all forms of family life should be encouraged and treated equally" (Schneider 1996:192, quoting *Michael H. v. Gerald D.*, 109 S. Ct. 2333, 2353 (1989)(dissent)). This hardly begins to state the contempt some writers have had for family institutions. Sullivan wrote, "Marriage of all institutions is to liberationists a form of imprisonment; it reeks of a discourse that has bought and sold property, that has denigrated and subjected women, that has constructed human relationships into a crude and suffocating form" (Sullivan 1995:87). Paula Ettelbrick invoked the wisdom of a t-shirt: "Marriage is a great institution ... if you like living in institutions" (Ettelbrick 1997:118).

These thoughtful reflections on same-sex marriage and marriage as a social institution are from social commentators. In what language does – can – the law respond? A landmark case – *Goodridge v. Department of Public Health* – is representative. The court eschewed the language of morality and invoked the language of legal doctrine and, especially, rights. In its first paragraph, the court recited a formula that hinted at the moral complexities we have been discussing, for it spoke not just of the "protections" and "benefits" of marriage, but also of its "obligations." The court expressly acknowledged that "[m]any people hold deep-seated religious, moral and ethical convictions" about whether "marriage should be limited to the union of one man and one woman." But then it reprovingly cited the Supreme Court's opinion in *Lawrence v. Texas*, 571: "Our obligation is to define the liberty of all, not to mandate our own moral code." The court concluded its prologue and introduced the language it would be using by invoking "the constitutional principles of respect for individual autonomy and equality under the law." The opinion's gravamen was that marriage "bestows enormous private and social advantages." The court spent over 1,200 words minutely listing those advantages. It then said that the principle of equal protection barred the state from granting some people such important benefits while denying them to others unless it had a sufficiently strong reason, which it lacked.

The court did call marriage a "social institution of the highest importance" (*Goodridge*). But the court looked only at the question of entry into that institution, not into its nature, much less its moral aspects. On the contrary, the court referred to the challenged statute as nothing more than "a licensing law" and spoke approvingly of the "historical aim of licensure generally" (*Goodridge*:952, 955). What one did after obtaining the license, the court suggested, was not at issue. Indeed, the court seemed to suggest, it could not be at issue because it was "among the most basic [elements] of every individual's liberty" (*Goodridge*:959) and a sphere of life protected from state interference. The court invoked the language of the therapeutic to help explain why: the decision to marry has a "central role . . . in shaping one's identity" (*Goodridge*:948). So the court said that it was not changing the social institution, but it was vague about the "obligations" it several times mentioned, and it invoked the "changing realities of the American family" (*Goodridge*:963).

If marriage becomes truly integrated, the way couples of all kinds behave in it would matter. It would matter because social institutions are primarily shaped by the way people in them think and act. It would matter because law might need to be adapted to accommodate the new participants in the institution. Even Sullivan and Eskridge seemed ambivalent about the new marriage they would create. Sullivan (1995:2003–04) found "something baleful about the attempt of some gay conservatives to educate homosexuals and lesbians into an uncritical acceptance of a stifling model of heterosexual normality. The truth is, homosexuals are not entirely normal; and to flatten their varied and complicated lives into a single, moralistic model is to miss what is essential and exhilarating about their otherness." More concretely, Chambers (1996:460) commented, "Many gay men and lesbians, particularly gay men, explicitly disavow sexual exclusivity within their long-term relationships . . . . [I]n those states that still have rules relating to adultery, some lesbians and gay men may find their taint a significant impediment to embracing legal marriage." Likewise, Sullivan (1995:196) remarked on "a difference that I think is inherent between homosexual and heterosexual adults. The latter group is committed to the procreation of a new generation. The former simply isn't." Eskridge (1996:11) was perhaps be reflecting this difference when he said, "In today's society the importance of marriage is relational and not procreational." How, then, would accommodating marriage to these views affect its socializing usefulness?

Broadening the definition of marriage in these ways might affect marriage in another way – by promoting further expansion of its definition. This might happen in the ordinary way of the slippery slope: Each extension of a principle makes the next step smaller and easier. But this particular slope is waxed by several factors that have already helped ease our slide down: Much of the argument for same-sex marriage draws on our contemporary discomfort with distinctions and judgments. Much of that argument partakes of the contemporary desire to accommodate within the term "family" what Kath Weston (1991) called the "families we choose." Furthermore, as Chambers (1996:491) speculated – and as Professor Stacey's contribution to this volume (Chapter 10) attests – "By ceasing to conceive of marriage as a partnership composed of one person of each sex, the state may become more receptive to units of three or more . . . and to units composed of two people of the same sex but who are bound by friendship alone. All desirable changes in family law need not be made at once." Finally, as Chambers's last comment reminds us, we slide down slopes faster when pushed.

However, it seems likely that the more broadly you define marriage, the less effective the demands you can make of people in it. Weston (1991:206) wrote that "most chosen families are characterized by fluid boundaries, eclectic composition, and relatively little symbolic differentiation between erotic and noneroticities." Where boundaries are fluid, where one family barely resembles another, where erotic and platonic ties are hardly distinguishable, marriage is no longer special. Yet making marriage special is part of making it work as a socializing institution.

Proposals that the state recognize same-sex marriage have tended to describe marriage as a benefit that is being denied. And so it is. But marriage is also a social institution the government recruits as part of a socializing strategy, as a way to regulate people's behavior in intimate relationships. The most intriguing argument for same-sex marriage rests on that fact. In evaluating that argument I have asked whether same-sex marriage would serve the classic marital socializing function for gays and lesbians and how it would affect that function for heterosexuals. And I have asked what languages we will have for answering them. I have found no answers, only more questions, some invitingly empirical, some implacably normative. "It was the devious-cruising Rachel, that in her retracing search after her missing children, only found another orphan" (Melville 1851:635).

REFERENCES

Bellah, R. N. et al. (1991). *The Good Society*. New York: Alfred A. Knopf.

Bellah, R. N. et al. (1996). *Habits of the Heart*. Berkeley: University of California Press.

Chambers, D. L. (1996). What If? The Legal Consequences of Marriage and the Legal Needs of Lesbian and Gay Male Couples. *Michigan Law Review*, 95, 447–91.

Eskridge, Jr., W. N. (1996). *The Case for Same-Sex Marriage: From Sexual Liberty to Civilized Commitment*. New York: Free Press.

Ettelbrick, P. (1997). Since When Is Marriage a Path to Liberation? In Sullivan, A. (Ed.), *Same- Sex Marriage: Pro and Con*. London: Vintage Books.

Friedman, L. M. (1990). *The Republic of Choice: Law, Authority, and Culture*. Cambridge, MA: Harvard University Press.

Garrison, M. (1991). Good Intentions Gone Awry: The Impact of New York's Equitable Distribution Law on Divorce Outcomes. *Brooklyn Law Review*, 57, 621–754.

Garrison, M. (1998). Autonomy or Community?: An Evaluation of Two Models of Parental Obligation. *California Law Review*, 86, 41–117.

Goodridge v. Department of Public Health, 440 Mass. 309, 798 N.E.2d 941 (Mass. 2003).

Jacob, H. (1988). *Silent Revolution: The Transformation of Divorce Law in the United States.* Chicago: University of Chicago Press.
Keynes, J. M. (1956). My Early Beliefs. In *Essays and Sketches in Biography*. New York: Meridian Books.
Lawrence v. Texas, 538 U.S. 559 (2003).
Marx, K. (1967). On a Proposed Divorce Law. In Easton, L. D. & Guddat, K. H. (Eds.), *Writings of the Young Marx on Philosophy and Society*. New York: Doubleday.
Melville, H. (1851). *Moby Dick.*, New York: Harper and Brothers.
Planned Parenthood of Southeastern Pennsylvania v. Casey, 505 U.S. 833 (1992).
Rieff, P. (1966). *The Triumph of the Therapeutic: Uses of Faith after Freud*. New York: Harper & Row.
Roe v. Wade, 410 U.S. 113 (1973).
Sarat, A. & Felstiner, W. L. F. (1995). *Divorce Lawyers and Their Clients: Power and Meaning in the Legal Process*. Oxford: Oxford University Press.
Schneider, C. E. (1985). Moral Discourse and the Transformation of American Family Law. *Michigan Law Review*, 83, 1803–79.
Schneider, C. E. (1988). Rights Discourse and Neonatal Euthanasia. *California Law Review*, 76, 151–76.
Schneider, C. E. (1991). Rethinking Alimony: Marital Decisions and Moral Discourse. *BYU Law Review*, 1991, 197–257.
Schneider, C. E. (1994). Bioethics in the Language of the Law. *Hastings Center Report*, 24 *(July-August)*, 16–22.
Schneider, C. E. (1996). The Law and the Stability of Marriage: The Family as a Social Institution. In Popenoe, D., Bethke Elshtain, J. & Blankenhorn, D. (Eds.), *Promises to Keep: Decline and Renewal of Marriage in America*. New York: Rowman & Littlefield.
Schneider, C. E. (1998). *The Practice of Autonomy: Patients, Doctors, and Medical Decisions*. Oxford: Oxford University Press.
Schneider, C. E. (2006). Elite Principles: The ALI Proposals and the Politics of Law Reform. In Wilson, R. F. (Ed.), *Reconceiving the Family: Critical Reflections on the American Law Institute's Principles of the Law of Family Dissolution*. Cambridge: Cambridge University Press.
Sullivan, A. (1995). *Virtually Normal: An Argument about Homosexuality*. New York: Alfred A. Knopf.
Tocqueville, A. de. (1994) *Democracy in America*. NewYork: Alfred P. Knopf.
Wardle, L. (1991). No-Fault Divorce and the Divorce Conundrum. *BYU Law Review*, 1991, 79–142.
Weston, K. (1991). *Families We Choose: Lesbians, Gays, Kinship*. New York: Columbia University Press.
Wilson, J. Q. (1991). *On Character*. Washington, DC: AEI Press.
Wilson, J. Q. (1993). *The Moral Sense*. New York: Free Press.

13

The Pluralistic Vision of Marriage

Shahar Lifshitz

INTRODUCTION

In what manner should the state design institutions for couples and influence couples' choices[1] among these institutions? The current legal discourse is polarized between two opposite approaches to this question: one supporting public channeling, the other preferring private neutrality.

The public-channeling approach is based on a monolithic-perfectionist philosophy that posits the state's authority and duty to foster certain ways of life and to prefer them over others. In the spousal context, application of this approach requires regulating intimate relationships based mainly on public interests and shared moral values. The public-channeling approach perceives marriage as a public institution and stresses the state's role in steering couples into traditional, legal marriage.

By contrast, the private-neutral approach is based on a liberal-neutralist philosophy. According to this view, the liberal state must maintain a neutral approach toward various lifestyles and refrain from preferring one over another. The application of this approach to spousal law requires the state to respect the conjugal pattern selected by the parties and to refrain from attempts to channel couples toward any specific affiliative pattern. In its radical versions, this approach seeks to abolish marriage as a legal institution, or at the very least to replace the perception of marriage as a public institution with a contractual account of marriage.

I find both of these approaches unconvincing and, in this chapter, I lay out the foundation for a new approach – the pluralistic model. The pluralistic model is based on perfectionist liberal philosophy that emphasizes the inherent value of pluralism as well as its role in enhancing individual autonomy. It underscores the idea that individual autonomy means not only the absence of formal limitations on

[1] In this article I use the term "spouses" not only for married partners but also for couples in nonmarital relationships, such as cohabitants or other unmarried couples.

individuals' choices, but also the existence of a range of plausible options. In light of the values of autonomy and pluralism, modern liberal approaches emphasize the duty of the liberal state to create a diversity of social institutions that enable the individual to make genuine and meaningful choices among various alternatives. This chapter argues that, in the spousal realm, the pluralistic approach provides an alternative to both the private-neutrality *and* the public-channeling approaches. On the one hand, similar to the public approach, the pluralistic approach rejects the pure, private vision of marriage and insists on the active role of the state in the design of marriage as well as alternative affiliative institutions. On the other hand, in contrast to the collective, social, and often traditionalist moral values that guide the public approach, this approach seeks to design affiliative institutions in light of the liberal values of pluralism and autonomy. Furthermore, whereas the public approach seeks to channel people toward one social institution (e.g., traditional marriage), the pluralistic approach requires the state to contribute to the creation of a diversity of valuable affiliative patterns that offer couples a meaningful choice among different possibilities.

This chapter explores the pluralistic approach by discussing three publicly debated topics: (1) the regulation of cohabitation relationships; (2) the legitimacy of legal privileges attached to civil marriage; and (3) legal acknowledgment of alternative marriage systems such as religious marriage or covenant marriage. Finally, this chapter discusses Israel's supposedly pluralistic system of spousal institutions. This case study sheds light on the risks inherent in adopting the pluralistic model without implementing the limitations and criteria that are recommended in the present chapter.

THE EXISTING DEBATE: PUBLIC CHANNELING V. PRIVATE NEUTRALITY

In recent years, prominent scholars have described the liberal transformation of marriage from a public institution to a private arrangement (Glendon 1989; Singer 1992; Witte 1997). Until the second half of the twentieth century, states controlled most aspects of spousal relations; government determined eligibility to marry, designed the marriage ceremony, and established the rules that regulated ongoing marriages (Glendon 1989). Fault-based divorce systems set forth public criteria for appropriate behavior, and these rules regulated divorce as well as its economic consequences (Phillips 1988). Paralleling public regulation of marriage, most legal systems opposed contractual regulation of the spousal relationship (Weitzman 1981). In addition, the law cultivated the exclusivity of legal marriage while continuously battling partners' attempts to conduct their conjugal relationships outside marriage (Cott 2000; Dubler 2006).

In stark contrast, many changes that have occurred within marriage and divorce law over the last few decades reflect a trend away from state regulation of conjugal relations in favor of granting control over these relations to the parties themselves (Singer 1992). This trend can be seen in almost all aspects of modern marriage law, including the lowering of capacity requirements and the establishment of same-sex marriage in some states (Case 2003; Dubler 2010; Wardle 2008). It is also evident within modern divorce law under which, in contrast to past practice, either spouse can unilaterally end the marriage (Glendon 1989). Another clear expression of the shift away from state regulation is increasing freedom to contractually define the terms of marriage. Through contract, the parties, instead of the state, determine their rights and obligations (Bix 2010; Garrison 1983). Beyond the deregulation of marriage, the traditional legal preference for marriage has weakened as the gap between legal marriage and other forms of conjugal relationships has narrowed (ALI 2002; Atkin 2008; Garrison 2005; Lifshitz 2009). In this way, the state avoids channeling partners toward a specific form of affiliative relationship (McClain 2007), leaving that choice to the concerned parties.

Beyond these rule changes, in several influential articles, Carl Schneider (1985, 1994) has contended that a significant decrease in "moral discourse" about family law has occurred. He maintains that even the nineteenth-century secularization of marriage in most Western countries did not release spousal law from collective value systems. This collective theology, partly rooted in religious doctrines, did not hesitate to define the "good life" with respect to family relationships and to condemn those who deviated from it. Contrary to the previous models, modern marriage law is not based on a collective moral concept and aims to avoid moral judgments (Teitelbaum 1985).

The privatization narrative is not monolithic, however; it is dynamic and characterizes a general trend. Some aspects of marriage law reflect a modern, private, morally neutral approach, while others embody a traditional, public, moralistic approach. In other instances, the law expresses a compromise or a balance in the power struggle between the different approaches (Katz et al. 2000). In addition, contrary to the linear impression implied by the privatization narrative, in recent years there has been a growing demand among Western lawmakers and scholars for counter-reform measures, including weakening the right to marry and to divorce, strengthening the institution of marriage, and reducing couples' freedom to regulate their own relationships, all in the spirit of the public approach (Bradford 1997; Galston 1991a; Wardle 2008). Nevertheless, the privatization narrative represents far more than simple historical description; it also demonstrates the ongoing struggle between the public and private approaches with respect to the state's role in regulating conjugal institutions.

The public-channeling approach, on the one hand, emphasizes the public interest in the regulation of conjugal relations, as well as the institutional aspect of marriage. Advocates of this approach posit that the state should channel citizens toward formal marriage, which is to be defined and regulated in a manner consistent with public interests and collective values (Hafen 1983; Regan 1999). In the political sphere, this approach has typically been advocated by conservative groups, although it has also received support from communitarian scholars (Sandel 1996).

The private-neutral approach, on the other hand, is driven by the liberal ideal of neutrality (Rawls 1993, 1999). It thus does not seek to channel people toward the institution of marriage or any other affiliative institution (Chambers 1985; Eekelaar 1998) and instead aims to demonstrate respect for a wide variety of family forms and lifestyles by reducing the privileges enjoyed by married partners at the expense of those in nonmarital relationships (Polikoff 2008). This approach views marriage as a private arrangement and seeks to increase the freedom of couples to marry, divorce, and define the content of their marriages.

The struggle between these two approaches in various contexts shapes current discourse regarding the law applicable to marriage and other affiliative forms (Lifshitz 2012).

TOWARD PLURALISTIC REGULATION OF THE SPOUSAL INSTITUTIONS

Beyond the Private-Public Debate

I find both the private and the public approaches to marriage unconvincing, for several reasons.

First, sociological research demonstrates both that families continue to perform important social functions in the modern world and that the content and form of a couple's relationship may have broad social implications beyond its consequences for the individual couple (Haddock & Polsby 1996; Murphy 2002; Wax 1996). Yet the private approach focuses strictly on the involved parties and does not take broader social consequences into account. By contrast, the traditional, public approaches emphasize only the public aspects of marriage and ignore its personal functions, the variety of affiliative lifestyles, and the liberal values of individual freedom and autonomy. As a result, both approaches have failed to attain a proper balance between individual autonomy and the public interest.

The "best interest of the child" principle demonstrates the problem with both approaches. At the heart of the private approach lies the perception of the conjugal relationship as a private matter. However, this view ignores the fact that partners' private arrangements have a considerable effect on the lives of their children (Cherlin et al. 1991; McLanahan & Sandefur 1994; Wallerstein & Blakeslee 1989). Under the private approach, the law takes into account the interests of the couple while ignoring those of their offspring (Scott 1991). The attempt to sharply distinguish between laws governing the relationship of the couple – to be regulated through a private-contractual prism – and parent-child laws focused on public responsibility for the "best interest of the child" is problematic, as certain domains, such as divorce law and marriage law, as well as the economic relationship between spouses, have dramatic consequences on children's lives (Lifshitz 2008b).

In contrast to the private approach, the public approach views children as a basis for a marriage law that reflects public interests. However, the public approach wrongly identifies the public interest with traditional legal regulation, in which children's interests were used to support limitations on divorce and eligibility to marry as well as the preference for legal marriage. Broader considerations demonstrate that, in many circumstances, the opposite policy (i.e., a more liberal policy) would be in the best interest of the children. Therefore, the best interest of the child should serve as an essential principle of family law, but the implementation of that principle should be compatible with modern understandings regarding adult relationships and their impact on children.

Even if we leave aside the concrete public effects of any given legal arrangement, the presentation of marriage as a private matter between the involved parties is insensitive to the meaning of marriage as a social institution and to the important role of law and society in the design of such institutions. Social institutions are essential in all societies as they grant human beings tools through which to arrange perceptions of identity, status, and relationships with other human beings (Geertz 1973; Posner 2000; Berger & Luckmann 2006). Societies develop a wide variety of legal and nonlegal norms meant to design the social institutions within them (Scott 2000). The social institution of "marriage" gives tangible meaning to the decision to marry, the marriage ceremony, the roles of husband and wife, expectations of one's partner, and the status of being married.

The role of marriage as a social institution requires that individual desires must sometimes give way to the public interest. Consider a couple who want to marry but also to stipulate in an agreement that their relationship will automatically expire in a number of years. A private regulatory model would accept this type of contractual arrangement on the premise that the arrangement reflects the desires of both parties. But this approach fails take account of the fact that legal acknowledgment of such a "marriage" will affect not only the specific couple, but also public perceptions of the institution of marriage. This fact requires those who shape the law to examine not only the interests and desires of individual couples, but also the social meaning that society wishes to attribute to marriage. Similarly, recognition of same-sex marriage may affect not only the concerned couple, but also collective social understanding of the meaning of marriage. Therefore, public responsibility toward the social institution of marriage requires examining whether same-sex marriage has a positive or damaging influence on the public at large (Case 2003). This type of examination involves public considerations that are not taken into account by the private-neutral approach.

In current legal discourse, public considerations are typically found in the rhetoric of "traditionalists" who oppose the recognition of same-sex marriage. In my view, however, it is a mistake to assume that public considerations necessitate nonrecognition of same-sex marriages. To the contrary, one can think of a number of public considerations that favor officially recognizing same-sex relationships, including providing an appropriate legal framework for raising children growing up within this family unit, enhancing the economic stability of the partners, moderating the gender-related implications and patriarchal practices still identified with marriage, and, in doing so, designing marriage as an egalitarian institution (Case 2011). I merely wish to emphasize that any discussion of the recognition of same-sex couples must not only address individual rights, but also the social meaning of supposedly private arrangements and the manner in which recognition of same-sex relationships could affect the institution of marriage.

This discussion of same-sex relationships is connected to a broader issue: the dynamism of social norms, social institutions, and culture. Such dynamism is a welcome phenomenon as it allows existing social institutions to be constantly updated and improved. Therefore, I do not accept a conservative approach as a replacement for the private one, as it views deviation from the historical and social definition of marriage as problematic. To the contrary, precisely because marriage has become a recognized institution with a set of hallmarks, there is a public interest in preserving marriage's relevance by updating it.

In my opinion, neither the private approach – focused solely on individual rights – nor the public approach – sanctifying existing social institutions – rises to the challenge. What is needed is a new approach that identifies the modern public interests worthy of promotion through marriage law and the manner in which these interests should be integrated within the private arrangements of the couple.

The Philosophical Aspect: Spousal Institutions' Neutrality, Monolithic Perfectionism, and Pluralism

At the heart of the private approach is the liberal idea of a neutral state and opposition to state channeling toward any particular perception of the "good life." However, almost all modern philosophers, including liberal scholars, reject the idea of neutrality as either impossible or undesirable (Gardbaum 1991; Raz 1986, 1994). As Dagan (forthcoming) recently argued: "Every choice of a set of legal rules governing a particular type of interpersonal relationship facilitates and entrenches one ideal vision of the good of that particular institution. Because private law must allocate rights and entitlements on the basis of *some* ideal vision of the relationship at hand, there is no substantively neutral way to allocate them." The law of conjugal relationships is no different. Therefore, I do not hesitate to reject the private-neutrality approach here as well.

Unfortunately, the public-channeling approach in vogue today does not provide a worthy philosophical alternative to the private-neutrality approach. A primary deficiency is that it is driven by a perfectionist-monolithic philosophical stream. Within philosophical discourse, such an approach typically identifies one set of values and interests or a specific balance between values and interests that society should promote. On a political level, such an approach aims at social institutions that reflect the identified values or balance. In the context of conjugal law, the public-channeling approach has thus sought to strengthen the institution of marriage, attribute to it a uniform meaning, and confront alternative lifestyles with one another.

Even if we put aside the "conservative," traditionalist rhetoric that advocates of the public-channeling approach typically employ today and accept the possibility of a modern design for the institution of marriage, I am still opposed to the perfectionist-monolithic approach that seeks to channel the complexity of the conjugal relationships toward one model. My opposition is based on a variety of factors: First, the current diversity of family types makes it difficult to accept that there is one specific balance capable of supplying a suitable and proper solution for the wide variety of existing lifestyles. Moreover, much of the public structuring of marriage and other intimate relationships relates to their nature as frameworks for conducting an emotional and intimate relationship. Emotions and intimate relations require specific "tuning" and are not suitable to a one-size-fits-all model. Certainly, from a liberal vantage point, a preference for and strengthening of one particular lifestyle is disrespectful toward couples' choices of different lifestyles and runs counter to liberal values of freedom and autonomy.

Given these reasons for discontent with both the private-neutral and perfectionist-monolithic approaches, I would like to suggest an innovative pluralistic approach to conjugal relationships. My approach is based on a wider, institutional-pluralistic theory which requires that society and law contribute to the prosperity of a variety of existing social institutions – differentiated from one another in their core values – and occasionally assist in developing new social institutions (Raz 1994; Dagan forthcoming).

Before moving on, I would like to put this argument in its proper context within the philosophical debate regarding the morality of pluralism (Kekes 1993). According to one view, pluralism stems from moral relativism, or at the very least an attempt to adopt moral neutrality in the political sphere. Practically, it leads to the adoption of the private-neutral approach. This chapter's institutional-pluralistic theory, however, is based on two moral-philosophical foundations, both significantly different from the neutral stream. The first foundation, whose early sources are found in the writings of key liberal scholars such as John Stuart Mill (1942) and Isaiah Berlin (1969), views pluralism as an intrinsic value reflecting the unique spirit of man and his dignity. Accordingly, this approach rejects monolithic approaches based on one set of values or even a specific balance between different values and instead supports a variety of institutions that strike different balances among different values in a manner that reflects and fosters the richness of human reality.

The second foundation, notably developed in Joseph Raz's (1986, 1994) scholarship, is based on perfectionist liberal values emphasizing individual autonomy. According to this approach, the state is obligated to actively allow its citizens to thrive and write their life stories in a free and rich manner. This approach further stresses that individual autonomy means not only the absence of formal limitations on individuals' choices, but also the existence of a range of plausible options. Thus, modern liberal approaches emphasize the duty of the liberal state to create a diversity of social institutions that enable individuals to make genuine and meaningful choices among various alternatives.

In the realm of intimate adult relationships, the pluralistic approach (whether based on the intrinsic value of pluralism or on the active value of autonomy) offers an alternative to both the private approach *and* the public approach. Whereas the public-channeling approach seeks to steer individuals toward one social institution and the private-neutral approach completely abandons the state's role in designing affiliative institutions, the pluralistic approach requires the state to contribute to the creation and design of diverse, valuable affiliative patterns that offer couples significant choice.

Of course, no state can design and promote an unlimited number of social institutions. What does the pluralistic approach take as criteria and limitations for designing its institutions for couples?

In my view, the state's choice among institutions ultimately requires perfectionist foundations, such as substantive moral evaluation of affiliative institutions and practice as well as consideration of public interests. Therefore, similar to the public approaches, the pluralistic approach will ultimately need to identify moral values and public interests. However, contrary to the existing public discourse, the pluralistic approach will be able to offer dynamic values and interests to guide the state in its design of affiliative institutions offered to couples.

Furthermore, despite the fact that both the public-monolithic and pluralistic approaches eventually need perfectionist standards, it would be a big mistake to assume that the difference between them consists merely of the one institution offered under the public-monolithic approach in contrast to the multiple institutions under pluralistic policy. In my view, the liberal values of pluralism, autonomy, and human dignity, which lie at the core of the pluralistic approach, distinguish it from the public-monolithic approaches; these values not only justify the state's involvement in designing a variety of social institutions, but also lay down the substantive cornerstone for designing affiliative institutions in at least four ways.

First, the pluralistic approach gives autonomy a central role in the moral evaluation of various institutional possibilities; thus (in contrast to private-neutrality approaches that are sometimes tolerant of non-liberal marital institutions and public-channeling approaches that traditionally support such institutions), this approach prefers egalitarian institutions that can assist couples progress and develop their life plans over institutions that are potentially repressive and exploiting. Second, the pluralistic approach requires that both partners enjoy substantive freedom of choice among the affiliative institutions offered by the state. Third, despite the fact that intimate relationships often create extremely complex human connections, the pluralistic approach demands that individuals who are no longer interested in their relationships have the right to exit them (Dagan & Franz 2004). Finally, although the pluralistic approach recognizes the need to consider public interests and values while designing affiliative institutions (and in promoting specific social institutions, as we will learn shortly), it nonetheless requires legislators to ensure that these interests and values, as well as the privileges accorded some institutions to promote them, do not profoundly undermine the autonomy of couples to choose the lifestyle that suites them best.

LEGAL APPLICATIONS OF THE PLURALISTIC APPROACHES

Legal Commitments between Cohabitants

Traditionally, the law in most Western countries sharply distinguished between marriage and cohabitation, to the extent of invalidating contracts in which the cohabitants explicitly took upon themselves marriage-like commitments. Civil law's hostility toward cohabitation was part of the public-monolithic approach that viewed this relational choice as immoral and defended marriage as the core social institution through which sexual relationships must be conducted. Influenced by the liberal transformation of Western family law during the second half of the twentieth century, most jurisdictions now respect couples' private choices and validate explicit contracts in which cohabitants assume marriage-like commitments (Bowman 2010). Furthermore, during the last decades of the twentieth century, a variety of legal doctrines, such as implied contract, restitution, unjust enrichment, and constructive trust, have been used to impose marital commitments on cohabitants. New legislation and court rulings in Western countries such as Canada, New Zealand, Sweden, and Israel, as well as the Domestic Partnerships chapter in the American Law Institute's Principles of Family Dissolution, may reflect a movement toward the total equation of the regulation of the internal relationship between unmarried cohabitants with that of married partners (American Law Institute 2002; Atkin 2008; Lifshitz 2009).

A thorough examination reveals that both justification and rejection of the distinction between marriage and cohabitation have been based on the same regulatory theories – contractual-private-neutral and perfectionist-monolithic-public-status – that I have already described. For example, in the famous California case of *Marvin v. Marvin*,[2] as well as cases in other states, courts justified the imposition of marital commitments on cohabitants through the doctrines of express and implied contract (Estin 2001). Elizabeth Scott (2004, 2006) went one step further in suggesting that, as a default rule, the law should impose marital financial obligations on cohabitants in a long-term relationship. Yet, at the same time, many of those who object to applying marital commitments to cohabitants base their arguments on the idea of

[2] See *Marvin v. Marvin*, 557 P.2d 106, 110 (Cal. 1976).

contractual freedom, or rather freedom from contracts. According to the latter claim, the absence of a formal marriage reflects the rejection of marriage laws. Therefore, imposing marriage laws on cohabitants does not respect their choice not to get married (Garrison 2005; Brinig 2006).

Public-perfectionist approaches also may lead to the opposite conclusion in this matter. On the one hand, the perfectionist school of thought historically distinguished between the obligations of married and unmarried couples in order to highlight the uniqueness of marriage and to channel couples to this institution. On the other hand, in many cases the demand to equate marital commitments and those of cohabitants is founded not on contractual arguments, but instead on public values and extra-contractual considerations of justice, fairness, and equality (Blumberg 2001; Ellman 2001). Furthermore, jurisdictions such as New-Zealand and Israel – and in some aspects even the ALI Principles – adopt a status model and impose marital commitments on cohabitants regardless of, or even against, their will (Lifshitz 2010).

In spite of the matrix of options created by the private-contractual-neutral and public-monolithic approaches, the pluralistic approach offers a unique perspective. Consider a world in which the law distinguishes between marriage and cohabitation. In such a world, a couple may choose between two different legal regimes. Such a framework offers individuals a range of options. On the other hand, consider a legal regime that has adopted the supposedly liberal position equating the legal status of cohabitants to that of married couples. In such a world, couples desiring to maintain a residential, intimate relationship are automatically subject to the system of marriage laws. Such a framework does not offer couples social institutions with meaningful differences and the possibility of making genuine choices.

The pluralistic approach is therefore close to the contractual-neutralist argument for distinguishing marriage and cohabitation. Nonetheless, in contrast to the passive liberal inclination of the neutralist approach, the pluralistic approach is based on an active perception of the state. The state's active role obliges it to construct the institution of cohabitation in a fair and just manner. As a result, even if the approach opposes the full imposition of marriage law on cohabitants, it supports the selective imposition on cohabitants of suitable elements of marriage law in order to construct the institution of cohabitation in a fair and just manner. In this sense, the pluralistic approach accepts the argument that freedom from contract militates against the imposition of marriage law as a whole on cohabitation relationships, but does not accept the claim that cohabitants should have absolute freedom from the imposition of legal obligations.

The comprehensive development of cohabitation law as derived from the pluralistic model is beyond the scope of this chapter.[3] However, I present here a number of principles from which a wide, complete, and coherent legal model can be derived.

[3] In earlier work (Lifshitz 2010) I propose a coherent model of cohabitation laws inspired by the pluralistic model.

First, the pluralistic model for cohabitation regulation rests on the premise that cohabitation and marriage law should be distinguished from one another.

Second, while the prevailing models address marriage law as a "package deal" with respect to cohabitants, the pluralist model offers a nuanced approach that selectively applies elements of marriage law.

Third, the pluralist model provides a means of identifying those components of marriage law that can appropriately be applied to cohabitants. In my view, cohabitation law should impose on cohabitants the *responsive* components of marriage law that aim to prevent exploitation and protect weaker parties from marriage ex-post as well as the *autonomy-based* components of marriage law, especially those compatible with the *right of exit*. But cohabitation law should not impose the communal aspects of marriage law on cohabitants; the pluralistic model rejects the imposition of regulations on cohabitants aimed at guiding couples, ex ante, to behave according to society's vision of marriage.

Fourth, beyond its menu of default rules, the pluralistic model supports cohabitants' freedom of contract. Yet, at the same time, the model's sensitivity to power gaps and exploitation enables it to adopt a nuanced approach, distinguishing between aspects of cohabitation law and the circumstances under which contracts were created.

Finally, the pluralistic model is based on the ability of the parties to choose between various affiliative institutions. Therefore, in the absence of a marriage option for same-sex couples, it is not possible to discuss providing a significant choice for this group. Hence, if marriage is unavailable to same-sex couples, a special legal regime should be offered to same-sex cohabitants that takes into account their ineligibility to marry.

Pluralism and the Legal Privileging of Marriage

The regulation of marriage extends beyond the relationship between the spouses and includes a wide variety of economic subsidies, costs, and privileges, such as tax benefits (and penalties), social security, mortgage eligibility, pension rights, bereavement benefits, protected tenancy, and housing rights that typically are unavailable to nonmarital families.[4]

Traditionally, these privileges were part of the monolithic-public approach, which sought to channel couples into marriage (McClain 2007). Alongside the historical justifications for strengthening marriage, based at least in part on moral and religious foundations, many lawmakers and scholars have urged that these privileges are justified based on the public interest – related to the welfare of the couple, their

[4] See Fineman (1995: at 104–105): "married couples receive hundreds, if not thousands, of subsidies and privileges from the state that are unavailable to other, supposedly less autonomous, family forms." See also Chambers (1996).

children, and society in general – in encouraging stable relationships with a high level of commitment. Relying on legal, psychological, economic, and sociological analyses, these advocates contend that marriage constitutes a more stable bond than cohabitation and that the level of commitment between two legally married partners is higher than that between mere cohabitants. Accordingly, they suggest that it is appropriate to promote legal marriage and to grant married couples rights not granted to cohabitants. Pointing to the advantages of marriage over other family forms for both the concerned families and society as a whole, they also argue that it is appropriate to privilege marriage over other patterns of family life (Galston 1991; Haddock & Polsby 1996; Murphy 2002; Waite & Gallagher 2002; Wax 1996). Finally, they argue that public *registration* of commitment has intrinsic and functional value as it clarifies the nature of the relationship, its obligations, and reinforces the commitment (Scott 2007).

While most legal systems continue to privilege marriage, the existence of these privileges is being challenged in modern legal discourse (Crane 2006; Zelinsky 2006). The modern challenge to privileging marriage comes in two versions. The mild version opposes privileging marriage without also privileging cohabiting couples. This approach is not opposed to providing tailored legal rights on the basis of taking part in an intimate relationship, but instead supports granting marital rights to nonmarital conjugal relationships (Polikoff 2003, 2008). The radical version denies the relevance of adult relationships to any given legal right. According to this position, neither cohabitants nor married couples should be entitled to special legal treatment. This approach aspires to a world that does not distinguish among various types of adult relationships (marriage, cohabitation, casual relationships, solitary life, etc.). In its most extreme version, it calls for the abolition of marriage as a legal category (Fineman 1995; Stacey, Chapter 10).

Obviously, the mild version of this argument opposes the perfectionist-public approach toward marriage; under the latter approach, the rights of spouses are intended to promote commitments and behavioral patterns embodied in legal marriage, and a person who has not assumed the obligations of marriage cannot demand marital rights. Certainly, a couple who choose a relational pattern that differs markedly from marital norms (for example, a couple who live apart, are not monogamous, and do not intend to maintain a stable relationship) cannot argue that their relationship reflects the values and interests embodied in legal marriage. By contrast, the neutralist approach requires the law to respect different choices and not to channel people into marriage by granting various rights only to those who get married. Consequently, granting marital privileges to every couple – married or not – seems to suit the neutralist approach. However, if the state may not favor any one lifestyle, what justification is there for granting marital rights to those who maintain a spousal relationship, while discriminating against those who do not maintain such a relationship? Accordingly, the legal application of the neutralist approach should be that any privileges granted to those involved in couple relations – married couples and quasi-married couples (e.g., cohabiting couples) alike – are illegitimate because they substantively discriminate against those who adopt different lifestyles. It follows that a sincere and coherent neutralist approach will lead not to the application of marital privileges to spouses in any type of relationship but, rather, as the radical approach suggests, to the complete negation of any consequence or benefit ensuing from the maintenance of an intimate relationship.[5]

What about the pluralistic approach? The question of privileging marriage highlights the internal tension embedded in this approach between perfectionism and autonomy. On the one hand, the pluralistic approach is based on a perfectionist philosophy holding that, at times, public interests and values may justify a preference for one lifestyle over another. Hence, on the basis of the psychological, economic, and sociological advantages of marriage, pluralism recognizes the state's authority and responsibility to prefer marriage over other relational forms that are less beneficial to society and to individuals. On the other hand, the pluralistic approach is grounded in autonomy, including the individual's right to choose between different institutions. The denial of all marital rights to cohabiting couples or other types of family relationships is liable to create considerable pressure to marry. Such pressure, even if it does not constitute absolute coercion, does not respect the choices and personal freedom of such couples. Thus, providing external incentives as a means to channel spouses toward marriage undermines the pluralistic approach, as the choice of one institution over the other no longer may no longer reflect the couple's authentic choice. Finally, privileging marriage and steering couples toward that institution ultimately clashes with the internal value of pluralism, which seeks to encourage social diversity.

So how should the pluralistic approach balance between the state's legitimate aim, and even responsibility, to foster certain relationship patterns, on the one hand, with the value of autonomy and the desirability of fostering social diversity on the other?[6] In my opinion, in light of the perfectionist philosophy in general and the specific

5 As I have shown within existing legal literature, the neutral approach often leads to the demand to abolish marriage as a legal institution. In contrast to that position, Case (2005), guided by the liberal-neutral approach, suggested an approach seeking to maintain legal marriage as a "license" for creating spousal relationships recognized by the state. Considering that one's spousal relationships affect one's relationships with external parties, the state should offer a public registry through which those who are interested may announce the existence of their spousal relationships. Case's attempt to justify the existence of marriage as a legal institution while maintaining a neutral worldview is indeed impressive. However, in my opinion, the need to define contractual default rules regarding the spousal relationship, as well as the fact that Case herself posits that it will not be possible to register all types of spousal relationships, ultimately requires a moral perfectionist decision between various spousal and familial lifestyles.

6 While most legal scholarship is divided between the private approach, opposing preference of marriage, and the public approach, seeking to prefer marriage as a desirable legal institution, there has been some recent literature attempting to combine the public value of marriage and the desire to respect people's alternative choices and defend various lifestyles (see McClain 2007; Eichner 2007). In many cases the motivation behind this type of literature is similar to that guiding the present chapter.

analysis of the importance of spousal institutions and of marriage in particular, granting unique rights to married couples is legitimate and even necessary.

However, the following techniques should be adopted in order to restrain the threat embodied in such rights to the values of pluralism and autonomy:

First, the autonomy and pluralistic aspects of the institution of marriage itself should be expanded. For example, the law should broaden the current eligibility requirement for marriage and include, under the category of marriage, unions of same-sex couples who are willing to take upon themselves marital values and commitments. In addition, as I argue later in the chapter, the law should permit a few parallel marriage "tracks," such as regular marriage and covenant marriage.

Second, the law should construct social institutions, such as civil unions, that provide alternatives to legal marriage and develop legal constructs for emerging social phenomena involving, for example, intimate nonsexual relationships between relatives (for example, siblings living together). In a legal world based on the pluralistic approach, these institutions would not serve as an inferior alternative for those disqualified to marry, but rather would offer an equally acceptable alternative for all couples. However, in contrast to the neutralist approach (that demands the automatic equation of these institutions to marriage) and to the monolithic-perfectionist approach (that seeks, a priori, to prefer legal marriage), the pluralistic approach will construct a specific – and different – package of rights and obligations that suits the nature of each institution, the different choice made by the couples in each case, and the ensuing social benefits from each institution.

Third, the law should avoid moral condemnation or punishment of those seeking alternatives to marriage. Therefore, even when the law chooses for public reasons to favor one social institution over another, as in favoring marriage over cohabitation, the law should clarify that cohabiting is legitimate and that the preference for marriage is based on a "package deal," in which the couple who assumes certain obligations that reduce society's burden will also be entitled to benefits or subsidies from society. In the spirit of the suggested correlation between spouses' rights and duties, in some cases there is no justification for imposing on cohabitants who are not entitled to marital rights those duties or burdens that are normally imposed on married couples (such as the obligation to carry the debt of the married spouse to third parties or tax burdens that are known as the marriage penalty).

Fourth, the law should distinguish between its directive and responsive functions. The directive aspect of the law seeks to channel couples toward successful affiliative institutions by privileging those institutions. Consequently, even if it is deemed appropriate to encourage couples to marry, the law ought not to leave unmarried couples or their children to their own fate. Thus, it is necessary to distinguish between those legal principles the primary role of which is to encourage couples to enter into long-term family relationships (directive principles), which ought not be applied to cohabitants, and those principles aimed at responding to problems and needs arising as a result of shared living arrangements, which can be relevant to cohabitation relationships (responsive principles). An important, albeit not absolute, indication of the guiding rationale of a given principle in marriage law is the time at which it is applied. For example, those legal principles that confer rights on married couples before or during the course of their relationship are generally more directive in nature, whereas those that confer rights on a married person after the death of the spouse are, in many cases, responsive in nature.[7]

Finally, children's welfare should be a guiding principle in determining whether or not to privilege married couples. While in some circumstances the interests of the children may be best served by promoting marriage, in most circumstances those interests may be best served by supporting children regardless of their family's affiliative model.

The Multi-Marriage System

So far we have addressed relational forms that are alternatives to marriage. We will now deal with a situation where the state recognizes or even offers various marriage tracks. As long as these tracks satisfy liberal standards, their recognition is not controversial from a pluralistic perspective. This is not the case, however, when it comes to marriage tracks that are not regulated by liberal norms, such as hierarchical marriage relationships or marriage tracks that limit the right of exit. In these instances, tension arises between the pluralistic concern for cultural diversity and commitment to individual autonomy and human dignity. The question of religious and covenant marriage illustrates these tensions and their policy implications.

Religious Marriage

In several countries (such as India, Kenya, Israel, and South Africa), the state offers religious regulation of marriage and divorce along with or instead of civil marriage (Nichols 2007). Even in Western countries, many citizens still choose to marry and divorce in religious ceremonies, and, in a deeper sense, perceive themselves as being subject to communal and religious legal systems. Consequently, courts often address the validity of private arrangements in which the spouses have applied religious law or jurisdiction to their relationships (Estin 2004). Furthermore, in the spirit of multicultural theories, Joel Nichols (2007:135–136) recently proposed that "civil government should consider ceding some of its jurisdictional authority over marriage and divorce law to religious communities that are competent and capable of adjudicating the marital rites and rights of their respective adherents."

Legal recognition of one or more religious marriage tracks alongside the civil track is seemingly consistent with the pluralistic approach, which seeks to enrich

[7] This distinction does not work however in all cases. For example, the right to make medical decisions for an incompetent spouse is responsive.

the existing menu with new affiliative institutions. But the substantive content of significant parts of religious marriage law must satisfy the pluralistic requirements of substantive freedom of choice, prevention of exploitation, and right of exit. First, the pluralistic approach demands substantive freedom of choice among the various institutions; it thus requires safeguards to ensure that the religious marriage track is not selected as a result of social and family pressures, which could potentially eliminate an individual's ability to choose between the secular and religious tracks. Second, religious family law systems are, in some cases, characterized by gender inequality; these systems may deny women the right to family property, express a double standard in sexual morality, and sanction polygamy.[8] Such rules do not conform to the pluralistic approach's commitment to prevent exploitation and inferiority within the affiliative institutions that it offers. Finally, the severe restrictions on dissolution of the marital relationship that are characteristic of certain religions are inconsistent with the pluralistic approach's commitment to the right of exit. The theory's stance toward religious regulation of spousal relationships is thus contingent upon the existing cultural background and the specific content of the religious laws. Should a religious community and its law satisfy the demands of free entry, equality within the relationship, and a reasonable exit option, then the law should validate private agreements to apply religious marriage law, and the pluralistic theory might even support the state's offering these religious tracks as options.

Furthermore, despite my reservations concerning a state-sponsored religious marriage track, a liberal, pluralistic state must respect the religious significance of marriage in the eyes of large segments of the population. For example, in communities in which a religious ceremony is the conventional way to formalize marriage, it is proper to authorize religious leaders to conduct marriage ceremonies and ensure their proper legal registration.

Moreover, at times, disregard for the religious aspect of marriage (and religious arrangements between the parties) and an exclusive focus on the secular, civil aspects of marriage might harm the values of individual autonomy and equality that the pluralistic approach seeks to defend. Take, for example, the case of an Orthodox Jewish divorce. According to Jewish law, spouses who were married in a religious ceremony are deemed married until they obtain a religious divorce. The religious divorce ceremony requires the voluntary grant of a divorce bill (*Get*) by the husband to the wife; spouses are considered, under Orthodox Jewish law, to be married as long as a *Get* has not been granted. This can lead to an outrageous situation in which a Jewish man, who married in a religious ceremony and obtained a divorce in a civil court, exploits his wife's need to receive a religious *Get* by making his cooperation in granting the *Get* conditional upon payment (Broyde 2001). Secular disregard for the religious dimension of marriage that enables this type of coercion contravenes the values of autonomy and equality. The pluralistic

[8] For the emerging debate on the legitimacy of consent polygamy, see Davis (2010).

approach thus supports civil recognition of religious arrangements obligating the husband to cooperate in obtaining a *Get* in order to reduce or eliminate such coercion (Stone 2000), as well as extensive use of contractual doctrines, such as duress and unconscionability, to invalidate divorce settlements that are a product of purchased *Get* bargains.[9] Finally, the pluralistic approach's commitment to the value of autonomy and the prevention of exploitation supports legislation, such as New York's statutory "Get Law,"[10] which imposes civil sanctions on Jewish spouses married in a Jewish ceremony who refuse to cooperate in obtaining the religious dissolution of their marriages.

To conclude: the pluralistic approach applies caution and suspicion in recognizing religious marriage as an official marriage track. In certain instances, however, it would recognize private arrangements that contain religious elements, while subjecting them to judicial review and supporting civil actions to prevent exploitation and harm to individual autonomy, even when these actions cooperate with religious arrangements and practice.

Covenant Marriage

In the late twentieth century, Louisiana and a few other states added a new marriage track called covenant marriage. In these states, spouses may choose either a regular marriage that is subject to standard marriage law or a "covenant marriage." Covenant marriage laws have three key features: (1) mandatory premarital counseling that stresses the seriousness of marriage; (2) the premarital signing of a Declaration of Intent requiring couples to make "all reasonable efforts to preserve the marriage, including marriage counseling" in the event of difficulties; and (3) limited grounds for divorce (Nichols 2007; Spaht 1998). In conventional political discourse, this special track has been perceived as a conservative victory and, accordingly, it has been criticized by liberals. The pluralistic approach, however, sheds a different light on covenant marriage.[11]

First, covenant marriage was not accepted in any state as the sole marriage track, but instead as an additional option alongside the regular marriage track. Consequently, covenant marriages can be viewed as a pluralistic method of enriching the range of available social institutions instead of a conservative approach to marriage. Second, unlike traditional family law and certain religious laws, covenant marriage does not entail double standards for men and women and does not include exploitative components. Third, even though covenant marriage extends the waiting

9 See *Golding v. Golding*, 176 A.D. 2d 20 (N.Y. App. Div. 1992).

10 There are actually two *Get* laws. For the 1983 Get Law (as amended substantially in 1984), see N.Y. Dom. Rel. Law § 253 (McKinney 1999 & Supp. 2010). For the 1992 Get Act, see N.Y. Dom. Rel. Law § 236B(5)(h), (6)(d) (McKinney 1999 & Supp. 2010).

11 For the pluralistic approach toward covenant marriage, see Nichols (1998).

period before divorce beyond what is common in the conventional track, it enables a determined party to demand and obtain a divorce in no more than two years.

Prior to covenant marriage legislation, the legal literature contained trenchant debates as to whether extending the waiting period before entry of a divorce was worthwhile (Scott 1990). The conventional legal approaches maintain that the state must clearly decide in favor of one of these positions. The pluralistic approach, by contrast, enables the spouses to decide between the available options. Just as the pluralistic approach refuses to choose for the parties between the package deal of marriage and the package deal of cohabitation, offering both possibilities to the spouses, it also offers spouses two available marriage tracks.

THE FAILURE OF THE SEMI-PLURALISTIC SYSTEM – THE CASE OF ISRAEL

Although the legal system in Israel is primarily secular and liberal, marriage and divorce laws, which were derived from the *millet* system as established under the Ottomans, are adjudicated in religious tribunals and subject to religious law. Therefore, marriage and divorce are subject not to a unified system, but instead to a variety of religious systems, each with different substantive rules and procedures.

Parallelling the religious regulation of marriage, Israeli civil regulation of cohabitation has led Israel to become one of the leading countries in abandoning condemnation of cohabitation and recognizing the rights of cohabitant partners – same sex as well as opposite sex. Thus, some scholars view Israel as a model of pluralistic regulation of marital relations (Nichols 2007). Unfortunately, however, Israel does not properly apply the pluralistic approach. On the contrary, Israel illustrates the dangers of adopting a *semi-pluralistic system* without the checks and balances contained in the pluralistic model, which should be based on the values of pluralism and autonomy as developed in this chapter.

Let us start with the most basic premise: the pluralistic model is fundamentally based on the availability of choice among various paths. However, in Israel, in the absence of civil marriage, couples are forced to marry and divorce in accordance with their official religions, without having any choice in the matter and regardless of their authentic beliefs.

Second, some potential spouses are not permitted to marry one another. These are mixed-faith couples (where each spouse adheres to a different religion), persons having no recognized religious affiliation, persons ineligible to marry (in the case of Jews, the most common example concerns *Kohanim*[12] wishing to marry divorcees), and same-sex couples. Israeli law does not offer these couples any official marriage track (Lifshitz 2008b; Rubinstein 1973).

[12] Those whose ancestors hailed from the clan in charge of the Temple, thus holding special religious status by birth.

Third, the religious laws of many of Israel's dominant religions contain rules that are gender-based and hierarchical, which is incompatible with the pluralistic commitment to human dignity and the prevention of exploitation. Finally, divorce laws of the various religious communities severely restrict freedom of exit from the spousal relationship, especially that of women (Halperin-Kaddari 2004; Lifshitz 2005).

Although there are no official civil marriages in Israel, Israeli secular law has developed a variety of civil alternatives to marriage. The most prominent alternatives are cohabitation and civil marriage outside of Israel. These alternatives vest in the couple a range of civil rights similar to the rights vested in married couples. Yet, a deeper analysis reveals that these solutions are not comprehensive and many problems remain unresolved.

First, cohabitation rights are granted retroactively, after the termination of the couple's relationship, and therefore often require lengthy litigation in order to obtain them. Cohabitation rights thus do not provide an answer for couples who wish to be recognized as spouses at the beginning of their conjugal relationships. The recognition of civil marriages conducted outside of Israel also does not provide a real substitute for a civil marriage track. Such a marriage entails an economic burden and is therefore not available to all persons who demand civil marriage. Moreover, while the secular alternatives to marriage and divorce may solve certain problems, in some cases they create new difficulties and obstacles. For example, Israeli law applies marriage law to cohabitant relationships not only in the context of external rights – that is, rights of cohabitants against third parties – but also in the context of the spouses' mutual commitments. Consequently, in contrast to the recommendations of the pluralistic model to selectively apply marriage commitments to cohabitants so as to maintain these as two distinct legal categories, Israeli law equates cohabitants' inheritance, property, and alimony rights with those of married spouses. Furthermore, despite the fact that recognizing a couple as cohabitant partners imposes on them quasi-marriage obligations, the threshold requirements for entering the institution of cohabitation is very low; no formal registration is required, and there is not even a requirement of living together for any minimum amount of time. In one case, living together for three months was found to be sufficient grounds to grant a widow inheritance rights, and, in another, couples living in two nearby apartments and sleeping together some of the time were considered cohabitants by the courts (Lifshitz 2005, 2008b).

The unique position of Israeli cohabitant law stems from the institution of cohabitation as a *secular alternative to religious marriage*. Thus, cohabitation is not viewed as a general rejection of the religious institution of marriage, but instead as a kind of secular marriage for those unable or unwilling to marry with a religious ceremony. However, *at least some* cohabitant partners in Israel choose to live in a cohabitant relationship for *universal* reasons, such as their desire to subject themselves to an experimental period (trial marriage) or their rejection of marriage commitments for reasons that do not necessarily stem from the specific Israeli context (the inability or unwillingness to take part in a religious marriage ceremony). Unfortunately, Israeli courts do not distinguish between different types of cohabitants. Consequently, they apply marital obligations to all cohabitants, not only those in marriage-like unions who are unable or unwilling to wed religiously. In certain situations, Israeli courts did so even when circumstances demonstrated that the concerned parties were generally reluctant to undertake a marriage commitment, rather than being reluctant to enter into a religious marriage specifically. Finally, Israeli courts have recently adopted a status model, holding that a couple were cohabitant partners even though they explicitly stipulated in an agreement that they objected to this legal status.[13] Therefore, neither the religious regulation embodied in the law nor the secular alternatives developed by the courts serves the pluralistic model.

CONCLUSION

This chapter has addressed the role of the state in designing institutions for couples and in influencing the choices couples make in choosing among these institutions.

The chapter criticized the two dominant approaches in current legal discourse: public-monolithic-channeling and private neutrality. The private approach was criticized both because it regulates spousal relationships without regard to public interests, including the influence of a couple's relationship on the interests of their children, and because of its disregard for marriage as a fundamental social institution and public responsibility for establishing such institutions. On a philosophical level, the chapter demonstrated that a neutral philosophical approach is in fact impossible and would not even be appropriate either as a general policy or in the specific context of conjugal relationships. The public approach was criticized on a few levels: First, it adheres to conservative interests and values that are fixed in the traditional marriage institution; instead, marriage should be designed as a dynamic institution that can be constantly renewed and that balances contemporary public values and interests against the needs and autonomy of the concerned parties. On a deeper level, the problem does not lie with the proper balance, but rather with the monolithic perfectionists' view that there exists a specific balance which should serve as the basis for the establishment of one spousal institution suitable to all couples.

The chapter proposed a third, pluralistic approach that supports the establishment of multiple affiliative institutions by the state. The pluralistic approach holds that it is the state's right and obligation to establish a variety of institutions that serve proper values and interests. However, at the perfectionist core of this approach lie the liberal values of autonomy and human dignity, as well as pluralism as an intrinsic value. These liberal values lead to certain important consequences. First, the state should provide a variety of institutions rather than offering only one spousal institution.

[13] C.A. 7021/93 *Bar-Nahor v. Estate of Osterlitz (deceased)* (Tak-El 943) 1512.

Second, the state must grant individuals substantive freedom of choice among these institutions. Third, the state should prevent oppression and exploitation. Fourth, subject to concern about exploitation, the state should foster freedom of contract within the various institutions. Finally, the state should insist on couples' right of exit from their particular relationships.

The pluralistic approach has been applied to various contexts. First, the approach supported the distinction between the regulation of marital relationships and those of cohabitant partners. But the significance of the distinction between marriage and cohabitation was shown not to justify the state's elimination of all responsibility toward cohabitant partners, but instead to support the establishment of a different legal regime. Second, the chapter reviewed the legitimacy of granting special privileges to married spouses. This issue clarified the tension between the perfectionist perspective of the approach, which encourages and even requires the establishment of institutions with a social benefit, and the damage to autonomy and pluralism that may result from such encouragement. I have suggested a few arrangements that reflect a proper compromise among these values, such as changing the marriage institution itself to a pluralistic institution, establishing a variety of institutions, and offering package deals that are specifically designed for each institution. Finally, the chapter explored whether a liberal state should recognize or even suggest a number of marriage tracks. This issue triggers an internal tension between the intrinsic value of pluralism and the value of autonomy, as those who ground pluralism on the value of autonomy will be more careful to legitimize marriage tracks that do not satisfy liberal perfectionist criteria, such as marriage tracks that significantly delay, even if they do not completely prevent, the right to exit the spousal relationship. The chapter proposed a set of criteria that may produce a balance among the different alternatives and be applied in the cases of religious and covenant marriages.

Finally, the chapter presented the example of Israeli marriage law as an illustration of the disastrous results that may ensue when the pluralistic approach is applied without a commitment to the values of autonomy and pluralism as sources of internal value and human dignity.

REFERENCES

Amato, P.R. (1993). Children's Adjustment to Divorce: Theories, Hypotheses and Empirical Support. *Journal of Marriage and Family*, 55, 23–38.

American Law Institute (ALI). (2002). *Principles of the Law of Family Dissolution: Analysis and Recommendations*.

Atkin, I. (2008). The Legal World of Unmarried Couples: Reflections on "de Facto Relationships" in Recent New Zealand Legislation. *Victoria University of Wellington Law Review*, 39, 793–811.

Berger, P.L., & Luckmann, T. (1966). *The Social Construction of Reality: A Treatise in the Sociology of Knowledge*. New York: Anchor Books.

Berlin, I. (1969). *Four Essays on Liberty*. New York: Oxford University Press.

Bix, B. (2010). Private Ordering and Family Law. *Journal of the American Academy of Matrimonial Lawyers*, 23, 249–285.
Blumberg, G.G. (2001). Unmarried Partners and the Legacy of *Marvin v. Marvin*: The Regularization of Non-Marital Cohabitation: Rights and Responsibilities in the American Welfare State. *Notre Dame Law Review*, 76, 1265–1310.
Bowman, C.G. (2010). *Unmarried Couples, Law, and Public Policy*. New York: Oxford University Press.
Bradford, L. (1997). The Counterrevolution: A Critique of Recent Proposals to Reform No-Fault Divorce Laws. *Stanford Law Review*, 49, 607–636.
Brinig, M.F. (2006). Domestic Partnership and Default Rules. In Wilson, R.F. (Ed.), *Reconceiving the Family*. New York: Cambridge University Press.
Broyde, M.J. (2001). *Marriage, Divorce and the Abandoned Wife in Jewish Law: A Conceptual Understanding of the Agunah Problems in America*. New Jersey: Ktav Publishing House.
Case, M.A. (2003). Of "This" and "That" in *Lawrence v. Texas*. *The Supreme Court Review*, 2003, 75–142.
Case, M.A. (2005). Marriage Licenses. *Minnesota Law Review*, 89, 1758–1797.
Case, M.A. (2010). What Feminists Have to Lose in Same-Sex Marriage Litigation. *UCLA Law Review*, 57, 1199–1233.
Case, M.A. (forthcoming). Why Evangelical Protestants Are Right When They Claim that State Recognition of Same-Sex Marriage Threatens Their Marriages and What the Law Should Do about It. In Sullivan, W.F. (Ed.), *Sacred/Secular Divide: The Legal Story*. Palo Alto, CA: Stanford University Press.
Chambers, D.L. (1985). The "Legalization" of the Family: Toward a Policy of Supportive Neutrality. *University of Michigan Journal of Law Reform*, 18, 805–827.
Chambers, D.L. (1996). What If? The Legal Consequences of Marriage and the Legal Needs of Lesbian and Gay Male Couples. *Michigan Law Review*, 95, 447–491.
Cherlin, A.J., Furstenberg, F.F., Morrison, D.R., and Robins, P.K. (1991). Longitudinal Studies of Effects of Divorce on Children in Great Britain and the United states. *Science*, 252, 1386–1389.
Cott, N.F. (2000). *Public Vows: A History of Marriage and the Nation*. Cambridge, MA: Harvard University Press.
Crane, D.A. (2006). A "Judeo-Christian" Argument for Privatizing Marriage. *Cardozo Law Review*, 27, 1221–1259.
Dagan, H. (forthcoming). Pluralism and Perfectionism in Private Law. *Columbia Law Review*, 113.
Dagan, H., & Franz, C.J. (2004). Properties of Marriage. *Columbia Law Review*, 104, 75–133.
Davis, A.D. (2010). Regulating Polygamy: Intimacy, Default Rules, and Bargaining for Equality. *Columbia Law Review*, 110, 1955–2046.
Dubler, A. (2006). Immoral Purposes: Marriage and the Genus of Illicit Sex. *Yale Law Journal*, 115, 756–812.
Dubler, A. (2010). Sexing *Skinner*: History and the Politics of the Right to Marry. *Columbia Law Review*, 110, 1348–1376.
Eekelaar, J.M., and Thandabantu, N. (Eds.) (1998). *The Changing Family: Family Forms and Family Law*. Oxford, Hart Publishing.
Eichner, M. (2007). Marriage and the Elephant: The Liberal Democratic State's Regulation of Intimate Relationships between Adults. *Harvard Journal of Law & Gender*, 30, 25–66.
Ellman, I.M. (2001). "Contract Thinking" Was *Marvin*'s Fatal Flaw. *Notre Dame Law Review*, 76, 1365–1380.

Emens, E.F. (2004). Monogamy's Law: Compulsory Monogamy and Polyamorous Existence. *New York University Review of Law & Social Change*, 29, 277–376.

Emens, E.F. (2011). Regulatory Fictions: On Marriage and Counter-Marriage. *California Law Review*, 99, 235–272.

Emery, E. (1988). *Marriage, Divorce and Children's Adjustment*. Newbury Park, CA: Sage Publications.

Estin, A.L. (2001). Ordinary Cohabitation. *Notre Dame Law Review*, 76, 1381–1408.

Estin, A.L. (2004). Embracing tradition: Pluralism in American family law. *Maryland Law Review*, 63, 540–604.

Fineman, M.A. (1995). *The Neutered Mother, the Sexual Family and Other Twentieth Century Tragedies*. New York: Routledge.

Galston, W.A. (1991a). A Liberal Democratic Case for the Two-Parent Family. *The Responsive Community*, 1, 145–155.

Galston, W.A. (1991b). *Liberal Purpose – Goods, Virtues, and Diversity in the Liberal State*. New York: Cambridge University Press.

Gardbaum, S.A. (1991). Why the Liberal State Can Promote Moral Ideals After All. *Harvard Law Review*, 104, 1350–1371.

Garrison, M. (1983). Marriage: The Status of Contract. *University of Pennsylvania Law Review*, 131, 1039–1062.

Garrison, M. (2005). Is Consent Necessary? An Evaluation of the Emerging Law of Cohabitant Obligation. *UCLA Law Review*, 52, 815–897.

Garrison, M. (2007). The Decline of Formal Marriage: Inevitable or Reversible? *Family Law Quarterly*, 41, 491–520.

Geertz, C. (1973). *The Interpretation of Cultures*. New York: Basic Books.

Glendon, M.A. (1989). *The Transformation of Family Law – State, Law and Family in the United States and Western Europe*. Chicago: University of Chicago Press.

Haddock, D.D., & Polsby, D.D. (1996). Family as a Rational Classification. *Washington University Law Quarterly*, 74, 15–46.

Hafen, B.C. (1983). The Constitutional Status of Marriage, Kinship, and Sexual Privacy: Balancing the Individual and Social Interests. *Michigan Law Review*, 81, 463–574.

Halperin-Kaddari, R. (2004). *Women in Israel: A State of Their Own*. Philadelphia: University of Pennsylvania Press.

Katz, S.N., Eekelaar, J.M., & Maclean, M. (Eds.) (2000). *Cross Currents: Family Law and Policy in the U.S. and England*. New York: Oxford University Press.

Kekes, J. (1993). *The Morality of Pluralism*. Princeton, NJ: Princeton University Press.

Kymlicka, W. (1989). *Liberalism, Community and Culture*. New York: Oxford University Press.

Lifshitz, S. (2005, Hebrew). *Cohabitation Law in Israel from the Perspective of a Civil Law Theory of the Family*. Haifa: Haifa University Press.

Lifshitz, S. (2008a). The Best Interest of the Child and Spousal Laws. In Ronen, Y., and Greenbaum, C.W. (Eds.), *The Case for the Child: Towards a New Agenda*. Cambridge, UK: Intersentia Publishing.

Lifshitz, S. (2008b). A Potential Lesson from the Israeli Experience for the American Same-Sex Marriage Debate. *Brigham Young University Journal of Public Law*, 22, 359–382.

Lifshitz, S. (2009). A Liberal Analysis of Western Cohabitant Law. In Verschraegen, B. (Ed.), *Family Finance* pp. 305–20. Vienna: Jan Sramek Verlag.

Lifshitz, S. (2010). Married against Their Will? Toward a Pluralist Regulation of Spousal Relationships. *Washington and Lee Law Review*, 66, 1565–1634.

Lifshitz, S. (2012). The Liberal Transformation of Spousal Law: Past, Present and Future. *Theoretical Inquiries in Law*, 13, 15–74.
McClain, L.C. (2007). Love, Marriage, and the Baby Carriage: Revisiting the Channeling Function of Family Law. *Cardozo Law Review*, 28, 2133–2184.
McLanahan, S., & Sandefur, G. (1994). *Growing Up with a Single Parent: What Hurts, What Helps*. Cambridge, MA: Harvard University Press.
Mill, J.S. (1942). *On Liberty*. New York: Oxford University Press.
Murphy Jr., R.D. (2002). A Good Man Is Hard to Find: Marriage as an Institution. *Journal of Economic Behavior & Organization*, 47, 27–53.
Nichols, J.A. (1998). Louisiana's Covenant Marriage Statute: A First Step toward a More Robust Pluralism in Marriage and Divorce Law? *Emory Law Journal*, 47, 929–1001.
Nichols, J.A. (2007). Multi-Tiered Marriage: Ideas and Influences from New York and Louisiana to the International Community. *Vanderbilt Journal of Transnational Law*, 40, 135–196.
Phillips R. (1988). *Putting Asunder: A History of Divorce in Western Society*. New York: Cambridge University Press.
Polikoff, N.D. (2003). Ending Marriage as We Know It. *Hofstra Law Review*, 32, 201–232.
Polikoff, N.D. (2008). *Beyond (Straight and Gay) Marriage: Valuing All Families under the Law*. Boston, MA: Beacon Press.
Posner, E.A. (2000). *Law and Social Norms*. Cambridge, MA: Harvard University Press.
Rawls, J. (1993). *Political Liberalism*. New York: Columbia University Press.
Rawls, J. (1999). *A Theory of Justice*. Revised Edition. New York: Oxford University Press.
Raz, J. (1986). *The Morality of Freedom*. New York: Oxford University Press.
Raz, J. (1994). *Ethics in the Public Domain: Essays in the Morality of Law and Politics*. New York: Oxford University Press.
Regan, M.C. (1999). *Alone Together: Law and the Meanings of Marriage*. New York: Oxford University Press.
Rubinstein, A. (1973, Hebrew). The Rights to Marriage. *Tel-Aviv Studies in Law*, 3, 433–458.
Sandel, M.J. (1996). *Democracy's Discontent: America in Search of a Public Philosophy*. Cambridge, MA: Harvard University Press.
Schneider, C.E. (1985). Moral Discourse and the Transformation of American Family Law. *Michigan Law Review*, 83, 1803–1879.
Schneider, C.E. (1994). Marriage, Morals, and the Law: No-Fault Divorce and Moral Discourse. *Utah Law Review*, 1994, 503–585.
Scott, E.S. (1990). Rational Decision Making about Marriage and Divorce. *Virginia Law Review*, 76, 9–94.
Scott, E.S. (1994). Rehabilitation Liberalism in Modern Divorce Law. *Utah Law Review*, 1994, 687–740.
Scott, E.S. (2000). Social Norms and the Legal Regulation of Marriage. *Virginia Law Review*, 86, 1901–1970.
Scott, E.S. (2004). Marriage, Cohabitation and Collective Responsibility for Dependency. *University of Chicago Legal Forum*, 2004, 225–272.
Scott, E.S. (2006). Domestic Partnerships, Implied Contracts, and Law Reform. In Wilson, R. F. (Ed.), *Reconceiving the Family* pp. 337–349. New York: Cambridge University Press.
Scott, E.S. (2007). A World without Marriage. *Family Law Quarterly*, 41, 537–566.
Singer, J.B. (1992). The Privatization of Family Law. *Wisconsin Law Review*, 1992, 1443–1567.
Shifman, P. (1995, Hebrew). *Civil Marriage in Israel: The Case for Reform*. Jerusalem: Jerusalem Institute for Israeli Studies.

Spaht, K.S. (1998). Louisiana's Covenant Marriage: Social Analysis and Legal Implications. *Louisiana Law Review*, 59, 63–130.
Stake, J.E. (1992). Mandatory Planning for Divorce. *Vanderbilt Law Review*, 45, 397–454.
Stone, L. (1990). *Road to Divorce – England 1530–1987*. New York: Oxford University Press.
Stone, S.L. (2000). The Intervention of American Law in Jewish Divorce: A Pluralist Analysis. *Israel Law Review*, 34, 170–210.
Teitelbaum, L.E. (1985). Moral Discourse and Family Law. *Michigan Law Review*, 84, 430–441.
Thornton, A. (1994). Comparative and Historical Perspectives on Marriage, Divorce, and Family Life. 1994 *Utah Law Review*, 1994, 587–604.
Waite, L., & Gallagher, M. (2000). *The Case for Marriage: Why Married People Are Happier, Healthier and Better Off Financially*. New York: Broadway Books.
Wallerstein, J.S., & Blakeslee, S. (1989). *Second Chances: Men, Women, and Children a Decade after Divorce*. New York: Houghton Mifflin.
Wardle, L. D. (1998). *Loving v. Virginia* and the Constitutional Right to Marry, 1790–1990. *Howard Law Journal*, 41, 289–347.
Wardle, L.D. (2008). A Response to the "Conservative Case" for Same-Sex Marriage: Same-Sex Marriage and "The Tragedy of the Commons." *Brigham Young University Journal of Public Law*, 22, 441–474.
Wax, A.L. (1996). The Two-Parent Family in the Liberal State: The Case for Selective Subsidies. *Michigan Journal of Race & Law*, 1, 491–550.
Weitzman, L.J. (1981). *The Marriage Contract: Spouses, Lovers, and the Law*. New York: The Free Press.
Weitzman, L.J. (1985). *The Divorce Revolution: The Unexpected Social and Economic Consequences for Women and Children in America*. New York: Simon & Schuster.
Witte Jr., J. (1997). *From Sacrament to Contract: Marriage, Religion, and Law in the Western Tradition*. Louisville, KY: WJK Press.
Zelinsky, E.A. (2006). Deregulating Marriage: The Pro-Marriage Case for Abolishing Civil Marriage. *Cardozo Law Review*, 27, 1161–1221.

Comments

14

The Growing Diversity of Two-Parent Families

Challenges for Family Law

Andrew J. Cherlin

One of the most striking characteristics of heterosexual marriage as a social institution today is that it must share its legitimacy with several other types of intimate partnerships, all of which are increasingly accepted as families throughout most of the industrialized world. For instance, acceptance is growing for cohabitation as a respectable alternative to marriage and for same-sex marriage as a respectable alternative to heterosexual marriage. These newer forms of partnership represent substantial changes from the way family life was organized a half-century ago, when heterosexual marriage was dominant. The emergence of these alternatives introduces the issue of whether society will not only recognize them culturally but also support them in law. In particular, it raises the question of how to extend family law to cohabiting couples, same-sex or different-sex, and to same-sex married couples. The answers to this question are surprisingly complex, as the chapters in this volume show.

The acceptance of alternative forms of two-parent families is a relatively new development. Until the middle of the twentieth century, heterosexual marriage was the only socially acceptable, two-parent setting in which to raise children. Cohabitation – living with a partner without marrying – was shameful, except perhaps among the poor and the bohemian. Marriage was predominant in all countries, throughout the class structure, and among all major racial and ethnic groups. Moreover, starting with the rise of "separate spheres" marriage in the nineteenth century, marriage evolved into an institution based on the specialization of men in paid work in the labor market and women in housework and child care. This so-called breadwinner-homemaker marriage peaked in the 1950s, when the postwar prosperity allowed more couples to keep wives out of the labor market.

Much of the existing law concerning families in the 1950s had been developed by the late nineteenth century. Hendrik Hartog compared four U.S. family law casebooks published in the early 1950s with four published in the 1890s and concluded that three of the four 1950s books were very similar to the 1890s books. While there had been some change, husbands still had the right to make marital decisions such as how to spend money and where the family would live; wives were still entitled to support; and domestic violence remained a largely private matter (Hartog 2000). This largely nineteenth-century conception of family law was still intact, just as the breadwinner-homemaker marriage itself was still intact as the dominant family form. By giving this particular model of marriage a central place, family law in the 1950s both reflected and reinforced its strength.

But since the 1950s we have seen breathtaking changes in family life across the Western, industrialized world – probably a greater amount of change than in any previous half-century. It is clear that marriage is no longer as dominant an institution as it once was. It is still held in high regard, and most heterosexuals will still marry at some point. There are, however, other acceptable options: Unmarried couples may raise children without marrying. Same-sex couples, with and without children, still face disapproval in some quarters but are increasingly accepted. In fact, a recent report by the Pew Research Center (2011), based on telephone interviews in 2010 with a national sample of American adults, suggests widespread acceptance of many types of partnerships. Respondents were asked whether they thought each of several family trends were "generally a good thing for our society, a bad thing for our society, or doesn't make much difference." Fifty-nine percent thought that "more mothers of young children working outside the home" was a good thing or did not make much difference, whereas just 21 percent thought it was a bad thing. As for "more people living together without getting married," 55 percent had a positive or neutral view, as against 43 percent who saw the trend as negative. The same 55 percent to 43 percent split obtained for "more unmarried couples raising children." And a majority – 53 percent – were even positive or neutral about "more gay and lesbian couples raising children," as against 43 percent who were negative. (Only 28 percent had positive or neutral views about "more single women having children without a male partner to help raise them," but that is another story.)

Similarly, Americans cast a broad net over what they consider to be a family. In the same survey, 80 percent thought that an "unmarried couple with children" constituted a family, and 64 percent thought that a "same-sex couple with children" was a family. This acceptance of multiple forms of two-parent families means that we have moved beyond the time when what Dorothy Smith (1993) called the "standard North American family" dominated our discourse about family life. The SNAF, as it has come to be known in the literature, consists of a heterosexual married couple with children, in which the man is the primary earner and the woman is the primary caregiver. While this is still a potent image, other conceptions of the family are commonplace and increasingly recognized.

Moreover, the marital bargain is changing. The specialization model, in which men traded market work for women's home work, is giving way to an income-pooling model in which both spouses work. In 1949, 25.2 percent of married women were in the paid labor force (Oppenheimer 1970); by 2009, the figure was 61.7 percent

(U.S. Bureau of the Census 2011). Bargaining between the two earners is replacing men's prerogative as the basis for family decision making. When a U.S. national survey asked married couples whether the wife or the husband controlled several daily decisions, a third of the respondents, without prompting by an answer category, responded that the decision was joint. Marriage patterns reflect this shift: Under the old bargain, women with less education were more likely to marry because they had more to gain from specializing in home work. But under the emerging new bargain, it is women with more education who are more likely to marry (Sweeney 2002), at least in part because they have more earning potential to bring to the marriage.

In addition, the meaning of marriage is changing. As Amato (Chapter 6) argues and I have written elsewhere (Cherlin 2004), we are now in the midst of a second transition in the meaning of marriage. The first transition, as labeled by family sociologist Ernest Burgess in the first half of the twentieth century (Burgess and Locke 1945), was a shift from an institutional marriage, based on the authority of the husband as family head, to a companionate marriage, in which love and friendship are more important and husband and wife derive satisfaction from playing the gendered roles of parent and spouse. The second is a shift toward an individualistic marriage, in which one's own sense of self-development and personal fulfillment is the most important determinant of whether one's marriage is a success. It is consistent with what Lifshitz (Chapter 13) calls the privatization narrative of marriage, as marriage has become less of a public and more of a private institution.

The rise of the individualistic marriage has occurred during a period when cohabitation has become commonplace. By the 2000s, two-thirds of married women under age forty-five had lived with a partner before marrying in the United States (Kennedy and Bumpass 2011) and even higher percentages report cohabitation before marriage in the United Kingdom (Probert, Chapter 4). As I noted, a majority of the public accepts this change as either beneficial or inconsequential. Together, the cultural shift toward individual fulfillment as the criterion for relationship satisfaction and the growing prevalence and acceptability of cohabitation have changed the place of marriage in the life course. A half-century ago, marriage was the first step into adulthood: a couple first got married and then rented an apartment and then had a child while the husband solidified his place in the labor market. Today, marriage is often the last step: one gets married after most or all of the other markers of adulthood have been achieved. Because marriage comes later in this process, it cannot serve as the basis for achieving adulthood, as it did in the mid-twentieth century. Instead, marriage has become more a symbol of achieving a successful personal life – a capstone experience, the last brick put in place.

Currently, then, marriage is a social institution that is less dominant but still highly valued. In fact, as marriage has become less necessary, it has become, if anything, more important symbolically as a marker of a social status. We also see greater acceptance of alternative family forms than in the past; marriage is no longer the only acceptable context for intimate partnerships and for raising children. And we see a newer, more egalitarian relationship between spouses based on pooling two incomes and more joint decision making. This is the social context in which one must evaluate marriage today.

THE GROWING SOCIAL CLASS GAP

Although the trends that I have just described are found across most of the industrialized world, there is, of course, regional variation. One trend that appears to be particular prominent in the United States is a growing social-class gap in family life. As legal scholars June Carbone and Naomi Cahn (Chapter 2) and social scientists Sara McLanahan and Irwin Garfinkel (Chapter 8) demonstrate, marriage has weakened among Americans without college educations while remaining strong among the college-educated. This class-based divergence in marriage patterns is perhaps the most striking family trend of the past few decades. The children of college-educated parents are advantaged not only in terms of income and wealth, as Carbone and Cahn note, but also in terms of parental time and attention because they are more likely to be raised in a stable, two-parent family.

This divergence has both economic and cultural roots. Economically, it represents a response to the globalization and automation of the American economy. Manufacturing jobs – once the backbone of the labor market for high-school-educated young men – have declined sharply. What is left for people without college degrees is a modest number of decent-paying opportunities, such as in the health sector (X-ray technicians) or the skilled trades (electricians), and a large number of low-wage, manual jobs. Of late, the Great Recession has worsened this situation. The result is that fewer young adults can find the kinds of good, steady jobs that most people still think are a prerequisite for getting married, especially for men. Instead, they take insecure jobs that do not pay well, and they postpone marriage.

What they increasingly do instead is live together – a response made possible by cultural change. A half-century ago, when cohabitation was shameful, a premarital pregnancy often led to a shotgun wedding. But today it is increasingly acceptable for unmarried couples to raise children together. The acceptability of this living arrangement has long been strongest among the poor, but in recent decades the moderately educated middle of the population has come to accept it as well. Consequently, romantically involved couples who do not see the possibility of a strong financial footing are more likely to decide to have a child or accept an unplanned pregnancy than to postpone having children until they have the means to marry. Similarly, single parents are more likely to move in with romantic partners without immediate thoughts of marrying.

The rise of cohabitation is now a major factor in how children are being raised. Consider the proportion of births that are to unmarried women: According to provisional data from the National Center for Health Statistics, 41 percent of U.S. births in 2009 were to unmarried women, an all-time high – up from 37 percent in 2005 and 33 percent in 2000 (U.S. National Center for Health Statistics 2011). To most observers the rise brings to mind a surge of births to young mothers living alone or with their own mothers. But that image is inaccurate. The National Center for Health Statistics compiles this information from birth certificates, which do not differentiate between an un-partnered mother ("single," in popular usage) and a woman who is living with a man at the time of the birth, most often the father. Both the single and the cohabiting women are counted as unmarried in the official statistics.

In fact, nearly all of the increase in childbearing outside of marriage over the last two decades has occurred because of the growing number of cohabiting women who are giving birth, according to analyses of several waves of the National Survey of Family Growth, from 1995 to 2008 (Kennedy and Bumpass 2011). The growth has been especially rapid among women with a moderate level of education – a high school degree and perhaps some college education but not a four-year college degree. The percentage of women who were cohabiting at birth has tripled to about 35 percent of those with a high school degree but no further education and about 20 percent of those with some college experience but no four-year degree. In contrast, less than 5 percent of women with a college degree are either single or cohabiting at birth. A large social-class gap exists between the more "traditional" childbearing patterns of the college-educated and the less traditional patterns of those without a college degree.

The moderately educated women who (along with their potential spouses) have been most affected by the collapse of the middle of the American labor market tend to be in their twenties, and their numbers are so large (there are far more people in the middle of the educational distribution than in the lower end) that they have been driving the overall upward movement in the percentage of nonmarital births. Two generations ago, their grandparents might have been embarrassed to cohabit; a generation ago, their parents might have cohabited but would have been embarrassed to have had children; today, the new generation will increasingly go ahead and have children with their cohabiting partners. Overall, I would estimate that nearly one-fourth of all children in the United States today are born to parents who are cohabiting.[1]

Is the rising number of children who are born to cohabiting couples a problem? After all, there are other advanced nations where an even greater proportion of children is born to cohabiting couples – a majority of children in Sweden, for example – without generating much social concern. But those cohabiting relationships tend to last much longer than do the ones in the United States. In fact, Americans' cohabiting relationships – and their marriages – are more prone

[1] Kennedy and Bumpass (2011) report that about 60 percent of unmarried mothers are cohabiting at birth. If 41 percent of all births in the United States are to unmarried (single or cohabiting) women, this implies that about one-fourth (60 percent of 41 percent) of all mothers are cohabiting at birth.

to quick disruption than is the case elsewhere and, after their marriages and cohabiting relationships end, Americans find new partners faster (Cherlin 2009). Moreover, single parents form numerous nonresidential romantic relationships that can result in pregnancies and childbirth.

The result, as McLanahan and Garfinkel (Chapter 8) show, is a greater instability in living arrangements for the children who are involved. In their Fragile Families study of births in urban hospitals, only 52 percent of the children born to cohabiting parents were living with both of their biological parents by the time they were age five, a much higher breakup rate than children of married parents are exposed to (Bendheim-Thoman Center for Research on Child Wellbeing 2007). The unstable nature of family life is worrisome because studies suggest that children may be as affected by frequent changes over time in who is living in their households as they are by whether or not they live with a single parent at any one point in time. For instance, Fomby and Cherlin (2007) and Osborne and McLanahan (2007) found that the greater the number of transitions that parents had in and out of marriages, cohabiting relationships, and, in the latter study, nonresidential romantic relationships, the more behavior problems their children showed. Cavanagh and Huston (2006) showed a similar relationship between more parental transitions and less competence in interacting with peers at school.

In addition, as McLanahan and Garfinkel also argue, the accumulation of different living arrangements creates much greater complexity of family and kin than in the past. Veering in and out of marriages and cohabiting relationships, an increasing number of adults have children with more than one partner (Carlson and Furstenberg 2006). Their children accumulate ties to half-siblings, stepsiblings, and stepparents in their households and to parents living elsewhere. These complicated households and complex ties to kin outside the households stretch adults' obligations and strain their resources.

In sum, the problem of childbearing outside of marriage today is related not only to family structure – the number of parents in the home – but also to family dynamics: the movement of adults and children in and out of relationships and households. Family instability and complexity are still highest among the poor and near-poor, but in recent decades they have increased among the moderately educated, the group we used to call the working class. In contrast, college-educated Americans – who are best positioned to gain from the globalized economy – still overwhelmingly wait until after they are married to have children. The growing split between the family patterns of the college-educated and those without college degrees is creating a troubling social-class gap in how American parents and children live their personal lives.

COHABITATION AND FAMILY LAW

How should family law respond to the increase in cohabiting unions? This, it seems to me, is one of the central questions of this volume. Currently, there is far less law that is relevant to cohabiting partners than to married partners. One response would be to make the legal status of cohabitation very similar to marriage. This was essentially the recommendation of the American Law Institute in a 2002 report. It would treat all unmarried couples who meet certain criteria, such as living together for two or three years, intermingling their finances, or assuming joint responsibility for a child, as if they were married (American Law Institute 2002). If the relevant state and federal laws were changed in this way, the inequalities in the legal treatment of cohabitation relative to marriage would be largely eliminated. Not everyone agrees, however, that the legal differences between cohabitation and marriage should be minimized. A group of legal scholars, concerned that such changes would undermine the status of marriage by sending a cultural signal that marrying is no longer important, issued a report opposing the ALI recommendations. Because marriage, they asserted, was the best context for raising children and promoting responsible behavior among adults, "The state must exercise special care not to undermine this web of meanings sustaining our increasingly fragile marriage culture" (Institute for American Values and Institute for Marriage and Public Policy 2006; see also Wilson 2006).

Along with this objection from the right, there is an objection from the left. It is that some individuals may have chosen to cohabit precisely to avoid the strictures of the law pertaining to marriage, and they should not be forced to marry. This line of reasoning has been more common in Europe, where the institution of marriage is weaker. In Britain and France, for instance, civil partnerships were enacted that formalized cohabiting relationships but did not make them equivalent to marriage (Probert, Chapter 4.) The Civil Solidarity Pact, a type of partnership that has had a legal status in France since 1999, is immediately ended if a partner marries someone else. No divorce is necessary, and many of the legal protections provided to divorcing spouses do not apply (Martin and Théry 2001).

Both critiques suggest that cohabitation should not be treated as identical to marriage – either because marriage is deemed to be the better environment for children or because cohabiting adults should have the freedom to enter into and exit from informal unions. But one must juxtapose against these two critiques the rising percentage of births to cohabiting couples, which often lead to unstable unions and complex family networks. While we might not wish to make cohabitation exactly like marriage, the state's interest in the well-being of children would seem to suggest that some of the rights and protections afforded to marriage by family law should be extended to cohabitation.

But which ones? Lifshitz (Chapter 13) addresses this question. He grants that marriage may, on average, provide a better foundation for child-rearing, but he also argues that individuals and children in cohabiting unions need the guidance and protections of family law. His solution is a pluralistic model of marriage in which the state would offer a range of marital institutions. Lifschitz would extend some legal provisions to cohabiting unions but retain others for marriage. In particular, he would extend to cohabitants the components of marriage law that protect the more vulnerable parties from exploitation. However, he would preserve autonomy by not imposing the idea of a community, with its support for equal division of property, no matter which partner earned it and when. He would also preserve the legal right of immediate exit from a cohabiting union. This selective extension of rights and protections, he argues, is justified because the law should both support the position of vulnerable adults and children in partnerships and preserve as much individual autonomy as possible. One could debate the exact division of law that Lifshitz advocates, but he has done a service in raising the issue of a possible middle-ground position for cohabitation law, neither as tightly regulated as marriage nor as free of the law as informal unions are now.

SAME-SEX MARRIAGE

The debates about same-sex marriage could be seen in a similar light: whether the state should provide rights and protections for children who are being raised by same-sex couples and rights for the more vulnerable adult partners. Child-rearing is common among lesbian partners and is modest but visible among gay male partners. According to several surveys conducted in the 2000s in California during which people were asked their sexual orientation (unlike Census Bureau surveys, which do not ask about that), 14 percent to 31 percent (depending on the survey) of partnered lesbians said that they had children in the household, as did 3 percent to 5 percent of partnered gay men (Carpenter and Gates 2008). States vary widely in laws regarding the rights and responsibilities of a second parent in lesbian and gay partnerships, such as by allowing or prohibiting second-parent adoption.

In addition, same-sex couples are seeking a range of rights and benefits that are available only to married couples even when no children are present in the household. Goldberg (Chapter 11) refers to the quest for equal rights as the "tangible benefits" reason many gay and lesbian activists seek same-sex marriage. Except for states that have legalized same-sex marriage or established domestic partnerships, little law guides and protects cohabiting same-sex adults. And even in states that allow same-sex marriage, no federal benefits to marriage, such as joint federal income tax filing, are currently available to same-sex couples. (Nevertheless, the commonly cited statistic that the federal government confers 1,049 benefits and rights on married couples is erroneous – that is the number of federal statutes that *mention* marriage (Cherlin 2010)).

Yet a close look at the debate over same-sex marriage reveals that the parties are not just arguing over legal rights and responsibilities. After all, if the debate were restricted in this way, then the enactment of domestic partnership or civil union law (I will use the two terms interchangeably) on a state or federal level would be enough to satisfy the advocates for same-sex marriage. Clearly, even universal acceptance of domestic partnerships would not be sufficient to end the debate. This situation leads Goldberg to theorize that achieving "equal status" is a second, important reason why same-sex marriage is desired. Status, she explains, means not just one's material situation but also one's social and political equality. Marriage, as I have argued elsewhere, has, if anything, increased in its symbolic value over the past few decades (Cherlin 2004). A half-century ago, when 95 percent of the population married, it was a mark of conformity – the only acceptable way to live a full adult life. Today, when there are alternatives, one might have expected that marriage would be fading away. Instead, it has become the preferred way to have an intimate partnership, provided that the partners can make a go of it economically. It has therefore become a notable achievement – a mark of status.

Studies show that young adults are increasingly deferring marriage, but not cohabitation, until one or both partners have stable earnings – an increasingly difficult achievement for non-college-educated adults. In a study of working-class and lower-middle-class adults in the Toledo, Ohio, area in 2002, a recently unemployed, twenty-nine-year-old man who was cohabiting, when asked why he had not married his partner, responded, "I don't really know 'cause the love is there uh . . . trust is there. Everything's there except money" (Smock, Manning, and Porter 2005). The individuals in the Toledo study also had a strong preference for a public wedding. They often distinguished between a "church" wedding and a "downtown" wedding at a courthouse and expressed the desire to postpone marriage until they could afford the former. One cohabiting woman said, "I'm not going downtown. . . . I say, you don't want a big wedding, we're not going to get married" (Smock, Manning, and Porter 2005). Unlike couples in the past, whose parents paid for weddings, today's cohabiting couples often pay for part or all of the wedding expenses themselves. The wedding becomes less of an occasion where parents allow their children to join in matrimony and more of a celebration of the couple's secure lifestyle. Thus, heterosexual couples who marry after having lived together for years and having children together will still throw a large wedding party as a public statement to their relatives, friends, and themselves they have achieved a successful family life.

I therefore agree with Goldberg that advocates for same-sex marriage are seeking access to the symbolic status of being legally married. They are responding to the continued value Americans place on marriage, even though it is now the capstone of young adulthood rather than the foundation. Advocates of same-sex marriage want same-sex partners to have access to this symbolic status. Without it, they argue, lesbian or gay partners cannot match the level of self-worth and dignity of heterosexual partners. It is an argument that courts consider and sometimes accept. For instance, the majority of the Massachusetts Supreme Court, in its 2003 decision in favor of same-sex marriage, adopted the celebratory view when they wrote, "Civil marriage is at once a deeply personal commitment to another human being and a highly public celebration of the ideas of mutuality, companionship, intimacy, fidelity, and family." Without access to marriage, they argued, "one is excluded from the full range of human experience" (*Goodridge v. Department of Public Health* 2003).

When the Massachusetts legislature subsequently asked the court whether civil unions with access to all the state benefits of marriage would suffice, the court said it would not. Civil unions without the possibility of marriage, they wrote, would create a "stigma of exclusion" because they would deny same-sex couples access to "a status that is specially recognized in society and has significant social and other advantages." Denying same-sex couples access to marriage, they told the legislature, would effectively create a lesser category of citizenship, and the Massachusetts constitution "forbids the creation of second-class citizens." In other words, irrespective of legal rights and responsibilities, individuals cannot become first-class citizens if they are denied access to this specially recognized status.

This appeal to the sense of dignity, respect, and self-worth that supposedly resides in marriage makes some gay and lesbian intellectuals uneasy. Franke (Chapter 5) is wary of what she calls a "turn to values," even though others (Schneider, Chapter 12) praise it. Same-sex marriage, according to Franke and others, could slight those in the gay and lesbian community who cannot, or choose not to, marry. More broadly, its ascendance as a goal of gay and lesbian activists, Franke and others write, represents a lost opportunity to support alternatives to marriage. Implicit in this line of reasoning is the view that marriage is a traditional, patriarchal institution that ought to be allowed to decline rather than being invigorated by an influx of gays and lesbians. "After all," Franke writes, "through history the institution of marriage has not been all that great for women."

The view of marriage as an oppressive institution that should be allowed to wither away is more prominent among gay and lesbian writers and activists in Europe (Probert, Chapter 4). They reside in nations such as France and Sweden, where marriage is not as strong an institution as it is on the other side of the Atlantic and where decades-long cohabiting relationships are common. In 2000, the World Values Survey asked samples of adults in many countries whether they agreed with the statement, "Marriage is an outmoded institution." Only 10 percent of Americans agreed, compared to 20 percent of Swedes, 26 percent of the British, and 33 percent of the French (Inglehart et al. 2004). Britain and France enacted their national domestic partnership laws without much controversy in the case of the former country (Eekelar 2003) and with controversies that were unrelated to marriage in the latter (Martin and Théry 2001). But neither country has legalized same-sex marriage, in part because the gay and lesbian communities are less enthusiastic about it than is the case in the United States. Even in the Netherlands, which recognizes same-sex marriage, there is substantial suspicion of marriage (Badgett 2009).

The oppositional view leads to the position that the state should withdraw from marriage altogether, abolishing it as a legal form, as Stacey (Chapter 10) argues. It should be left, so this argument goes, to religious and cultural groups that wish to conduct ceremonies to bestow the title on its adherents. Meanwhile legal partnerships should be open to a variety of forms. "A democratic state has no business dictating or even favoring any particular brand of intimacy or family life," Stacey writes. "It should value the quality and substance of relationships over their form." Thus, Stacey and others urge the "disestablishment" of civil marriage, much as the early American colonists and early citizens of the nation disestablished the Anglican church.

I think the disestablishment argument has two problems. First, it is rather tone-deaf to the powerful theme of marriage in American culture. As the World Values Survey responses I noted earlier suggest, marriage matters more to Americans than to citizens of most other Western countries. And, I would suggest, it always has. Prior to the revolution, the colonists in New England and some middle-Atlantic areas built their societies around the civil status of marriage rather than abandoning it. The Calvinists were influenced by Luther, who viewed marriage as the foundation of civil society. A series of historical events, such as the decades-long nineteenth-century struggle over polygamy, strengthened Christian monogamous marriage (Cott 2000). Although its meaning has changed, it remains a potent public symbol of a successful private life. The American public is coming to accept multiple kinds of marriage – breadwinner-homemaker, dual-earner, and even same-sex – but it is a great stretch to suggest that the public would support backing away from marriage entirely. In this sense, the Massachusetts Supreme Court was reading American culture correctly when it argued that access to marriage was necessary to be a first-class citizen.

Second, the discourse about the disestablishment of marriage and the acceptance of alternatives tends to be adult-centered. It is an argument about adult preferences rather than children's well-being, whereas the public interest centers on the latter. Stacey, to her credit, addresses this issue when she writes of the state: "It has a legitimate interest in promoting responsible, committed care and protection for children and other dependents." But she is content to argue that adults in any type of relationship can provide responsible, committed care. I would argue that, given the seeming importance of stability in children's living arrangements, there is a public interest in supporting the types of partnerships that are most likely to produce long-term stable bonds. And to this date in the United States, marriage has provided a more stable foundation for children than has cohabitation. It would seem, then, that a better strategy for providing stability would be for the state to expand the boundaries of marriage to same-sex couples rather than to get out of the marriage business. To be sure, providing greater legal support to cohabiting relationships, as domestic partnerships do, could reduce breakup rates. Scott (2007) writes that if domestic partnerships were to replace civil marriage, the law surrounding partnerships should include all of the protections of the more vulnerable partners that marriage law provides today. This is not the case in national domestic partnership laws in some other countries, which tend to allow easy and immediate dissolution without a full, community-property basis for the division of assets between the separating spouses. Scott argues that if such highly structured domestic partnerships were enacted, then it would be possible for domestic partnership to become an acceptable substitute for marriage. But she concludes that abolishing civil marriage in the current American environment would risk undermining the higher commitment and stability found in marriage.

I do not think that the law can get too far ahead of the public in this matter. Cohabiting unions are very unstable in American culture, and until and unless American cohabiting relationships come to resemble the long-term relationships in Sweden or France today, I think that expanding marriage rather than abandoning marriage is the less risky way to respond to the rise of same-sex partners raising children.

The third motivation that Goldberg cites for same-sex marriage is to transform the institution of marriage itself. This position is hardly visible in public debates but reflects the views of some academic and cultural critics of marriage as it currently exists. It has been largely an internal issue within the gay and lesbian community, a way for advocates of marriage to argue to skeptics of marriage that its extension to same-sex couples will lead not to an expansion of patriarchal relations but rather to a newer, more liberating form. Yet the idea that same-sex marriage will transform the institution of marriage has the historical story backward. It is the existing transformation of heterosexual marriage, as Goldberg notes, that has made same-sex marriage viable as a social and political issue. The emergence of the individualistic marriage, with its focus on autonomy and individual rewards, has made it plausible to consider marriage separately from gender roles and reproduction. Because contemporary marriage centers on an intimate relationship grounded in self-development and personal satisfaction – rather than on specialized roles and reproduction – the argument for limiting it to a woman and man is weakened. Heterosexuals, then, have already transformed marriage in a way that can include same-sex couples.

Still, one could envision further changes. Heterosexual marriage remains gendered: Although husbands have increased the amount of housework and child care that they do, wives still do about two-thirds of it (Brinig, Chapter 3; Fisher et al. 2007). Would an influx of same-sex marriages lead to a further movement toward fully egalitarian marriage? After all, the principal basis for a specialized division of labor, the union of a man and a woman, no longer applies. One would expect that most same-sex marriages will be more egalitarian. Yet some modest degree of role specialization in a marriage may be efficient. One could take this position without accepting the overwhelming gender-based specialization of mid-twentieth-century marriage as the most efficient and fair bargain, as sociologist Talcott Parsons (Parsons and Bale 1955) and economist Gary Becker (1991) did.

It will be an interesting empirical question to see how tasks are divided in the typical same-sex marriage. So far the evidence is mixed. Carrington (1999) found that, among many of the gay couples he observed, one partner did more than half of the household work while the other earned more than half of the income. Among African-American lesbian couples with children, the birth mother often emerged as the partner with more authority (Moore 2008). But other studies have found an egalitarian relationship without much specialization (Kurdek 2007). I would not be surprised if the division of labor in both different-sex and same-sex marriage trended asymptotically toward a 60/40 or 55/45 split in the specialization of labor market production and home production roles, rather than a 50/50 split, representing substantially more equality in the past while also reflecting modest efficiency gains, and perhaps the personal preferences of spouses.

CONCLUSION

It appears that American culture is moving toward the position that any two intimate partners who are either (a) married or (b) raising children together, or both, are acceptable as a family, regardless of the sexual orientation of the partners. To be sure, this view is not universally held; there are, and will continue to be, pockets of resistance, both geographical and cultural, in which only heterosexual marriage is acceptable. But public opinion surveys suggest that a majority of Americans already support the broader view. It encompasses cohabiting partners, both same-sex and different-sex, who are raising children; and it includes married partners, both same-sex (where legal), and different-sex, whether or not they are raising children. This is a great shift from the prevailing view a half-century ago.

During that time, family law has changed greatly, too. The major trend has been toward recognizing individual rights rather than protecting the authority of the head of the household or the preeminence of the marital bond (Katz 2000). For instance, the unilateral right to divorce, with few restrictions, has been established everywhere. Although there have been some extensions of rights and protections to cohabiting couples, by and large family law has left cohabiting couples alone. But today, with perhaps one in four children being born to cohabiting couples, the challenge is to extend the law in a way that respects the individualistic preferences of the cohabitants but protects vulnerable partners and children. In the event of a breakup, does the nonbiological parent have the right to visit the child? And, correspondingly, does the child have a right to continued support from the nonbiological parent? There is a lack of consensus, both in the legal sphere and the larger public sphere, on how such questions should be resolved.

Same-sex marriage is so new that little law pertaining to it exists. There is still, of course, a substantial body of law that provides privileges, protections, and responsibilities to individuals in heterosexual marriages. Yet the extension to same-sex spouses of laws developed with heterosexual marriage in mind may be problematic. Although much has changed, the assumptions behind these laws still reflect cultural conceptions of the differences between men and women. But those conceptions are inapplicable to marriages that involve only one gender. Consider divorce: In the event of a breakup of a same-sex marriage, should the legal system endeavor to determine which spouse has been the primary caregiver of the children, or is the very concept of "primary caregiver" gendered and therefore irrelevant? Is the concept of "alimony" similarly irrelevant? Historically, it was directly tied to compensating the more vulnerable partner – almost always the wife. While it still is a topic of interest in family law, as Ellman and Braver (Chapter 9) demonstrate, it already has faded away in social science. The word "alimony" has not been in the title of an article in the *Journal of Marriage and Family* since 2000.

At present, marriage remains important in American family life – so important that a political battle is being fought over whether same-sex couples should have access to it. But it is difficult to predict what will happen to marriage because we are still in the midst of a great transition that has encompassed, so far, the last half of the twentieth century and the beginning of the twenty-first. Will marriage remain strong or will it decline in importance, relative to cohabitation, as it may be doing in some northern European nations? Demographers tend to assume that the social trends occurring in family life at any given time will continue indefinitely into the future. But that is not always the case. The prophets who issued jeremiads about the demise of (different-sex) marriage in the latter-third of the twentieth century did not foresee that the institution, transformed as it is, would still be the experience of the vast majority of young adults. Observers alarmed by the rise in divorce among all social classes in the 1960s and 1970s were caught unaware of the divergent trends of the college-educated versus the rest of the population. Almost no observers of family life in the 1960s and 1970s foresaw same-sex marriage. If marriage has paused at the crossroad, it is only to catch its breath. Which road it will choose to take now is difficult to predict.

REFERENCES

American Law Institute. (2002). *Principles of the Law of Family Dissolution: Analysis and Recommendations*. Philadelphia: American Law Institute.

Badgett, M.V.L. (2009). *When Gay People Get Married: What Happens When Societies Legalize Same-Sex Marriage*. New York: New York University Press.

Becker, G.S. (1991). *A Treatise on the Family (Enlarged Edition)*. Cambridge, MA: Harvard University Press.

Bendheim-Thoman Center for Child Wellbeing. (2007). Parents' Relationship Status Five Years after a Nonmarital Birth. *Fragile Families Research Brief*, no. 39 Retrieved June 12, 2010, from http://www.fragilefamilies.princeton.edu/briefs/ResearchBrief39.pdf.

Burgess, E.W. and Locke, H.J. (1945). *The Family: From Institution to Companionship*. New York: American Book Company.

Carlson, M.J. and Furstenberg, F.F., Jr. (2006). The Prevalence and Correlates of Multipartnered Fertility among Urban U.S. Parents. *Journal of Marriage and Family*, 68, 718–732.

Carpenter, C. and Gates, G.J. (2008). Gay and Lesbian Partnership: Evidence from California. *Demography*, 45, 573–590.

Carrington, C. (1999). *No Place Like Home: Relationships and Family Life among Lesbians and Gay Men*. Chicago: University of Chicago Press.

Cavanagh, S.E. and Huston, A.C. (2006). Family Instability and Children's Early Problem Behavior. *Social Forces*, 85, 551–581.

Cherlin, A.J. (2004). The Deinstitutionalization of American Marriage. *Journal of Marriage and Family*, 66, 848–861.

Cherlin, A.J. (2009). *The Marriage-Go-Round: The State of Marriage and the Family in America Today*. New York: Alfred A. Knopf.

Cherlin, A.J. (2010). One Thousand and Forty-Nine Reasons Why It's Hard to Know When a Fact Is a Fact. In Risman, B.J. (Ed.), *Families as They Really Are* pp. 10–14. New York: W. W. Norton.

Cott, N.F. (2000). *Public Vows: A History of Marriage and the Nation*. Cambridge, MA: Harvard University Press

Eekelaar, J. (2003). The End of an Era? *Journal of Family History*, 28, 108–122.

Fisher, K., Egerton, M., Gershuny, J.I., and Robinson, J.P. (2007). Gender Convergence in the American Heritage Time Use Study (AHTUS). *Social Indicators Research*, 82, 1–33.

Fomby, P. and Cherlin, A.J. (2007). Family Instability and Child Well-Being. *American Sociological Review*, 72, 181–204.

Goodridge v. Department of Public Health, 440 Mass. 309, 798 N.E.2d 941 (2003).

Hartog, H. (2000). *Man and Wife in America: A History*. Cambridge, MA: Harvard University Press.

Inglehart, R., Basáñez, M., Díez-Medrano, J., Halman, L., and Luijkx, R. (2004). *Human Beliefs and Values: A Cross-Cultural Sourcebook Based on the 1999–2002 Values Surveys*. Mexico City: Siglo Veintiuno Editores.

Institute for American Values and Institute for Marriage and Public Policy. (2006). Marriage and the Law: A Statement of Principles. Retrieved September 6, 2008, from http://www.americanvalues.org/html/mlawstmnt2.html.

Katz, S.N. (2000). Individual Rights and Family Relationships. In Katz, S.N., Eekelaar, J. and Maclean, M. (Eds.), *Cross Currents: Family Law and Policy in the United States and England* pp. 621–635. Oxford: Oxford University Press.

Kennedy, S. and Bumpass, L.L. (2011). Cohabitation and Trends in the Structure and Stability of Children's Family Lives. Paper presented at the Annual Meeting of the Population Association of America, Washington, DC, April 1.

Kurdek, L.A. (2007). The Allocation of Household Labor by Partners in Gay and Lesbian Couples. *Journal of Family Issues*, 28, 132–148.

Martin, C. and Théry, I. (2001). The PACS and Marriage and Cohabitation in France. *International Journal of Law, Policy and the Family*, 15, 135–158.

Moore, M.R. (2008). Gendered Power Relations among Women: A Study of Household Decision Making in Black, Lesbian Stepfamilies. *American Sociological Review*, 73, 335–356.

Oppenheimer, V.K. (1970). *The Female Labor Force in the United States*, Population Monograph Series, 5. Berkeley: Institute of International Studies, University of California.

Osborne, C. and McLanahan, S. (2007). Partnership Instability and Child Well-Being. *Journal of Marriage and Family*, 69, 1065–1083.

Parsons, T. and Bales, R.F. (1955). *Family, Socialization, and the Interaction Process*. New York: The Free Press.

Pew Research Center. (2011). The Public Renders a Split Verdict on Family Structure. Retrieved February 19, 2011, from http://pewsocialtrends.org/files/2011/02/Pew-Social-Trends-Changes-In-Family-Structure.pdf.

Scott, E.S. (2007). A World Without Marriage. *Family Law Quarterly*, 41, 537–566.

Smith, D.E. (1993). The Standard North American Family: SNAF as an Ideological Code. *Journal of Family Issues*, 14, 50–65.

Smock, P.J., Manning, W.D., and Porter, M. (2005). "Everything's There Except Money": How Money Shapes Decisions to Marry among Cohabitors. *Journal of Marriage and Family*, 67, 680–696.

Sweeney, M.M. (2002). Two Decades of Family Change: The Shift in Economic Foundations of Marriage. *American Sociological Review*, 67, 132–147.

U.S. Bureau of the Census. 2011. *2011 Statistical Abstract*. Retrieved June 9, 2011, from http://www.census.gov/compendia/statab/2011edition.html.

U.S. National Center for Health Statistics. (2010). Births: Preliminary Data for 2009. National Vital Statistics Reports, Vol. 59. No. 3. Retrieved February 27, 2011, from http://www.cdc.gov/nchs/data/nvsr/nvsr59/nvsr59_03.pdf.

Wilson, R.F. (Ed.). (2006). *Reconceiving the Family: Critique on the American Law Institute's Principles of the Law of Family Dissolution*. New York: Cambridge University Press.

15

Legal Regulation of Twenty-First-Century Families

Marsha Garrison and Elizabeth S. Scott

A primary theme of this volume is that recent sweeping changes in marriage and family life present important challenges for family law. Half a century ago, both law and deeply entrenched social norms prescribed marriage as the only acceptable family form. Marriage was exclusively heterosexual, and both marital roles and entitlements were based on spousal gender. As the various contributors to this volume have explained, much has changed. Across most of the industrialized world, the proportion of families based on marriage has declined substantially. Increasingly, couples choose to live together before marriage or as an alternative to marriage. A 2011 survey found that barely 50 percent of American adults were married – a record low (Pew 2011). A growing number of children are born to unmarried mothers, who often live in informal unions with their children's fathers. As a result of higher divorce rates and the dissolution of nonmarital families, many more children live in a succession of households involving a single parent, that parent's new partner, and, sometimes, the children of the partner or of the parent and the new partner. Same-sex couples also form families and raise children today in a way that was uncommon fifty years ago and, increasingly, these couples have been successful in advocating for legal recognition of their unions.

Several contributors describe how the institution of marriage itself has changed dramatically over the past half-century. Differentiated social roles for husband and wife are no longer prescribed in the way that they once were, and the law has taken a strong stand in support of gender equality (Goldberg, Chapter 11). The new equality norm is associated with increasing equality in spousal earnings and a somewhat more egalitarian apportionment of household work (Brinig, Chapter 3). Moreover, the meaning of marriage has evolved from a role-based, "institutional" model to one based on companionship or, more recently, individual personal fulfillment (Amato, Chapter 6). Under modern divorce law, spouses have unprecedented freedom to leave unhappy marriages, and public opinion increasingly favors such freedom (Schneider, Chapter 12).

Attitudes toward family and familial obligation have also changed. Today, most adults, particularly young adults, are either neutral or positive toward nonmarital and same-sex couples, with or without children. For example, in a recent U.S. poll, a majority of respondents expressed positive or neutral views toward a diverse range of family arrangements, disapproving only of single women having children without a partner (Pew 2010). Reflecting this attitude change, many individuals would be willing to extend "spousal" support and grant a property-division entitlement to at least some unmarried partners; marital status played a role in the thinking of the adult Americans polled by Ellman and Braver (Chapter 9), but not a determinative role.

This account of family change seems straightforward, but on closer inspection, the trends are complex in ways that pose important challenges for legal policy.

First, the general trends mask class-based variation in family-formation behavior. In the United States, Russia, and most of Western Europe, nonmarital birth is associated with lower educational attainment and "a pattern of disadvantage" (Perelli-Harris et al. 2010). This variation is particularly striking in the United States, where nonmarital birth and marriage are now highly correlated with race and class, creating the possibility that variation in family-formation norms reinforces the already large disadvantages of minority status and poverty.

Second, the trend away from marriage masks continuing public support for marriage. Indeed, as both Cherlin (Chapter 14) and McLanahan and Garfinkel (Chapter 8) explain, the decline of marriage seems to be attributable, at least in part, to the fact that marriage is increasingly idealized as a marker of success. The high priority advocates for gay and lesbian rights have placed on access to civil marriage also suggests that marriage remains a core social institution. As Goldberg (Chapter 11) and Franke (Chapter 5) point out, the strong emphasis on this goal is controversial in the gay and lesbian community, and yet it has absorbed the attention of many advocates.

THE POLICY CHALLENGES

The various shifts in public opinion and behavior that the contributors to this volume recount pose important questions for policy makers, questions that continue to provoke profound disagreement. Some commentators long for a return to traditional marriage (Blankenhorn 2007), while others have welcomed the decline of what they view as an outdated institution (Fineman 2001; Polikoff 2008). Representing the latter group, Stacey (Chapter 10) points to the variety of nonmarital families as evidence that many family types can satisfy the needs of their adult and child members. She argues that traditional family law has unfairly privileged marriage by granting public and private rights based on marital status; the solution, in her view, is for the state to abolish marriage as a legal category.

On one level, few would disagree with Stacey's conclusion that the trend toward family diversity is to be applauded; the trend represents a decline in stigmatization of and discrimination against nontraditional relationships and families. A reduction in social prejudice is valuable in its own right. So is the increase in freedom and autonomy that it supports. Lifschitz (Chapter 13) discusses these advantages of family diversity, but argues, in contrast to Stacey, that the state can best support pluralism by making available a variety of family-status options that supplement marriage instead of replacing it. Cherlin (Chapter 14) also sounds a cautionary note, pointing out that, because marriage remains an important life goal for a large segment of the population, it is possible that abolishing marriage would restrict choice rather than expand it.

This debate over the desirability of access to marriage as a legal status is also evident in the literature on same-sex marriage. As Goldberg and Franke observe, the gay and lesbian community has been divided on the importance of marriage as a political goal. Some share Stacey's sense that marriage is a regressive, gendered institution that harms other families and cannot meet the needs of same-sex couples. Others see access to marriage as an essential aspect of full membership in society.

The question of how the state can best support diverse, autonomous choices about family life is not an easy one. It is complicated by two other concerns.

First, cohabitation is, everywhere, less stable than marriage and, as several contributors to this volume make clear, unstable relationships are associated with a variety of risks to children. If marriage plays a *causal* role in promoting stable relationships and reducing child welfare risks, policy makers should be wary of adopting legal rules that deter or disadvantage marriage. This issue is particularly salient where, as in the United States, marriage is strongly associated with race and class; family law and policy should not further worsen the prospects of children who are already disadvantaged. Whether marriage offers unique benefits that other relational forms cannot is also important to the debate over same-sex marriage. If marriage provides benefits (beyond those conferred by government) that informal relationships cannot match, then the case for making marriage available to all citizens is enhanced. At the same time, it is important to recognize that many couples will not marry and many children will be born into nonmarital families. Thus, a critical policy issue is how the law can best support the full spectrum of children and their families.

Second, marital status has long served as the basis for a variety of legislative assumptions about relational expectations and equities. Rules governing spousal inheritance rights and the division of property and support on divorce, for example, assume that spouses are an integrated economic unit with understandings and expectations about the sharing of property and continuing support (Scott and Scott 1998); the law does not make these assumptions about nonmarital cohabitants. Increased family diversity raises the challenge that formal marriage may no longer serve as an accurate marker of expectations and equity. But if this is the case, another means of accurately and fairly classifying couples – in divorce law, probate law, and across a wide range of obligations and entitlements – may be needed.

In sum, the decline of formal marriage poses two different challenges to policy makers. Family law and policy should aim to reduce risks to adult and child well-being. Legal rules dealing with both public status and private rights should also seek to accurately classify couples to ensure that relational expectations and equities are met.

A premise of this interdisciplinary volume is that empirical research on marriage and family relationships can, and should, inform policy making. Within this framework, the contributors offer a range of thoughtful views on the future status of legal marriage and how the law can best support children and adults in nonmarital families. The views that we offer in this comment are grounded in this empirical perspective. To preview our conclusions, the social science evidence is persuasive that stable, low-conflict marriage offers benefits to family members (Amato 2005; Emery 1999); thus, we favor retaining the special status of marriage and argue that its historic harms can be (and to some extent have been) ameliorated through policies of gender equality and nondiscriminatory access. But not all marriages are beneficial, and efforts to promote marriage (or deter divorce) are potentially both ineffective and harmful. Moreover, many couples will continue to live together in informal unions – a reality that poses other challenges for lawmakers. On questions about the conditions under which informal relationships generate rights and obligations, we are not in agreement. But we are in agreement that the public has an important interest in ensuring that parents in all families can meet their children's needs, and we explore some policies that could further this goal.

DOES MARRIAGE MATTER?

Some commentators have argued that the decline of marriage signals its growing irrelevance. For example, the American Law Institute (ALI) (which does not favor the abolition of marriage) has argued that "the absence of formal marriage may have little or no bearing on the character of the parties' domestic relationship and on the equitable considerations that underlie claims between lawful spouses at the dissolution of a marriage" (ALI 2002). This and similar claims hint at the possibility that declining marriage rates and the increase in cohabitation may evidence no more than a shift in family-formation norms in which informal unions that share all, or most, of the characteristics of marital relationships are replacing formal marriages.

However, the research evidence does not support the supposition that marriage and cohabitation typically are equivalent in terms of relational expectations. First, cohabiting relationships are varied in ways that make classification very difficult; demographers have identified six or seven different cohabitation "types," ranging from a casual affiliation, to a stage in the marriage process, to informal "common-law" marriage (Heuveline and Timberlake 2004; Kiernan 2001). Although some cohabiting couples share a marriage-like bond, cohabitation often signals a lack of readiness for or interest in marriage, not marital intentions. The diversity of cohabiting relationships also ensures that cohabiting couples have varied understandings about important aspects of their relationships, including the level of commitment and economic interdependency (Brown 2000; Sassler and McNally 2004; Scott 2004). In short, the fact that two people are cohabiting does little to reveal their understandings and relational expectations (Nock 1995).

In contrast to cohabitation, marriage typically is grounded in a set of clear expectations, the most important of which are commitment and sharing; these expectations underlie many legislative classifications. Married couples overwhelmingly report that they share economic resources and that such sharing is a product of love, trust, and commitment (Blumstein and Schwartz 1983; Pahl 1989; Stocks et al. 2010) Cohabitants are much less likely to express commitment toward or support for their partners (Nock 1995; Stanley 2004); across a wide range of nations, they are more likely to split expenses instead of pooling their resources (Hamplova and Le Bourdais 2009; Knudsen and Wærness 2009; Lingstadt et al. 2011; Vogler et al. 2006). Indeed, surveyed cohabitants often describe the advantages of cohabitation as a function of noncommitment (Coast 2009; McRae 1993). These patterns persist even in Scandinavia (Heimdal and Houseknecht 2003; Lingstadt et al. 2011), where there are few economic incentives to marry and cohabitation is "widely accepted as a way of living together, even when there are children" (Wiik et al. 2009: 466). That many cohabitants do not view their unions as the equivalent of marriage is also suggested by the fact that the vast majority of cohabitants also report that they plan to marry a current or future partner. Even in Sweden, survey data shows that the majority of cohabitants expect to marry within the next five years (Bernhardt 2004), and most people do marry at some point (Andersson and Philipov 2002).

In sum, policy makers cannot assume that cohabitation and marriage are substitutes, with similar expectations of commitment and sharing. To be sure, marriage no longer serves as well as it once did as a means of ascertaining expectations and equities; some cohabiting unions are marriage-like and some marriages are based on little more than formality. Moreover, in some areas of regulation – domestic violence comes immediately to mind – marital status is clearly not an appropriate classification device. In other instances, as we discuss later, a more nuanced scheme may be required.

The Marital Advantage: Correlation or Causation?

As Emery, Horn, and Beam (Chapter 7) explain, formal marriage has long been associated with a range of benefits to adult partners. Researchers have found that married individuals typically live longer and healthier lives than their unmarried counterparts (Wilson and Osborne 2005) and that they do better economically (Ellwood and Jenks 2004; Grossbard-Schechtman 1993). Marriage is also associated with advantages for children. First, marriage tends to be far more stable than cohabitation, and relational instability is associated with financial, physical, and educational risks during childhood and extending into adulthood (Cherlin 2009; McLanahan and Beck 2010; McLanahan and Garfinkel, Chapter 8). Growing up in a single-parent household is negatively, and significantly, correlated with adult income, health, and emotional stability (Amato 2005; Sigle-Rushton and McLanahan 2004). Men and women who experience single-parent households as children are more likely, as adults, to experience marital discord and to divorce or separate (Amato and Cheadle 2005; Hetherington and Elmore 2004). There is also evidence that the advantages conferred by marital childbearing and rearing extend beyond the specific benefits associated with residential and economic stability: married fathers appear to be more involved and spend more time with their children than unmarried fathers; if parental separation occurs, they see their children more often and pay child support more regularly (Brown 2004; Carlson et al. 2005; Hofferth and Anderson 2003).

This is not to say that marriage is invariably correlated with benefits. First, the marital advantage appears to be concentrated in low-conflict relationships. The continuation of a high-conflict marriage is *negatively* associated with health and happiness for both adults and children (Emery 1999). Indeed, longitudinal surveys show that "parents' marital unhappiness and discord have a broad negative impact on virtually every dimension of offspring well-being" (Amato and Booth 1997:219). Second, remarriage does not seem to confer the same advantage as a first marriage either for adults (Nock 1999:66–82) or children. Children living in step-families, for example, tend to score lower on tests of emotional and social well-being than children living with both parents in intact families (Brown 2004; Hofferth 2006).

Finally, a large portion of the marital advantage is explained by "selection effects." As both Cahn and Carbone (Chapter 1) and McLanahan and Garfinkel (Chapter 8) explain, married couples tend to be older, better educated, and better off than cohabiting couples. At least in the United States, cohabiting couples also have more physical, mental health, and substance abuse problems than married couples (DeKleyn 2005; McLanahan 2004); moreover, a large number (40 percent) of U.S. unmarried fathers have been incarcerated at some point (McLanahan and Garfinkel). Thus, to a significant extent, the advantages associated with marriage can be explained by partner characteristics that precede family formation; indeed, it is possible that instead of *producing* advantages, marriage results from them. A key question for policy makers is thus whether, and to what extent, marital status *itself* affects the well-being of adult partners and their children. If it does not, then the decline of formal marriage presents no particular cause for concern (although it may still give rise to classification problems).

A number of the contributors to this volume shed light on this controversial and important question. First, Emery, Horn, and Beam's twin study (Chapter 7) supports the view that marital status matters. The novel design that Emery and his colleagues employed enabled them to largely eliminate both nature and nurture as potentially confounding variables for their identical-twin subjects. That marriage was associated with some advantages (less depression and some differences in general health) in this research sample provides evidence that marriage itself promotes partner well-being.

The various contributors who tackled the problem of determining whether marriage benefits children did not have the advantage of such an optimal sample. However, they show that marital relationships are more stable than nonmarital cohabitation even after controlling for a wide range of demographic variables, and their conclusions on this point have been replicated in numerous other research reports (Crawford et al. 2011; Osborne et al. 2004; Sigle-Rushton and McLanahan 2004).

The persistence of the marital advantage across national and cultural boundaries also suggests that it does not derive solely from selection effects. In Scandinavia, which has the longest experience with cohabitation as a mainstream family form, demographers continue to find that marital childbearing is associated with greater childhood stability, smaller risks to youthful and adult well-being, and lower rates of divorce and nonmarital childbearing among children. For example, in Sweden, where state policies "tend to view cohabitation as equal to marriage, and many of the regulations of marriage are applied to cohabiting relationships" (Heimdahl and Houseknecht 2003:527), cohabiting parents are still more than four times as likely as married parents to separate before their first child turns five (Kiernan 2000). And despite a high level of public assistance to single parents – assistance that produces a child poverty rate of less than 5 percent – single parenthood remains a risk factor for children even after controlling for a wide range of demographic variables (Breivik and Olweus 2006; Garrison 2008b; Weithoft 2003).

Separating advantages produced by marriage from selection effects is difficult, and a large portion of the marital advantage can be explained by partner characteristics, economic factors, and other variables; the more that researchers are able to control for these other explanatory variables, the more the marital advantage diminishes (Crawford 2011; Emery, Horn, and Beam, Chapter 7). However, the evidence to date supports the claim that marriage itself potentially generates some benefits for adults and children.

How Is the Marital Advantage Produced?

Why is marriage associated with personal benefits? Could family policies improve the likelihood of these advantages in nonmarital relationships? Again, some of the contributors to this volume offer useful data on these important questions.

First, it seems likely that the stability associated with marriage is key. Family dissolution typically is associated with reductions in both income and parental attention. It also sets the stage for new relationships. As McLanahan and Garfinkel (Chapter 8) argue, these transitions are often emotionally disruptive, distracting, and stressful for both parents and children – and they can undermine familial bonds that are important to healthy child development. A mother is likely to be less focused on parenting her children from earlier unions when she is building a relationship with a new partner – and perhaps with his children and, ultimately, with children born to the new union. In these circumstances, parents may be less attentive to their children's needs at the very time the children themselves are dealing with stressful new family relationships. Moreover, when either parent finds a new partner or spouse, the child's relationship with his nonresidential parent often becomes attenuated – a serious loss for many children (Cherlin, Chapter 14). In sum, the instability of relationships in serial families pose stressful challenges and demanding adjustments for both parents and children, and it is not surprising that children's welfare often is negatively affected.

So, if marital stability is a key source of the marital advantage, how and why does marriage tend to produce more stable relationships? Most experts have concluded that the public commitments associated with marriage play an important role. The decision by a couple to enter formal marriage represents an agreement to undertake a commitment that involves (relatively) well-defined responsibilities to one another and to any children the couple may have; the registration of such a commitment is likely a more secure foundation for a stable union than the tentative step of cohabiting (Scott 2007). Indeed, as Ellman and Braver point out, often it is not obvious when cohabitation begins. By contrast, in exchanging marital vows, a couple "agrees to be subject to a complex set of behavioral expectations defining the roles of spouse and parent, expectations that will restrict their freedom and guide their behavior in the relationship" (Scott 2000:1907). Of course, the social norms regulating marriage and the role expectations attached to marital status are weaker today in an era of more individualistic marriages and readily available divorce (Amato, Chapter 6). Nonetheless, these norms and expectations continue to inhibit opportunities to participate in other sexual relationships and to prescribe behavior that likely reinforces relational stability, commitment, and mutual interdependency (Scott 2000).

Cohabitation often does not produce these attitudes. In the Fragile Family Study described by McLanahan and Garfinkel, "most of the . . . cohabiting pairs espouse[d] a strong *individualistic* ethic . . . in which personal happiness and fulfillment hold the highest value" (Edin et al. 2004:1011). The researchers offer two quotes from cohabitants that "illustrate this ethos particularly well, and describe how sharply cohabitation differs from marriage":

> The first tells us, "Most people feel like with their boyfriend or girlfriend, when they get into an argument they can just leave. Most of them feel like, OK, when you're married you can't just walk away and leave like that." The second says, "With me and Victor, we have a commitment. But he can still decide this is not working for 'him.' But if you go as far as getting *married*, there you need to know you're really *with* the person" (Edin et al. 2004).

Of course, the sense that marriage is a commitment from which spouses "can't just walk away" has declined. Many married couples get divorced and, in recent years, "individualistic" marriage, in which the marriage partners hold views much like those of the Fragile Family Study cohabitants, have become much more common. Indeed, Amato (Chapter 6) reports that fully 28.5 percent of American marriages were individualistic in the year 2000. Unsurprisingly, spouses in individualistic marriages (both in 1980 and in 2000) were most likely to think that their relationships were in trouble, to think about divorce, and the least likely to report a high level of happiness in their relationship.

In sum, the marital advantage appears to stem, in large part, from commitment, sharing, and the greater stability that these attitudes promote. Despite the rise of individualistic marriage, these advantages appear to persist, but they are far weaker today than in earlier generations.

Why Has Formal Marriage Declined?

Marriage is a malleable and inclusive institution; it can accommodate individualistic marriages along with companionate and traditional, institutional marriages. So why has marriage declined?

One reason seems to be a shift in the meaning of marriage. Cherlin, for example, has urged that marriage "has evolved from a marker of conformity to a marker of prestige" (Cherlin 2004:855). Survey and interview data support this claim. As one interviewee put it, "Marriage is something you earn.... If [she] graduates and [I] graduate, you can start working and we can afford [a wedding] and that's when you get married. It's not just cause we have a child and all of a sudden we need to go out and do it" (Kefalas et al. 2011). Of course, the fact that there has been an attitudinal shift toward marriage does not explain why this is so.

One set of explanations relies on economic factors. As Brinig (Chapter 3) explains, Professor Gary Becker's path-breaking economic model of marriage posits benefits from marital role specialization; it thus predicts that factors diminishing the incentive to specialize – for example, a convergence in male and female wages – will produce diminished gains from marriage and a lower marriage rate (Becker 1981). Economic models also emphasize the importance of sex ratios; if women are in relatively short supply, the models predict a higher marriage rate, and if men are in short supply, they predict a lower marriage rate (Ellwood and Jenks 2004; Grossbard-Schectman 1993).

Empirical researchers have charted many of the correlations predicted by economic theory (Ellwood and Jenks 2004; Smock et al. 2005), and the class divide in marriage behavior described by contributors to this volume supports the importance of economic factors as an explanatory variable. College-educated Americans – the only group whose economic prospects have improved during the past few decades – have continued to bear children within marital relationships during the same period in which the nonmarital birth rate has skyrocketed (Cahn and Carbone 2010). The college-educated group is also the only population sector in which male wages have not stagnated. Most researchers have thus concluded that the increase in nonmarital families is, in part, a product of a decline in the availability of good, working-class jobs for men (Wilson 2002; McLanahan and Garfinkel, Chapter 8). This conclusion is supported by research finding that many individuals in nonmarital families view marriage as a union in which husbands are wage earners who can care for their families.

The racial divide in marriage behavior in the United States also supports the importance of economic factors, as Richard Banks explains in his important recent book (2011). African Americans have the lowest marriage rate of all U.S. ethnic groups. The gap between male and female earnings is also lower for black Americans than any other group; indeed, on average, black women earn almost 95 percent of what black men earn (Banks 2011:42–43). Banks observes that black women face a shortage of available men at all educational levels and that college-educated black women face a particularly acute shortage.

Economic factors alone cannot explain the magnitude of the recent decline in marriage, however. Researchers who measured the impact of changing economic conditions on the marriage rate in the United States between 1986 and 1997 found that wage and employment shifts explained only about one third of the decline during that period (Lichter 2002). Further, the retreat from marriage in the United States also continued throughout the 1990s, despite dramatic increases in economic growth.

At least as important as an explanation for the decline of marriage are changing social norms that began with the sexual revolution of the 1960s; because of these changes, couples can freely choose between marriage and cohabitation without fear of social sanctions. This was not always true. In the 1950s, and even later, couples who chose to live together, and particularly to have children together outside of marriage, could expect to confront disapproval in most communities. Strong social norms prescribed marriage as the only socially acceptable setting for intimacy and raising children (Scott 2000). Not surprisingly, most couples seeking an intimate relationship chose marriage. These social norms have now been largely abandoned in the developed world (Thornton, Chapter 1), a shift that has surely contributed to the increased numbers of nonmarital families – and to the decline in marriage.

The importance of social influence is apparent in the fascinating case of Quebec, where the marriage rate is about half, and the nonmarital cohabitation rate about double, that of the other Canadian provinces (Lachapelle 2007; Laplante 2006). A half-century ago, Quebec's marriage rate was higher than the Canadian norm (Le Bourdais and Marcil-Gratton 1996). Although economic conditions undoubtedly explain some of this shift – Quebec's already high unemployment rate rose steeply during the same period that the marriage rate began to decline sharply – most demographers have concluded that the more important factor is hostility by

Francophone, predominantly Catholic, Canadians to the conservative attitudes of the Catholic Church. Evidence for this claim comes from two facts: the Quebecois marriage rate is much lower than that of neighboring provinces with comparable unemployment figures, and Francophones have a higher cohabitation rate than Anglophone Canadians no matter where they live in Canada (Lachappelle 2007).

The case of Quebec is particularly intriguing because non-Catholic, Anglophone Canadians who live in Quebec also have a higher cohabitation rate than Anglophones who live in the other provinces (Lachappelle 2007). This could result from economic factors, or from a "bandwagon effect" in which majority Francophone sentiment influences minority Anglophone attitudes.

Quebec may be somewhat unusual in that hostility toward marriage rather than acceptance of cohabitation seems to have driven changes in family formation – but the dynamic interaction between changing attitudes and behavior is not unusual. Bandwagon effects generally influence public opinion, and, over time, public attitudes play an important role in shaping private attitudes and behavior (Coleman 1998; Kuran 1995). Those without strong views on a subject may be swayed by perceptions about the views and behavior of others, and "[e]ach new person on [an] . . . upward bandwagon induces additional people to climb on" (Marsh 1984). In this way, dramatic attitudinal and behavioral changes can occur in a relatively brief period. For example, in the early 1960s, 80 percent of the public agreed that "a couple should stay together" for the sake of the children. By the 1980s, agreement with this statement had dropped to 50 percent (Axinn and Thornton 2000).

The recent decline in marriage thus can be attributed, at least in part, to a dynamic process through which more favorable public attitudes toward cohabitation as an alternative to marriage have encouraged couples to cohabit, which in turn has increased the acceptability of cohabitation and influenced more couples to choose cohabitation over marriage in a self-reinforcing pattern.

THE ROLE OF LAW IN SUPPORTING TWENTY-FIRST-CENTURY FAMILIES

So, how should the law respond to the growing diversity of modern families?

As a preliminary matter, it is useful to note the general goals of contemporary family law and policy and the principles we think should animate the legal regulation of families in the twenty-first century. The primary goal is to ensure that the needs of dependent members of society, particularly children, are met. Society has an important interest in the healthy development of children, who will be the next generation of adult citizens. Society also has an interest in ensuring that families meet the needs of their dependent adult members; if families perform these important functions adequately, the burden on government (and on taxpayers) is reduced. In regard to adults, public policy should also support and respect personal autonomy and choice in intimate relationships; it should thus avoid discrimination against particular types of families and acknowledge the legitimacy of a diverse range of family types. Finally, the law should protect family members from harm, including harms associated with detrimental reliance on relational obligations and commitments.

Should the State Eliminate Legal Marriage or Expand Access?

A key question raised by this book is the future status of legal marriage. In addressing this issue, we think it important to note that the most prominent argument against marriage today is different from the concerns that animated marriage critics a generation ago. Beginning in the 1970s, this earlier generation of opponents challenged marriage as a hierarchical institution that oppressed and subordinated women (Fineman 1995; Olson 1983; Olson 1984). Although this critique has not disappeared, it is not the primary objection of most marriage critics today (Stacey, Chapter 10). In part, as Goldberg (Chapter 11) explains, this may be attributable to law reforms that have systematically abolished differential legal treatment of husbands and wives.

Today's hostility to legal marriage is typically grounded in the claim that a "special" status for marriage is harmful to other families – and that all families should be treated with the same respect under the law. This critique stems, in part, from the law's long-standing exclusion of gays and lesbians from marriage. It also has roots in traditional family law's harsh treatment of nonmarital families. Until the 1960s, "illegitimate" children of unmarried mothers were ineligible for a range of legal benefits (including inheritance rights) enjoyed by children whose parents were married (*Levy v. Louisiana* 1968). Cohabiting adults were deemed to be in immoral, "meretricious" relationships – outside of the law's protection; in some jurisdictions, even their contracts were unenforceable (*Marvin v. Marvin* 1975; *Hewitt v. Hewitt* 1979). The law thus reflected and reinforced the social stigma attached to nonmarital relationships and birth. Marriage critics point to this history of discrimination and urge that any continued differential legal treatment of marital and nonmarital families undermines the legitimacy of nonmarital families.

Although differences in the legal treatment of marital and nonmarital families require careful scrutiny and justification, we think the evidence shows that this critique is misguided. First, in recent years, constitutional and statutory reforms have abolished overtly discriminatory policies toward nonmarital children and relationships. Second, public attitudes have changed dramatically, and survey evidence suggests little or no stigmatization of nonmarital families today (Pew 2010). Third, as McLanahan and Garfinkel point out (Chapter 8), differential treatment of marriage results in penalties for married couples as well as benefits – and marriage also carries obligations as well as rights. Finally, the evidence shows that cohabitation does not typically entail the same type of sharing and commitment as marriage; differential treatment of marriage and cohabitation thus often reflects the different expectations and behaviors of married and unmarried couples.

Our conclusion that differential treatment of marriage and cohabitation is warranted does not, of course, apply to same-sex couples who cannot marry. But the answer, in our view, is to make marriage available to all couples seeking to register their commitment, not to eliminate marriage. Public attitudes toward marriage are positive, and a majority of adults continue to marry. At least in the United States, even those who are unmarried typically express the hope to marry at some point in their lives.

With the abolition of overtly discriminatory policies toward nonmarital families and the adoption of policies making marriage available to same-sex couples, marriage becomes an option that all couples are free to choose. Over time, marriage critics' concern that the law's "special" treatment of marriage harms other families may diminish in response to legal reforms and to changing social attitudes, just as concerns about gender hierarchy have faded.

Indeed, today's positive public attitudes toward marriage may be attributable, at least in part, to the fact that both marriage and marriage law have evolved to reflect changing social values. These changes are reflected in the gender-equality reforms noted earlier, in the availability of no-fault divorce, and (indirectly) in legal changes ending discrimination against nonmarital families. In this evolution, law and social norms have interacted in a dynamic process and, we think, this is as it should be. Legal marriage must be responsive to changing social values, or it will become a moribund institution inconsistent with current goals for intimate and family life. Today, lawmakers are challenged to extend marriage to same-sex couples – a group that historically has been excluded. Responding positively to this challenge represents the type of adaptation and evolution through which the institution of marriage has retained its robustness as a family form.

We thus believe that civil marriage should be opened to same-sex couples and that it should continue to be available to all couples who want to register their commitment. As Lifshitz suggests (chapter 13), the state's nondiscriminatory stance and commitment to pluralism could be underscored by offering a menu of status options in addition to informal cohabitation.

Should the State Continue to Grant Benefits and Impose Burdens Based on Marital Status?

This is a hard question given the importance of avoiding discrimination toward nonmarital families. Government programs that aim to benefit children should not (and generally do not) discriminate among families on the basis of marital status. But spouses receive benefits not available to cohabitants, including inheritance rights, estate tax advantages, Social Security survivor benefits, and a testimonial privilege, among others. It is well accepted that this package of benefits (and obligations) has both tangible and expressive value as a signal of the social importance of marriage.

We think rules distinguishing marriage from cohabitation, and at least some of the benefits that accompany the formal status, can be justified on several grounds. First, as Lifshitz suggests, the special legal status of marriage can be justified as a quid pro quo for the couple's agreement to formally undertake marital obligations such as mutual support and sharing. Although these duties are seldom enforced during marriage (except occasionally under the necessaries doctrine), they are embodied in divorce law rules that regulate spousal support and property distribution; they also underlie many of the classifications that distinguish marriage from cohabitation (Scott and Scott 1998; Scott 2006).

Second, encouraging committed couples to marry may be desirable to the extent that marriage reinforces commitment and relational stability. Today, as McLanahan and Garfinkel point out, some committed couples may be deterred from marrying because they will lose government benefits.

Third, classification schemes that impose marital status, without consent, on couples who do not have marital understandings needlessly reduce individual autonomy. As we have pointed out, many couples cohabit *because* cohabitation does not entail marital obligations (Garrison 2005; Scott 2007). Moreover, under current law, intimate partners can designate one another as will beneficiaries, enter into contracts, take joint title to property, and otherwise individualize their expectations.

Finally, marriage performs an important notarial function in that it clearly signals a couple's commitments and expectations. Given the range of cohabiting relationships, factually distinguishing marriage-like informal unions from casual affiliations that do not warrant special legal treatment may be difficult and costly; indeed, differences in the wording of questions have been shown to affect self-reports of cohabitation status among cohabiting couples and couples with nonmarital children, and even classification by researchers (Knab 2005). "Common-law" marriage – which relied on a private marital agreement and public "holding out" as a married couple instead of a marriage ceremony – has been abolished in most states precisely because of the difficulty of separating spurious from genuine marital claims. It is thus desirable for committed couples to formally marry so that their expectations can be recognized without expensive, time-consuming, and potentially inaccurate fact finding (Garrison 2008b).

This is not to say that the law should never make some form of relief available to cohabitants who do not register marital intentions or individualize their expectations through a contract or other means. The question is when and how. The rapid rise of cohabitation has produced a wide variety of schemes. Some jurisdictions grant relief based on the couple's informal agreement(s) (United States), while others focus on compensating for disadvantage arising from the relationship (Ireland). A third group treat unmarried couples as married for some or all purposes, based on one or more relational facts (e.g., the duration of cohabitation or having a common child) (Australia, Canada, New Zealand, Scotland).

The lack of consensus on when and how to grant relief to cohabitants who have not formalized their relational intentions reflects different balances among competing policy goals and variation in background factual assumptions. We expect that it may be some time before consensus on the right approach emerges. Indeed, this is an issue on which we are not in agreement ourselves.

Scott favors an approach under which cohabitants would assume marriage-like financial obligations based on the birth of a common child or a period (perhaps five years) of cohabitation, with the possibility of opting out. In her view, the state's interest in promoting family stability and ensuring that parents provide financially for their children justifies imposing marital obligations on partners when a couple has a common child. Optimally, the birth of a child will motivate the couple to consider making a formal commitment to one another. Indeed, assigning marital obligations when a couple has a child together may encourage them to marry, if the reluctance of either was attributable to a desire to avoid financial responsibility. But even if they do not marry, the birth of a child should signal to parents that they now have obligations toward one another that they were free to reject previously. The child's financial security is likely to be interwoven with that of both parents, and if they separate, that security is not likely to be achieved through child support alone. As Ellman and Braver (2011) report, public opinion now favors imposing partner support obligations on unmarried parents.

Scott also views the imposition of marital obligations on long-term cohabitants (couples who have lived together five years or more) as justified. In her view, these couples (a group representing a small percentage of cohabiting couples) are more likely than other cohabitants to be in marriage-like relationships and may often have an implicit understanding about financial sharing or support – or the more sophisticated partner may allow the other to believe that they do. A default rule creating marital financial obligations after an extended period of cohabitation would put the burden on the reluctant party to disclose his preference to avoid mutual obligations and persuade his partner to opt out by contract. This approach would avoid misunderstandings by vulnerable partners while preserving the freedom of couples who want to avoid mutual financial obligations (Scott 2006).

Garrison favors an approach, like that recently adopted in Ireland, which focuses on disadvantage flowing from the relationship as a basis for relief. In her view, the evidence fails to support the assumption that either the birth of a child or relational duration create marital expectations: even in Scandinavia, the birth of a child is not significantly correlated with the seriousness of a cohabiting relationship (Wiik et al. 2009), and cohabiting couples are significantly less likely than married couples to pool resources even after the duration of the relationship, the presence of children, and other socioeconomic variables are taken into account (Lyngstadt et al. 2011). The imposition of marital status based on relationship duration or parenthood thus creates serious risks of misclassification and reintroduces all the problems with fraud and uncertainty that have led states that formerly permitted fact-based, "common-law" marriage to abandon the doctrine. The fact that cohabitants often fail to agree about the nature of their relationship enhances these risks. Garrison is skeptical that the stability and other welfare benefits associated with marriage can be obtained when a couple fails to make formal, public commitments. And she fears that schemes which impose marital status retrospectively without such formal commitments may accelerate nonmarital parenting both through bandwagon effects and by signaling that formal marriage does not matter. Given that targeted legislation focused directly on remedying relationship-induced disadvantage can prevent unjust enrichment, she sees no reason to risk such negative effects (Garrison 2005, 2007, 2008a, 2008b).

Although we have not reached consensus on how the state should regulate nonmarital cohabitants who have not registered their intentions, we agree that the state should encourage couples with marital intentions to formally marry. We also agree that the state should facilitate marriage by providing an efficient, inexpensive registration process and streamlining the process through which individuals' legal status is changed.

Should the State Promote Marriage?

If it makes sense to support the registration of marital intentions, should the government also promote formal marriage?

In recent years, marriage advocates have urged a diverse array of marriage-promotion initiatives (Blankenhorn 2007; Waite and Gallagher 2000). Some focus on divorce reform while others promote public education. Some proposals aim to increase the marriage rate either through direct incentives or the elimination of marriage "penalties" like those described by McLanahan and Garfinkel. Advocates have also advanced initiatives that aim to reduce marital conflict or deter nonmarital births, particularly among teenage mothers. Although these initiatives have not attracted much attention outside the United States, the George W. Bush administration funded a number of marriage-promotion programs, and state governments have funded others.

In our view, the evidence does not support governmental efforts to advance marriage per se. Because only low-conflict, enduring relationships offer significant benefits to adult partners and their children, only programs or reforms aimed at promoting this narrow category of marriages are justifiable. Those that aim to encourage marriage more broadly should be resisted. Indeed, for high-conflict relationships, the data suggest that government policy should aim to discourage marriage and facilitate divorce (Amato 2005; Emery 1999).

Several marriage-promotion initiatives – including divorce reform, marriage "incentives," and public information campaigns extolling the benefits of marriage – clearly fail this test. The revival of fault grounds and other restrictions on access to divorce have the potential to enhance and prolong marital stress in high-conflict relationships. Moreover, the problem of spousal collusion – a fact of life that played an important role in legal reforms eliminating the necessity of establishing fault as a precondition to divorce – also greatly undermines the ability of courts to separate marriages worth preserving from those that should be terminated; spouses who agree can evade the formal requirements, and the law is powerless to prevent them from doing so. Marriage incentives are a bad idea for similar reasons. Incentive programs that encourage marriage per se are not calibrated to foster enduring, low-conflict partnerships. This problem is particularly acute if incentives are targeted at poor people, who have the lowest marriage rate. Low-income unmarried mothers often report that they have not married their children's fathers because of serious relationship problems such as violence, addiction, criminal misbehavior, and chronic conflict (Edin and Kefalas 2007), problems that are strongly associated with both relationship failure and poor outcomes for children (Sigle-Rushton and McLanahan 2004). There is no reason to encourage marriage in the context of such relationships. Even public information campaigns that extol the benefits of marriage sweep too broadly; it is far from clear how government could deliver a pro-marriage message without promoting undesirable marriages as well as healthy ones. The opinion-poll evidence also suggests that education about the benefits of marriage is not needed. These surveys find positive attitudes about marriage and widespread appreciation of its benefits.

Some marriage-promotion strategies do have appropriate goals. For example, conflict reduction and relationship skills programs, also included in the Bush administration's Healthy Marriage Initiative, aim at promoting relational stability and quality. These programs, and similar projects aimed at encouraging parental cooperation before and after separation, may benefit participants. Programs seeking to reduce teenage pregnancy (almost invariably nonmarital) and to encourage young women to postpone childbearing until they have completed their educations are also appropriate and potentially among the most beneficial initiatives. By providing counseling and access to contraceptives, these programs may assist in reducing the substantial social costs of adolescent childbearing — for mothers, children, and society.

It is notable that these initiatives with appropriate goals do not entail marriage promotion per se. Instead, they focus directly on problems with which the decline of marriage is associated. In our view, this is the approach that policy makers should follow, although further research is needed to evaluate the efficacy of particular programs.

Equally desirable, in our view, are programs that focus directly on the disadvantages with which nonmarital birth and relational failure are correlated. The research described by contributors to this volume indicates that many forms of disadvantage – economic, educational, and psychological – are correlated with increased risk of nonmarital childbearing, unsuccessful partnering, and deficiencies in parenting that undermine child well-being. The data also suggest that the underlying stresses which promote relational dysfunction and instability also contribute to other, arguably far more serious, deficits in family functioning. Single and adolescent parenting, substance abuse, mental health problems, adult family violence, child maltreatment, lack of social support, and low socioeconomic status are all highly correlated (Garrison 2008b; Huston 2003). In short, relational dysfunction and instability are often symptoms, as well as causes, of emotional and economic stresses that should be addressed directly.

Government policies that reduce the disadvantages associated with poverty thus offer the possibility of providing a range of benefits to children and their parents (Currie 2006). For example, high-quality, intensive preschool education is significantly associated not only with long-term educational and social advantages to the children who attend such programs, but also with a lower rate of child maltreatment and teen pregnancy within the educated group (Garfinkel and McLanahan, Chapter 8). These programs also free parents to seek employment and thus increase their family's economic well-being. In our view, such programs should play a central role in any government policy aimed at reducing family instability.

Programs that focus on improving the job prospects of adults who lack a college education are also important. As we have seen, this is the group that has experienced the most family instability and the most economic stress. Reversing this negative economic trend could play a valuable role in reversing the trend toward family instability as well as ensuring that families' basic economic needs are met. In the United States, changes in sentencing policy could also play a valuable role. As McLanahan and Garfinkel point out (Chapter 8), the extraordinarily high incarceration rate of young black men not only disrupts their lives and prospects of productive employment, but also reduces the likelihood that they will become responsible parents and husbands.

Many factors contribute to the challenges faced by unmarried parents and their children – and government cannot solve every problem. But the relatively greater stability of nonmarital families in Europe, particularly in Scandinavia, where nonmarital birth rates are as high as or higher than those in the United States, suggests that government policies aimed at ensuring that families can adequately provide for their children – educationally, emotionally, and economically – will promote family stability and child well-being in a range of dimensions.

We are also persuaded by McLanahan and Garfinkel that, for the most part, programs available to all children will best advance the welfare of children in nonmarital families. Some services should, of course, target those most in need. But eligibility for programs that support parents and children should not be contingent on nonmarital status; a clear lesson of the research, in our view, is that discouraging parents from marrying is counterproductive as a policy matter. Beyond this, programs for which all children and families are eligible are likely to enjoy broader public and political support. The experience with the Individuals with Disabilities Education Act – a federal law creating an entitlement to special education services for children – demonstrates that middle-class families constitute a powerful interest group in support of social and educational programs (Pasachoff 2011).

CONCLUSION

As lawmakers consider how to respond to family change at this critical juncture, we think that the evidence supports some policy directions: Although fewer couples choose to marry, marriage continues to be an important goal for many individuals and to offer social and personal benefits; thus, we favor retaining marriage as a special legal status, but one that is available to all couples ready to undertake marital commitment. We also favor a pluralistic regime that respects the freedom of adults to make choices about their intimate relationships and which generally is not inclined to impose nonconsensual marital obligations on cohabitants. Although children in nonmarital families are disadvantaged relative to children in marital families in ways that are likely to increase in the future without intervention, neither high-conflict marriage nor remarriage to a new partner is associated with benefits to children; we thus do not support initiatives to promote marriage per se. Instead, we favor policy reforms directed toward supporting the growing number of fragile families – and all families. Educational, employment, and public health programs that contribute to the ability of unmarried parents to raise their children in a stable, nurturing family setting will benefit these families and the rest of society as well.

REFERENCES

Amato, P.R. (2005). The Impact of Family Formation Change on the Cognitive, Social, and Emotional Well-Being of the Next Generation. *Future of Children*, 15, 75–96.

Amato, P.R. and Cheadle, J. (2005). The Long Reach of Divorce: Divorce and Child Well-Being across Three Generations. *Journal of Marriage and Family*, 67, 191–206.

American Law Institute (2002). *Principles of the Law of Family Dissolution*. American Law Institute.

Andersson, G. and Philipov, D. (2002). Life-Table Representations of Family Dynamics in Sweden, Hungary, and 14 Other FFS Countries: A Project of Descriptions of Demographic Behavior. *Demographic Research*, 7, 67–144.

Axinn, W.G. and Thornton, A. (2000). The Transformation in the Meaning of Marriage. In Waite, L.J. (Ed.), *The Ties That Bind: Perspectives on Marriage and Cohabitation*. New York: Aldine de Gruyter.

Banks, R.R. (2011). *Is Marriage for White People? How the African American Marriage Decline Affects Everyone*. New York: Dutton.

Becker, G. (1981). *A Treatise on the Family*. Cambridge, MA: Harvard University Press.

Bernhardt, E. (2004). *Cohabitation or Marriage? Preferred Living Arrangements in Sweden*. Austrian Institute for Family Studies.

Blankenhorn, D. (2007). *The Future of Marriage*. Encounter Books.

Blumstein, P. and Schwartz, P. (1983). *American Couples: Work, Money, Sex*. New York: Wm. Morrow & Co.

Breivik, K. and Olweus, D. (2006). Adolescents' Adjustment in Four Post-Divorce Family Structures. *Divorce and Remarriage*, 44, 99–124.

Brown, S.L. (2000). Union Transitions among Cohabiters: The Significance of Relationship Assessment and Expectations. *Journal of Marriage and Family*, 62, 833–46.

Brown, S.L. (2004). Family Structure and Child Well-Being. *Journal of Marriage and Family*, 66, 351–67.
Brown, S.L. and Booth, A. (1996). Cohabitation versus Marriage: A Comparison of Relationship Quality. *Journal of Marriage and Family*, 58, 668–78.
Cahn, N. and Carbone, J. (2010). *Red Families v. Blue Families*. Oxford: Oxford University Press.
Carlson, M., McLanahan, S., and Brooks-Gunn, J. (2005), *Unmarried But Not Absent: Fathers' Involvement with Children after a Nonmarital Birth*. CRCW working paper 2005–07.
Cherlin, A.J. (2009). *The Marriage-Go-Round: The State of Marriage and the Family Today*. New York: Alfred A. Knopf.
Coast, E. (2009). Currently Cohabiting: Relationship Attitudes and Intentions. In Stillwell, J. et al. (Eds.), *Fertility, Living Arrangements, Care and Mobility*. Dordrecht: Springer.
Coleman, J.S. (1998). *Foundations of Social Theory*. Cambridge, MA: Harvard University Press.
Crawford, C. (2011). *Cohabitation, Marriage, Relationship Stability and Child Outcomes: An Update*. London: Institute for Fiscal Studies. Retrieved from http://www.ifs.org.uk/comms/comm120.pdf.
Currie, J. (2006). *The Invisible Safety Net: Protecting the Nation's Poor Children and Families*. Princeton, NJ: Princeton University Press.
DeKlyen, M. et al. (2006). The Mental Health of Parents with Infants: Do Marriage, Cohabitation and Romantic Status Matter? *American Journal of Public Health*, 96, 1836–41.
Edin, K. and Kefalas, M. (2005). *Promises I Can Keep: Why Poor Women Put Motherhood Before Marriage*. Berkeley: University of California Press.
Edin K., Kefalas, M., and Reed, J. (2004). A Peek Inside the Black Box: What Marriage Means for Poor Unmarried Parents. *Journal of Marriage and Family*, 66, 1007–14.
Ellman, I. and Braver, S. (2011). Lay Intuitions about Family Obligations: The Case of Alimony. Working Paper Series, Arizona State University. Retrieved from http://ssrn.com/abstract=1737146.
Ellman, I. et al. (2010). *Family Law: Cases, Texts, Problems*. LexisNexis.
Ellwood, D.T. and Jencks, C. (2004). The Uneven Spread of Single-Parent Families: What Do We Know? Where Do We Look for the Answers? In Neckerman, K. M. (Ed.), *Social Inequality*. New York: Russell Sage Foundation.
Emery, R.E. (1999). *Marriage, Divorce, and Children's Adjustment*. Thousand Oaks, CA: Sage Publications.
Fineman, M.A. (1995). *The Neutered Mother, the Sexual Families and other Twentieth Century Tragedies*. New York: Routledge.
Fineman, M.A. (2001). Why Marriage? *Virginia Journal of Social Policy & the Law*, 9, 239–71.
Garrison, M. (2005). Is Consent Necessary? An Evaluation of the Emerging Law of Cohabitant Obligation. *UCLA Law Review*, 52, 815–97.
Garrison, M. (2007). The Decline of Formal Marriage: Inevitable or Reversible? *Family Law Quarterly*, 41, 491–520.
Garrison, M. (2008a). Nonmarital Cohabitation: Social Revolution and Legal Regulation. *Family Law Quarterly*, 42, 309–31.
Garrison, M. (2008b). Reviving Marriage: Could We? Should We? *Journal of Law and Family Studies*, 10, 279–335.
Grossbard-Shechtman, S. (1993). *On the Economics of Marriage: A Theory of Marriage, Labor, and Divorce*. Boulder, CO: Westview Press.

Hamplova, D. and LeBourdais, C. (2009). One Pot or Two Pot Strategies? Income Pooling in Married and Unmarried Households in Comparative Perspective. *Journal of Comparative Family Studies*, 40, 355–85.
Heimdal, K.R. and Houseknecht, S.K. (2003). Cohabiting and Married Couples' Income Organization: Approaches in Sweden and the United States. *Journal of Marriage & Family*, 65, 525–38.
Hetherington, E.M. and Elmore, A.E. (2004), The Intergenerational Transmission of Couple Instability. In Chase-Landsdale, P.L. et al. (Eds.), *Human Development across Lives and Generations: The Potential for Change*. Cambridge: Cambridge University Press.
Heuveline, P. and Timberlake, J.M. (2004). The Role of Cohabitation in Family Formation: The United States in Comparative Perspective. *Journal of Marriage and Family*, 61, 1214–30.
Hofferth, S.L. (2006). Residential Father Family Type and Child Well-Being: Investment versus Selection. *Demography*, 43, 53–77.
Hofferth, S.L. and Anderson, K.G. (2003). Are All Dads Equal? Biology versus Marriage as a Basis for Paternal Investment. *Journal of Marriage and Family*, 65, 213–32.
Huston, A.C. et al. (2003). *New Hope for Families and Children: Five-Year Results of a Program to Reduce Poverty and Reform Welfare*. New York: MDRC.
Kieman, K. (2001). The Rise of Cohabitation and Childbearing Outside Marriage in Western Europe. *International Journal of Law, Policy and the Family*, 15, 1–21.
Kiernan, K. (2000). European Perspectives on Union Formation. In Waite, L. (Ed.), *The Ties That Bind*. New York: Aldine de Gruyter.
Knab, J. (2005). Cohabitation: Sharpening a Fuzzy Concept. Princeton Center for Research on Child Wellbeing Working Paper # 04–05-FF.
Knudsen, K. and Wærness, K. (2009). Shared or Separate? Money Management and Changing Norms of Gender Equality among Norwegian Couples. *Community, Work & Family*, 12, 39–55.
Kuran, T. (1995). *Private Truths, Public Lies: The Social Consequences of Preference Falsification*. Cambridge, MA: Harvard University Press.
Lachapelle, R. (2007), The High Prevalence of Cohabitation among Franco-phones: Some Implications for Exogamous Couples. Canadian Population Society Annual Meeting.
Laplante, B. (2006). The Rise of Cohabitation in Quebec: Power of Religion and Power Over Religion. *Canadian Journal of Sociology*, 31, 1–24.
Lawrence v. Texas, 539 U.S. 558 (2003).
LeBourdais, C. and Marcil-Gratton, N. (1996). Family Transformations Across the Canadian/ American Border: When the Laggard Becomes the Leader. *Journal of Comparative Family Studies*, 28, 415–36.
Levy v. Louisiana, 391 U.S. 68 (1968).
Lichter, D.T. (2002). Economic Restructuring and the Retreat from Marriage. *Social Science Research*, 31, 230–56.
Lyngstad, T.H., Noack, T., and Tufte, P.A. (2011). Pooling of Economic Resources: A Comparison of Norwegian Married and Cohabiting Couples. *European Sociological Review*, 27, 624–35.
Marsh, C. (1984). Back on the Bandwagon: The Effect of Opinion Polls on Public Opinion. *British Journal of Political Science*, 15, 51–74.
Marvin v. Marvin, 557 P.2d 106 (1976).
McLanahan, S. (2004). Diverging Destinies: How Children Are Faring under the Second Demographic Transition. *Demography*, 41, 607–27.
McLanahan, S. and Beck, A.N. (2010). Parental Relationships in Fragile Families. *Fragile Families*, 20, 17–37.

McRae, S. (1993). *Cohabiting Mothers*. London: Policy Studies Institute.
Nock, S. (1995). A Comparison of Marriages and Cohabiting Relationships. *Journal of Family Issues*, 16, 53–76.
Nock, S. (1999). *Marriage in Men's Lives*. Oxford: Oxford University Press.
Olson, F. (1983) The Family and the Market: A Study of Ideology and Legal Reform. *Harvard Law Review*, 96, 1497–1578.
Olson, F. (1984). The Politics of Family Law. *Law and Inequality*, 2, 1–21.
Osborne, C. et al. (2004). *Instability in Fragile Families: The Role of Race-Ethnicity, Economics, and Relationship Quality*. CRCW Working Paper 2004–17FF.
Pahl, J. (1989). *Money and Marriage*. New York: Palgrave McMillan.
Pasachoff, E. (2011). Special Education, Poverty, and the Limits of Private Enforcement. *Notre Dame Law Review*, 85, 1413–1492.
Perelli-Harris, B. et al. (2009). How Does Childbearing Change the Meaning of Cohabitation? A Study of Nine European Countries. Paper presented at the Population Association of America meetings, Detroit, MI, April 30 to May 2.
Perelli-Harris, B. et al. (2010). The Educational Gradient of Nonmarital Childbearing in Europe. *Population and Development Review*, 36, 775–801.
Pew Research Center (2010). *The Decline of Marriage and Rise of New Families*. Retrieved from http://pewresearch.org/pubs/1802/decline-marriage-rise-new-families.
Pew Research Center (2011). *Barely Half of U.S. Adults are Married – A New Low*. Retrieved from http://www.pewsocialtrends.org/2011/12/14/barely-half-of-u-s-adults-are-married-a-record-low/?src=prc-headline.
Polikoff, N. (2008). *Beyond (Straight and Gay) Marriage: Valuing All Families under the Law*. Boston: Beacon Press.
Sassler, S. and McNally, J. (2004). Cohabiting Couple's Economic Circumstances and Union Transitions: A Re-Examination Using Multiple Imputation Techniques. *Social Science Research*, 32, 553–78.
Scott, E.S. (2000). Social Norms and the Legal Regulation of Marriage. *Virginia Law Review*, 86, 1901–70.
Scott, E.S. (2004). Marriage, Cohabitation and Collective Responsibility for Dependency. *The University of Chicago Legal Forum* 225–64.
Scott, E.S. (2006). Domestic Partnerships, Implied Contracts, and Law Reform. In Wilson, R.F. (Ed.), *Reconceiving the Family* pp. 331–349. New York: Cambridge University Press.
Scott, E.S. (2007). A World without Marriage. *Family Law Quarterly*, 41, 537–566.
Scott, E.S. and Scott, R.E. (1998). Marriage as Relational Contract. *Virginia Law Review*, 84, 1225–1332.
Sigle-Rushton, W. and McLanahan, S. (2004). Father Absence and Child Well-Being: A Critical Review. In Moynihan, D. P., Smeeding, T., and Rainwater, L. (Eds.), *The Future of the Family* pp. 116–158. New York: Russell Sage Foundation.
Smock, P.J. et al. (2005). "Everything's There Except Money": How Money Shapes Decisions to Marry Among Cohabitors. *Journal of Marriage and Family*, 67, 680–96.
Stanley, S.M. et al. (2004). Interpersonal Commitment and Premarital or Nonmarital Cohabitation. *Journal of Family Issues*, 25, 496–519.
Stocks, J. et al. (Eds.) (2007). *Modern Couples: Sharing Money, Sharing Life*. Houndsmill Basingstoke: Palgrave.
Vogler, C., Brockmann, M., and Wiggins, R.D. (2006). Intimate Relationships and Changing Patterns of Money Management at the Beginning of the Twenty-First Century. *British Journal of Sociology*, 57, 455–82.

Waite, L.J. and Gallagher, M. (2000). *The Case for Marriage: Why Married People are Happier, Healthier, and Better Off Financially*. New York: Broadway Publishers.

Weitoft, G.R. et al. (2003). Mortality, Severe Morbidity, and Injury in Children Living with Single Parents in Sweden: A Population-Based Study. *Lancet*, 361, 289–95.

Wiik, K.A., Bernhardt, E.M., and Noack, T. (2009). A Study of Commitment and Relationship Quality in Sweden and Norway. *Journal of Marriage and Family*, 71, 465–77.

Wilson, C.M. and Oswald, A.J. (2005). How Does Marriage Affect Physical and Psychological Health? A Survey of the Longitudinal Evidence, IZA Bonn Discussion Paper No. 1619.

Wilson, J.Q. (2002). *The Marriage Problem: How Our Culture Has Weakened Families*. New York: HarperCollins.

Index

Abecedarian program, 158
abortion
  legalization of, 39
  moral claim to abort, origin of, 249
  opposition to, 20
  rates, declines in, 21
  right of access to, *Roe v. Wade*, 13
Adams, John and Abigail, letters of, 109
adoption, second-parent, 229
Adoption and Children Act 2002, 81
adultery, in New York State, 101
advertising problem, regarding marriage, 137
AFDC (Assistance to Families with Dependent Children), 122
Africa, European colonization of, 37
African Americans
  failure to form respectable families, 95
  high school dropouts, 10
  lesbian couples with children, 298
  link between marriage and childbearing, 22
  marriage rate of, 312
  Moynihan's analysis of black family, 203
  right to marry in immediate postbellum period, 97
age
  of majority changing, 13
  of marriage increasing, 10
agenda, of marriage, 90
alimony, 173, 174–178, 179
  decreasing importance of, 300
American Freedmen's Inquiry Commission, 90
American Law Institute (ALI)
  2002 report, 293
  on absence of formal marriage, 306
  Principles of the Law of Family Dissolution, 244
antenuptial agreements, permissible scope of, 243
anti-Catholic sentiment, increase in cohabitation rates and, 312
Assistance to Families with Dependent Children (AFDC), 122
asthma rates, among children living with single mothers, 149
attitudes, about what law should be
autonomy, 267, 270, 272

baby boom, 12
bandwagon effect, 313
Banks, Richard, 312
Bayesian Information Criterion (BIC), 114
Becker, Gary, 57
Bernard, Jessie, 54
best interest of the child, role of, 263
Beyond (Straight and Gay) Marriage (Polikoff), 213
Beyond Conjugality (2001), 219
"Beyond Same-Sex Marriage: A New Strategic Vision for All Our Families and Relationships," 217, 219
Bibb, Henry, 89
bigamy, crime in every state, 97
biological father, 229
biological time clock, 145
births outside marriage, percentage of US, 143
bisexual and transgender rights advocates, debates about marriage, 228
Bishop, Bill, 19
Blankenhorn, David, 205
blended families, 154
blue approach, 20
blue collar manufacturing jobs, moved overseas, 15

"blue" states vs. "red" states distinction, 20, 24
abortion rates of, 21
elections, 43
middle class strategy, 11
Bowers v. Hardwick, 93, 236
breadwinner/homemaker marriage, 17, 287
breastfeeding, 158, 159
British Columbia in Canada, anti-polygamy laws, 46
Brown, Murphy, 204, 206
Brown v. Board of Education, 232
Browning, Don, 205
Burger, Warren, Chief Justice, 93
Burgess, Ernest, 108, 289
Bush, Laura, 227
Bush administration, 2, 318

California Proposition 8, 94
California Supreme Court, on civil unions, 230
Canada
Anglophone Canadians, living in Quebec, 313
Canadian Parliament, same standards applying to married and "common-law" partners, 2
car rental companies, providing breaks to married renters, 229
Catholic Church, in Quebec, 313
child of divorce, 215
child support
considering with alimony, 173
determining, 178–186
enforcement by state of, 159, 163
from fathers with low and irregular earnings, 160
Federal law, requiring all states to establish numerical guidelines, 179
permitting child to share in better livinig standard of the father, 183
Child Support Act 1991, 76
child support amount, 181, 184
benefitting the custodial parent, 179, 185
guaranteeing minimum, 160
in "one night" or no-relationship cases, 184
for two bookend cases, 184
child support assurance, 158, 159
child wellbeing, 149
"Childcare and Parental Employment in Fragile Families" project, 166
child-custody disputes, courts resolving, 252
children
adding costs to divorce, 58
advantages of marriage to, 307
cognitive development, 78
custody disputes, 243, 252
direct investments in, 156–158
divorce, 58, 215
healthy development of, 313
investment in, 155
majority of U.K. born into two-parent households, 75
not central to individualistic marriages, 112
with a parent in state or federal prison, 162
rights of, 35
sharing in the living standard of higher-income obligor, 180
in single-parent families, 24, 303
in two-parent families, 23
unstable relationships associated with a variety of risks, 305
well-being of, 149, 297
Children Act 1989, extension or rights to unmarried fathers in, 76
China, 37
and Chinese families, 35–36, 37
one-child policy, 36
Christian monogamous marriage, strengthened by struggle over polygamy, 297
church wedding, 295
civil alternatives to marriage, in Israeli secular law, 278
civil law, hostility towards cohabitation, 268
civil marriage. *See also* legal marriage
abolishment and disestablishment of, 296, 297
as a public celebration, 295
Civil Partnership Act (2004), 81, 82
civil partnerships and unions, 82, 217–221, 230–232, 293
civil recognition, 276
civil solidarity pact (PACS), 230, 293
Civil Union Review Commission, in New Jersey, 231
civil unions, 217–221, 230–232
enactment of law, 294
preference over marriage, 99
"stigma of exclusion," 296
class divide
in attitudes toward marriage, 18
in family formation, 24
in marriage and family life, 2, 290, 311
class lines, remaking of society along, 25
Clinton, William, 206, 215
cluster analysis
creating a typology of institutional, companion, and individualistic marriages, 112
described, 114–115
grouping marriages, 107
more straightforward than LCA, 114
producing three distinct groups of marriages, 119
cohabitation, 78, 278, 306
acceptance growing for, 287, 290

accepted in Scandinavia, 307
almost universal in England and Wales, 74
asset sharing, 79
consequences of, 78
countries providing minimal protection for, 78
division of labor, 57, 60
in England and Wales prior to the 1970s, 74, 77, 78
expressing commitment toward or support for partners, 307
family law and, 171, 268–270, 292–294
greater instability associated with, 67, 305
in Israel, 278
legal planning involved, 171
less stable than marriage, 79, 305
long-term, marriage-like relationships, 317
proposed assumption of marriage-like financial obligations, 317
rates increasing, 128, 307, 316
in Scandinavia, 307
types of, 306
in the United States, 170, 291, 298
college graduates
changing marriage patterns reflecting blue strategy, 11
divorce rates, 10, 16
finding new employment more quickly, 15
as parents, 10
Commission on European Family Law, 73
common law marriages, 39, 77, 171, 306
decline, 316
communal and exchange relationships, theoretical work on, 121
Communist party, adopting developmental idealism in China, 36
community and family well-being, interrelated, 26
community organizations, decline in, 25
companionate marriages, 109, 123
comparatively high level of marital happiness and low divorce rates, 118, 120, 122
compared with other marriage types, 109, 123
held together by bonds of affection and mutual support, 111
involving a communal model, 121
less patriarchal than institutional marriages, 109

rate of, 115, 116, 120, 289
complex households, mothers negotiating with several different fathers, 155
condoms, media campaigns encouraging men to use, 164
Connecticut, allowing same-sex couples to marry, 98
consent, as a human right, 33
"The Conservative Case for Gay Marriage," 95
Conservatives, 19, 178
attitudes toward move away from marriage, 18, 23
contraband camps, 96
contraception, 13, 38, 39
Contract with America, 204
Convention of the Elimination of All Forms of Discrimination Against Women (CEDAW), 34
Convention on the Rights of the Child (CRC), 34
corporations, as persons, 250
courts, treating spouses' economic relationships, 243
covenant marriage, 243, 276–277
coverture doctrine, 233
cross-cultural research, on love, sex, and family, 216
cultural clashes
within country, 42–43
created by spread of developmental idealism, 42
within individuals and within families, 42–46
international, 43–44
in United States, 42
cultural conceptions, of cultural models, 30–31, 34
cultural norms, conformity to, 93
culture
American increasingly individualistic, 110
changing definition of human perfection, 245
culture war, 11
differences between men and women, 299
differences in, 150
culture of poverty, evidence for, 143
custody issues, as matters of the child's interest, 252

decision to marry, shaping one's identity, 257
decision-making equality, companionate characteristic, 121
Defense of Marriage Act (DOMA), 206, 207, 229
Deficit Reduction Act of 2005, reauthorizing TANF, 122
deinstitutionalization, of marriage, 109, 256
demographic trends, in marriage, divorce, and cohabitation, 74–75
depression, 132, 133
de-registration, simpler than divorce, 81
de-regulation, of marriage, 262
developing countries, adopting family planning programs, 38
development, models of, 32–33
developmental idealism
around the world, 35–37
clashes within, 45–46
conflicting with local cultural models, 43

developmental idealism (*cont.*)
  continuing influence and tension, 47
  endorsement by ordinary people, 41
  future effects of, 46–49
  impact on family life in the developing world, 3
  influence on family and marriage, 34
  introduction of, 34
  mechanisms spreading internationally, 31
  past effects of, 35–42
  possible limitations on, 47–48
  providing new goals and methods, 33
  specifying universal rights, 33
Devlin, Patrick, 93
differentiated social roles, for husband and wife, 303
direct investments, in children, 156–158
disciplinary effects, of marriage, 99–101
discipline, harsh, 148
discourses, competing, 244
diseases history, measures of, 132
disestablishment, of civil marriage, 217, 296, 297
disparities revealed by fragile families, 149–154
division, of property, 190
divisions, over marriage, 14–22
divorce
  American Revolution, easing of divorce laws following, 40
  changes in, 16
  costs of, 58
  covenant marriage, limited gruonds for in, 276
  in England and Wales, 80
  Jewish Orthodox, 275
  law, 252
  limited grounds for, 276
  morality of, 251
  predictors of, 117
  Southern states, opposed to, 12
  spousal collusion in, 319
  spousal fault, evidence of, 80
  technical requirements of, 100
  trend towards easier and more frequent, 40
  unilateral right established everywhere, 299
  waiting period, requirement of, 277
  widespread perception of "quickie," 80
divorce gene, 129
divorce law, no-fault
  exemplifying trend away from moral discourse, 243
  in revolutionary France, 40
divorce rate
  declining, 14, 74
  dramatic increase in, 40
  in England and Wales, 74
  increases in, 40
  in individualistic marriage, 118
  judicial, adopted by New England colonists, 12
  leveling off, 16
  by marriage type, 119
  rising steeply, 74
  of well off and not so well off heading in opposite directions, 16
Divorce Reform Act 1969, 74
dizygotic (DZ) or fraternal twins, 130
Dobson, James, 204
domestic partners, in California, 95
domestic partnership, 230
domestic partnership law, 99, 294
Domestic Partnerships chapter, in Principles of Family Dissolution, 268
drug offenders, 162
dual-earner model, 17

Early Childhood Longitudinal Study – Birth Cohort 2000 (ECLS-B), 165
Early Head Start, 165
Eaton, John, 96
economic change, effects of, 15–16
economic disadvantage, fragile families both a consequence and cause of, 154
economic discourse, talking about almost anything, 244
economic factors, importance as an explanatory variable, 311
economic inequality, dramatic increase in, 14
economic model
  of marriage, 57, 311
  of marriage and divorce, 59
economic relations, of parties in economic terms, 243
economic status, of unmarried parents, 146
economy, globalization and automation of American, 290
education
  and division of family responsibilities, 17
  early childhood, 157
  predictor of earnings and family stability
  predictor of marriage, 18, 170
educational attainment, predictor of earnings and family stability, 163
Edwards, John, 213, 214, 216
effect size comparisons, 132, 133, 134
egalitarian attitudes, toward women, 42
egalitarian institution, designing marriage as, 265
egalitarian marriage model, proponents of, 59
Egypt, ideas about proper family life, 42
emancipation, right to marry one of most important ramifications, 90
empirical evidence, shaping family policy, 3
empirical studies, data from a series of, 172

employers
insisting on marriage in jurisdictions where same-sex couples are eligible to marry, 87, 230
providing family health care coverage, 229
employment statistics, men and women (2000–2010), 61
England, marriage at the crossroads in, 73–84
Enlightenment
principles of freedom, equality, and consent, 34
trend towards easier divorce, 40
Ensign, John, 216
entry into marriage delayed, 128
environmental experiences, correlated with genetic make-up, 129
equal division, for equal earners in shared property study, 189
equal earners variant, regarding property division, 187
Equal Love campaign, 82
equal marriage rights, 230
Equal Rights Amendment (ERA), 204
equal-division presumption, 186
equality, as a human right, 33
Equality Act (2010), 81
equitable distribution
introduced in New York to produce awards more favorable to women, 252
of marital property, 186, 251
Eskridge, William, 254
Ettelbrick, Paula, 227
Eunice Kennedy Shriver National Institute of Child Health and Human Development, 142
Europe
low fertility, 38
marriage-rate declines, 170
relatively greater stability of non-marital families in, 320
European Court of Human Rights, 73, 82
European Court of Justice, 73
exchange relationships, spouses in, 121
expectations, attached to marital status weaker today, 310
expressive individualism, ethic of, 109
externalizing behavior, 149, 154

Falwell, Jerry, 204
familial closeness, degree of before marriage, 234
families
attributes and definition of, 32, 204, 299
clashes of culture within, 45
composition, 19
proportion based on marriage declining substantially, 303
reuniting after emancipation, 96
social functions of, 208, 263
three-parent, 211
family and familial obligation, attitudes toward, 304
family change, 16–18, 288
family diversity
ideology and morality of, 77, 426
as normal, 202
obtaining broader recognition of, 235
family dynamics, 292
family form
formation norms, shift in, 306
relationship with political loyalty, 19
family instability, consequences of, 152–154
Family Justice Review, 80
family law
assigned to the states, 12
change in, 299
response to increase in cohabiting unions, 292–294
revealing moral attitudes, 242
Family Medical Leave Act, men's access to, 65
family planning
federal funding of, 13
international movement, 37–39
family relationships, strengthening, 161
family scholars, describing types of marriage, 108
family stability, range of benefits to children, 2
family stress, changes in, 16
family structure, 292
family system, types of, 218
family types, many satisfying needs of their adult and child members, 218
family-law casebooks, 1890s compared 1950s, 287
fatherhood programs, 122, 161
Fatherless America (Blankenhorn), 205
fathers. *See also* biological father; unmarried fathers
arrearages (debts) during periods of unemployment, 160
harsh treatment of, 159
involvement at time of birth, 145
involvement declining when either the mother or father has a new partner, 154
prior children reducing quality and stability of mother-father relationship, 154
role of, 208
fault allegations, exacerbating hostilities, 80
fault-based divorce systems, 261
Federal Freedmen's Bureau, 92
federal government, campaign to promote marriage, 126

Federal law, numerical child support "guidelines," 179
Federal Marriage Initiative, 207
federal officials acting as guardians of moral practices of black people, 91, 96
federal statutes, number mentioning marriage, 294
female circumcision (genital cutting), 44, 46
The Feminine Mystique (Friedan), 203
feminist commitment, to gender justice, 220
feminists, quest for intimate equality never speaking to or for all women, 219
Ferguson, Jane, 98
fertility, 38
fertility rates
  Latino, 22
  older populations, 38
fetus, moral status of, 249, 250
fidelity, 215–217
finances, of married adults, 126
financial inequality, respondents caring about, 194
financial stress, increased effect of, 17
Fleming, Patsy, 204
Focus on the Family, 204
footbinding, eliminating, 36
fragile families. *See also* non-marital childbearing
  capabilities of, 146–147
  child wellbeing in, 149
  defined, 142
  disparities revealed by, 149–154
  dissolution of, 147, 310
  health insurance, 157
  investing in parents in, 158–161
  multi-partnered fertility, prevalence, 146
  parental relationships in, 145–146
  reducing prevalence of, 155
  supporting, 158–161, 321
"Fragile Families and Child Health" project, 166
Fragile Families and Child Wellbeing Study, 144, 165
  births into, 292
  children born to unmarried parents, 157
  data from, 4, 146
  described, 144
  individualistic ethic, 310
  parent interviews, 165
  uniqueness of, 165
  website, 166
"Fragile Families and Public Policy: Fathers' Ties to Unmarried Mothers and Their Children" project, 166
France
  national domestic partnership laws, 230, 296
  pacte civil de solidarité, 81
Francophones, higher cohabitation rate than Anglophone Canadians, 313
Frankfurter, Felix, 12
free choice, 245
freed men and women
  experienced moving from outlaws to inlaws, 89
  marriages, immediate post Civil War regulation of, 88
  need to civilize, 91
Freedmen's Bureau agents, solemnizing marriage among Freedmen, 96
freedom
  of a contract, pluralistic model, 270
  from contracts, 269
  as a human right, 33
French Revolution, produced equal inheritance, 40
Friedan, Betty, 203
functional families, various proposals to treat, 252
future change, decisions and pathway in regard to developmental idealism, 47

Gallagher, Maggie, 205
gatekeeper for marriage, state functioning as, 232
gay, lesbian, bisexual, and transgender (LGBT)
  communities, 227, 305
  constituencies, 227
  couples transforming marriage, 235
  decriminalization of sexual relations, 41
  hostility toward, 226
  rights movement, 237
gay marriage. *See* same-sex marriage
"*Gay Marriage: A Must or a Bust?*," 227
gay men
  families formed by, 210
  managing sexual jealousy, 215
  tension between desire and domesticity, 215
gay politics, of the 1990s, 93
gay rights movement, 202
gender attitudes, measuring, 113
gender effects, significant interaction for property division, 192
gender equality
  ameliorating historic harms of marriage, 306
  law supporting, 303
  long-term efforts for in Western societies, 41
gender equity, emphasis shifted to, 38
The Gender Family (Berk), 63
gender mistrust, levels of, 150
gender roles, 109, 188
  household work, 54–57
  premarital specialization, 58
gender segregation, elimination of, 37
gendered differences, in comparative advantage, 58

gene-environment correlation, 129
genes, influencing personality characteristics and physical characteristics, 129
genetic selection, 129, 130
geographical mobility, of young adults, 108
Germany, constitutional protection conferred on marriage, 73
Gingrich, Newt, 204, 207
Glick, Deborah, 218
Goodridge v. Department of Public Health, 256
government
  fulfilling many "family" functions, 139
  policies designed to support children, 139
  promoting formal marriage, 318–320
Government Accountability Office (GAO), 228
Great Britain, national domestic partnership laws, 296
Great Compression (1941 to 1979), 12
Great Divergence, 1980s and 1990s, 14
Great Recession, effects of, 290
Green, Tom, 214
Grimké, Angelina, 89

Habits of the Heart, 248
harm principle, application of, 93
harmful cultural practices, 44
Harris, James H., 92
harsh parenting, increases in, 153
Hart, H.L.A., 93
Hartog, Hendrik, 287
Hartwell, David, 100
Hawaii, reciprocal beneficiaries status, 230
Hawaiian Supreme Court, ruling in 1993, 207
health care legislation, 157
health clubs, singling out married couples, 229
health insurance coverage, 157
health limitations, of unmarried parents, 146
Healthy Marriage Initiative, in the Bush Administration, 319
heterosexual marriage, 287, 288, 298
heterosexual normality, model of, 257
heterosexual women, preferences of, 220
heterosexuals, having transformed marriage, 298
hierarchical institution, marriage as, 314
high-conflict marriage, negatively associated with health and happiness, 308
high-conflict relationships, discouraging marriage and facilitating divorce, 318
higher earners, awarding more property, 189
home environment, of children, 148
homemaker-breadwinner marriages, of the 1950s, 109
homophobia, 88, 101
homosexuals, marriage an unqualified social good for, 255
hostility, *Roe* provoked enormous, 251
household labor
  division of, 54–68
  gendered division of, 56, 113
household routines, maintaining stable, 148
household work, 57, 303
households
  joint consumption items, 179
  short of males or of females, 210
human capital, 58, 146, 163
Human Fertilization and Embryology Act 2008, 81
Human Potential Movement, 109
husbands
  in individualistic marriages, 115
  retaining role of "senior partner," 109
hybridization, 34, 45

ideational factors, focus on, 30
identical twins, 129
ideological differences, reflecting and reinforcing demographic differences, 21
illegitimate children. *See* non-marital births
imprisonment
  effects of, 162
  for non-payment of support, 160
incarceration
  and family resources, 160
  reducing, 158, 162
incarceration rate, of young black men, 320
income disparity, alimony principle grounded on partners,' 178
income disparity principle, in child support, 181
income inequality
  current level, 10, 15
  decline during the fifties, 12
income-pooling model, 288
incommensurability, of histories of oppression, 101
India, over-turned prohibitions against sex-sex relations, 41
individual personal fulfillment, marriage based on, 303
individualistic marriages
  distinguished from institutional marriages, 112
  holding together, 111
  rise of, 109, 116, 289, 311
  spouses in most likely to think relationships in trouble, 118
  spouses likely to adopt an exchange perspective, 121
  wives in, 115
individualistic unions, tending to be unstable, 110
Individuals with Disabilities Education Act, 320
industrial and urban societies, called modern or developed, 32

Infant Health and Development Program (IHDP), 165
infidelity
concept of, 216
ethical breach of trust, 217
informal unions. *See* cohabitation; non-marital births
information economy, remaking women's roles, 10
infrastructure, creating an, 20
inhibition, of moral discourse, 252
instability
high levels of for many children, 152
increasing asthma and obesity, 153
range of risks to children, 2
reducing children's life chances, 151
reducing health and increasing mental health problems for fathers and mothers, 153
reducing quantity and quality of fathers' investments in children, 153
Institute for American Values, 205
Institute for Marriage and Public Policy, 205
institutional marriage
Burgess describing, 108
decline in, 116
holding together, 111
rate of, 116, 120, 289
traditional unions with characteristics of, 115
internalizing behavior, associated with depression, 149
international agreements, spreading developmental idealism, 34–35
international culture clashes, 43–44
international family planning program, initiated after WW II, 37
international financial resources, 38
investments, in children, 155
Iowa, contemporaneous median guideline amounts, 185
Ireland
divorce availability, 80
donstitutional protection conferred on marriage, 73
legislation giving economically disadvantaged or dependent cohabitants a claim in the event of separation, 79
irretrievable breakdown, establishing, 80
Israel, failure of semi-pluralistic system, 277–279

Jacobs, Edom, 100
Japan, campaign of modernization, 37
jealousy, serious problem for many unmarried couples, 154
Jeffs, Warren, 214
Joaquín (gay man), 211, 212, 214
job programs, 320
job stability, 15
Johnson, Dan, 92
judicial divorce, adoption of, 12

Kennedy, Justice, 93
Kenya, family planning, 37
Keynes, John Maynard, doctrine of original sin and, 253
Kohanim, wishing to marry divorcées, 277

labor, kinds of, 57
labor saving devices, 10
Lambda Legal, lawsuit challenging New Jersey's ongoing denial of marriage rights, 231
latent class analysis (LCA), 114
Latino families, structure changing rapidly, 22
Law Commission of Canada, 219
law of marriage, languages of, 241–258
Law of Unintended Consequences, 203
Lawrence v. Texas, 93, 101, 256
LDS Church, repudiating polygamy, 219
legal aid, in private family law cases, 76
legal applications, of pluralistic approaches, 268–277
legal commitments, between cohabitants, 268–270
legal marriage. *See* marriage
legal paternity, marriage less important in establishing, 178
legal principles, conferring rights on married couples, 274
legal privileges, legitimacy for civil marriage, 261
legal privileging of marriage, pluralism and, 270–274
legal scholars, opposed to ALI recommendations, 293
legal systems, continuing to privilege marriage, 271
lesbian and gay couples, and marriage's evolution to a non-gendered institution, 236
lesbian and gay parents, denied contact with children, 229
lesbian and gay partnerships, rights and responsibilities of a second parent in, 294
lesbian- and gay-parent families, large local community of, 212
lesbian partners, childrearing common among, 294
lesbians, many explicitedly disavowing sexual exclusivity, 257
liberal state, 260, 261
liberal values, at core of pluralistic approach, 267
liberal-neutralist philosophy, 260

liberationist view, espoused by some homosexual writers, 256
licensing law, 257
literacy activities, 148, 153
living-standard disparity, 194
Locke, John, 41
Loscocco, Paul, 217
love and parenting, Mosuo approach to, 210
love-makes-a-family ideology, 213
low-income couples, decline in marriage among, 18
low-income fathers, more likely to be ordered to pay amounts exceeding state guidelines, 160
low-income women, placing a high value on children, 151
Luther, Martin, viewed marriage as foundation of civil society, 297

macro economy, decline in jobs for low-skilled men, 150
maintenance, 174, 251
Malawi, 37, 43
male breadwinner role, 18
male employment prospects, improving, 24
male high school dropouts, income decreasing, 15
male unemployment, followed by marital strain or dissolution, 150
Manning Up (Hymowitz), 25
manufacturing jobs, decline, 290
marital advantage
  appearing to stem from commitment, sharing, and greater stability, 311
  concentrated in low-conflict relationships, 308
  correlation or causation, 307–309
  persistence of across national and cultural boundaries, 309
  selection effects, 309–311
marital bargain, changing, 288
marital birth rate, for women with some college education, 11
marital commitments, 268
marital happiness
  based on 10 items, 117
  marriage types and (1980 and 2000), 118
  mean levels for, 118
marital infidelity, as a virtue, 101
marital instability, continuing high levels of, 122
Marital Instability over the Life Course, study of, 112
marital obligations, 316, 317
marital privileges, granting to every couple, 271
marital property, division of, 186, 251
marital prospects, changes in, 16
marital quality
  central indicators of, 112
  differences in, 117–119
  improving, 123
  measures of, 132
marital relationships, more stable than nonmarital cohabitation, 309
marital separation, causing a period of grieving marked by increased depression, 133
marital stability
  promoting greater, 24
  values and beliefs forming foundation of, 111
marital status
  alimony amount and, 176
  child support amount and, 182
  imposition based on relationship duration or parenthood, 317
  interaction with paternal income, 182
  measures of, 132
  property division and, 193
  state granting benefits and imposing burdens based on, 315–318
marital stress, in high-conflict relationships, 318
marital timing and processes, 39–40
market production, 57
marriage
  abolishing as a legal category, 79–81, 271, 296, 304, 314–315
  added benefits of, 135
  advantages of, 307
  age, increasing, 170
  age, minimum, 234
  age at, 10, 14, 21, 38, 39, 40
  agenda of, 90–95
  alternative marriage systems, 261
  Alternatives to Marriage Project (2011), 229
  American adults, percentage married, 303
  arranged marriage, declines in, 39
  attitudes toward, 296, 304
  becoming a symbol of disunion, 9
  benefits, 307
    confounding of selection and causation, 127
    empirical findings, 126
    formula, complicating, 128
    long-term, 137, 256
    MZ twins, 134
    physical and mental health, 135–136
    private sector entities, allocating benefits based on, 229
    short-term, 138
    tangible goods and material protections, 225, 228–230
  broadening elibibility requirement for, 273
  broadening the definition of, 257
  child marriages, declines in, 39

marriage (*cont.*)
child welfare, not necessary to promote, 209–212
civilizing institution, 91
for lesbians and gay men, 93
class, education and race, highly correlated with in the United States, 290, 304, 305
class and success, a marker of, 18, 304
cohabitation, not equivalent to, 306
commitment, marriage as, 311
commitments and expectations, clear signals, 316
consequences of, 95, 234
contract, freedom to define rules of, 262
correlated with race and class in the U.S., 304
corresponding to a country's political and economic climate, 12
costs of, hidden, 128, 137–139
at a crossroads, 237
decline of, 40, 311–313
in England and Wales, 74
definition, as union for life of one man and one woman, 82
disciplinary effects of, 99–101
as discipline and punishment, 99
divisions over, 23
efforts to increase age at, 39
eligibility rules, changing regarding age and blood relations (consanguinity), 234
England, New Labour government (1997–2020), statements on, 75
evolution, 41–42, 233–234
in gendered nature of, 234, 235, 237
of love as basis for, 109
from a public institution to a private arrangement, 261
as traditional, patriarchal institution, 296
two divergent directions, moving in, 122
expanding access to, 314–315
failure from hasty searches, 58
first, percentage intact, 16
foundational to a strong society, 236
future status of, 314–315
law cultivating exclusivity of, 261
meaning of, 107, 311
changing, 289
tied to ideas of loyalty, commitment, and personal responsibility, 252
moral theory of, 251
obligations of, 256
oppressive outmoded institution, 23, 296
opting out of, 77–79
personal growth, 246
pluralism and legal privileging of, 270–274
pluralistic vision of, 260–280
political and economic climate, correspondence, 12
prioritization, as a movement goal, 228
privileges challenged in modern legal discourse, 271
pro-marriage ideology, gains of, 203
promoting personal growth of the spouses, 246
promotion by state, 83, 318–320
promotion typically linked to political right, 126
as a public institution, 260
public support, continuing for, 304
ratios, of men to women correlated with rates, 311
reduced risks of, 135
Reformation, Protestant
campaign to tighten control after, 39
criticism of marriage system, 39
regional, class and ideological differences, 11
relational and not procreational, 257
relevance of, 195, 306–307
remaining a prominent and leading priority, 225
remaining important, 225, 300
remaking in ways more likely to gain consensu, 25
requiring a male and a female as an artifact of an earlier time, 234
responsibilities of, 97
resulting from advantages, 308
retaining special status of, 306
same-sex, access to, 81–83
seeming to matter so much, 224
shift in the meaning of, 311
shift in the nature of, 237
signaling a couple's commitments and expectations, 316
skewing differences in children's development, 24
as social institution, 289
social institution, as a
less dominant but still highly-valued, 289
preeminent institution of family life, 254
retaining special status of, 306
role as a social institution, 254
stability, 25
stereotypes abounding in public discussion, 83
symbolic role in transformation of status from slave to citizen, 91
symbolic value over past few decades, 295
third parties, treatment by, 171
types of, 4
value-laden institution, 90
marriage advocacy, complicated, 228
marriage allowance, 76
marriage and fatherhood programs, 158

marriage and nuclear families, no longer efficient mechanisms, 139
marriage bar, 17
marriage clusters, differences between over time, 116–117
marriage constraints, general movement toward loosening, 256
Marriage Convention (MC), 35
marriage education, 76, 123
marriage grant program, initiated by President Bush in 2002, 161
marriage incentives, as a bad idea, 319
marriage law and policy
  changing language of, 242–248
  enforcement of, 91, 242
  and politics, 75–77
  revealing moral attitudes, 242
marriage license, 97
marriage market, 57, 138
Marriage Matters, at the University of Virginia, 205
"Marriage Movement," ideological campaign, 205
marriage paradox, 136–137
marriage "penalties," elimination of, 318
marriage premium
  in child support, 182
  greater for the more educated, 178
  in property allocation, 189
  shrinking, 176
The Marriage Problem (Wilson), 150
marriage rates, declining, 311
marriage types
  cluster analysis of three, 114
  indirect indicators of, 111
  percentage of respondents in, 116
  study of, 111–122
The Marriage-go-Round (Cherlin), 21, 219
marriage-promotion initiatives, 2, 318, 319
marriage-rights movement, 95
married adults, 126, 134
married couples
  benefits and penalties, 314
  sharing economic resources, 307
  social relationships of, 126
  tax allowances for, 83
married women, and share of housework, 64
"Marrying in Haste," counseling Black women against, 92
Marvin v. Marvin, 268
Marx, Karl, on divorce, 246
Massachusetts Supreme Court, 2003 decision in favor of same-sex marriage, 295
maternal stress, increases in, 153
McConico, Celia, 100
Means, Sam, 100
Medicaid expansion, highest benefit-cost ratio, 164
men
  depression appearing to be more sensitive to marital status, 133
  enjoying sexual access to women without demands, 25
  percent of 29–60-year-old unemployed, 15
  power relative to women, 65
  viewed as primary breadwinners, 150
mental health, measures of, 132
middle class model, for marriage, 9
middle class parents, more resources to invest in children's cognitive development, 24
middle class strategy, designed to meet needs of information age, 20
Middle East, 43
millet system, 277
minimum living standard approach, 185
miscegenation laws, 88
mixed faith couples, 277
models
  cultural, 30–31
  of development, 32–33
moderators, analyzing, 136
modernists, 19, 23
modernization ideas, in many international settings, 34
modernization models
  elements under heavy academic criticism during recent decades, 33
  positing a trajectory of development, 32
monolithic perfectionists' view, of establishment of one spousal institution suitable to all couples, 279
monolithic-public approach, marriage privileges part of, 270
moral and religious arguments, disappearance from debates about marriage, 76
moral crisis, moving away from traditional family values as, 20
moral discourse
  concerning modern family law, 262
  diminution, costs of, 248–254
  eliminating to make courts more easily managed, 244
  generally requiring discretion, 244
  tainted, 248
moral hazards, 89, 102
moral issues
  central to family life and family self-governance, 242, 251
  commanding special attention from marriage law, 242
moral language, 253

moral life, American in process of revisng itself, 241
Moral Majority, conservative family values of, 204
moral sentiments, influencing lawmakers unawares, 242
moral thinking, as intolerant thinking, 245
morality
  denying, 245
  of pluralism, 266
Mormon polygamists, granting women the right to vote in the Utah territory, 219
Mosuo kinship rules, 209
Mosuo people, 209
mothers. *See also* unmarried mothers
  having children with new partners, 154
  objecting to fathers spending time with children in other households, 154
  parenting, 148
  parenting quality differing by marital status, 148
  reducing access to friends and relatives willing to provide support, 154
Moynihan, Daniel Patrick, 142, 203, 204, 206
The Moynihan Report, 95, 203
multi-marriage system, 274
Murphy Brown story, 145
MZ twins, 129, 130

National Institute of Child Health and Human Development (NICHD), 165
National Marriage Project, 205
National Organization for Marriage, 205
National Survey of Families and Households (NSFH), 55, 60, 62
National Survey of Family Growth, 291
National Survey of Midlife Development in the United States (MIDUS), 132–134
Nationalists, adopting developmental idealism in China, 36
The Negro Family: The Case for National Action (Moynihan), 95, 142, 203
Nepal, endorsement of development widespread, 37
Netherlands, substantial suspicion of marriage, 296
neutral philosophical approach, 272, 279
neutralist approach, 265, 271
New Families – No Families (Goldscheider and Waite), 64
New Jersey, 231
New Right, 204
New York statute, "Get Law," 276
New Zealand, de facto partners, 3
night visiting, system of, 209
Nock, Steven, 205
nonbinding commitment, marriage becoming, 246
non-cohabiting fathers, showing high levels of involvement, 146
non-discriminatory access, ameliorating historic harms of marriage, 306
non-interference, in family and marriages, 244
non-marital birth rates, increased for the country through the end of the 1960s, 14
non-marital births
  cause for concern, 144–149
  changes in demography of, 143
  as a consequence of disadvantage, 155
  contributing to social disorganization, 143
  debate over consequences of, 142
  exacerbating pre-existing disadvantage, 155
  extending beyond lower-class African American population, 143
  giving rise to fragile families, 142
  increase in, 9, 14, 18, 303
  as product of casual relationships, 145
non-marital childbearing. *See* non-marital births
nonmarital cohabitation. *See* cohabitation
non-marital families, traditional family law's harsh treatment of, 314
non-marital sexuality, punishing women for, 25
non-resident fathers, 148, 153
non-resident parents, relationships with, 166
Nordegren, Elin, 215
NSFH. *See* National Survey of Families and Households (NSFH)

Obama, Barack, 207, 218
Obama, Michelle, 218
Obama administration, 122
Oklahoma Marriage Initiative, 123
Olson, Ted, 94, 95
Ottoman Empire, 36

Palin, Bristol, 216
Palin, Sarah, 201, 216
parental courtship, four-way, 211
parental income, significant effect in child support vignettes, 180
parental investments, quality of, 148
parental leave, paid, 158
parental relationships, in fragile families, 145–146
parent-child relationships, 165, 229
parenting, of mothers, 148
parents. *See also* unmarried parents
  demographic characteristics and human capital, 147
  in fragile families, 158–161
parents' approval, required prior to marriage, 108

parents' material conditions, differences in, 150
parolees, 162
partnership instability. *See also* instability
effects on children, 153
high levels of, 151
reducing quality of mothers' parenting, 153
partnerships, 152, 288
paternity, 219
Patterson, Orlando, 150
perfectionist liberal values, 266
perfectionist philosophy, 260, 272
perfectionist school of thought, 269
perfectionist-monolithic approach, opposition to, 266, 267
perfectionist-monolithic philosophical stream, 265
permanence, 9, 244
Perry v. Schwarzenegger, case challenging Proposition 8, 94
Personal Responsibility and Work Opportunities Reform Act (PRWORA) 1996, 122, 206
"Persons of Color," Georgia's 1866 law relating to, 98
physical and mental health, marriage benefitting, 135–136
physical health
of married adults, 126
measures of, 132
overall rating of, 134
self-rating of overall, 132
Planned Parenthood of Southeastern Pennsylvania v. Casey, 251
pluralism
as an intrinsic value, 266
recognizing state's authority and responsibility to prefer marriage, 272
stemming from moral relativism, 266
pluralistic approach
alternative to both private and public approach, 260, 267, 269
based on an active perception of the state, 269
demanding substantive freedom of choice, 275
diversity, seeking to encourage, 272
ensuring both partners enjoy freedom of choice, 267
foundation for, 260
legal applications of, 268–277
needing to identify moral values and public interests, 267
preferring egalitarian institutions, 267
supporting extensive use of contractual doctrines, 276
tension embedded between perfectionism and autonomy, 272
policies, to improve marriage, 123
policy makers, questions for, 304–306
policymaking, informing with empirical research, 306
political parties, American differing in ideological terms currently, 19
politics of recognition, investing heavily in, 88
polygamy
criminalizing doing more harm than good, 213–215
hostility to, 213
not inherently harmful, 219
opposition to, 45
patriarchal history of, 219
religious freedom not extending to these marriages, 44
in South Africa and the United States, 213
strong opposition as a barbaric practice, 44
United States Congress, harsh laws to eliminate, 44
polygyny, advocating tolerance of, 220
poly-parenting families, 210, 211
poor man's marriage model, 145, 146
poor parenting, undermining children's opportunities, 155
Pop Luck Club, 211, 214
Popenoe, David, 205
poverty, reducing disadvantages associated with, 320
pregnancy rates, reducing among unmarried couples, 164
premarital counseling, 276
premarital pregnancy, leading to a shotgun wedding, 290
pre-school education, high-quality, intensive, 320
presidential candidates, politically obliged to oppose gay marriage, 207
Principles of European Family Law, 81
Principles of the Law of Family Dissolution, 244
private-neutral approach, 260, 263, 265
privatization narrative of marriage, 262, 289
professional women, running up against biological time clock, 145
Promises I Can Keep (Edin and Kefalas), 151
property
allocation when partners separate, 186–193
division, unequal earners' variant, 187
division of, 174
rules governing division of, 305
transmitting to men's heirs, 219
Proposition 8, campaign to defeat, 212
psychological adjustment, of married adults, 126

public approach
  criticized, 279
  emphasizing public interest in the regulation of spousal relations, 264
  identifying public interest with traditional regulation, 264
  pointing to advantages of marriage-based over other family patterns, 271
  seeking to channel people towards marriage, 261
public channeling v. private neutrality, as the existing debate, 261–263
public commitments, producing stability, 310
public goods, children as, 58
public registration, of commitment, 271, 272
public weddings, types of, 295
public-channeling approach, 260, 265
punishment
  associating with morality, 247
  avoiding for those seeking alternatives to marriage, 273

quasicausal studies, 130
Quayle, Dan, 204, 206
Quebec, cohabitation rate, 312

race, 22, 58
racial divide, in marriage behavior in the United States, 312
radical challenge, against privileging marriage, 271
Red Families v. Blue Families, 19, 20
red values, associated with traditional religious teachings, 11
refugee camps. *See* contraband camps
regional data, for marriage and family patterns, 19
regional differences
  in birth rates reflecting state policy, 21
  interacting with race and class to vary the role of marriage, 21
  in patterns of marriage, divorce and cohabitation, 18
registered-partnership regimes, extent modeled on marriage, 81
regression analysis, estimating mean levels of marital happiness and divorce proneness, 117
relational dysfunction and instability, often symptoms of emotional and economic stresses, 320
relational instability, associated with risks during childhood, 308
relationship quality, marriage influence on, 78
relationship stability, children's exposure, 152
relationship-related benefits, delinking marriage from, 230
relationships, low-conflict, enduring, 318
religion
  church wedding, 295
  marriage not homogeneous with respect to, 58
  playing only minor roles in individualistic marriages, 112
  providing an important institutional foundation, 111
Religion, Family and Culture Project, at the University of Chicago, 205
religious affiliation, 277
religious and cultural groups, leaving marriage to, 296
religious communities, 274, 278
religious companionate group, 119
religious control, decline in, 108
religious divorce ceremony, 275
religious family law systems, characterized by unequal gender practices, 275
religious groups, conservative, 123
religious laws, gender-based and hierarchical in Israel, 278
religious marriage, 274–276, 278
religious services, frequency of attendance, 113
religious view of marriage, accepting, 65
remarriage, not seeming to confer same advantage as a first marriage, 308
Report on the Negro Family (Moynihan), 142
reproduction, outside of marriage, 23
reproductive freedom, theme across recent decades, 38
reproductive health, emphasis shifted to, 38
reproductive technologies, complicating assignment of paternity, 179
Republicans, self-identified, 178
Research Triangle, attracted better educated migrants to North Carolina, 18
right of exit
  described, 270
  marriage tracks limiting, 274
  not always protected in religious marriage, 275
  preserving, 268
right of privacy, 249
right to marry, collapsing into an obligation, 95–99
rights
  conferring on a married person after the death of a spouse, 274
  gap between married and cohabiting couples, 78
  language of, 245
  obtaining not always resulting in justice, 228
rights *inter se*, 171
Rituals of Blood (Patterson), 150

Roe v. Wade
remaining at the moral center, 249
therapeutic viewpoint, 249
rules, of marriage, 99
Russia, nonmarital birth, 304

Saez, Emmanuel, 15
safety net programs, 156
same-sex couples, 40, 255
acceptance of, 67, 288
adopting a child together, 81
automatic marriage of, 98
effects of denying marriage to, 232, 296
entering into a institution perceived as heterosexual and patriarchal, 83
entering into a registered partnership, 81
extending marriage to, 1, 81–83
finding they must marry to retain rights, 99
forming families and raising children, 303
in Israel, 277
registering as civil partners in England and Wales, 81
seeking range of rights and benefits available only to married couples, 294
wanting marriage because of what it currently offers, 237
same-sex marriage, 95
access to symbolic status of being legally married, 295
changing marriage as a socializing institution, 255
concepts of "primary caregiver" and "alimony," 299
contemporary arguments about, 89, 225
contemporary discomfort with distinctions and judgements, 257
described, 254, 294–299
division of tasks, typical, 298
hostility toward, 95
influence on public, 264
legalization, 207, 212–213
likely to be more egalitarian, 298
movement, 213
in New York, 87
promoting social equality, 207, 212
symbolic status of, 295
tangible benefits of, 237, 294
transforming institution of marriage, 23, 233–237, 255, 298
Sanford, Mark, 207, 216
Savage, Dan, 101
Savannah Tribune, formerly The Colored Tribune, 92
Scalia, Justice, 11
Scandinavia
demographers continue to find marital advantage, 309
few economic incentives to marry, 307
relatively greater stability of non-marital families in, 320
Scandinavian model, 144
Schlafly, Phyllis, 204
Schwarzenegger, Arnold, 213, 214, 216
Scotland, 79
secular alternatives
to marriage and divorce, 278
to religious marriage, 278
secular institutional group, 119
secular marriage movement, 205
selection effects, and marital advantage, 308
self-development, replacing companionship and team effort, 110
Semi-Weekly Louisianan, 92
separate but (un)equal, civil unions as, 230
"separate spheres" marriage, in the nineteenth century, 287
serial families, instability of relationships in, 310
sex, consent requirement for, 39
sex outside of marriage, 23, 150
sex ratios, importance of, 311
sex roles and rules, in marriage, 233
"the sexual family," 210
sexual freedom, support for, 45
sexual integrity, ethic, 216, 217
sexual intercourse, minimum age for, 48
sexual morality, one aspect of family morality, 242
sexual practices, remaking of, 13
sexual relationship, refusal to engage in, 82
sexual revolution
of the 1960s, 312
beginning of, 12
shared environmental selection, 129
shot gun marriages, 14, 58
sin, living in, 76
"Since When is Marriage a Path to Liberation?," 227
single parenthood, 147, 309
single-parent households, disadvantages for children, 24, 308
slave marriages, laws legitimizing, 96
slavery, inability to marry, 89
social expectations, of responsibilities within marriage, 235
social institutions
defined, 253
essential in any society, 264
existing without moral language, 254
law constructing alternative to legal marriage, 273

social institutions (*cont.*)
marriage as, 257
moral language and, 254–258
social meaning, attributing to marriage, 264
social norms, 310, 312
changing at glacial speed, 67
social institutions and culture, dynamism of, 265
social prejudice, reduction in, 305
social stigma, attached to nonmarital relationships and birth, 314
social-class gap
in how American parents and children live their lives, 292
in U.S. family life, 290
socializing function, of marriage, 254
society
American built around civil status of marriage, 297
remaking along class lines, 25
soul mate marriages, 110, 119
South Africa, and polygamy, 215
South Carolina, statutory duty of election, 98
special procedure, for undefended divorces, 80
special status for marriage, harmful to other families, 314
specialization avoided by childless couples, 68
specialization of household tasks model, 57, 59, 288
Spitzer, Elliot, 215, 216
spousal income, combinations of in studies, 175
spousal law, 261, 262
spousal relationships, 107, 260
spousal support, as post-separation alimony, 174
spouse(s)
assumed to be an integrated economic unit, 305
contracts relieving courts of some burden of decision, 243
fulfillment of complementary marital roles, 109
granting unique rights to, 273
in institutional marriage, 108, 118
leaving for a trophy wife, 23
legitimacy of granting special privileges to, 280
making most of the important decisions, 113
receiving benefits not available to cohabitants, 315
supportive partners replaced with "soul mate," 110
unilaterally deciding to end a marriage, 262
usage of the term, 260
St. John's Lodge of Odd Fellows, 92
stability
associated with marriage, 111, 151, 309
benefits to children, 2, 297
of the family in an institutional system of marriage, 108
of marriage and cohabitation, social factors, associated with
stable marriage, 111, 151
standard North American family (SNAF), 288
state(s)
active role in pluralistic approach, 269
best supporting pluralism, 305
as imperfect parent, 139
state assumption, of traditional family functions, 137
state law, marital status affecting legal recognition as a parent, 229
state of nature, 33
status, indicating social and political equality, 294
status equality, 230–233
status model, Israeli courts recently adopted, 279
"stigma of exclusion," 296
stigmatization
of non-marital families, 314
sense of, 232
Stoddard, Thomas, 227, 236
Sullivan, Andrew, 254
support awards, to cohabitating couples compared to those with no relationship, 195
Survey of Marriage and Family Life (2000), 112
surveys, measuring marital characteristics, 113
Sweden
cohabiting parents more likely to separate, 309
majority of children born to cohabitating couples, 291
marriage not as strong an institution, 296
marriage undergoing a revival, 75
neutrality stance toward different types of family relationships, 73
pioneer in assimilating cohabitation to marriage, 78
Swedish model, 146

tangle of pathology, 142, 203
"Tax Problems for Illinois Civil Unions," 229
teamwork, emphasis in companionate marriage, 121
teen pregnancies and births, 319
proportion of, 146
rates, 16, 18, 21
teen pregnancy programs, expanding, 164
Teenage Parent Demonstration, 165
Temporary Assistance to Needy Families (TANF), 122
tenancy in common, versus joint tenancy, 193
Texas sodomy statute, demeaning lives of homosexual persons, 93
therapeutic discourse, 244, 245

therapeutic function, of marriage, 110
three-cluster solution, providing an optimal fit to data, 114
time horizons, 136, 138
tisese (night visiting), 209, 210
TLC3 project, 166
traditional family, as relatively new phenomenon, 12
traditional marriage, advocates longing for a return to, 304
traditionalists
  blue model as afront to, 20
  described, 19
  emphasis on unidimensional metric, 24
  seeing marriage as a divinely ordained institution, 23
  viewing children's interests as reason for viewing marriage law as a public matter, 264
trial marriages, 151
true effects, suppressed by selection, 130
The Truly Disadvantaged (Wilson), 143, 150
Trumbull, Lyman, 89
Tuchman, Gary, 220
Tucson, Arizona jury pool, as an excellent cross section of county's citizens, 173
Turkey, developmental idealism in, 36
twin method, 129–130, 133
twin studies, 127, 130, 308
twins
  comparing, 127
  controlling for selection effects, 131
  using to parse the marriage benefit, 128–129
two-parent families
  acceptance of alternative forms of, 287, 288
  growing diversity of, 287–300
Two-Step Clustering procedure, used for analysis, 114
typological (or person centered) approach, 107

U.K. Law Commission, 79
U.K. residents, travelling abroad to marry, 83
underclass, pathology of, 203
unfaithfulness, of one partner, 82
Unhitched: Love, Marriage and Family Values from West Hollywood to Western China (Stacey), 202
UNICEF, targeting female circumcision, 44
Uniform Premarital Agreement Act, 243
United Kingdom
  divorce laws varying, 79
  nonmarital births, effects of
United States
  cultural clashes in, 42
  nonmarital births, effects of, 304
United States Congress, harsh laws to eliminate polygamy, 44
United States Sentencing Commission, 162
universal health insurance system, for children, 156
universal pre-school, for three- and four-year-olds, 157
universal programs, superior to targeted programs, 155
universal rights, developmental idealism specifying, 33
unmarried couples
  instability among, 152
  much more likely than married couples to end their relationships, 155
  raising children, 288, 290
unmarried fathers
  information lacking about, 144
  large number incarcerated at some point, 308
  pattern of, 152
unmarried mothers
  large oversample of, 144
  much younger than married mothers, 146
  percent cohabiting at birth, 291
  proportion of births, 290
  public attitudes toward, 304
unmarried parents
  with a college degree, 146
  in committed relationships at the time of their child's birth, 145
  families formed by, 142
  nature of parental relationships and capabilities in families formed by, 144
  optimistic about future of their relationship, 146
  percentage living together five years after child's birth, 170
  placing a high value on marriage, 151
  relationship status at child's birth, 145
  relationships, dissolution of, 151
  unmarried mothers, health problems, 153
unmarried participants, significantly more depressed, 132
unmarried white mothers, percentage of in early 1980s, 203
U.S. Constitution, reserving authority over marriage and divorce to the states, 12
U.S. Federal District Court, ruling on California's ban against same-sex marriage, 41
U.S. Supreme Court
  on abortion, 249
  on contraception right of single women, 13
  on interracial marriage (*Loving v. Virginia* 1967), 233
  on marriage, 225
  and same-sex marriage, 47

veils, 37, 46
Vermont, first state to offer civil unoins to same-sex couples, 230
voting patterns, related to geographical distribution of behaviors, 43
vows, revising, 219–221

Waddell, Alfred M., 91
wage inequality, 18
wage-earner husband, 9
Wales, marriage at the crossroads in, 73–84
Walmart family, competing with marriage, 139
Wardle, Lynn, 244
Washington state, 186
wealthy, in blue states likely to vote Republican, 19
wedding
  mass ceremonies, in the postwar South, 97
  white dresses, in China, 36
welfare benefits, reducing by one dollar for each dollar of child support paid, 160
Welfare Reform Act (1996), 122, 206
welfare-reform legislation, 1996 Federal, 2
Western Europe, nonmarital births, 304
Western values and practices, exportation and imposition of, 48–49
Whitehead, Barbara Dafoe, 206
Williams, Elizabeth, 100
Williams, Joan, 55
Williams v. Georgia, 100
Wilson, William Julius, 143, 150
within-individual culture clashes, resolving, 45
women
  comparative advantage in household production, 58
  depression more sensitive to marital quality, 133
  doing less housework as they obtain more power, 65
  dress as focus of a developmental idealism clash, 46
  employment exacerbating relationship between financial distress and divorce, 17
  graduate school attendance, 14
  incomes increasing, 16
  with more education more likely to marry, 289
  positions improved vis-à-vis men, 15
  presence of children augmenting age-based loss of marriage-market value, 59
  rights and status of, 42
  and sex before marriage, 13
  status of an indicator of development levels in a society, 42
  veils and, 37
women's work
  cohort of older women doing, 63
  hours above the average destabilizing marriage, 56
  reduction for women of about two hours per week, 60
  valuing through higher market wages, 67
Woods, Tiger, 215
working age population, reductions in, 38
working class, skeptical of making marriage work, 20
world
  culture, 31
  models, 32–34
  portrayed as dynamic, 32
world culture, 31
World Values Survey (2000), 296

young adults, increasingly deferring marriage, 295
"young children" condition, in alimony studies, 175

Z good production, 57
Zarrillo, Jeff, 94
Zuma, Jacob, 214